HISTORY OF THE
GREAT CIVIL WAR
Vol III

Samuel Rawson Gardiner was one of Britain's most distinguished historians. His *History of the Great Civil War* and *History of the Commonwealth and Protectorate* are among the finest achievements of British historiography. Gardiner was born in Ropley, in Hampshire, on 4 March 1829 and educated at Winchester and Christ Church, Oxford. Both his parents belonged to the Irvingite church and Gardiner himself married the youngest daughter of Edward Irving in 1856.

He supported his writing career by teaching and lecturing, first at Bedford College, London (1863–81), then at King's College, London (1872–77, becoming professor of modern history there in 1877), and the Society for the Extension of University Teaching in London (1877–94). Gardiner published numerous influential books and articles on what he termed 'the Puritan Revolution', but was only slowly rewarded with official recognition. His cause was championed by Lord Acton who persuaded Gladstone to grant Gardiner a civil list pension in 1882. He was elected a fellow of All Souls, Oxford in 1884, and was later appointed a fellow of Merton College, but refused the Regius professorship when it was offered by Rosebery in 1894.

Samuel Rawson Gardiner died on 23 February 1902. He had finished only one chapter in what was to be the fourth and final volume of *History of the Commonwealth and Protectorate*, a project completed for him by his friend and disciple C.H. Firth. Firth summed up his friend's achievements after his death: 'He sought to interest his readers by his lucid exposition of facts and the justice of his reflections rather than by giving history the charms of fiction, and was content with the distinction of being the most trustworthy of nineteenth-century historians.'

BOOKS BY S.R. GARDINER

History of the Great Civil War
(four volumes) (Phoenix Press)

History of the Commonwealth and Protectorate
(four volumes) (Phoenix Press, forthcoming)

HISTORY OF THE
GREAT CIVIL WAR
1642–1649

Volume III – 1645–1647

S.R. Gardiner

**PHOENIX
PRESS**

5 UPPER SAINT MARTIN'S LANE
LONDON
WC2H 9EA

A Windrush Press Book

A PHOENIX PRESS PAPERBACK

First published in Great Britain
by Longmans, Green & Co in 1889
Reprinted by The Windrush Press in 1987
This paperback edition published in 2002 by
The Windrush Press in association with Phoenix Press,
a division of The Orion Publishing Group Ltd,
Orion House, 5 Upper St Martin's Lane,
London WC2H 9EA

Phoenix Press
Sterling Publishing Co Inc
387 Park Avenue South
New York
NY 10016-8810
USA

The Windrush Press
Windrush House
12 Adlestrop
Moreton in Marsh
Glos GL56 0YN

A CIP catalogue record for this book
is available from the British Library.

Printed and bound in Great Britain by
Clays Ltd, St Ives plc

ISBN 1 84212 642 3

CONTENTS

OF

THE THIRD VOLUME.

———◦◦———

CHAPTER XXXVIII.

A DIPLOMATIC TANGLE.

CHAPTER XXXIX.

GLAMORGAN AND RINUCCINI IN IRELAND.

CHAPTER XL.

THE LAST CAMPAIGN IN THE WEST.

CHAPTER XLI.

THE KING'S FLIGHT TO THE SCOTS.

CHAPTER XLII.

THE FIRST MONTHS OF THE KING'S CAPTIVITY.

CHAPTER XLIII.

THE NEWCASTLE PROPOSITIONS

CHAPTER XLIV

THE FAILURE OF THE IRISH PEACE.

CHAPTER XLV.

THE DEPARTURE OF THE SCOTS.

CHAPTER XLVI.

FINANCIAL AND ADMINISTRATIVE DISORDER.

CHAPTER XLVII.

THE PRESBYTERIANS AND THE ARMY.

CHAPTER XLVIII.

THE AGITATORS.

CHAPTER XLIX.

THE ABDUCTION OF THE KING.

CHAPTER L.

THE MANIFESTOES OF THE ARMY.

CHAPTER LI.

THE ELEVEN MEMBERS.

CHAPTER LII.

THE HEADS OF THE PROPOSALS.

CHAPTER LIII.

THE MILITARY OCCUPATION OF LONDON.

CHAPTER LIV.

CROMWELL AND THE KING.

CHAPTER LV.

THE AGREEMENT OF THE PEOPLE.

APPENDIX.

MAPS.

THE GREAT CIVIL WAR.

CHAPTER XXXVIII.

A DIPLOMATIC TANGLE.

ALREADY, before his return to Oxford, Charles had been playing with each of the two parties into which his opponents were

Charles
plays with
both
parties.

divided. The attempt to open a correspondence
with Leven and the Scottish army was now of old
date.[1] There is more obscurity as regards the intercourse between Charles and the Independents, but there is
strong reason to believe that he had given a favourable response
to overtures made to him from that quarter for an understanding on the basis of liberty of conscience.[2] On the whole, however, the King inclined to the Presbyterians. He was afraid
of the democratic tendencies of the army, and he underesti-
mated the tenacity with which the Presbyterians clung to their
ecclesiastical system.

Circumstances were bringing both the Scots and the English
Presbyterians to contemplate an understanding with the King,
as affording them a rallying-point against the Independents.

[1] See vol. ii. p. 385.
[2] It is true that nothing of this appears in the printed papers taken at
Sherburn, or in the notes in Yonge's Diary of others read in Parliament.
The Scottish Dove, however (E. 308, 25), says that 'the chief champions
of our sectaries, or furious factious men, have been tampering with the
Royal party,' and this, which in itself would not be of much weight, is
confirmed by the reiterated allegations of Montreuil.

Though, as far as liberty of conscience was concerned, the Presbyterians had the mastery in the House of Commons, the Independents carried all before them whenever any question arose bearing on the conduct of the war, or on the relations between the English Parliament and its Scottish auxiliaries. Towards the end of September there was much bickering between the House and the Scots. On the 23rd the Commons voted that Leven should be asked to lay siege to Newark, that 1,400*l.* a week should be paid to his infantry, and that he should not be allowed to levy taxes or contributions in any part of England. The Scottish commissioners reminded the House that it was one thing to vote money and another thing to pay it, and that of the large sums which had been already voted, very little had ever come into their hands. If their soldiers were neither paid nor allowed to levy contributions, they must either starve or disband. This sharp reply was accompanied by a request that Presbyterian government might be established and negotiations opened with the King.[1]

Marginal notes:
Presbyterians and Independents in the Commons.

Sept. 23. Leven's army asked to come south.

Sept. 30. Reply of the Scots.

Almost at the same time that the gulf between the Scots and the House of Commons was thus widening, Holland made a proposal to Montreuil that the King should seek refuge with the Scottish army. Montreuil passed on the project to Balmerino, who was one of the Scottish commissioners, and Balmerino adopted it warmly. Holland was hardly the man to invent such a stroke of policy, and it is likely enough that he had in some way learnt that the proposal had already been made by Charles to Leven and Callander. At all events, he now took it up with the utmost enthusiasm. "I am but a poor gentleman," he told Montreuil, "with a scanty following, but I should be able to go to the King with 10,000 men."[2]

Marginal note:
Holland proposes that the King shall go to the Scots.

Knowing nothing of the proposed scheme, the Commons proceeded to act as if their express design had been to irritate the Scots. It is true that they voted them 30,000*l.* to be paid

[1] *C.J.* iv. 283; *L.J.* vii. 619.
[2] Montreuil to Brienne, Oct. $\frac{2}{12}$. *Carte MSS.* lxxxiii. fol. 101.

on November 1, on condition that their army was actually before Newark on that date, but they took no notice of any of

Oct. 6.
Money
vote.l to
the Scots. the complaints of the Scottish commissioners. They treated Leven's troops as hired auxiliaries who were expected to obey orders without question.[1] They complained, and justly complained, of the devastation wrought by the Scottish army in the northern counties, but they could not be induced to remember that it was their own slackness in sending pay which had been the main cause of

Oct. 13.
Fault
found with
them. the evil. On the 13th they passed a new series of resolutions, protesting against the conduct of the Scots, and demanding the immediate withdrawal of their garrison from the northern towns. It is true that they added a resolution to set apart two days a week to the consideration of propositions of peace, but the Scots were likely to doubt whether their deliberations would lead to a speedy result.[2]

Under these affronts the Scots were growing more inclined than they had hitherto been to listen to direct overtures from

Oct. 9.
Leven
refuses to
negoliate
with the
King. Charles. Leven, indeed, was too cautious to engage in political intrigues, and he had recently forwarded to Westminster a letter in which Digby, immediately on his arrival with the King at Newark, had pressed him for an answer to his former proposals.[3] The commis-

Oct. 17.
The terms
of the
Scottish
commis-
sioners. sioners in London were, however, less reserved, and on October 17, having adopted the view already expressed by Balmerino, they placed in Montreuil's hands a paper expressing the terms of peace to which they were prepared to consent. The King, according to these terms, was to agree to establish ecclesiastical affairs in the manner agreed on by the Parliaments and Assemblies of both kingdoms. If he did that, his wishes would, as far as possible, be complied with in all other respects. When he had signified his acceptance of this proposal, the Scots would use all their power in his support. Fearing to commit themselves, the

---

[1] *C.J.* iv. 298.   [2] *Ibid.* iv. 305.

[3] Digby's letter was dated Oct. 4, and was read with Leven's answer in the House of Lords on Oct. 15. *L.J.* vii. 638.

commissioners requested Montreuil to take a ciphered copy of their paper for transmission to France, and to return the original into their hands.   They had, in fact, no sort of warrant from any public authority in Scotland to do what they were doing, and the Scottish Parliament would be able to disavow them with a good conscience if it saw fit to do so.

It was agreed that the Queen's support should, if possible, be obtained before her husband was directly approached, and

The terms to be carried to the Queen by Sir R. Moray. Sir Robert Moray, who had recently been appointed colonel of the Scottish guard in France, and who would consequently be able to cross the sea without exciting attention, was selected as the bearer of so important a communication.   Moray, who, after the Restoration, became the first president of the Royal Society, was a man of singular force and delicacy of character ; but, like all his countrymen, he was quite unable to understand how anyone could entertain a conscientious objection to take part in the abolition of Episcopacy.[1]

In fact, there was no need for a Scotchman to be a bigot to make him anxious to see Presbyterianism established in England.   The Scottish nobility and gentry did not so much dread either Episcopacy or Independency, in so far as they were ecclesiastical institutions, as they feared the establishment of a military organisation by their powerful neighbour under influences hostile to themselves.[2]   They believed, rightly or wrongly, that a negotiation was on foot between the King and the Independents,[3] and the prospect of a junction between Royalty, Independency, and the New Model army naturally filled them with alarm.

---

[1] Montreuil to Du Bosc, Oct. $\frac{17}{27}$; Transcript of a paper given to Montreuil ; Questions put by Montreuil, *Arch. des Aff. Étrangères*, li. fol. 284, 308, 315.

[2] Montreuil told Mazarin that the Scots asked for the establishment of Presbyterianism in England, 'ayans toujours à craindre de l'Angleterre tant qu'elle ne se gouvernerait point dans les choses de la religion par un mesme esprit que l'Escosse.'   Montreuil to Mazarin, Oct. $\frac{16}{26}$.   *Arch. des Aff. Étrangères*, li. fol. 317.

[3] Balmerino had told Montreuil 'que le Prince Robert avoit apporté de Bristo à Oxford les articles de la paix entre le Roy de la Grande

Some weeks would necessarily elapse before the success of Moray's mission could be known in England. Long before

Oct. 22.
Lord Digby's correspondence read.

that time arrived the Houses were in possession of information which strengthened their resolution to make no peace with the King on any terms short of his absolute submission. Lord Digby's correspondence had been captured at Sherburn, as his master's had been captured at Naseby, and during the last week in October the Houses learnt more than they had ever known before of the details of the negotiation with the Prince of Orange for his daughter's hand, and of the readiness of the Stadtholder to employ Dutch shipping against the English Parliament. Something too they discovered of aid implored by Charles from Denmark, and of contributions expected from the French clergy. Above all things it was clear that Charles continued to hope for the intervention of an Irish army, and that he had consented to the abolition of the penal laws. One passage struck nearer home. "We are," wrote some one, who was probably Digby himself, "in hourly expectation of an answer from the Scots' army to those overtures made unto them, whereof I advertised you formerly, and we have cause to hope well of that negotiation." [1]

It would evidently be unwise to publish letters in which so many foreign States, and possibly the Scots themselves, were

The Independent leaders strengthened.

compromised, and for the present at least they were allowed to remain unprinted. [2] Yet they could not but confirm the hold which the Independent leaders had acquired upon the House as the chief supporters of the war. Their influence, indeed, was now greater than ever, as, by a combination with a group of members which was not disposed to accept their whole programme, they had of

Bretagne et les Anglois Independans, et qu'on attendoit le dit Roy pour les signer.' Montreuil to Mazarin, Sept. $\frac{18}{28}$. *Arch. des Aff. Étrangères*, li. fol. 568. Later information connected the King more directly with the negotiation.

[1] *L.J.* vii. 666 ; *The Lord George Digby's Cabinet*, E. 329, 15.

[2] Till March 26, 1646. The passage about the Scots is in *L.J.* vii. 668.

late found themselves on the winning side even on questions
of religion. The Independents had long discovered that
it would be as imprudent as it would be useless to throw
obstacles in the way of the establishment of Presbyterianism.
They had, therefore, found it expedient to preserve silence on
the question of liberty of worship for sectarian congregations
outside the Presbyterian pale till a more convenient season

They find
common
ground
against
Scottish
Presby-
terianism.

should arrive. Yet if such a season was ever to
arrive, it was necessary to provide that the Presbyterianism to be established should not assume a
thoroughly Scottish character—that is to say, that it
should not be entirely in the hands of the clergy
and of the clerically-minded laity, but that it should be subjected to the influences which prevailed in distinctively lay
society. In working in this direction the Independents were
certain of the support of many who would not hear of toleration, especially as not only the lawyers but not a few of the
ordinary supporters of Presbyterianism were Erastian at heart,
and no more wished to be subjected to clerical Presbyterianism
than they had formerly wished to be subjected to Episcopacy.

The battle was fought out on a question sure to arise as
soon as any attempt was made to bring the Presbyterian system

May 9.
Discussion
on exclusion
from the
Lord's
Supper.

into action. As early as on May 9 the Houses
decided that the right of exclusion from participation in the Lord's Supper should rest, as the
Assembly had desired, in the eldership—that is to
say, in the lay elders combined with the minister. They
themselves, however, drew up a definition of the competent
knowledge to be required of communicants, as well as a list of
the moral offences which were to debar from communion.[1]

Aug. 4.
Claims of
the Assem-
bly.

To this the Assembly took exception. On August 4,
finding that the Houses persisted in refusing to
allow to the eldership an arbitrary and unlimited
power of exclusion, they stated their own view of the case in
reply. "How," they asked, "can that power be called arbitrary which is not according to the will of man, but the will
of Christ ; or how can it be supposed to be unlimited which is

[1] *L.J.* vii. 362.

circumscribed and regulated by the exactest law—the Word of God?"[1]

Such views obtained little, if any, support in either of the Houses. Both Lords and Commons went tranquilly on their way in drawing up rules for the choice of elders, and on September 29 the Lords insisted, not only on maintaining the list of offences, but on adding a clause to the effect that if there were any not specified which were thought by the elders to deserve excommunication, no action should be taken by them till the matter had been referred to a standing committee of both Houses, 'to the end that the Parliament, if need require, may hear and determine the same.'[2] This proposal was accepted by the Commons, and was finally, on October 20, embodied in an ordinance.[3]

Sept. 29.

A committee of both Houses on excommunication proposed.

Oct. 20. Ordinance authorising it.

The same spirit which prevailed in prescribing limitations to the authority of the elders prevailed in the rules laid down for their election. Pending the full introduction of the system in the counties, Parliament had resolved to set up a model in London. London was to be divided into twelve classes, to which a thirteenth, comprising the Inns of Court and other abodes of lawyers, was subsequently added. In each of these classes was erected a board of nine triers, without whose confirmation no election of elders by the congregations would have any validity. Each board of triers was to consist of three ministers and six laymen, and, what was of more importance, these triers were to be named not by any church assembly but by Parliamentary ordinance.

To the zealous Presbyterians of the Assembly the course taken by Parliament was a sore discomfiture. "Our greatest trouble for the time," wrote Baillie, "is from the Erastians of the House of Commons. They are at last content to erect presbyteries and synods in all the land. . . . Yet they give to the ecclesiastical courts so little power that the Assembly, finding their petitions not granted, are in great doubt whether to set up anything, till, by some

Baillie's lament.

---

[1] Petitions, Aug. 4, 12. *L.J.* vii. 523, 534.

[2] *L.J.* vii. 609.

[3] *Ibid.* vii. 649, 652.

powerful petition of many thousand hands, they obtain some more of their just desires. The only means to obtain this and all else we desire is our recruited army about Newark."[1]

Baillie's cry for 'some powerful petition' was evidently addressed to the City of London, which was already taking its stand with the Presbyterian Scots, if not in its zeal to subject the laity to the clergy, at least in its desire to free both laity and clergy when assembled for ecclesiastical purposes from the interference of Parliament. The Common Council represented, not the whole of the inhabitants, but the tradesmen and merchants of London. Their religion was a good average religion, and their morality a good average morality. Of the heights and depths of spiritual warfare, of the soul's travail, and of the eager quest for truth, they neither knew nor cared to know anything. Milton's scornful reference to the rich man who would fain be religious, and who, having found out some divine of note and estimation, made 'the very person of that man his religion,' and having feasted him and entertained him in the evening, and in the morning, gladly allowed him to walk abroad at eight, and to leave 'his kind entertainer in the shop trading all day without his religion,'[2] was doubtless a caricature, though not without a basis of truth. Yet there was another side from which a picture might be drawn. The religion of the London citizens on the whole implied an observance of those common rules of honesty and self-restraint, without which all religion is vain, and which in the eighteenth century continued to characterise them, after the zeal of Puritanism had melted away.

Religion of the London citizens.

Such men could not but be Presbyterian, though their Presbyterianism was likely to be more after Prynne's type than after Baillie's. The lay-elderships opened to them a whole sphere of disciplinary activity, and they would be quite ready to use their new powers in silencing the voices of those who, for any reason, were unwilling to tread the beaten paths. They had a horror of singularity, especially if singularity appeared likely to lead to disquiet.

Their Presbyterianism.

[1] *Baillie*, ii. 318.　　　　[2] *Areopagitica.*

Within the last few weeks a controversy had arisen in the City which served to disclose the temper of the citizens. A lectureship supported by voluntary contributions at the church of St. Mary's Aldermanbury, of which Calamy was the minister, was controlled by a committee representing the subscribers. The lecturer was Henry Burton, and for some time the congregation heard him gladly. Of late he had given offence by advocating the Independent system, but his culminating fault was that he called on his hearers to make sure of their religion by personal investigation, and not to take it on trust from Parliament or Assembly. On this the committee locked the door of the church in his face and put an end to his lectureship. In the controversy which followed no stress was laid by the committee on the scriptural argument for Presbyterianism. What was wanted was not a divinely appointed model of church government, but peace and quiet. The committee was quite ready to trust Parliament to make some arrangement which would satisfy all moderate men, and to which all who were not moderate must be compelled to submit. If their lecturer was to stir up troublesome questions, he would not only foster distractions in the congregation, but might drive influential subscribers to withhold their subscriptions.[1]

Controversy at St. Mary's Aldermanbury.

Burton's lectureship.

Sept. 23. His sermon gives offence.

Oct. 6. The door of the church locked against him.

To do the committee justice, it had not merely to be on its guard against the high champions of spiritual religion. Independency was apt to assume an unlovely shape in the eyes of the well-to-do citizen. The main danger, as far as he was concerned, did not lie in the enforcement of the ideas of the Dissenting Brethren concerning ecclesiastical organisation, but in the noisy ranting of the tub-preacher. Wild incoherency of ignorant speech was flowing from the mouths of men and women who had no sense of decorum and no capacity for grasping the relative importance of doctrines, while they regarded themselves as immensely superior to those who had hitherto been counted as their

Twofold aspect of Independency.

[1] *Truth shut out of doors*, by H. Burton, E. 311, 1 ; *The door of truth opened*, E. 311, 15.

betters. On one occasion at least this reversal of the old order led to the deliberate defilement of the pews in which the wealthier citizens ensconced themselves, and which were as hateful to the equalitarian zeal of the sectaries as they had been to Laud.[1]

Whilst Presbyterianism was obtaining a firm hold on the City, the Dissenting Brethren in the Assembly marked the growing influence of the Independents in the House of Commons. In April they had been bidden to produce their own scheme of church government. On October 13 they flatly refused to do anything of the kind. They declared that the majority of the Assembly had shown itself so hostile that it was hopeless to expect from it a fair construction of anything that they might propose.[2] It was the House of Lords, and not the House of Commons, which now took up the cause of the minority by ordering, on November 6, the revival of Cromwell's Accommodation Order for a committee to consider how an accommodation could be effected between the Presbyterian system and that of the Dissenting Brethren.[3] It can hardly be doubted that the Lords came to this resolution, not because they approved of it, but because they feared something worse. On the 14th the proposal of the Lords was accepted by the Commons. It was all in vain. What had been in September 1644, when Cromwell proposed it, a healing measure, was in November 1645 a mere retrograde expedient for shelving an inconvenient subject. The Dissenting Brethren would have none of it. The first meeting of the committee, on the 17th, showed that an arrangement on these terms was impracticable. The Independents declared for full liberty of con-

Oct. 13.
The Dissenting Brethren refuse to produce a scheme of church government.

Nov. 6.
The Lords revive the Accommodation Order.

Nov. 14.
Its acceptance by the Commons.

Nov. 17.
The Dissenting Brethren declare for full liberty of conscience.

---

[1] *A just defence of J. Bastwick*, p. 41. E. 265, 2.

[2] *A copy of a Remonstrance.* E. 309, 4. In *The answer of the Assembly*, E. 506, 11, this is said to have been dated Oct. 22, but see *The Minutes of . . . . the Westminster Assembly*, 148, where it is mentioned at the end of the sitting of the 13th.

[3] See vol. ii. p. 30.

science. They 'expressed themselves,' as Baillie sadly wrote, 'for toleration, not only to themselves, but to other sects.'[1]

This audacious demand roused the London citizens. On the 19th, by order of the Common Council, a batch of petitions was laid before the Houses. They asked for certain amendments in the Ordinance on Church Government, and especially that care might be taken for the maintenance of unity by the establishment of Presbyterian discipline. The Commons replied in a somewhat surly tone. The answer of the Lords was far more sympathetic.[2] The two views of Puritan ecclesiastical development were at last brought face to face.

Nov. 19. London petitions.

As long as the war lasted it would manifestly be impossible to bring so grave a question to an issue, and it was hard to see how the war could be brought speedily to an end without the assistance of the Scottish army. On November 13, therefore, the Houses postponed till March the date at which their irritating demand for the surrender of the northern fortresses was to be complied with.[3] They were rewarded by knowing that Leven's army had moved southwards. Before the end of November the Scots took up their quarters on the north side of Newark, whilst Poyntz completed the investment on the south.[4]

Nov. 13. Question of the surrender of the northern fortresses postponed.

Nov. 27. Newark invested.

If the Scots were to be satisfied, more would be needed than an abandonment for a time of an offensive proposal. On November 24 their commissioners again pressed for supplies for their army, for the settlement of religion, and for a speedy consideration of the terms to be offered to the King.[5] To settle religion, as matters stood, was plainly impossible; but, at least, the farce of preparing peace propositions which the King was certain to reject could be gone through, and for some weeks the Commons were hard at work on the

Nov. 24. Demands of the Scots.

Peace propositions to be prepared.

[1] *L.J.* vii. 679; *C.J.* iv. 338, 342; Whitacre's Diary, *Add. MSS.* 31,116, fol. 242; *Baillie*, ii. 326.

[2] *C.J.* iv. 348; *L.J.* vii. 713. [3] *C.J.* iv. 341.

[4] *Ibid.* 362. [5] *L.J.* viii. 9.

well-worn task. The categories of delinquency were extended,
Dec. 1.
Rewards
for the
Parliamen-
tary leaders.
and a demand was inserted that Essex, Northumberland, Warwick, and Pembroke should receive
dukedoms, that Manchester and Salisbury should
become marquises, Robartes, Say and Sele, Wharton, Willoughby of Parham, and the elder Fairfax earls. At
the same time Holles was to be created a viscount, and
Cromwell, the elder Vane, and Sir Thomas Fairfax were to be
raised to the peerage as barons. Sir Thomas was to have
5,000*l.* a year, Cromwell and Waller 2,500*l.*, Hazlerigg and
Stapleton 2,000*l.* apiece, Brereton 1,500*l.*, and Skippon 1,000*l.*
Evidently the House was bent on making no distinction between Presbyterians and Independents in this distribution of
honours and rewards.[1]

Even before these impossible terms of peace were discussed in the House of Commons, the Scottish commissioners
Nov.
A secret
negotiation
between the
King and
the Inde-
pendents.
learnt that the Independents were secretly negotiating with the King on far different conditions. The
Independents, it seemed, were ready to make over
to the King the New Model army and the fortresses
in its possession if he would ultimately allow them
to retreat to Ireland, and to enjoy there the liberty of worship
which they would be the first to refuse to the Irish Catholics.[2]
The knowledge of this negotiation made the Scots all the
more anxious to learn the result of Moray's mission to the
Sir R.
Moray's
report.
Queen. When at last the news arrived, a little
before the end of November, it was far from being
as satisfactory as they had hoped. For some time
the Queen had obstinately refused to give any support to the
establishment of Presbyterianism, and though she ultimately
gave way before Mazarin's entreaties so far as to promise to
write to the King in favour of the Scottish demands, it was only
on condition that Moray should not be told of her promise.[3]

---

[1] *C.J.* iv. 359.

[2] Montreuil to Mazarin, Nov. $\frac{13}{23}$. *Arch. des Aff. Étrangères,* li. fol. 356.

[3] Montreuil to Mazarin, Nov. $\frac{20}{30}$; Mazarin to Montreuil, $\frac{\text{Nov. 21}}{\text{Dec. 1}}$; Moray
to the Scottish commissioners. Copied $\frac{\text{Nov. 27}}{\text{Dec. 7}}$, written about a fortnight
earlier. *Arch. des Aff. Étrangères,* li. fol. 359, 364, 369.

It is probable that the grounds of the Queen's disinclination to accept Moray's overtures are to be found in the eager-

Reasons of the Queen's disinclination to come to terms with the Scots.

ness with which she had for some months been seeking for help from the Continental Catholics on behalf of the Catholics in England. The Pope now on the throne was no longer Urban VIII., who during a long pontificate had striven to advance the interests of his Church by a politic moderation. Innocent X. had

Sept. $\frac{5}{15}$. Innocent X.

been chosen as his successor in September 1644. Though Innocent was a slave to his sister, and his own household a prey to disorder, yet in dealing with the outer world he showed conspicuous firmness of a kind which, for want of knowledge of the ways of men, was likely to prove more disastrous to the causes which he advocated than to those which he opposed. He was a fair type of the administrative ecclesiastic, without spiritual aspirations or priestly subtlety.[1]

In the winter succeeding his election the new Pope received Bellings, the secretary of the Irish Confederate Catho-

1645. Bellings in Rome.

lics, who had come to solicit help in money. Much to the surprise of Bellings, Innocent resolved to send a representative to Ireland, who would act directly in his name, and would give him information on the state of affairs uninfluenced by Irish parties. Early

March $\frac{5}{15}$. Rinuccini's mission.

in March he announced that he had chosen Rinuccini, Archbishop of Fermo, to be his Nuncio in Ireland.

Rinuccini was a churchman of resolute character, with a power of bending others to his will which would stand him in good stead in Ireland if his inflexibility did not drive from his

May. He reaches Paris.

side those whom it was to his interest to gain. In May he arrived in Paris, bringing with him a store of money from Rome, which he hoped to increase with the help of a contribution from Mazarin. It was long before he could obtain a favourable answer from the Cardinal. The Pope had already given grave offence to Mazarin by his

Visitors to the Loan Exhibition of 1886-7 will not be likely to forget the marvellous portrait of this Pope by Velasquez.

leaning to the Spaniards, and the French statesman was probably anxious to know the issue of the conflict in England before committing himself even in secret to a decided policy.

The Nuncio therefore found the summer months slipping away, whilst his purpose was still uneffected. Between him

Rinuccini
and the
Queen. and the Queen of England there soon sprang up that feeling of tacit hostility which shows itself clearly beneath the veil of outward courtesy. Rinuccini wished to advance the authority of the Papal See, without caring whether Charles remained a king or no. Henrietta Maria wanted to combine her pious devotion to her Church with a vigorous effort on behalf of her husband and

July.
She cannot
receive him. herself. She was unable even to receive a visit from the Archbishop, as he refused to visit her except in the state of a Nuncio, and she knew well that his appearance in her presence in such a guise would compromise her in the eyes of all Protestant Englishmen. The Nuncio, on his part, was glad to avoid the visit which he pretended to desire, as he feared lest he should be wheedled out of some promise which he might find it inconvenient to fulfil when he

Aug. 15.
Mazarin
gives him
shipping
and money. arrived in Ireland. At last, on August 15, Mazarin gave him 25,000 crowns and shipping for transport. The Cardinal had probably no desire to waste his energies in Ireland, but it was important to him to keep a hold on the affections of the people, if it were only to prevent them from falling under the influence of the King of Spain.[1]

Rinuccini had thus been delayed in France for many weeks by his negotiations with Mazarin. Though it was evident that when he arrived in Ireland he would not be eager to work in the interests of Charles, the Queen had not lost hope of winning the Pope to her side. At the beginning of the summer she had at last despatched Sir Kenelm Digby to

June.
Mission of
Sir Kenelm
Digby. Rome to negotiate for an advance of money on her own behalf, and on behalf of the mixed committee of English and Irish Catholics which met at Paris.[2] On his arrival at Rome he was full of hope that his request

[1] Rinuccini, *Nunziatura*, 7-47.   [2] See vol. ii. p. 170.

for pecuniary assistance would be shortly granted. For a moment his torrent of words appeared to carry everything before it. Innocent himself declared that the Englishman spoke not merely as a Catholic, but as an ecclesiastic. Rome, however, had not so lost her cunning as to be carried away by the promises of a sanguine enthusiast who gave glib assurances that, if Charles owed his success to Catholic aid, the hearts of the King and of his chief supporters would return to the one fold and the one shepherd. Digby was asked what warrant he had to produce from the King. As soon as it appeared that he had none to show, cold looks convinced him that his mission was likely to fail. The paper on which he had couched his demands was forwarded to Paris for Rinuccini's criticism, and the utmost that he could obtain was an order for 20,000 crowns, to be spent in munitions of war.[1]

In the beginning of the winter Henrietta Maria had still hopes of Digby's success. She continued to correspond with the French Catholics who had talked of supporting foreign troops in England, and she thought it possible that Mazarin might be induced, now that the troops of the continental powers had retired into winter quarters, to lend her some soldiers from the French army itself.[2] It must have been therefore a severe wrench to her mind to have to apply herself to a project for establishing Presbyterianism in England, especially as she knew well that she would be favouring the system which was of all others the most hostile to a Catholic propaganda.

Nov.
The Queen's hopes from France.

Half-hearted as the Queen's support was, the Scots in London and their English Presbyterian allies could not afford to reject it. Knowing that Charles was already engaged in a negotiation with the Independents, their fears inclined them to regard that negotiation as more serious than it really was. Generous as were the offers which the Independents were making, it is unlikely that Charles would have responded to them at all but for

Oct.
Charles negotiates with the Independents.

---

[1] Rinuccini, *Nunziatura*, 32, 445, 446; *Lord Leicester's MS.* fol. 856.

[2] The Queen to the Duke of Orleans, Nov. ? *R.O. Transcripts.*

the pressure put upon him by his own partisans. Yet before the end of October, whilst he was still at Newark, he had Vavasour's authorised a Royalist officer, Sir William Vavasour, mission. to surrender himself a prisoner in order that he might discuss terms of peace with the leading Independents. When the King reached Oxford, however, little belief was entertained of his intention to accept a peace. In vain did Dorset, Southampton, Hertford, and Lindsey conjure him to put an end to the miserable war. He answered fiercely that he would place the crown on his head, and would defend it with his own sword, if the swords of his friends failed him. If, as there is little doubt, the terms offered by the Independents were known in Oxford, as they were known to Montreuil in London, it is easy to understand the irritating effect produced by the King's words upon men who would have been delighted to find peace thrown in their way without the necessity of bowing their necks under the Presbyterian yoke. Unless Montreuil was misinformed, the Independents offered

Nov.
Terms
offered by
the Inde-
pendents.

before the end of November to allow the King to regulate matters of religion in concurrence with his Parliament after his return to Westminster, and to leave at his disposal half the places of authority in the realm. They asked in return that after the army had conquered Ireland he would establish Independency there, and tolerate it in England.[1] If the Parliament threw any difficulty in the way of this arrangement, the army would place itself at the King's

Nov.
Alleged plot
against the
King.

disposal and force it to give way.[2] So incensed were the earls at Charles's rejection of these proposals, that they sent to Westminster offering to deliver up the King on the sole condition that their own properties might be secured to them.

---

[1] This has passed through the mind of a Frenchman, but it probably means that neither the Roman Catholic nor the Presbyterian organisation was to be allowed to exist in Ireland, if indeed the contrast between establishment and toleration is more than a flourish.

"J'en ai apris ces particularitez qu'ils offrent audit Roy, de luy laisser regler les choses de la Religion quand il sera de retour en son Parlement, de luy donner la disposition de la moitié des gouvernemens et

In some way or another the plot became known to Vavasour, who at once sent information of it to Charles.[1]　On

Dec.
Charles is
informed
of it, December 5, accordingly, the King, anxious to disarm this dangerous opposition in his own camp, wrote to Westminster and proposed that the Houses

Dec. 5.
and offers
to negotiate
with Parliament. should send commissioners to open negotiations.[2] As it soon appeared that the commissioners were to propose that Charles should come to Westminster to treat in person,[3] the Houses naturally drew back, fearing lest

Dec. 9.
Vavasour
arrested, his presence would be a mere centre of intrigue. For some time they hesitated to send any answer

Dec. 17.
and
banished. whatever. On the 9th the House of Commons ordered the arrest of Vavasour, and on the 17th they expelled him from England.[5]

The Houses were undoubtedly right in their suspicions. Vavasour's mission had, as one of his companions informed

Charles
wishes to
gain time. Montreuil, been contrived merely to spin out time till foreign troops could arrive in England,[5] and it was hardly likely that the King's proposal to visit Westminster had any other end in view. His mind was now full of a combination between the scheme of Willis, which he had rejected in October,[6] and a scheme for the landing of

des charges de son Royaume, et de luy pourvoir des forces suffisantes pour se rendre maitre d'Irlande à condition que l'Independance sera establye et sera soufferte en Angleterre, et que, si le Parlement d'Angleterre n'est pas satisfaict de ces conditions, ils pretendent donner leur armée au Roy d'Angleterre pour les forcer à les recevoir."—Montreuil to Brienne, Nov. $\frac{20}{30}$. *Carte MSS.* lxxxiii. fol. 111.

[1] Montreuil to Mazarin, Dec. $\frac{4}{14}$. *Arch. des Aff. Étrangères,* li. fol. 383. Vavasour had received permission to come to London on Oct. 30. *C.J.* iv. 326. Montreuil derived his information from a messenger employed by Vavasour.

[2] The King to the Speaker of the House of Lords, Dec. 5. *L.J.* viii. 31.

[3] Charles's intention is mentioned on the 11th in *The Diary.* E. 311, 23. Compare *The Scottish Dove.* E. 313, 6.

[4] *C.J.* iv. 370, 379.

[5] Montreuil to Mazarin, Dec. $\frac{4}{14}$. *Arch. des Aff. Étrangères,* li. fol. 383.

[6] See vol. ii. p. 366.

French troops which was in favour with the Queen. On

Dec. 7.
The Prince
to leave
England.

December 7 he reiterated his orders to the Prince to leave England, so that the rebels, if they succeeded in capturing himself, might know that the heir to the

The Duke
of York to
go to Ire-
land.

crown was beyond their reach.[1]   The Duke of York was to be conveyed as soon as possible to Ireland. Orders were sent to the governors of Worcester, Exeter, Newark, Chester, and Oxford to destroy their fortifica-

A mar-
vellous plan
of campaign.

tions simultaneously on February 20, and to concentrate on Worcester.   In this way the King hoped to be at the head of an army of 3,000 foot and 2,500 horse.   He might then either march to the West to relieve his overmatched forces in Devon and Cornwall, or might turn towards Kent and Sussex, where, as it was believed, the inhabitants were prepared to 'rise with great cheerfulness' if only the King appeared amongst them.   It was expected that by April 1 Astley, who, now that South Wales was lost, had been sent to take up Prince Maurice's command in the Border counties, would have succeeded in raising at least 2,000 recruits in Worcestershire and in the neighbouring districts.   The Queen's foreign forces would serve to fill up the numbers of the army.[2]

Charles was never content with a single project, and simultaneously with this scheme for a renewed military effort he had embarked heartily on another scheme which might give him the assistance of the Scottish army.   He had doubtless been made aware before his message was sent to the Houses, on December 5, that the Scottish and English Presbyterians in

His object
in wishing
to come to
Westmin-
ster.

London wished to come to an understanding with him.   He was therefore anxious to be allowed to appear at Westminster, not because he expected to come to terms with Parliament, but because he hoped to come to terms with the Scots.   If the Scots rejected

---

[1] The King to the Prince, Dec. 7.   *Clarendon,* ix. 114.

[2] Jermyn to Hyde, Nov. 17 ; Ashburnham to Culpepper, Dec. 13, *Clar. MSS.* 2,029, 2,046.   Mutilated portions of the latter are printed in *Clar. St. P.* ii. 196.   The allusions to the foreign forces are somewhat veiled, but there can be no doubt as to their meaning, especially as the intention comes out more clearly afterwards.

his offer, he might fall back on his military plan. He was prepared to ask permission to remain at Westminster for forty days, and he calculated that, as that permission could not reach him before the end of the year, his proposed visit would come to an end not long before February 20, the day fixed for the concentration of his forces at Worcester. He had therefore asked to be allowed, if the negotiation failed, to retire in safety to Oxford, Newark, or Worcester. The reason why these places were named is not difficult to guess. If Charles came to terms with the Scots he would join their army at Newark. If he did not, he would put himself at the head of his own army at Worcester. Oxford can only have been spoken of to disarm suspicion.[1]

When projects so wild were entertained, the fact that Rupert was once more at his uncle's side could have no mili-
Rupert's return to Oxford. tary or political significance. As he had declined to engage never more to draw his sword against Parliament, and the Houses had refused him a passport to go beyond sea on these conditions, he cut his way through their armies to Woodstock, and on December 8 humbled himself sufficiently to ask forgiveness from the King. Charles was well pleased to receive him at Oxford, but he never gave him his confidence again.[2]

Of the two contradictory policies in which Charles was involved, the negotiation with the Scots assumed a more prominent position than the wild military scheme—so impossible to carry into execution—over which he sometimes brooded. On
Dec. 6.
Sir R.
Moray's
return. December 6, the day after the King's message was despatched to Westminster, Sir Robert Moray returned to England, bringing with him the Queen's tardily given consent to the greater part of the Scotch demands.[3] Though Montreuil was in hopes that the religious difficulty might be smoothed away, he had first to deal with an obstacle

---

[1] Ashburnham to Culpepper, Dec. 13. *Clar. St. P.* ii. 196.

[2] *Warburton*, iii. 208. Dorset's letter, printed by Warburton at p. 213, should have been dated Nov. 25, not Dec. 25, and Nicholas's letter of June 10 was written in 1645, not in 1646.

[3] See p. 12.

in the King's refusal to employ Will Murray in Scotland,
though the Scottish commissioners had expressed
a wish that he might be sent there by the Queen,
the ground of Charles's refusal being that Murray
was distasteful to Montrose, who 'was principally to
be consulted in that business.'[1]

Suggested employ-ment of Will Murray

Charles's feeling towards Montrose did honour to his heart.
"Be assured," he had written to him early in November, "that
your less prosperous fortune is so far from lessening
my estimation of you that it will rather cause my
affection to kythe the clearlier to you."[2]   In anyone
but Charles the adoption of the notion that it was possible to
combine the services of Montrose and the Scottish Presbyterians might fairly be set down as a symptom of an unsound
mind.   The Scots had certainly shown themselves unsparing
to Montrose's followers.   On October 21 Sir William
Rollock, his companion in his daring ride across the
Lowlands from England, was beheaded in Glasgow.
On the 22nd two more, Sir Philip Nisbet and Alexander Ogilvy, of Inverquharity, shared his fate.
Ogilvy's appearance on the scaffold aroused almost
universal commiseration.   He was but a lad of eighteen, and
singularly attractive in the flush of opening manhood, but the
Kirk had been too terrified to be merciful.   David Dickson,
the moderator of the Assembly of 1640, who had wept tears of
joy when Episcopacy was abolished, triumphed in the deed of
cruelty.   "The work," he cried, "goes bonnily on."   Such
words were not easily forgotten in the land.[3]

Charles and Mont-rose.

Oct. 21. Execution of Rollock at Glasgow,

Oct. 22. and of Nisbet and Ogilvy.

Other victims were reserved for a yet more solemn sacrifice
when the Scottish Parliament next met.   To Charles it seemed
easy to bring the slayers and the kinsmen of the slain to make
common cause in his behalf.   The Scots, in England at least,

---

[1] Montreuil to Mazarin, Dec. $\frac{12}{22}$, *Arch. des Aff. Étrangères*, li. fol.
397 ; Ashburnham to Culpepper, Dec. 13, *Clarendon MSS.* 2,046.

[2] *i.e.* to show itself more plainly to you.   The King to Montrose,
Nov. 3.   Napier, *Memoirs of Montrose*, ii. 614.

[3] *Guthry's Memoirs*, 166.   For the dates, see Napier, *Memoirs of Montrose*, ii. 589.

were profuse in expressions of devotion. On December 13
Charles received from Lord Sinclair and David Leslie a direct
Charles
hopes much
from the
Scots.
invitation to the Scottish camp. Yet, if Charles was
to bend the Scots to his will, it was necessary for
him to visit Westminster that he might employ his
powers of persuasion with the Scottish commissioners there.
Dec. 15.
He urges
the Houses
to nego-
tiate.
He therefore on the 15th repeated his request for a
safe-conduct for the persons whom he proposed to
send to prepare the way for his own visit.[1] His
diplomacy seemed likely to be wrecked on the incur-
Dec. 17.
Mildmay's
speech.
able distrust which he had awakened on every side.
On the 17th Mildmay expressed the feeling which
prevailed in the House of Commons. Their affairs, he said,
were now in good condition. Let them keep the advantages
which they had gained, and renounce all further treaties.
Dec.
Balme-
rino's
doubts.
Balmerino, one of the Scottish commissioners, almost
at the same time declared his belief that the King's
overtures to them were only made in order to induce
the Independents to bring their negotiation to a satisfactory
end.[2] Yet neither the English Parliament nor the Scottish
commissioners liked to announce openly that a breach was
unavoidable, and during the greater part of December a warm
discussion was carried on between these two bodies. In the
Proposed
negotiation.
course of the dispute the Scots urged that the proposed negotiation should be so conducted as to make
it comparatively easy for the King to accept the terms offered
him, whilst the English wished the proposals to be made as
unacceptable as possible.

The time was rapidly approaching when Charles would
have no course open to him but submission to the conquerors.
Dec. 17.
Hereford
surprised.
One fortified post after another was falling into the
hands of his enemies. On December 17 the important city of Hereford was surprised by Morgan
and Birch,[3] and Charles's project of sending his second son

---

[1] *L.J.* viii. 46.

[2] Montreuil to Mazarin, Dec. $\frac{18}{28}$. *Arch. des Aff. Étrangères*, li. fol.
411.

[3] *Several Letters.* E. 313, 17.

to Ireland[1] had of necessity to be abandoned.   Chester was
strictly blocked up, and except in the improbable contingency

Chester
and
Newark
blocked up. of the landing of an Irish army to relieve it, it could
not hold out much longer.   The surrender of
Newark was a mere question of time unless Charles
could induce the Scots to come round to his side.

At last, on December 23, the Houses, with the assent of
the Scots, positively refused to admit the King's commissioners

Dec. 23.
Answer of
the Houses. to Westminster.   They were busy, they said, in preparing terms of peace, which would be presented to
him as soon as they were ready.[2]   Before this answer
reached Charles he had despatched, as he had previously

Dec. 26.
The King
proposes to
come to
Westmin-
ster, planned, a fresh letter, in which he offered to come
in person to Westminster for forty days, if security
were given that at the end of that period he might
retire to Worcester, Newark, or Oxford.   He also
sketched out a plan for dealing with the militia, and on

Dec. 29.
and makes
further
offers. the 29th he further offered to give satisfaction
about Ireland and the public debt.   Up to this
time he had not spoken a word upon the subject
of religion.[3]

Montreuil perceived that if his scheme was not to break
down altogether, it would be necessary to appeal in person to

Montreuil
resolves to
intervene. Charles.   Already there had been signs of a diver-
gency of opinion between the Scots and their Eng-
lish Presbyterian allies.   Before Christmas Balmerino
had been growing impatient because the King did not throw
himself, without further question, into the Scottish army, whilst
Holland, who had been deeply irritated at the refusal of the
House of Commons to grant him 1,000*l.* a year in compensation for the losses which he declared himself to have suffered
in their cause, talked of effecting a Royalist rising in the City
if only Charles could be brought in safety to Westminster.[4]

On January 2 Montreuil arrived at Oxford to urge Charles

---

[1] See p. 18.   [2] *L.J.* viii. 64.

[3] *Ibid.* viii. 72.

[4] *C.J.* iv. 380; Montreuil to Mazarin, $\frac{\text{Dec. 25}}{\text{Jan. 4}}$, *Arch. des Aff. Étrangères*,
lii. 9.

to accept the proposals which he was now commissioned to

lay before him on behalf of the Scots. Charles was to accept the propositions rejected by him at Uxbridge, and then to betake himself to the army

Jan. 3.
Lays the
Scottish
proposals
before the
King.

before Newark. In his reply, the King compared favourably the zeal of the Scots for his person with the resolution of the Independents to place the monarchy in bonds, but he would hear nothing of an arrangement which would virtually establish Presbyterianism in the Church of England. He would, he said, lose

his crown rather than his soul. He was, however, quite ready to go to Leven's army if the Scots would engage themselves for his safety, and if the Queen Regent of France and Mazarin would give security for the fulfilment of that engagement. Of Montrose he spoke with unqualified praise. "From henceforth," he said, "I place Montrose amongst my children, and mean to live with him as a friend, and not as a king."

A further conversation gave Montreuil the key to Charles's readiness to trust himself to the Scots, whilst refusing the con-

cession which they most eagerly demanded. He found him convinced that the Scottish negotiators had no conscientious motives in urging the establishment of Presbyterianism in England, and that they merely wanted the security of the bishops' lands for the payment of their own arrears, or at the most were afraid lest, if bishops were re-established in England, they would be re-established in Scotland as well. To meet the second difficulty he proposed to offer the security of the French Government for the maintenance of the existing church government in the Northern kingdom. With respect to the first, he offered to the Scots lands in Ireland in place of church property in England. How far this proposal would affect the negotiation which he was still carrying on with the Confederate Catholics, he probably did not care to inquire.

Stubborn as Charles was, he at last discovered that some concession must be made to the religious feeling which even the Scots might be supposed to possess. The restored Church

of England, he told Montreuil on the 5th, should grant toleration to English Presbyterians and to Scottish visitors. He

Jan. 5.
Charles
proposes to
tolerate
Presby-
terianism. had, in fact, rightly discerned that the Scottish
nobles were not entirely dominated by religious
enthusiasm ; but he had failed to understand that
they were anxious to see a Presbyterian Church
established in England because such a Church would
be not only through its system friendly to Scotland, but
would, from its very weakness, be driven to seek support in
Edinburgh.

When Montreuil returned to Westminster he found that
the reception of Charles's proposals was even worse than he

Reception
of this pro-
posal by
the Scots. had expected.[1] The Scottish commissioners had
recently been joined by Lauderdale, and Lauder-
dale, keen of vision and firm of purpose, was not
likely to favour the acceptance of a mere toleration for Presbyterians, which would allow a restored Cavalier England to
grow up and hold out a hand to the Royalist nobility of
Scotland.

If Charles failed to conciliate the Scots, he also failed to
conciliate the English Parliament. On January 3 the House

Jan. 3.
Reply
drawn up
to the
King's pro-
posal to
come to
Westmin-
ster. agreed to a further answer to Charles's proposal to
come to Westminster. "Concerning the personal
treaty desired by your Majesty," they declared,
"there being so much innocent blood of your good
subjects shed in this war by your Majesty's commands and commissions ; Irish rebels brought over
into both kingdoms, and endeavours to bring over more to
both of them, as also forces from foreign parts, and the Prince
at the head of an army in the West, divers towns made
garrisons and kept by your Majesty against the Parliament
of England, there being also forces in Scotland against that
Parliament and kingdom by your Majesty's commission ; the
war in Ireland fomented and prolonged by your Majesty,
whereby the three kingdoms are brought to utter ruin and
destruction ; we conceive that, until satisfaction and security

---

[1] Montreuil to Mazarin, Jan. $\frac{5}{15}$, Arch. des Aff. Étrangères, lii. fol. 45 ;
The King to the Queen, Jan. 8, Charles I. in 1646 (Camden Soc.), 3.

be first given to both your kingdoms, your Majesty's coming
hither cannot be convenient or by us consented to." To
accept the propositions which would shortly be despatched
to him would 'be the only means' to give satisfaction.[1] To
the last phrase the Scottish commissioners, who had another
project of their own, took exception, and it was only after it
had been somewhat toned down that they consented to the
despatch of the reply. It was not till January 13
that this reply was at last sent off.[2] Even then it
must have been offensive enough to Charles. It
refused to admit to the position of a constitutional king one
who had been a promoter of foreign invasion.

Jan. 13.
The reply
sent to
Charles.

Charles had no conception of the injury done to his cause
by these foreign entanglements. On January 10, in a letter to
the French Agent, he had committed to writing the
concessions which he was prepared to make to
the Scots. The religious disputes in England were
to be composed by a national synod, which, although
some Scottish divines were to be admitted to it, would certainly
be a very different body from the existing Westminster Assembly. Toleration was to be accorded to the Presbyterians.
Charles was the more confident that he would carry his point,
because he was aware that the Presbyterian system adopted by
the House of Commons did not altogether tally with that
which existed in Scotland, and he seems to have fancied that
the Scots would therefore be disinclined to press for the lukewarm system which found favour with the English Parliament.
How little he knew of the motives which influenced the Scottish nobility was, however, clear from the words in which he
pressed for their union with the man of whom they were most
jealous. "Lastly," he wrote, "concerning the Marquis of
Montrose, his Majesty's resolution is that he and his party
shall be received into this conjunction with all possible freedom
and honour without any reservation." [3]

Jan. 10.
The King's
formal
overture to
the Scots.

Whatever the Scottish commissioners might be induced to
say, their countrymen in Scotland had set their minds in a very

---

[1] *L.J.* viii. 81.   [2] *Ibid.* viii. 91, 99.
[3] The King to Montreuil, Jan. 10. *Clar. St. P.* ii. 209.

different direction.　Sitting at St. Andrews amidst the howls
of the Kirk for blood, the Scottish Parliament opened its proceedings on December 23 by ordering that all Irish
captives still remaining in prison should be put to
death without form of trial.[1]　On January 16 they
condemned to death Nathaniel Gordon, William
Murray, Andrew Guthry, and Sir Robert Spottiswoode, the latter being the brother of the Archbishop, and guilty of having, as Charles's Secretary
of State, prepared Montrose's commission, and of
having brought it down to Scotland.　Every one of these
had been admitted to quarter after Philiphaugh, and Spottiswoode could plead that he had taken no part in operations of war.　On the 20th three of the number—
Gordon, Guthry, and Spottiswoode—were executed.
Murray received a respite, as his brother, the Earl of
Tullybardine, pleaded for his life on the ground of his youth,
and even alleged him to be insane.　The appeal for mercy
was, however, rejected, and on the 22nd the young
Murray followed his comrades to the scaffold, claiming it as his highest honour to die for a king who
was the father of his country.

Lord Ogilvy escaped, but not through the mercy of the
Covenanters.　He owed his life, as many another has done, to
the brave devotion of a woman.　His mother, his
wife, and his sister were permitted to visit him in
prison.　When the time for parting came, the keepers conducted, as they supposed, three weeping ladies from the cell.
One of these figures was that of young Ogilvy himself, whose
sister had exchanged clothes with him, and had taken his place
in bed.[2]

Ignorant of the doom impending over his loyal subjects at
St. Andrews, Charles, having prepared the way by his communications with the Scottish commissioners, addressed himself for the first time on January 15 to the English Parliament

Marginal notes:

1645.
Nov. 26.
The Parlia-
ment at St.
Andrews.

Dec. 23.

1646.
Jan. 16.
Sentence on
Montrose's
followers.

Jan. 20.
Three
executions.

Jan. 22.
Murray
executed.

Ogilvy's
escape.

---

[1] Balfour, *Hist. Works*, iii. 341.
[2] *Ibid.* iii. 358; *Wishart*, ch. xix.

on the subject of religion. The government of the Church,
he now openly said, was to be restored to its condition in

Jan. 15.
Charles's
offers to
Parliament
on religion.

the happy times of Elizabeth and James, but there
was to be 'full liberty for the ease of their consciences who will not communicate in that service
established by law, and likewise for the free and public
use of the Directory prescribed, and by command of the two
Houses now practised in some parts of the City of London.'
With respect to Ireland and the militia, he would endeavour to
give satisfaction.[1]

It looked as if Charles was really working himself round to
that principle of toleration through which the difficulties of the

Jan. 18.
His expla-
nation to
the Queen.

time ultimately received their solution ; but even if
the Houses had been at all ready to accept his proposal, his diplomacy was too crooked to achieve
success. "For Ireland and the militia," he wrote to the
Queen, "it is true that it may be I give them leave to hope
for more than I intended, but my words are only to 'endeavour
to give them satisfaction in either.' . . . Now, as to the fruits
which I expected by my treaty at London. Knowing assuredly
the great animosity which is betwixt the Independents and
Presbyterians, I had great reason to hope that one of the
factions would so address themselves to me that I might without difficulty obtain my so just ends, and questionless it would
have given me the fittest opportunity for considering the Scots'
treaty that would be ; besides, I might have found means to
have put distractions among them, though I have found
none."[2]

Charles's method of proceeding had been condemned in
advance by Montreuil. On the 15th the Frenchman had

Jan. 15.
Montreuil's
remon-
strance.

warned him not to play with the Scots. They would
be content, he wrote, with nothing short of the three
propositions of Uxbridge, implying the establishment
of Presbyterianism, the abandonment of Ireland, and the

---

[1] The King to the Speaker of the House of Lords, Jan. 15. *L.J.*
viii. 103.

[2] The King to the Queen, Jan. 18. *Charles I. in 1646,* 11.

appointment of Parliamentary commissioners permanently to control the militia, with the assistance of Scottish commissioners not exceeding a third part of their number. As for Charles's expectation that the Scots would quarrel with the English because their Presbyterianism was too Erastian, Montreuil besought him to put that notion aside. Both the Scots and the City had already expressed their approbation of the system adopted by Parliament, and Charles's only chance of safety lay in his acceptance of that which had been adopted at Westminster.[1]

The Scottish laity wanted, in short, to be assured that England would be governed by persons whom they could

The temper of the Scots, and of the City. trust, not that its Church should assume the exact form which might satisfy Henderson or Baillie. Presbyterian as the City was, it was quite content with Parliamentary Presbyterianism, and was not likely to quarrel with the House of Commons in order to set Episcopacy on its feet again. In a petition presented to

Jan. 15. The City petition against toleration. the House of Commons on the 15th, the City declared against any sort of toleration. The existing state of things was declared to be unbearable. Private meetings for religious worship were constantly held. In one parish there were as many as eleven. Godly ministers were evil spoken of, and their discipline was compared to that of the prelates. Women and other ignorant persons were allowed to preach. Superstition, heresy, and profaneness were increasing. Families were divided and God was dishonoured. The Commons, Independent on questions of policy, but Presbyterian on questions of religion, heard and approved.[2] It was evident that Charles had addressed himself to the wrong persons in seeking Presbyterian support for a scheme of tolerationist Episcopacy.

---

[1] Montreuil to the King, Jan. 15. *Clar. St. P.* ii. 211.

[2] Petition of the City. *L.J.* viii. 104. Though the elections of the preceding December had undoubtedly strengthened the anti-tolerationists, they had made no thorough change in the predominant party in the City, as the November petitions (see p. 11) had been couched in similar terms.

On the 16th the King's proposal for a religious compromise

Jan. 16. The King's proposal read. was read in the Houses. It was nearly certain to be rejected in any case; but on the same day news arrived which seemed to make all further negotiation with the King impossible. The secret of Glamorgan's mission was at last disclosed.

CHAPTER XXXIX.

GLAMORGAN AND RINUCCINI IN IRELAND.

EARLY in August Glamorgan landed in Dublin. He came, there can be little doubt, to smooth away the difficulties in the

1645.
August.
Glamorgan
in Ireland. way of Ormond's negotiation, and to induce the Confederates to content themselves with the repeal of the penal laws, instead of asking for the additional repeal of the statutes which threw obstacles in the way of the exercise of Papal jurisdiction in Ireland. When Glamorgan arrived he found the situation greatly changed. It is possible that Charles's unwise instruction to Ormond to keep back the secret of the permission given him to promise the repeal of the penal laws [1] had weakened the hands of the moderate party at Kilkenny. At all events, the Irish clergy were already asking

May 31.
The Irish
clergy refuse
to abandon
the churches. for much more than that. On May 31 they had pronounced emphatically against any peace which did not leave in their hands all the churches at that time in their possession, and by implication all the property of those churches as well, a concession which would have surrendered to them almost all the ecclesiastical property

June 9.
Concurrence
of the Gene-
ral Assem-
bly. existing in Ireland. On June 9 the General Assembly expressed its concurrence with this resolution, with some formal modifications, and when on the 13th the Agents of the Confederates received

June 19.
Resumption
of negotia-
tions. authority to reopen the negotiation with Ormond, they carried with them instructions to stand firm on this point, as well as on that of the absolute liberation of the Catholics from all ecclesiastical jurisdiction except

[1] See vol. ii. p. 174.

that derived from the Pope.[1] The negotiations were reopened on the 19th, and were carried on at Dublin during the following weeks.

To the Confederates peace was in every way desirable. In the middle of July it was known in Dublin that Monro with

July.
Sligo stormed.

the Scots and their English allies had pressed on through Ulster, had stormed Sligo on the 8th, and

March 19.
Surrender of Duncannon.

had massacred not only the Irish garrison, but the women and children as well.[2] It was true that in the South the fort of Duncannon, important from its

Castlehaven in Munster.

command of the entrance to the harbour of Waterford, had been reduced by Preston on March 19,[3] and that Lord Castlehaven, at the head of 5,000 foot and 800 horse, had been subsequently carrying on a successful cam-

Financial distress.

paign in Munster.[4] Castlehaven, however, was calling aloud for money, and money was hard to find. It was, indeed, known that, though the mission of Bellings had failed,[5] Rinuccini, when he arrived, would bring with him a certain amount of supplies, but, unless he arrived soon, it would be difficult to hold out.

Dangerous as their situation was, the Irish Agents refused to give way on the two points now at issue. With them it was

A fruitless negotiation.

a point of honour not to surrender churches which had already been restored to Catholic worship, and, though Ormond asserted that the King demanded no more than a theoretical acknowledgment of his jurisdiction, he was reminded that the Protestant clergy put forward a practical claim to the power of the keys, carrying with it the right of excommunication and absolution, a right the exercise of which was followed by civil consequences.[6] Nor was it likely to

---

[1] *Lord Leicester's MS.* fol. 688–708b.

[2] Scarampi to ——, July 14, *Ibid.* fol. 708b ; Captain Dillon to Sir Ulick Bourke, *Carte MSS.* xv. fol. 238.

[3] Examinations on the siege of Duncannon Fort. Gilbert's *Hist. of the Irish Confederation,* iv. 210.

[4] Castlehaven to the Supreme Council, June 17 ; Castlehaven to the Mayor of Limerick, June 17. *Ibid.* iv. 281, 286.   [5] See p. 13.

[6] Negotiations in Gilbert's *Hist. of the Irish Confederation,* iv. 289, 309. See also *Carte MSS.* xv. fol. 198–315.

conduce to the success of the negotiation that Ormond, con-
ceiving himself still bound by the King's instructions, persisted
in keeping secret Charles's readiness to assent to the repeal of
the penal laws.[1]

Under these circumstances Glamorgan, as long as he continued to act in conformity with Ormond's wishes, could not

August.
Glamorgan's
position.

possibly be of any service to his master. He was
confronted with the difficulties of a situation for
which nothing in his instructions had prepared him.
The question about the churches had arisen since he had had
an opportunity of speaking with Charles, or even of receiving
written directions from him.

For some time Glamorgan did his best to tide over the
difficulties. As long as he remained with Ormond, he kept

Interruption
of the nego-
tiation.

within his instructions, consulting as opportunity
arose with the Lord Lieutenant. It was not, however, long before he was called upon to act on his
own judgment. There was to be a meeting of the General
Assembly at Kilkenny on August 7, and the Agents of the
Confederates left Dublin to attend it. In order that the thread
of the negotiations might not be dropped, Glamorgan was

Aug. 11.
Glamorgan
goes to Kil-
kenny.

directed to follow them, and on August 11 he set
out on his journey, hoping that he might succeed in
inducing the Confederates to abandon their pretensions. The letter which he carried to them from Ormond
commended him to their confidence in the warmest possible
terms.[2]

Of discussions between Glamorgan and the Confederates
during the first fortnight of his visit to Kilkenny we have no

Glamorgan's
difficulties.

record, and the motives which determined his action
can only be conjectured in the light of his subsequent proceedings. Yet it may safely be supposed that he
was anxious to overcome the obstacle about the churches, and
he may very well have reasoned with himself that it would be
fit for him to spare the King by taking upon himself the
responsibility of yielding. Though his instructions had im-

---

[1] Fitzwilliam to Digby, July 16. *Gilbert,* iv., lxii.
[2] Ormond to Muskerry, Aug. 11. *Lord Leicester's MS.* fol. 717b.

plied that he was to place himself at Ormond's service,[1] he had, on the other hand, unlimited powers, and it can hardly be doing him wrong to hold that he thought very little of instructions which had been given him five months before under circumstances different from those which now embarrassed him,[2] and very much of powers which authorised him to do almost anything he pleased. As a Catholic he would be little inclined to sympathise with Charles's scruples about the abandonment of churches which had once been in Protestant keeping, whilst he was most anxious to gather under his command that Irish army which was to relieve his master from his difficulties in England, but of which not a man would ever be levied unless he could come to terms with the Confederates.

If such thoughts passed through Glamorgan's mind, it is easy to understand the motives which induced him to sign on August 25 a secret treaty with the Confederate Catholics in virtue of the powers granted to him in the preceding March.[3] In this treaty the grant of the free and public exercise of the Roman Catholic religion may perhaps be regarded as giving no more than Ormond was empowered to give, though in a more complete and definite manner. Two other concessions went far beyond anything to which Charles had consented. In the first place the Catholics were to enjoy all the churches which they had possessed at any time since the outbreak of the rebellion in Ulster, and all those—apparently those which were lying vacant in consequence of the war—'other than such as are now actually enjoyed by his Majesty's Protestant subjects.' In the second place all Roman Catholics were to be exempted from the jurisdiction of the Protestant clergy, and the Roman Catholic clergy were not to be molested 'for the exercise of their jurisdiction over their respective Catholic flocks in matters spiritual

Aug. 25. A treaty signed by Glamorgan.

---

[1] See vol. ii. p. 166.

[2] The power on which Glamorgan acted was that of March **12**. See my article in *The English Historical Review* for October 1887, to which I must again refer my readers for a more complete discussion of this question.

[3] See vol. ii. p. 175.

and ecclesiastical'[1]—a stipulation which left untouched the question how far the clergy themselves were subjected to the jurisdiction of the See of Rome. No doubt it was clearly stated that the jurisdiction of the clergy was to be confined to 'matters spiritual and ecclesiastical,' but there must be some authority to decide where the border line between civil and spiritual cases was to be traced, and it is hardly likely in the existing circumstances in Ireland that this authority would have been allowed to rest with the crown.

That Glamorgan had secret instructions from Charles, empowering him to act as he did, is a notion which may be promptly dismissed. Charles had not heard of the demand about the churches till after Glamorgan left England. His first reference to it is in a letter to Ormond on July 31, and his reception of the proposal was not such as to give encouragement to Glamorgan's enterprise.

Had Glamorgan secret instructions?

He was indeed ready to take one step in the direction in which the Irish Confederates wished to drag him, and to allow the Catholics to build chapels for their worship wherever they were in a decided majority, but he absolutely refused to allow them the enjoyment of the existing churches. "I will rather choose," he declared, "to suffer all extremity than ever abandon my religion."[2] There is always something arbitrary in the selection of a limit to concession, but that limit had now been reached by Charles.

Charles offers to allow the Catholics to build chapels.

It may possibly be said that Charles merely intended to conceal his real intentions from Ormond, and it may be acknowledged that if his refusal to abandon the churches had been embodied in a proclamation or in a message to Parliament there would have been little reason to give credence to it. On the other hand, for Charles to use strong language on the subject to Ormond and at the same time to authorise Glamorgan to do that which was forbidden to Ormond would have been to pile up unnecessary difficulties

Was Charles sincere?

---

[1] Cox, *Hib. Anglicana,* ii. XXVII.

[2] The King to Ormond, July 31. Carte's *Ormond,* vi. 305. The original is in the possession of Mr. Alfred Morrison.

against himself. Even if he had been unwilling to trust Ormond with his whole secret, if such a secret in reality existed, he would at least have attempted to smooth the way for its subsequent revelation.

The simplest explanation of the facts is here, as usual, undoubtedly the best. It was characteristic of Charles to shrink from the abandonment of the churches as equivalent to the abandonment of religion, and it was no less characteristic of Glamorgan to act on the spur of the moment, in accordance rather with his own wishes than with the wishes of his master.

Contrast between Charles, Glamorgan, and Ormond.

Ormond in similar circumstances would have written for fresh instructions, but it may not unfairly be presumed that Glamorgan neglected even the instructions which he had already received, and fixed his eyes solely on his powers. He was not, as Ormond was, a man of one devotion. Chivalrously loyal to Charles, he was even more chivalrously loyal to his Church. To save Charles for the sake of the Church was the great ambition of his life, and there was nothing in his scheming, impulsive, and most indiscreet mind to make it improbable that he resolved to save the Church on her own terms, and Charles in spite of his petty hesitations. He doubtless hoped to purchase Charles's condonation of his disobedience by the levy of 10,000 Irish soldiers for his service, as Raleigh had once hoped to purchase from Charles's father the condonation of a similar act of disobedience by a sample of gold from Guiana.

Strong as is the evidence derived from Glamorgan's character in favour of the view that he acted without Charles's knowledge, there exists evidence more conclusive still. On the day after that on which he signed the main treaty he signed another document, which he called a defeasance, in which he declared that he had no intention of binding the King to any concession 'other than he himself shall please, after he hath received these ten thousand men, being a pledge and testimony' of the loyalty of his Irish subjects. This defeasance was, however, to be kept secret even from Charles till Glamorgan had done everything in his power to induce him to accept the treaty, and had failed to persuade him. Such a stipulation is the strongest possible evidence that Charles had yet to be converted—partly, it would seem, by the presence of 10,000 Irish soldiers in England—to Glamorgan's views on the point at issue.[1]

It was hardly within the bounds of possibility that Glamorgan's action should prove beneficial either to his master or to the Irish people; but he was surely right in thinking that if a military alliance was to be formed with the Confederates, it could only be by the acceptance of their own terms. It was childish to expect to gain the hearty co-operation of the Irish if their Church was to be maintained in the position of a merely tolerated sect, the organisation of which was in constant danger of a sudden application of the Statutes of Appeals and Præmunire; and if the ecclesiastical lands and buildings set apart for religious use by their ancestors, and now recovered after a deprivation of less than a century, were to be forcibly torn from them, and restored to the professors of an alien creed from whom they had nothing but persecution to expect.

Nature of Glamorgan's compact.

As Glamorgan, at all events, had still to force the hand of Charles, he could not venture to mention what had been done until he could emphasise his words by his appearance in England at the head of an Irish army. Whether such an army would really be entrusted to him might reasonably be doubted. It was significant that Scarampi looked on him with grave suspicion, holding that the powers exhibited by him did not give him sufficient authority to conclude the treaty, and that Charles, if he were so minded, would have no difficulty in disavowing his agent.[2] It had indeed been arranged that the negotiation with Ormond should be continued, in the hope that he might be induced to make the required concessions in a regular way, and it is not unlikely that Glamorgan at first thought it possible to carry Ormond with him.

Scarampi distrusts Glamorgan.

The negotiation with Ormond to be carried on.

The Supreme Council proceeded at once to test the value

---

[1] Cox, *Hib. Anglicana*, ii. App. XXVII.

[2] Panfilio to Rinuccini, $\frac{Oct. 26}{Nov. 5}$. *Nunziatura*, 458.

of the new alliance which they had formed.   On August 29

Aug. 29.
The
Supreme
Council
offers its
forces to
Ormond.
they proposed to combine their forces with those of
Ormond against the Scots in the North.[1]   Finding
that Ormond made no response, they betook them-
selves to Glamorgan.   Glamorgan could not press
Ormond to consent to the junction of forces, but on

Sept. 9.
Glamorgan
is assured
that he shall
take an army
to England.
September 9 he assured him that the General Assembly had agreed to give the 10,000 men of which
so much had been said, for service in England, and
that it was now proposed to resume the negotiation

in Dublin.   The Confederates, he added, hoped that Ormond
would yield as much as possible, and would leave them to
appeal to the King for the rest.   Glamorgan had, in short,
induced the Confederates to believe that they would get all
that they wanted from Charles, and they were consequently
ready to accept from Ormond such an instalment of their
demands as he thought fit to give.   To prevent Ormond from
becoming aware of the real state of the case, Glamorgan professed entire ignorance of the requests which would now be
made by the Agents of the Supreme Council.[2]

For two months the discussion between Ormond and the

Irish Agents was kept up in Dublin.   Though
Ormond was strongly urged to give way on points
relating to religion, he refused to go a single inch
beyond his instructions.[3]

On November 20 Glamorgan, after visiting Dublin to take
part in the debates, returned to Kilkenny.   He found that the

Nov. 20.
Agreement
between
Glamorgan
and the
Supreme
Council.
resolutions of the Confederates were shaping themselves according to his wishes.   The Supreme
Council agreed that, if Ormond refused to concede
the articles relating to religion, the political ones
should be published alone, whilst those which had
been agreed on with Glamorgan should be kept secret till they
had received Charles's approval.   They further promised that

[1] The Supreme Council to Ormond, Aug. 29.   *Carte MSS.* xv. fol.
526.

[2] Glamorgan to Ormond, Sept. 9.   *Carte MSS.* xv. fol. 580.

[3] See the *Carte MSS. passim* from September to November.

the army of 10,000 men should be despatched under Glamorgan's command without waiting for the King's acceptance of these articles. After he had landed with them—so Glamorgan· assured the Supreme Council upon oath—not only would he make no use of them till the King's consent had been given, but, in the event of a refusal, he would either compel him to assent by force of arms or would bring the whole force back to Ireland.[1] In writing to Ormond Glamorgan not only gave no hint of this secret negotiation, but assured him with the most fulsome expressions of devotion that he was but carrying out the directions which he had received at Dublin. His precipitate zeal to effect Charles's objects in Ireland was already transforming itself into an eager desire to impose upon Charles by force of arms concessions which he was never likely voluntarily to make.[2]

Charles to be forced or deserted.

By this time Glamorgan had to count on another power in Ireland besides that of the Supreme Council. A new actor had appeared on the stage. On October 11 Rinuccini, the Papal Nuncio,[3] landed at Kenmare.[4] On November 12 he entered Kilkenny amidst the applauses of a shouting throng.[5] On his journey he had been struck by the hardihood and activity of the men and by the beauty and modesty of the women. The fecundity of the latter struck him with amazement. There were married couples, he related with

Oct. 11. Arrival of Rinuccini at Kenmare,

Nov. 12. and at Kilkenny.

His impressions on the journey.

---

[1] "Il quale si è obligato di più con suo giuramento avanti il Consiglio Supremo, che egli non imbarazzerà la soldatesca predetta in alcuna fazione, prima che il Rè ratifichi ; e quando non lo volesse fare, che egli lo constringerà con quelle forze, o vero rimetterà nell' Ibernia tutti i 10,000 soldati."—Rinuccini to Panfilio, Dec. 23. *Nunziatura*, 76.

[2] Glamorgan to Ormond, Nov. 28. *Carte MSS.* xvi. fol. 264.

[3] See p. 13.

[4] Rinuccini to Panfilio, Oct. $\frac{15}{25}$. *Nunziatura*, 63. This letter is dated Oct. 25, 'stile nuovo d'Ibernia,' which is unintelligible. In the Latin translation in *Lord Leicester's MS.* we have 'stylo novo, nam imposterum ad alterum, quo in hac patria utuntur, me semper accommodabo,' an indication useful in dating subsequent letters.

[5] *Nunziatura*, 68–71 ; *Lord Leicester's MS.* fol. 93, 1,026.

surprise, which were blessed with no less than thirty children still living, whilst families of fifteen or twenty were—so at least he had been told—of common occurrence.[1]

Glamorgan's first impression of the Nuncio was that he would throw no obstacles in his way. "Before Sunday night,"

Nov. 28.   he wrote to the Lord Lieutenant on the 28th, "I am
Glamorgan's   morally certain a total assent from the Nuncio shall
expecta-   be declared to the propositions for peace, and in the
tions.
very way your Lordship prescribes."[2]   The approbation of the

Rinuccini's   Nuncio was not so easily gained.   He brought with
character   him a firm will, an exclusive devotion to the interests
and
position.   of his Church, coupled with a disability to enter into
the feelings with which even Catholic laymen regarded questions in which both ecclesiastical and political interests were involved.   He held in contempt all projects aiming at the employment of the resources of a Catholic country to buttress up the tottering throne of an heretical king.   As he brought with him a considerable sum of money, as well as a large store of arms and munitions, he was able to speak with even more authority than he could derive simply from his position as representative of the Pope.

Rinuccini was not long in discovering that a large number of the influential members of the Supreme Council were

Rinuccini   attached to Ormond by ties of affinity or dependence,
and the   and he at once held them in suspicion as lukewarm
Supreme
Council.   defenders of the cause confided to their keeping.
He distrusted too the natural desire of wealthy landowners to regain peace, and thus to preserve their estates, though at some sacrifice of the claims of religion ; and he was easily convinced that such men would shrink from continued suffering in vindication of the full privileges which he demanded for the Church, and would not take it much to heart if she were even forced to content herself with the clandestine celebration of her rites.

Rinuccini was the more ready to take alarm as he had reason to believe that the Agents of the Supreme Council were

---

[1] *Lord Leicester's MS.* fol. 944.

[2] Glamorgan to Ormond, Nov. 28. *Carte MSS.* xvi. fol. 264.

at last on the point of coming to an agreement with Ormond on the basis of the acceptance by the Lord Lieutenant of the
Approaching agreement with Ormond.　political articles, whilst the religious articles were to be reserved for Charles's own judgment—an arrangement which, as he firmly believed, would ultimately result in the entire abandonment of the religious articles.
Rinuccini's protest.　He therefore openly protested against the course taken by the Supreme Council.[1]　His next step was to win over Glamorgan.　The impressionable Eng-
Dec. 20. He wins over Glamorgan.　lishman became as wax in his hands, and on December 20 engaged on the King's behalf that, even if Ormond accepted the political articles, they should not be published till the religious questions at issue had been settled by Charles's confirmation of the secret treaty which had been signed by Glamorgan on August 25, and that he would demand this confirmation as soon as he landed with his army on English soil.

Even this engagement was not enough for Rinuccini.　He drew Glamorgan on to expand his original promises into what
The second Glamorgan treaty.　can only be fitly described as a second treaty.　The Earl now undertook, in the name and by the authority of the King, that Charles would bind himself never again to appoint a Protestant Lord Lieutenant, would admit the Catholic bishops to their seats in the Irish Parliament, would allow Catholic statutes to be drawn up for a Catholic university which was about to be founded, and would grant to the Catholics the churches and ecclesiastical revenues, not only in all places taken by the Confederates before the date on which the political articles were signed by Ormond, but also in those taken subsequently to that signature up to the confirmation of the treaty of August 25 by the King. Finally, Glamorgan promised that the Supreme Council should not be superseded in its jurisdiction till this confirmation had been given.[2]

---

[1] The Nuncio's speech.　*Lord Leicester's MS.* fol. 1,005b.

[2] 'Donec privatæ concessiones ratæ habeantur.' This means, as far as can be gathered from the use of 'privatæ concessiones' in the earlier

Even if it were possible to entertain doubts about the first
treaty, it is certain that this second one was not founded on
Glamorgan's anything more explicit than the general powers
motives. which Glamorgan possessed. It was drawn up by
him on the spur of the moment, and is only to be explained
by his intense eagerness to lead Irish troops to Charles's help.
If Irish soldiers could effect anything but mischief in England,
Chester in their presence was sadly needed now that Chester
danger.
A force to was in imminent danger, and, in view of the incon-
be given to veniences which would result from the loss of a port
Glamorgan
for its relief. so important for the traffic with Ireland, the Supreme
Council agreed to allow Glamorgan to take with him at once
3,000 men as an advanced guard.[1] Yet Glamorgan could not
embark a single man till he had procured Ormond's consent
both to his own appointment to command this force, and to
Dec. 24. the arrangement by which the expected political
Glamorgan treaty was to be kept back for a time from publica-
in Dublin. tion. With this object in view he set out for
Dublin, and arrived in that city on December 24.[2]

Before two days were over Glamorgan's dazzling vision of
his own triumphant intervention in England melted away. On
Dec. 26. the 26th he was summoned before Ormond and the
Glamorgan
ar. ested. Privy Council at the demand of Digby, who had
Oct. 17. recently reached Dublin from the Isle of Man.[3] On
His treaty
brought to October 17 the Scottish garrison of Sligo had made
light. a sally, in which the Catholic Archbishop of Tuam
was killed.[4] On his person was found a copy of Glamorgan's
original treaty, which after some time passed into Ormond's
He is hands. Digby, who now saw the treaty for the first
denounced time, raised his voice loudly in the council against
by Digby, Glamorgan. He was especially scandalised at the
Earl's claim to have the King's authority for his engagements.

---

part of the document, the treaty of August 25. See *Engl. Hist. Review*,
Oct. 1887, p. 706.

[1] Rinuccini to Panfilio, Dec. 23. *Nunziatura*, 75.

[2] *Lord Leicester's MS.* fol. 1,033b; Muskerry to Ormond, Jan. 3;
Glamorgan to Ormond, Jan. 10, *Carte MSS.* xvi. fol. 380, 409.

[3] See vol. ii. p. 371.   [4] *Rushw.* vi. 239.

That authority, declared the Secretary, 'must be either forged or surreptitiously gained,' as it was certain that the King would never grant to the Irish 'the least piece of concession so destructive to his regality and religion.' The Coun-

and by the Irish Council.

cil took up the note, and declared the treaty 'to import no less than absolute giving up the King's ecclesiastical supremacy within this kingdom, and in lieu of it, introducing the fulness of papal power of vast prejudice to all the Protestant clergy, and that not only to their utter ruin in point of subsistence, but also to the absolute taking away of their churches and ecclesiastical es-

*1646.
Jan. 5.
The matter referred to the King.*

tates, possessions, rights, interests, jurisdiction, and government.' On these grounds the Council committed Glamorgan to prison, and referred the whole matter to the King.[1]

On January 16, before the despatches of the Irish Council reached Charles, copies of the incriminating documents had

*Jan. 16.
The Glamorgan treaty known at Westminster.*

been received at Westminster, having been forwarded by some commissioners who had been sent by Parliament to Ulster to watch over English interests in the North of Ireland. The Commons at once ordered them to be sent to the press, together with the papers which had been captured at Sherburn.[2] Some motives, however—probably those of prudence—held back the House from allowing the latter documents to be printed in accordance with this order, and for the present the Glamorgan mystery alone was unveiled to the public gaze.

In the House itself sharp words were spoken against the person of the King. They had, it was said, the example of

Sharp words spoken of Charles.

earlier Parliaments, and they knew how kings had been used by them in similar cases. At a meeting held by four or five of the Independent leaders it was resolved to give point to these words by agitating for the King's deposition. When that had been effected, the

---

[1] Digby to Nicholas, Jan. 4, *Rushw.* vi. 240 ; Ormond and the Council to Nicholas, Jan. 5, Carte's *Ormond,* vi. 333 ; Glamorgan's examination, *Carte MSS.* xvi. fol. 341, 356.

[2] *C.J.* iv. 408.

Prince of Wales was to be declared an enemy of the State, and the Duke of York summoned to present himself at Westminster. In the probable case of his refusal the little Duke of Gloucester was to be crowned, and Northumberland declared Lord Protector of the realm.[1]

It may seem strange, after all that had passed, that the Houses made no reply to an angry letter received on the 19th

Charles asks for a reply. from the King,[2] in which he demanded an immediate answer to his last communication.[3] Their silence was, perhaps, due to their wish to know their whole peril before further negotiation was attempted. It was not only from Ireland that they were threatened with danger. During

Reports from France. the last weeks of the year the reports which the Committee of Both Kingdoms derived from their agents in Paris, Robert Wright and Sir George Gerard, had been reassuring. The Queen, they were told, had been doing all that was in her power to engage the French court to assist her husband, but it did not appear likely that as long as the war with the House of Austria lasted the Queen-Regent would be in a position to give serious aid. Mazarin would no doubt

---

[1] "Et ce qui n'est pas moins secret qu'il est estrange que quatre ou cinq des chefs des Independants s'etant assemblés vendredi dernier, ils arresterent qu'il falloit travailler promtement à la deposition du Roy de la Grande Bretagne, à quoy les lettres qu'ils avoyent de luy et sa declaration en faveur des Catholiques d'Irlande qui avoit eté lue le mesme jour au Parlement donneraient assez de sujet qu'on declareroit le Prince de Galles enemy de l'Estat aprés le refus qu'il auroit fait de poser les armes, qu'on sommeroit le Duc d'York de venir au Parlement, et que n'aiant pas voulu obeir, on couronneroit le petit Duc de Glocester et on feroit le Comte de Northumberland protecteur de ce Royaume.

"Ce mesme jour diverses choses furent dittes dans la maison basse du Parlement qui ne s'éloignoient pas bien fort de cela, puisqu'il y en eut un qui remontra sur le sujet de cette declaration en faveur des Catholiques d'Irlande qu'ils avoient les examples des precedens parlemens, et qu'ils sçavoient comme on en avoit usé envers d'autres Roys d'Angleterre dans de semblables rencontres."—Montreuil to Mazarin, $\frac{\text{Jan. 22}}{\text{Feb. 1}}$. *Arch. des Aff. Etrangères,* lii. fol. 81.

[2] The King to the Houses, Jan. 17. *L.J.* viii. 108.

[3] See p. 29.

do his best to weaken England by a prolongation of the civil war, but this at least was no revelation at Westminster.[1]

On January 17, however, far more startling news reached the Committee. Sir Kenelm Digby had returned to Paris upon the completion of his negotiation with the Pope.

Jan. 17.
The Queen
to be helped
by the
French
clergy. In the Queen's name—so much at least had oozed out—he had engaged that Charles should abolish the penal statutes in England as well as in Ireland.

Sir Kenelm
Digby's
treaty. In consequence of the hopes thus raised, an assembly of the French clergy, which was then in session, had offered 1,500,000 francs, or about 150,000*l*., for

Offers of
the French
clergy. the expenses of an expedition which on the lowest computation was to consist of 5,000 foot and 2,000 horse, and was to be placed under the command of the Duke of Bouillon. Emery, a Frenchman of Italian origin, who had risen under Mazarin to be comptroller-general of finance, and who for the most part employed his ingenuity in contriving fresh means of wringing money out of the poor for the benefit of the treasury,[2] now posed as an enthusiastic devotee, and became the Queen's principal adviser in the matter. It was even

The
Channel
Islands to
be pledged. said that Henrietta Maria had offered to pledge the Channel Islands and some towns in the West of England to those who would now come to her help.

Matri-
monial
schemes. She was further hoping to get possession of her son, the Prince of Wales, and thinking of abandoning her project of marrying him to the daughter of the Prince of Orange,[3] in the hope of securing for him the hand of her niece, the daughter of the Duke of Orleans. The young lady, afterwards known as the Great Mademoiselle, was three years older than the Prince, but she would be one of the wealthiest brides in Europe.[4]

---

[1] Wright to St. John, Nov. $\frac{14}{24}$; N. N., *i.e.* Sir G. Gerard, to S. G., Nov. $\frac{22}{Dec. 2}$, Nov. $\frac{29}{Dec. 9}$, *Tanner MSS.* lx. fol. 339, 342, 344.

[2] See *Nouvelle Biogr. Générale, s. v.* Particelli.

[3] The negotiation with the Prince of Orange was finally broken off in the following April. Goffe to the Prince of Orange, April 9. *Groen. van Prinsterer*, iv. 152.

[4] N. N. to S. G. Jan. $\frac{9}{19}$. News from France read in the House,

This intelligence, alarming as it was, fitted in too well with the news from Ireland to cause much surprise. Far more sur-

The Scots' treaty revealed. prising was the revelation contained in other letters from Wright, that the Scottish commissioners were treating through Will Murray with the Queen, and that they were ready, under certain conditions, to direct their army to 'do no service before Newark.' Though it is certain that the Scots were aiming at the establishment of Presbyterianism and not at the establishment of the Papal Church in England, their junction with the Queen and Mazarin, at a time when the forces of Papal France and Papal Ireland were sharpening all their weapons against England, may well have seemed to Englishmen to be treason of the deepest dye. The

Jan. 24. Protest of the Scots. Scots at once perceived how the accusation was telling against them, and with unblushing effrontery they publicly declared that the charges were absolutely false from beginning to end. They then, with every expression of injured innocence, called on the English Parliament to produce its informants in order that they might be compelled to answer for their calumnies.[1] The House of Commons was

Jan. 29. Votes of the Commons. not so easily misled. On the 29th it voted that the members of the Committee of Both Kingdoms who had supplied the information had done no more than their duty, and directed the preparation of an answer to the Scottish protest.[2]

Charles's disavowals were made in a different style, though at the bottom they were no less false. He was accustomed to

Charles disavows Glamorgan, strive to give as much as possible the semblance of truth to what was in itself untrue. He now, writing from Oxford on the 29th, after he had had knowledge of the publication of Glamorgan's treaty, assured the Houses :—

Jan. 29. *Tanner MSS.* lx. fol. 362. Other letters from France, read on the 29th, were before the Committee on the 17th, and I have therefore supposed this to have been read there with them ; but the date is of no consequence.

[1] The Scottish commissioners to the Speaker of the House of Lords, Jan. 24. *L.J.* viii. 122.   [2] *C.J.* iv. 421.

"That the Earl of Glamorgan, having made offer unto him to raise forces in the kingdom of Ireland, and to conduct them into England for his Majesty's service, had a commission to that purpose, and to that purpose only.

"That he had no commission at all to treat of anything else without the privity and directions of the Lord Lieutenant, much less to capitulate anything concerning religion, or any propriety [1] belonging either to Church or laity."

It can be no matter of surprise that Charles should have acknowledged what he could not help acknowledging, and should have sought to cast a discreet veil over that
and offers to abandon the Irish. which could yet be concealed.   His really unpardonable fault was that, after engaging in such a negotiation with the Irish Catholics, he should now have announced his 'resolution of leaving the managing of the business of Ireland wholly to .the Houses, and to make no peace there but with their consent.' [2]   What sort of peace the Houses would establish in Ireland he knew full well.   Rinuccini had looked into his heart and had estimated his motives to more purpose than Glamorgan.

No wonder that the Houses declared themselves dissatisfied.   There was a talk of sending to the King a copy of the
Feb. 2.
The Commons dissatisfied. warrant on which Glamorgan had rested his authority, and which, together with the treaty founded on it, had fallen into the hands of the Scots when the Archbishop of Tuam was slain ; [3] but in the end the proposal was allowed to drop, probably because those who made it felt that it was useless to continue the altercation.

To Ormond Charles could not venture to prevaricate on the subject of Glamorgan's commission.   He could not say to
Jan. 30.
Charles explains to Ormond, him, as he had said to the Houses, that he had given him no authority to treat without the Lord Lieutenant's privity, but he was able to say what in all probability was strictly true, that his intention had never been that Glamorgan should treat without Ormond's approbation,

---

[1] *i.e.* property.   [2] *L.J.* viii. 132.
          [3] *C.J.* iv. 426.

much less without his knowledge.[1]   In a public despatch to
the Irish Council he allowed himself to cast doubts upon the
genuineness of his warrant to Glamorgan [2] by speaking of it as a credential which he might possibly have
given, whilst he permitted Nicholas at the same
time to call attention to its defects as an official
document.   "Your Lordships," concluded the Secretary, "cannot but judge it to be at least surreptitiously gotten,
if not worse; for his Majesty saith he remembers it not."[3]

*Jan. 31.
but throws
doubts on
the
genuineness
of his
warrant.*

Whatever he may have been to others Charles was always
perfectly truthful in his letters to his wife.   "It is taken for
granted," he wrote to her, "the Lord of Glamorgan
neither counterfeited my hand, nor that I have
blamed him more than for not following his instructions."[4]   This may perhaps be accepted as the final verdict of
history on the subject.

*He ex-
plains to
the Queen.*

It remained to be seen how Glamorgan would take his disavowal.   It struck heavily on the ears of his aged father.   "It
was the grief of his heart," complained Worcester to
one who reached Raglan with a comforting message
from Charles, "that he was enforced to say that the
King was wavering and fickle, and that at his
Majesty's last being there he lent him a book to read"—
Gower's *Confessio Amantis* [5]—"the beginning of which he

*Feb. ?
Worcester
complains
of his son's
treatment.*

[1] The King to Ormond, Jan. 30.   Carte's *Ormond*, v. 16.

[2] The one of March 12 is always intended.

[3] The King to the Irish Council, Jan. 31 ; Nicholas to the Irish
Council, Jan. 31.   Carte's *Ormond*, vi. 347, 349.

[4] The King to the Queen, March 22.   *Charles I. in* 1646, 28.

[5] That the book was Gower's appears from Bayly's *Golden Apo-
phthegms*, p. 5.   E. 184, 3.   The lines referred to are, I suppose, those
near the end of the *Confessio Amantis* (ed. Pauli), iii. 381 :—

> "So were it good, that he" (*i.e.* the King) "therefore
> First unto rightwisnesse entend,
> Wherof that he himself amende
> Toward his God and leve vice,
> Which is the chefe of his office.
> And after all the remenaunt
> He shall upon his covenaunt

knows he read, but if he had ended it, it would have showed
him what it was to be a fickle prince ; for was it not enough
. . . . to suffer . . . . the Lord of Glamorgan to be unjustly
imprisoned by the Lord Marquis of Ormond for what he had
his Majesty's authority for, but that the King must in print
protest against his proceedings, and his own allowance, and not
yet recall it ; but I will pray for him, and that he may be the
more constant to his friends." [1]

However harshly Charles's conduct may be judged, he at
least did not make a scapegoat of Glamorgan as Elizabeth did

Glamorgan
is not to be
seriously
prosecuted. of Davison. In his public despatch, indeed, he
directed that the charge against him should be dili-
gently prosecuted,[2] but in a private letter to Ormond
he ordered that the execution of the sentence should be suspended till his pleasure was known. Glamorgan, he added,
had sinned through misguided zeal rather than from malice.[3]

Feb. 3.
Charles
assures him
of his
favour. To Glamorgan himself he declared his whole mind.
"I must clearly tell you," he wrote on February 3,
"both you and I have been abused in this business,
for you have been drawn to consent to conditions
much beyond your instructions, and your treaty hath been
divulged to all the world. If you had advised with my Lord
Lieutenant, as you promised me, all this had been helped ; but
we must look forward. Wherefore, in a word, I have commanded as much favour to be shown to you as may possibly
stand with my service or safety ; and if you will trust my advice, which I have commanded Digby to give you freely, I will
bring you so off that you may be still useful to me, and I shall
be able to recompense you for your affliction." [4]

> Governe and lede in such a wise
> So that there be no tirannise,
> Wherof that he his people greve.
> Or elles may he nought acheve
> That longeth to his regalie."

[1] Narrative of Allan Boteler. *Carte MSS.* xxx. 307.

[2] The King to Ormond and the Irish Council, Jan. 31. *Carte's
Ormond,* vi. 349.

[3] The King to Ormond, Jan. 30. *Ibid.* v. 16.

[4] The King to Glamorgan, Feb. 3. *Dircks,* 134.

Before these lines were written Glamorgan had regained his freedom. He had made strong representations to Ormond

Jan. 21.
Glamorgan
liberated,

that the continuance of his imprisonment would be of the greatest disservice to the King, and on Janu-

Jan. 24.
and arrives
at Kil-
kenny.

ary 21 he was liberated on bail.[1] On the 24th he was once more at Kilkenny, urging the Supreme Coun- cil to push on the political treaty with Ormond on which all parties were agreed, and to give him in all haste the

Jan. 29.
The Su-
preme
Council
agrees to
relieve
Chester.

3,000 men needed for the relief of Chester. On the 29th he was able to announce to Ormond that, as to his first request, the Council was only waiting for the meeting of the General Assembly to be empow- ered by it to conclude peace, and that, as to the second, the men would be ready to sail at a day's notice as soon as the treaty had been signed.[2]

Meanwhile the Nuncio's doubts of the solidity of a peace concluded by anyone professing to act by the King's authority

Attitude of
the Nuncio.

had been intensified by Digby's denunciation of Glamorgan. It now seemed that the Earl, by acting as intermediary between Ormond and the Supreme Council, had basely deserted his alliance with himself, and might even be expected, if only he could receive the regiments which he needed, to treat a merely political undertaking as a sufficient satisfaction of the whole of the demands of Ireland.[3] Rinuccini was the more anxious to hinder any understanding with

He receives
the articles
agreed on
between
the Pope
and Sir K.
Digby.

Ormond, as before the end of January[4] he received from Rome a copy of articles which had been pre- sented to Sir Kenelm Digby in the Pope's name, and he had thus learnt that the Queen's representa- tive had consented to terms which went far beyond not only anything that Ormond, but even anything that Gla- morgan, had hitherto been prepared to concede.

The articles brought from Rome by Sir Kenelm were even

---

[1] Glamorgan to Ormond, Jan. 10, 20; Act of Council, Jan. 21. *Carte MSS.* xv. fol. 409, 449, 455.

[2] Glamorgan to Ormond, Jan. 29. *Carte MSS.* fol. 465.

[3] *Lord Leicester's MS.* fol. 1,042.

[4] *Ibid.* fol. 1,056b.

VOL. III.

more trenchant than had appeared by the warning lately conveyed to the English Parliament.[1]   Not merely was

Nature of
these
articles.
entire liberty of the Catholic worship and a completely independent parliament to be granted to
Ireland, but Dublin and all other Irish fortresses still garrisoned
by the King's troops were to be placed immediately in the
hands of Irish, or at least of English Catholics, whilst the
King's forces were to join the Confederates in chasing the Scots
and the Parliamentary English out of the country. As soon as
this was done, and any additional demands which might seem
desirable to the Nuncio had been granted, the Pope would pay
to the Queen 100,000 crowns, or about 36,000*l.* [2] of English
money.   The remaining articles concerned England.   In that
country the King was to revoke all laws affecting the Catholics,
placing them on complete equality with his Protestant subjects.
At the next Parliament the change thus made was to be confirmed, and in the meanwhile the Supreme Council was to
send into England a body of 12,000 foot under Irish officers,
to be supported upon its landing by 3,000, or at least 2,500,
English horse commanded by Catholics.   As soon as the Irish
landed in England the Pope would pay another 100,000 crowns,
and the same payment would be continued during the two
following years, if it appeared to be desirable.[3]   Preposterous
as these terms were, Rinuccini was, from his own point of
view, perfectly right in adopting them.   Nothing would make
the Pope the master of Ireland which did not make him
master of England as well.

In the General Assembly, as soon as it met, Rinuccini
struggled hard for the postponement of any conclusion with
Ormond until it was known whether Sir Kenelm's articles were
accepted or not.   Whatever difficulty he had with the Irish,
he had none with Glamorgan.[4]   With the instinct of a weak

[1] See p. 44.

[2] The exchange in 1638, as given in Lewis Roberts' *Map of Commerce*,
was 7*s*. 3½*d*. for the Roman crown, making the sum 36,375*l*.

[3] Articles, *Nunziatura*, 459. Further proposals for managing this
army will be found at p. 154.

[4] *Lord Leicester's MS.* fol. 1,066.

and excitable nature, Glamorgan once more bowed before the
Nuncio's strength of will, and recognising at once that in no
other way could he hope to obtain immediately the
3,000 men who were to be sent in advance to the
relief of Chester, on February 8 he adjured Ormond
to give all content to Rinuccini. "Certainly," he
wrote, after referring to 'the expectance of a more
advantageous peace wrought by the powerful hand
of her Majesty,' "before I can put myself into a hand-
some posture to serve the King, my master, by sea and land,
and in some kind to supply his Majesty's private purse, I think
it will stand me in little less than 100,000*l.* within three
months ; all which whence can I have it but out of Catholic
countries? And how cold I shall find Catholics bent to this
service if the Pope be irritated, I humbly submit to your
Excellency's better judgment. And here am I constrained . . .
absolutely to profess not to be capable to do the King that
service which he expects at my hands unless the Nuncio here
be civilly complied with, and carried along with us in our
proceedings." [1]

*Feb. 7.
The Nuncio
urges these
articles on
the General
Assembly.*

*Feb. 8.
Glamorgan
appeals to
Ormond.*

Ormond's reply to this extraordinary letter was coolly
sarcastic. After declaring his inability to understand what
was meant by the advantageous peace to be obtained by the Queen's intercession, he went on to
define his own position. "My lord," he wrote,
"my affections and interest are so tied to his Majesty's cause
that it were madness in me to disgust any man that hath power
and inclination to relieve him in the sad condition he is in ;
and, therefore, your lordship may securely go on in the ways
you have proposed to yourself to serve the King without fear
of interruption from me, or so much as inquiring the means
you work by. My commission is to treat with his Majesty's
Confederate Catholic subjects here for a peace, upon conditions of honour and assistance to him and of advantage to
them ; which, accordingly, I shall pursue to the best of my

*Feb. 11.
Ormond's
reply.*

---

[1] Glamorgan to Ormond, Feb. 8. *Carte MSS.* xvi. fol. 502.

skill, but shall not venture upon any new negotiation foreign
to the powers I have received." [1]

Upon Glamorgan this dignified protest had no effect whatever. On the 16th he surrendered himself body and soul to
the Nuncio, swearing by all the saints that he would
obey every one of his commands and would never do
anything contrary to his honour and good pleasure. [2]
Glamorgan's profession of unlimited obedience was
accompanied by a compact between himself and the Nuncio on
the one part and the Supreme Council on the other,
in consequence of which the latter body agreed to
prolong the cessation till May 1. So much time was
to be allowed to the Nuncio to enable him to obtain the
original articles which Sir Kenelm Digby had brought from
Rome, signed and sealed by the Pope and the Queen, as the
Supreme Council refused, upon the mere sight of a copy, to
support the fresh demands upon Charles which they contained.
He, on his part, engaged that if he failed to produce the document within the specified time, he would content himself with
such terms as might be agreed on between Glamorgan and the
King. In the meanwhile he waived his objection to the
continuance of the Supreme Council's negotiations with Ormond, on the understanding that nothing should be made

Feb. 16.
Glamorgan
surrenders
himself to
the Nuncio.

Compact
with the
Supreme
Council.

---

[1] Ormond to Glamorgan, Feb. 11. Carte's *Ormond*, vi. 352.

[2] " Ego Eduardus Glamorganus Dominationi vestræ Ill^{mæ} promitto
et juro me prompte obtemperaturum omnibus suis imperatis sine ulla
reluctatione ex animo, et cum animi oblectatione. Et hanc protestationem
perpetuam positis genibus facio Dominationi vestræ Ill^{mæ} et R^{mæ} non
solum velut Papæ ministro sed etiam suæ personæ tam insigni, et mearum
in hoc purissimarum intentionum testes invoco Beatissimam Virginem
atque omnes Sanctos Paradisi. Præterea sincere spondeo me de[in] in
omnibus quibus honoris sui intersit fore non minus sollicitum nec minore
cura processurum quam circa memetipsum, nihilque me ipsi propositurum
nisi quod eidem congruat nec commissurum, vel aliquid suo honori vel
beneplacito contrarium fiat, sed conforme obligationi, qua tenear nunquam
non esse   " D.V. Ill^{mæ} et R^{mæ}

16 Feb. 1646.   Benevolentissimus et humilissimus servus
usque ad mortem,

Lord Leicester's MS. fol. 1,053b.   "GLAMORGANUS."

public till the result of Glamorgan's negotiation with Charles was known, so that both treaties—the political one concluded with Ormond, and the religious one concluded with the King in person—might be published at the same time.[1]

The immediate interest of the negotiation was thus transferred to the Continent, and on the 18th Glamorgan, leaving the conduct of the troops for Chester to others, and despatching his brother, Lord John Somerset, to England to urge Charles to compliance with the new terms, announced his intention of leaving Ireland for Rome in the hope of being able to induce the Pope to give his full support to the proposals already made by him to Sir Kenelm Digby. So certain was Glamorgan of being able to sway the resolution not only of the Pope but of the King as well, that though he had no fresh instructions from England, he referred Rinuccini to the powers which he had originally received from Charles as being sufficient to assure him that the royal ratification of these proposals could not possibly be refused.[2] It is incredible that this third Glamorgan treaty,[3] as we may fairly call it, emanated in any way from Charles.

Feb. 18.
Glamorgan to go to the Continent.

The third Glamorgan treaty.

An agreement having been thus temporarily come to between the Nuncio and the Supreme Council, it seemed as if there would be no further difficulties in the way of the despatch of troops to Chester. On February 24 Glamorgan was able to assure Ormond that not 3,000 but 6,000 men would be sent, and that he was himself starting for Waterford to expedite their embarkation.[4] On March 8 bad news arrived from Chester. The city had surrendered to Brereton on February 3. The port which was to have received Charles's Irish auxiliaries was closed against them.[5]

Feb. 24.
Troops to be sent over.

March 8.
Bad news from England.

Feb. 3.
Surrender of Chester.

[1] Articles between the Confederate Catholics and the Nuncio with Glamorgan, Feb. 16. *Lord Leicester's MS.* fol. 1,086b.

[2] Glamorgan to Rinuccini, Feb. 18. *Lord Leicester's MS.* fol. 1,084–1,086.   [3] For the other two see pp. 33, 40.

[4] Glamorgan to Ormond, Feb. 24. *Carte MSS.* fol. 546.

[5] Note by Glamorgan, March 9. *Ibid.* xvi. fol. 617.

As far as Glamorgan's plans were concerned, the only immediate result of the evil tidings was the transference of his intended port of landing from Chester to some point either in Wales or in Cornwall, where the Prince of Wales was still

March 18.
Glamorgan
learns that
Charles has
disavowed
him.
holding out. On March 18 a far worse blow overtook him. He then learned that Charles had not only disavowed him, but had published his disavowal to the world.[1] In his annoyance Glamorgan talked to Du Moulin, the French agent at Kilkenny, of abandoning the master to whom he had hitherto devoted himself, and of passing with the army which was being raised to champion Charles's cause in England into the service of the King of France.[2]

Glamorgan's chance of being allowed to carry any considerable force from Ireland was, however, now the less, as the Irish had fresh dangers to meet at home. A Parliamentary

The seizure
of Bunratty.
squadron had sailed up the estuary of the Shannon and had seized Bunratty Castle, a few miles below Limerick. The Earl of Thomond, whose influence in Clare was great, and who for some time had been hesitating between the parties, now threw his whole weight on the Parliamentary side. The members of the Supreme Council informed Glamorgan that unless Ormond would openly join forces with them they would neither make peace at Dublin nor send an army to England.[3]

Rinuccini, at least, was well satisfied with the turn events were taking. He thoroughly distrusted the Supreme Council,

Rinuccini
distrusts the
Supreme
Council,
believing it to be capable of sacrificing the Church for mere temporal expediency; but he still more thoroughly distrusted the King. "I consider," he

March 4.
and the
King.
had written a few weeks earlier, "that, with regard to the Faith, it is safer to treat with a prince who perhaps is not averse to concede what he can on this head, and who has had experience of the fidelity of the Irish, besides

---

[1] Glamorgan to Ormond, March 18. *Carte MSS.* xvi. fol. 666.

[2] Du Moulin to Mazarin, $\frac{\text{March }30}{\text{April }9}$. *R.O. Transcripts.*

[3] *Lord Leicester's MS.* fol. 1,145b; Glamorgan to Ormond, March 18, *Carte MSS.* xvi. fol. 666.

having a Catholic wife, and having intercourse in civil matters with all the other princes of Christendom. Yet, on the other hand, I am alarmed at the common belief of his inconstancy and untrustworthiness, on account of which it may be doubted that no concession made by him will live longer than he wishes, and that, unless a Catholic Lord Lieutenant is appointed, he will, in the end, by means of Protestant ministers, assert his claims by the sacrifice of the best heads in Ireland, and establish more atrociously than before the heretic reign of terror." [1]

The Supreme Council could not, however, make up its mind to abandon its negotiation with the representative of a

March 18. Attitude of the Supreme Council.

King who had not the power, even if he had the will, to fulfil engagements made in his name. There being as yet no sign of Charles's acceptance of Sir Kenelm Digby's articles, or even evidence that they had come under his notice, the Council bade their commissioners, who were now once more at Dublin, to propose that the conclusion of peace should be deferred to the middle of June, to enable Glamorgan to fetch from France and the Netherlands the ships and money of which he was in need for the transportation of his forces to England. In the meanwhile Glamorgan would send his brother to obtain from the King a confirmation under the great seal of his own treaty. If this were accepted, and if Ormond would agree in the meanwhile to combine with the Irish forces against the common enemy, the Council would allow him 3,000*l.* to meet his current expenses. [2]

On these terms, with some modification, Ormond agreed to conclude the peace, on the understanding that it was to be

March 28. The treaty of peace signed.

kept a profound secret, not till the middle of June, but till May 1. The articles of the treaty which related to the civil government were signed on March 28. They contained many valuable reforms, especially providing for the admission of Catholics and Protestants to office upon equal terms. The whole question of religious

---

[1] Rinuccini's Memoir, March 1. *Nunziatura,* 114.
[2] The Supreme Council to the commissioners, March 18. *Carte MSS.* xvi. fol. 668.

liberty was postponed till an answer had been received from Charles. The negotiators were, however, so expectant of a favourable reply that they appended to the treaty an agreement to send to England without delay the long promised army of 10,000 men. Six thousand were to start on April 1, and on May 1 the remaining 4,000 were to follow. On March 30 Ormond gave to the Irish commissioners a written promise that if they were attacked before the time appointed for the publication of the treaty, he would appear in arms against their assailants.[1]

The articles on religion postponed.

The 10,000 men to be sent at once.

Whatever hopes might be entertained at Dublin, Glamorgan had given up all hope of conducting the army to England till the day when the King should, as he fervently believed he would, acknowledge the articles signed in his name. In the meanwhile he would go abroad and gather support for the great enterprise. His short access of ill-temper had passed away, and he avowed his belief freely that the King's disavowal had been drawn unwillingly from him. Yet he also acknowledged frankly that for the time it rendered him incapable of doing him service. During his absence the men should be placed under Preston for operations in Munster.[2]

March 29. Glamorgan gives up the hope of commanding them at present.

No wonder that, in spite of the signatures of their commissioners in Dublin, the Supreme Council felt doubtful as to the prospects of the treaty. Within a few days after its conclusion, news arrived from England which rendered the prospects of the expedition hopeless. Chester had long been closed against it, and South Wales had since fallen into the hands of the Parliamentarians. Cornwall was now lost as well, and there was no longer a foot of English soil on which the army could land with any prospect of being able to maintain itself. Officers and soldiers alike refused to leave Ireland.[3] On April 3 Muskerry wrote to Ormond that

Prospects of the expedition.

[1] The Irish Treaty, *Rushw.* vi. 402, with the date of its subsequent publication, Agreement, March 28; Ormond to the commissioners, March 30, *Carte MSS.* xvi. fol. 610, xvii. fol. 28.

[2] Glamorgan's considerations, Mar. 29. *Lord Leicester's MS.* fol. 1,101.

[3] Digby to Ormond, April 3. Carte's *Ormond,* vi. 363.

the expedition must be abandoned for the present. It would be impossible to land 10,000 infantry in a hostile country where no cavalry was available for their protection.[1] A week earlier Charles had written to Ormond precisely to the same effect. The foot, he said, was to be kept back, as it would be lost if it should now attempt to land, 'we having no horse nor ports in our power to secure them.'[2]

April 3.
The expedition countermanded.

The bubble had burst. Irish help was not available for Charles. Excellent as were the motives of the Supreme Council, their expectation of being able to gain civil and religious liberty in co-operation with a Stuart king was a rock upon which wiser statesmen than themselves must infallibly have split.

[1] Muskerry to Ormond, April 3. *Carte MSS.* xvii. fol. 49.
[2] The King to Ormond, March 26. *Ibid.* xiv. 309.

CHAPTER XL.

THE LAST CAMPAIGN IN THE WEST.

LONG before Charles's Irish negotiation hopelessly collapsed, the only army which still kept the field for him in England had

1645.
November.
Goring
leaves Eng-
land.

begun to melt away. Before the end of November Goring betook himself to France, partly because he was in reality suffering in health from the effect of his debauches, and partly because he hoped for a high command in the army of foreigners which the Queen expected to muster in the spring.[1] During the remainder of

Fairfax
before Exe-
ter.

the year Fairfax, in spite of the sickness which was ravaging his army, was cautiously establishing his posts on the east side of Exeter, in the hope of being able ultimately to complete the investment and to starve the city into surrender.[2] Though Cromwell had rejoined the army in October, neither he nor his chief was disposed to undertake an active campaign during the rainy season in so impracticable a country as Devonshire, and Fairfax contented himself with sending detachments to occupy Fulford and Canonteign, with the object of hindering the introduction of supplies into Exeter by the Royalists in the West.

Fairfax could afford to wait better than the enemy. On December 26 the Prince of Wales was at Tavistock, where he had ordered his scattered forces to concentrate in order to

[1] Goring to the Prince of Wales, Nov. 20 ; Jermyn to Hyde, Nov. 27. *Clar. MSS.* 2,033, 2,038 ; *Clarendon*, ix. 99. His name is afterwards connected with the foreign forces by the Parliamentary newspapers, and he does not seem to have been blamed by the King for his desertion.

[2] For the operations before Exeter, see the map at vol. ii. p. 358.

fall upon the Parliamentary army whilst it was ·hampered by
the operations of the siege. He calculated that when every
available man had been brought into line he would

Dec. 26.
The Prince
at Tavi-
stock.

have 6,000 foot and 5,000 horse at his disposal.
Unfortunately for him, his body was formidable in

Condition
of his army.

numbers only. The brutalities of Grenvile in Cornwall, and the ravages committed in Devonshire by the
cavalry which had been deserted by Goring, had exasperated
even the most loyal subject who had anything to lose. The
army itself was little better than a mob. Scarcely an officer of
rank would take orders from his superior, and the men, stinted
of every kind of supply, were scattered in small groups, from
the neighbourhood of Exeter almost to the Land's End.[1]

Fairfax's own army was indeed somewhat weakened by the
necessity of despatching Fleetwood and Whalley to watch the

Dec. 25.
Fleetwood
and Whalley
to watch the
King.

motions of the King's cavalry at Oxford, but it was
still strong enough to continue the blockade of
Exeter, and to deal with the approaching enemy in

A change of
weather.

his existing state of disorganisation. A frost which
now set in made the roads slippery, and threw almost
as much difficulty in the way of an advance as the previous

1646.
Jan. 8.
Advance of
Fairfax.

rains. At last on January 8 orders were given to
advance. Whilst Sir Hardress Waller pushed on to
Bow to distract the enemy's attention, Cromwell

Jan. 9.
The surprise
at Bovey
Tracey.

surprised a part of Lord Wentworth's brigade at
Bovey Tracey by a night attack, and though the
men for the most part escaped in the darkness, four
hundred horses fell into the hands of the victors. So terrified
was Wentworth at the unexpected blow that he fled in hot
haste to Tavistock to tell the news of his misfortune. The

The Prince
retreats to
Launceston.

Royalist plan had crumbled away, and the Prince,
who had set out with the intention of advancing to
Totnes, fell back upon Launceston, sending orders
to Colonel John Digby, who had been watching Plymouth
from afar, to abandon the semblance of a blockade and to fall
back upon headquarters.[2]

---

[1] *Clarendon,* ix. 116.　　　[2] *Clarendon,* ix. 117 ; *Sprigg,* 176.

Insubordinate and tyrannical as Grenvile was, he was at
least a soldier, and his first impulse on hearing of Wentworth's
mishap was to urge the Prince to appoint a commander-in-chief—Brentford or Hopton—to whom
the officers would be bound to render obedience.
On January 15 the choice of the Prince—or rather
that of the counsellors by whose advice he was
guided—fell upon Hopton. Grenvile was to serve
under him in charge of the infantry, and Wentworth in charge
of the cavalry. In pure devotion Hopton accepted the heavy
burden. He knew well that nothing but defeat was possible. He
declared that he had often heard men say that it was against
their honour to do this or that, when, in reality, it was only
against their inclination. He for his part was ready to obey
his Highness, though by so doing he should lose his honour.

> *Grenvile asks for the appointment of a commander.*

> *Jan. 15. Hopton appointed.*

Never, in the eyes of all whose opinion was worth having,
had Hopton's stainless reputation stood higher than on that
day of self-surrender. He was not likely to find many to
follow him in his path of loyalty. Grenvile, after recommend-
ing his appointment, refused to serve under him,
and proposed to employ himself in Cornwall in
bringing up those who had deserted from the trained bands of
the county. The Prince and his council were at last weary of
his disobedience, and thrust him as a prisoner into Launceston
Castle, whence, before many days were over, he was removed
to safer custody to St. Michael's Mount.[1]

> *Grenvile's arrest.*

The new commander had indeed a hopeless task before
him. Fairfax, having secured himself from immediate danger
by dispersing the advanced parties of the enemy, wheeled to
the left, and, though the heavy snow made it impossible to
bring up the artillery, carried Dartmouth by storm
on the 18th. The general's clemency served him
even better than his valour. To the Cornishmen
taken in the place he gave two shillings apiece, and sent them
home to spread among their countrymen the news that the
Parliamentary soldiers were not robbers like those of Grenvile
and Goring.[2]

> *Jan. 18. Dartmouth stormed.*

[1] *Clarendon*, ix. 141.   [2] *Sprigg*, 179.

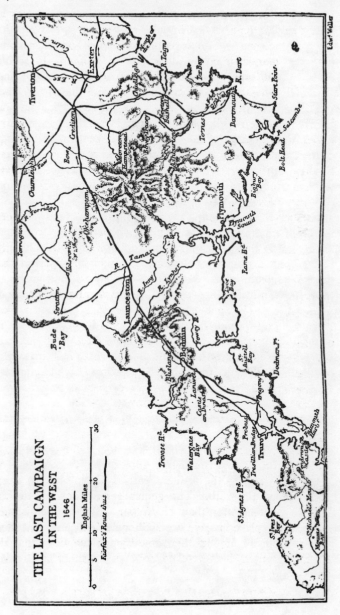

THE LAST CAMPAIGN
IN THE WEST

1646

English Miles

Fairfax's Route thus

In Devonshire, at least, the belief was spreading that peace and plenty were only to be recovered by the victory of the best

Jan. 24.
Devonshire
recruits for
Fairfax.

disciplined army. On the 24th, on his return to Totnes, Fairfax called on the county for 1,000 recruits to be employed in the defence of South Devon. Three times the number offered themselves willingly. " We are come," said Cromwell to them, " to set you, if possible, at liberty from your taskmasters." [1]

Having thus strengthened his position in South Devon, Fairfax returned to the work of encompassing Exeter. On

Jan. 26.
Powderham
Castle
surrenders.

the 26th his chain of forts round the city was completed by the surrender of Powderham Castle. On the same day news reached the army of a nature to strengthen, if possible, the grim resolution with which it had set itself to its appointed task. The captain of a French vessel sailed into Dartmouth, thinking the place to be still in

Intercepted
letters.

Royalist hands. As soon as he discovered his mistake he threw overboard a packet, which was, however, seized before it sank, and was found to contain letters written by the Queen and her principal adherents. [2]

After the reading of these letters at Westminster there could no longer be any reasonable doubt as to the correctness

The Queen's
projects.

of the information recently forwarded from Paris [3] as to the Queen's plans. In her letter to her husband Henrietta Maria wrote of the project of marrying their eldest

---

[1] *Sprigg*, 186 ; *The Moderate Intelligencer*, E. 320, 11.

[2] *Sprigg*, 188.

[3] "The treaty betwixt the King and Scots is with all industry prosecuted by Mr. William Murray with the Queen. She, to gain time, entertains it with great hopes of a fair and desired conclusion, and is resolved—if other expectations fail—to give them their desires. The obstacle at present is the difficulty of reconciling the party of Montrose with that of Hamilton and Argyle. Yet in case the Parliament should —upon the King's refusal of the propositions now desired—proceed to the deposing of him, the Scots commissioners in England do assure that those two parties shall reconcile and declare with one consent for the King, which is the only thing by her desired ; for having also assurance —in that case—of a party now with the Parliament, she is confident that that is the only way to re-establish the King to her content. The French

son to the daughter of the Duke of Orleans. Nor did she pass over in silence that negotiation with the Scots, the existence of which had been emphatically denied by the Scottish commissioners in London. She had sent, she said, 'Will Murray fully instructed with her mind about it.'[1] Of the other letters the most important was one from Jermyn. His

A French invasion proposed.

mistress, he said, had obtained leave to raise 4,000 foot and 1,000 horse in Brittany and Guienne, and she would have no difficulty in obtaining a larger number if she wished. This force would be ready about the end of February, and by that time the Dutch fleet, which was to transport them to England, would be ready to put to sea. "I had almost forgot," he concluded, "to observe to you that if the Scots' treaty be concluded it draws along with it another thing of equal importance, which will be the declaration of this Crown, and that may very probably be followed by that of the States United."[2] If the Houses had had any doubt before, they were now convinced that the Scots in their self-exculpation had spoken falsely.

The combination was, at least on paper, extremely formidable. The knowledge of its existence seems to have come through some other channel to Charles, who was now hoping

to entertain the war, until they have done their business in Flanders, give leave to raise 6,000 volunteers; 2,000 in Normandy, 3,000 in Brittany, and 1,000 in Poitou; for the setting forth of all which the Queen of France and Cardinal have this last week given 30,000 pistoles. The clergy gives the like sum, and both assurance of 5,000 pistoles monthly. Six hundred of the former number are within sixteen days to be shipped at Newhaven," *i.e.* Havre, "and conducted to Dartmouth by Sir William Davenant; the gross in March, all to be commanded by General Goring, who, having now passed his cure, will make his flourish for twenty or forty days in Paris." R. Wright to St. John [?], Jan. 17. *Portland MSS.* See also p. 44.

[1] See p. 20.

[2] Jermyn to Culpepper and Hyde, Jan. 17. *Clar. MSS.* 2,094. The signature is in cipher, but it is ascribed to Jermyn by Hyde. This is a duplicate of the copy taken at Dartmouth, which is, no doubt, the one now amongst the *Tanner MSS.* lx. fol. 371. That the Parliamentarians ascribed it to Davenant merely shows that they guessed the interpretation of the ciphered signature wrongly.

to do great things with the help of his foreign auxiliaries.
The notion of concentrating at Worcester [1] was for the time

Feb. 1.
Charles
hopes to
march into
Kent. abandoned, in all probability because the success of
Fairfax put an end to all hope of a junction with
the Prince's army. Charles, therefore, urged the
Queen to divert her French levies to the east of
England. If they could land at Hastings before the middle
of March, he would be able to gather a force of 2,000 horse
and dragoons. With these he would make a dash upon Kent,
seize Rochester, and hold out a hand to the invaders in
Sussex. [2]

Knowing nothing of this last wild scheme, Fairfax loitered
not in the execution of the duty before him. On February 8

Feb. 8.
Fairfax
before
Exeter.

Hopton
advances
towards
Torrington.

Fairfax's
precautions.

Feb. 10.
He advances
to meet
Hopton. he received the good news of the fall of Chester,
and at the same time learnt that the Prince's army
under Hopton's command was already on the march
for Torrington, in the hope of falling upon him
whilst he was engaged in the siege of Exeter.
Leaving a large part of his force under Sir Hardress
Waller to carry on the blockade, and despatching a
strong body of horse northwards to keep back the
Royalist garrison of Barnstaple from coming to
Hopton's assistance, he was still able to advance to
meet the enemy with 10,000 men.

Hopton reached Torrington on the 10th, the day on which
Fairfax broke up from before Exeter. The force at his dis-

State of
Hopton's
army. posal numbered little more than 5,000 men, of
which by far the greater part were cavalry. [3] In all
that constitutes an army he was miserably lacking.
His foot-soldiers had no heart in the cause for which they had
been dragged from their homes, and his horse, which had
been trained in Goring's evil school, utterly refused to submit
to discipline. They could seldom be induced to appear at

---

[1] See p. 18.

[2] The King to the Queen, Feb. 1.   *Charles I. in* 1646, p. 14.

[3] I follow Hopton's own account, Relation, *Carte's Orig. Letters*, i.
110, which gives 5,140; Hyde writing to the Queen on Feb. 17, *Clarendon St. P.* ii. 208, says he had 6,800.

the appointed rendezvous, and so slack were they in watching the enemy's movements, that it was only by accident that

Feb. 14.
Fairfax at
Chumleigh. Hopton learnt on the 14th that Fairfax had arrived at Chumleigh, and that an immediate conflict was therefore to be expected. Supplies too were slow in coming in, and, even if Fairfax left him unassailed, he would experience some difficulty in keeping his army together.

All that a brave soldier could do was done by Hopton. To abandon Torrington was to give up all hope of preserving

Hopton
resolves to
defend
himself. the West, and as the frost of the early part of the year had been succeeded by soaking rain, it was just possible that if the Prince's army could maintain itself in a strongly defensible position for a few days, Fairfax might be compelled by the weather to retreat. Such a position Hopton attempted to make for himself at Torrington. He blocked up with mounds of earth the entrances of the streets at the eastern end of the town, the side on which Fairfax was likely to approach, and threw out advanced guards to give warning of his coming. The Royalist general took care to quarter the greater part of his cavalry on a common to the north, so as to be ready to take the Parliamentary army in flank as soon as it was engaged in storming the town.

For two days there was skirmishing between the horse, always to the disadvantage of the Royalists. On the 16th

Feb. 16.
Advance of
Fairfax. Fairfax advanced in force. In the afternoon the weather temporarily cleared, and the Parliamentarians succeeded in establishing themselves at no great distance from Hopton's defences. After nightfall a re-

Torrington
stormed. connoitring party, fancying that the barricade at the end of the street had been abandoned, and creeping orward too far, was unintentionally drawn into an engagement. Other troops were pushed forward in support, and at last a general attack was ordered. After a sharp struggle the defences were carried. A body of horse, which had been kept in the town by Hopton to support his infantry, turned round and galloped down the long street which sloped westwards towards the Torridge. Their flight was the signal for disorder. Of the whole of the foot the Prince's guard alone maintained the struggle. Hopton himself, hurrying out to the common where the main body of his horsemen lay inactive, brought them back with him to turn the tide. The horsemen did their best, and drove the assailants back for a while, but not a foot-soldier could be induced to make a stand, and cavalry, unsupported, were at a hopeless disadvantage in a narrow street. Fifty barrels of powder, the whole of Hopton's remaining ammunition, which had been deposited in a church, now blew up with a terrific roar. Retreat was now inevitable, and under cover of the night the greater part of the Royalists who had not already fled made their way across the Torridge. The next day Hopton mustered the remains of his army at Stratton, the scene of his most successful exploit in happier days. Only 1,200 foot had rejoined him. The remainder had either stolen away to their homes or had enlisted in the ranks of the enemy.[1]

Hopton at Stratton.

The victory encouraged Fairfax to make short work of the enemy. The Prince, he knew, had retreated to Truro, and a deserter brought a rumour that the Queen's allies were to land in Cornwall in the middle of March. There was, therefore, no time to be lost. On the 25th Fairfax entered Launceston, driving the enemy before him. The Cornishmen had once risen as one man to drive intruders over the Tamar. Since that time the bitter lesson of Royalist plunderings had entered into their souls, and they welcomed the soldiers who robbed no one and paid their way.[2]

Feb. 20. Fairfax's further advance.

Feb. 25. Fairfax enters Launceston.

Hopton had fallen back upon Bodmin. It was no fault of his if he was unable to make a stand. Even his cavalry was now dissolving before his eyes. Those who did not desert to the enemy neglected to perform the commonest duties of military service. Regiments appeared at their posts with half their numbers absent, and those who thought fit to attend often arrived two hours after the appointed time. On March 1 a

Hopton's condition.

March 1. Misconduct of his cavalry.

[1] Hopton's Narrative, *Carte's Orig. Letters*, i. 109; Wogan's *Narrative, Ibid.* i. 126; *Sprigg,* 192; *A more full relation,* E. 325, 2.

[2] *Sprigg,* 207.

whole brigade of horse, posted on Bodmin Downs to check
the advance of the enemy, fell back upon the town
in direct defiance of their commander.   Hopton
was compelled to abandon Bodmin, and the place
was occupied by Fairfax on the following day.[1]

March 2.
Fairfax
occupies
Bodmin.

The advance of the Parliamentary army had rendered the
position of the Prince of Wales exceedingly precarious.   It
was true that on February 21 he had received letters
from France in confirmation of the rumour that
troops were being raised for his succour,[2] but it was
added that there would be a delay of two or three
weeks beyond the date which had been originally fixed for
their transportation, so that they could hardly be expected in
Cornwall before the latter end of March.[3]   Almost
at the same time those who had the charge of the
Prince's person learnt that that old trickster, Lord
Newport, had been attempting to curry favour with Parliament
by suborning a lieutenant of the Prince's guard to carry the lad
off to Westminster.[4]

Feb. 21.
French aid
promised
to the
Prince.

A plot to
seize the
Prince.

Before Fairfax reached Bodmin the heir to the crown had
taken refuge in Pendennis Castle, where a council was hastily
summoned to discuss the measures for securing his
safety.   There was a general disinclination to send
him to France, if it could possibly be avoided, and on
March 2, the day on which the Parliamentary troops
occupied Bodmin, the Prince embarked for the Scilly
Isles, where he would be out of reach of Fairfax, and would
yet be on English soil.

The Prince
at Penden-
nis Castle.

March 2.
He goes to
the Scilly
Isles.

As soon as the Prince had departed, Hopton ceased to
have any motive for prolonging an impossible
resistance.   When he left Bodmin he appointed
a rendezvous at Castle Dinas, an isolated hill at no
great distance, crowned with the ramparts of an ancient

March 1.
The rendez-
vous at Cas-
tle Dinas.

[1] *Clarendon,* ix. 144; Hopton's Narrative, *Carte's Orig. Letters,* i.
116.   [2] See p. 63, Note 3.

[3] Hopton's Narrative, *Carte's Orig. Letters,* i. 116.

[4] Montreuil to Mazarin, $\frac{Jan. 29}{Feb. 8}$, *Arch. des Aff. Etrangères,* lii. fol. 91;
Jermyn to Culpepper, Feb. 9, *Clar. MSS.* 2,125.

camp. Very few of his horse attended, and at a council of
war held on the 2nd every officer, except himself
and Major-General Webb, voted for an immediate
surrender. A letter from Fairfax offering honourable
terms arrived on the 6th, and Hopton, though he
resolutely refused to treat for the surrender of Pendennis and St. Michael's Mount, was driven by the
importunity of his own officers to open negotiations
on the 8th. Before it was too late he took care to
send to the two garrisons reinforcements out of the
infantry still remaining with him.

March 2.
A council
of war
votes for
surrender.

March 6.
A letter
from Fair-
fax.

March 8.
Hopton
agrees to
treat.

But for the forbearance of the Parliamentary soldiers
Hopton's desire to postpone the inevitable surrender might
have cost his followers dear. On March 10 a
party of Ireton's horse, near Probus, fell in with
some of the Royalist cavalry, who, fancying that they
were out of danger because negotiations had been opened,
made no preparations for resistance. Ireton had much
ado to persuade them that hostilities had not been suspended, but he had too much generosity to take advantage
of their error, and allowed them to retire without
injury. On the same day commissioners from both
sides met at Tresillian Bridge. Fairfax did not,
however, think it necessary to halt, and before night he entered
Truro.

March 10.
A peaceable
rencontre.

Commis-
sioners
meet.

It seemed as if Hopton's army would cease to exist before
the commissioners could agree. The gentlemen of the county
and the soldiers alike declared themselves to be weary of the
war, and to be desirous of living peaceably under the protection of Parliament. At last, on the 14th, the wrangle
over the terms of surrender was brought to a conclusion. Common soldiers, after giving up their arms
and horses, might return to their homes or go beyond sea.
Officers not specially excepted from pardon by the Parliament
were allowed the same choice, but might retain their horses
and their pistols. Even officers excepted might leave the
country, a reasonable time being allowed them to petition Parliament for their restoration to favour. All who remained in

March 14.
Hopton's
surrender.

England were to take an oath never again to serve against Parliament.

On the 20th the disbandment of what remained of the army of the West was carried out on these terms. The spirit which had once animated that army was as extinct as its organisation. The contrast between the vagabonds whom Goring had mustered and the disciplined warriors of the New Model was striking enough to counterbalance the local Western patriotism which at one time had stood Charles in good stead. No one who had anything to lose wished to see Goring back again, especially if he brought a pack of hungry Frenchmen at his heels,[1] No less distasteful was the prospect of an Irish invasion. A Waterford ship, taken at Padstow on March 5, had been found to contain letters from Glamorgan, in which he boasted that 6,000 Irish would soon land in England, to be followed in May by 4,000 more. In making its submission, Cornwall did not so much bow before the conqueror as rally round the national banner in the hands of Fairfax.[2]

March 20. Hopton's army disbanded.

March 5. A Waterford ship taken.

Charles had little left to rely on except his foreign intrigues. A few strong places held out for him, but he could not hope to maintain them for many weeks. Yet he could hardly expect to profit by his intrigues any more than he had profited hitherto. Before the end of January he knew that Glamorgan's negotiation had miscarried,[3] and that the Queen's negotiation with the Scots had been revealed.[4] Her letter, which had recently been intercepted at Dartmouth, referred to Will Murray as about to cross to England to inform the King what she had been doing in that matter, and on February 5 Will Murray was seized as he was passing through Canterbury in disguise, on his way to Oxford. The Houses sent him to the Tower, and attempted to extract his secrets from him. No revelations were, however, obtained and he was

Strongholds still unreduced.

Charles's intrigues breaking down.

Feb. 5. Will Murray arrested.

---

[1] *Sprigg*, 212; Hopton's Narrative, *Carte's Orig. Letters*, i. 117.
[2] *Sprigg*, 213, *The Earl of Glamorgan's negotiations*, E. 328, 9.
[3] See p. 45.　　　　　　　　　[4] See p. 63.

ultimately sent before a court-martial as a spy. The court

Tried as a
spy and
acquitted. very properly refused to adjudge him to be a spy and he recovered his liberty on bail in the course of the summer.[1]

Murray had brought with him an important letter from the Queen to her husband, of which the French Agent was able to

Montreuil
cannot get
leave to go
to Oxford. gain possession, as it had been directed to himself. Montreuil was anxious to carry it to Oxford, but the Houses, suspecting the object of his journey, threw every possible obstacle in his way.[2]   Charles, however, knew

The Queen
favours an
all'ance
with the
Scots. from other sources that his wife, who had by this time discovered the articles brought from the Pope by Sir Kenelm Digby to be hopelessly impracticable, had now set her heart on an understanding with the

Scots.   She seems to have said something about the probability that concessions made to them on the score of religion would be only temporary.   Charles replied bluntly that,

Feb. 19.
Charles
refuses to
make
religious
concessions. whether they were temporary or not, he would never make them. " I must confess to my shame and grief," he added, with evident reference to his abandonment of Strafford, "that heretofore I have, for public respects—yet, I believe, if thy personal safety had not been at stake,[3] I might have hazarded the rest—yielded unto those things which were no less against my conscience than this ; for which I have been so deservedly punished that a relapse now would be insufferable, and I am most confident that God hath so favoured my hearty though weak repentance, that He will be glorified either by relieving me out of these distresses—which I may humbly hope for, though not presume upon—or in my gallant sufferings for so good a cause, which to

---

[1] *L.J.* viii. 260, 416 ; *C.J.* iv. 641.

[2] *C.J.* iv. 430, 431 ; Montreuil to the King, *Clar. St. P.* ii. 213; Montreuil to Mazarin, Feb. $\frac{5}{15}$, $\frac{\text{Feb. 19}}{\text{March 1}}$, *Arch. des Aff. Étrangères*, lii. fol. 103, 126.

[3] This is a curious corroboration of the evidence in favour of the view that Charles's anxiety about his wife was a principal cause of his weakness in the case of Strafford. See *Hist. of England*, 1603-1642, ix. 365.

eschew by any mean submission cannot but draw God's further justice upon me, both in this and the next world." [1]

The words were well and bravely written, and there could be little doubt that they were well and bravely meant. Yet Charles could not fold himself in silence, or hold himself aloof from entanglement with men whom he never could conciliate. His resolution not to grant to the Presbyterians the only terms which they would accept merely led him to make fresh overtures to the Independents.

His resolution unalterable.

On March 2 Ashburnham wrote to Vane, by the King's orders, adjuring him to support his master's request for leave to visit London, there to obtain the acceptance of that offer of toleration which he had already made,[2] so amended as to make it applicable to all religious parties. "If Presbytery," urged Ashburnham, "shall be so strongly insisted upon as that there can be no peace without it, you shall certainly have all the power my master can make to join with you in rooting out of this kingdom that tyrannical government, with this condition, that my master may not have his conscience disturbed—yours being free—when that work is finished." [3]

March 2. His appeal to the Independents.

If no response was made to this offer—and at least no evidence exists that Vane ever replied—it is unnecessary to blame the Independent leaders. It was impossible for them to believe that Charles had no other object in coming to London except to establish a settlement of the kingdom on the basis of a general toleration. The knowledge of Glamorgan's treaty must have made them cautious, and, however loudly the Scots might protest, no reasonable person could doubt that Charles had been listening favourably to overtures from them, or that in those overtures they had stood out for exclusive Presbyterianism. It was not the fault of the Independents if they refused to believe that Charles could be negotiating with the Presbyterians without being prepared to grant their most indispensable demand.

No response made to it.

[1] The King to the Queen, Feb. 19. *Charles I. in 1646,* p. 18.
[2] See p. 17.
[3] Ashburnham to Vane, March 2. *Clar. St. P.* ii. 226.

This, however, was precisely what Charles was doing. On March 3, the day after Ashburnham's letter was sent to London, he wrote again to his wife. "For the Scots," he told her, "I promise thee to employ all possible pains and industry to agree with them, so that the price be not giving up the Church of England, with which I will not part upon any condition whatsoever. . . . Besides the nature of Presbyterian government is to steal or force the crown from the king's head ; for their chief maxim is . . . that all kings must submit to Christ's kingdom, of which they are the sole governors, the king having but a single and no negative voice in their assemblies, so that yielding to the Scots in this particular, I should both go against my conscience and ruin my crown." [1]   It was impossible for Charles to express more clearly the mixture of religious and political considerations which possessed his mind.

March 3.
Charles's attitude towards the Presbyterians,

The King's distrust of the Presbyterians had made him ready on the 2nd to seek the aid of the Independents. On the 12th it made him ready to seek the aid of the Catholics. "If the Pope and they," he wrote, "will visibly and heartily engage themselves for the re-establishment of the Church of England and my crown . . . against all opposers whatsoever, I will promise them, on the word of a king, to give them here a free toleration of conscience." Would it not be well, he added in a postscript, 'that all the English Roman Catholics be warned by the Pope's ministers to join with the forces that are to come out of Ireland?' [2] How was it possible to deal with a man so utterly out of touch with the world in which he lived?

March 12.
and towards the Catholics.

Whilst Charles was speculating on the choice of allies, Montreuil, with a Frenchman's incredulity of the existence of insuperable conscientious objections in the breast of a heretic, was pertinaciously striving to extract from the Scottish commissioners the lowest terms upon which they would receive Charles into their army, making no doubt that he would ultimately accept them without

Feb.
Montreuil's continued activity.

---

[1] The King to the Queen, March 3.   *Charles I. in* 1646, p. 22.
[2] The King to the Queen, March 12.   *Ibid.* p. 24.

difficulty.[1] He soon found, however, that the task of reconciliation was harder than he anticipated. In spite of all
his protestations, he was unable to obtain anything in writing
from a body of which Lauderdale was a member, and was
March.
Sir R.
Moray
declares the
terms of
the Scots. obliged to content himself with a verbal authorisation to Sir Robert Moray to set down in writing the
conditions demanded. Charles, it appeared, was not
only to accept the three propositions touching the
Church, the militia, and Ireland which he had rejected at
Uxbridge, but he was also to sign the Covenant. If he did
these things he would be received with honour and respect
into the Scottish army, and might be assured that the Scots
would do all in their power to reconcile his followers with the
English Parliament. If it were necessary to make exceptions
in the cases of five or six, then nothing worse than temporary
banishment should befall them. If the King accepted these
terms he must write two letters to that effect, the one to the
Parliament and the Scottish commissioners at Westminster,
the other to the Committee of Estates at Edinburgh.[2]

---

[1] Montreuil to Nicholas, Feb. 26, *Clar. St. P.* ii. 217 ; Montreuil to
Mazarin, Feb. 26, *Arch. des Aff. Étrangères*, lii. fol. 140.

[2] "Les Deputez d'Escosse m'ont autorisé pour asseurer la Reyne et
Mgr le Cardinal, ainsy que je fays par ce present escrit, que si le Roy de
la Grande Bretagne veut se retirer en l'armée des Escossois, il y sera
receu avec toute sorte d'honneur, et de respect, et y demeurera avec une
entière seureté, et que les Escossois s'interposeront efficacement pour faire
l'accomodement de ceux de son party avec le Parlement d'Angleterre à
la reserve de cinq ou six qui s'esloigneront seulement pour quelque temps,
pourveu qu'avant que d'aller en l'armée il plaise à sa dite Majesté de la
Grande Bretagne escrire deux lettres, l'une au Parlement d'Angleterre et
aux deputez d'Escosse à Londres, et l'autre aux commitez du Parlement
d'Escosse, par lesquelles il donne son consentement aux trois propositions
touchant Religion, la Milice, et l'Irlande, qui ont esté autrefois faites à
Uxbridge, et aux demandes de la Ville de Londres qui sont de peu de
consequence avec promesse de les ratifier par actes de ses Parlements, et
de faire tout ce que peut contribuer à l'establissement des affaires ecclesiastiques et civiles et à la paix et l'union de ses Royaumes par l'advis de
ses Parlements, et que sadite Majesté de la Grande Bretagne signe le
Couvenant devant qu'aller à l'armée des Escossois, ou en y arrivant à son
choix." Moray to Montreuil, March ? *Arch. des Aff. Étrangères*, lii. fol.
164.

Montreuil, sanguine as he was of bending Charles to his will, knew that it would be impossible to obtain his consent to

March 16.
The
Scottish
proposal
modified.

such terms as these, and he accordingly sought for an interview with Loudoun, the most influential of the commissioners who had lately returned from Scotland. He was told that an interview could not be granted, and that he must continue to treat through Sir Robert Moray. Moray, on being again addressed, assured the Frenchman that Loudoun had full powers from the Scottish Parliament to negotiate,[1] and on March 16 he announced that the commissioners would withdraw their demand for the acceptance of the whole of the three propositions of Uxbridge and for the signature of the Covenant, and would content themselves with a promise from Charles to accept the church settlement which had been already made and which should hereafter be made by the Parliaments and Assemblies of the two kingdoms. Charles was, however, to express a general approbation of the Covenant in the letters to the two Parliaments in which he was to accept these conditions. The first requirement, wrote Montreuil to Mazarin, was no more than had been proposed by Moray in France. As to the second, Charles would not, by writing a letter, bind himself to the Covenant as much as if he had actually signed it.[2] Montreuil was a young diplomatist, full of indiscreet zeal and anxious to distinguish himself by promoting the establishment of a weak government in England ; but he entirely failed to understand the very peculiar

Charles's
conception
of truth and
falsehood.

constitution of Charles's mind. Charles could explain away a promise which he had formerly made, or could couch a promise which he was making in words which he intended to explain away at some future time ;

[1] The only official powers given to him by Parliament were given to him as a member of the Committee of Estates, and they contained a clause ' that nane of the commities entir in treattie anent the poyntes and articles in questione betwixt his Matie and estates of this kingdome, or betwixt the kingdomes themselves, without consent of a quorum of the whole thrie committies.' *Acts of Parl. of Sc.* vi. 383. Probably Loudoun had this assent, but a foreigner easily makes mistakes in such matters.

[2] Montreuil to Mazarin, March $\frac{16}{26}$. *Arch. des Aff. Étrangères,* lii. fol. 164.

but nothing would induce him deliberately to use binding words with the express intention of disregarding them on the plea that the form in which his promise was made did not officially and legally amount to a contract. The distinction may appear to plain minds to be merely one between one form of falsehood and another, but there can be no doubt that it was a very real one to Charles himself.

Later in the day Moray handed to Montreuil a paper in which the final engagements expected by the Scottish Commissioners were written down, though merely in his own hand. The demand for even a general approval of the Covenant had disappeared entirely, but in other respects the obligations now required by Moray in the name of the Scots corresponded with that indicated in his own conversation in the morning.[1] On Charles's agreeing to

A final engagement proposed.

---

[1] " Les Deputéz de l'Escosse m'ont autorisé pour asseurer la Reyne et Monseigneur le Cardinal, que si le Roy de la G. B. veut se retirer en l'armée des Escossois il y sera receu avec toutes sortes d'honneur et de sureté, et y demeurera avec une entière sureté, comme aussy les Princes Robert et Maurice, le Secretaire Nicholas, et Mr. Ashburnham, et les Escossois s'interposeront efficacement pour faire l'accomodement de tous ceux de son party avec le Parlement d'Angleterre, à la reserve de trois ou quatre qui s'éloigneront pour quelque temps seulement, pourvu qu'auparavant que d'aller à la ditte armée : il plaise au Roy de la Gr. Br. escrire deux lettres, l'une au Parlement d'Angleterre et aux Deputez d'Escosse à Londres, l'autre au Comité du Parlement d'Escosse, qui sont en Escosse, et en l'armée des Escossois, par lesquelles il déclare qu'il consent que les affaires ecclesiastiques soient establies en la manière desja prescritte par les Parlements et Assemblées du Clergé des deux Royaumes, et qu'il approuvera tout ce qu'ils feront à l'advenir touchant les dittes affaires ecclesiastiques, consent que la Milice soit disposée en la manière qu'il a esté proposé par les Deputez d'Escosse et d'Angleterre à Oxbrige pour sept ans entre les mains de ses Parlements, comme leurs Deputéz l'ont proposé à Oxbrige, et qu'il accorde les demandes de la ville de Londres presentées à sa ditte Majesté à Oxford avec promesse de tout ratiffier et establir par actes de ses Parlements et de faire tout ce qui peut contribuer au bien des affaires ecclesiastiques et civiles par l'advis de ses Parlements, ce qui estant fait les Deputez d'Escosse sont résolus de faire en sorte, que sa ditte Majesté seroit reçue en son Parlement et remis en sa dignité, grandeur et autorité. A Londres le $\frac{19}{28}$ Mars 1646, signé Moray." *The second engagement of the Scots.* Ranke, *Engl. Geschichte,* viii. 174.

the terms as they now stood he would be received in the Scottish army.

Bearing this missive, Montreuil set out for Oxford on the following morning.   He had learnt from the Scots that they entertained no doubt of their ability to carry their point with the English Parliament.   The majority of the Peers was on their side, and the City was no less firmly attached to them.   The Presbyterian members of the House of Commons had bound themselves by oath that if, on the King's betaking himself to the Scottish army, the Independents should refuse their consent to a reasonable settlement, they would join the Scots with an army of 25,000 men.   These troops they hoped to levy in the associated counties, where Presbyterianism was now rampant, possibly because the Independents who found their way into the army at the beginning of the war were, after all, exceptions amongst their neighbours, and certainly because the eastern counties, as a seat of manufacture as well as of agriculture, were anxious for peace, and were annoyed at the burdensome taxation which had been imposed specially upon the Parliamentary counties for purposes in which they were not themselves immediately interested.[1]

Whatever might be the result of the proposed appeal to the associated counties, the support of the City seemed to be absolutely certain.   As usually happens when bodies of men are divided upon some wide question of principle, petty differences of opinion were aggravated into causes of grave dispute.   On February 13 the officers of the militia of the suburbs, the Tower Hamlets, Southwark, and Westminster, had remonstrated against a proposal for placing them at the orders of the City Committee of Militia.   The Commons did their best to smooth away the difficulty, and on March 13 appointed a committee to consider how the suburban forces could be placed under the command of the City authorities in some way which would avoid giving offence to either party.[2]   A far

March 17. Montreuil goes to Oxford.

Hopes of the Scots.

Collision between Parliament and the City.

Feb. 13. The command of the suburban militia.

March 5. Ordinance for Presbyterianism passed by the Commons.

[1] Montreuil to Mazarin, March $\frac{16}{26}$.   *Arch. des Aff. Étrangères.*

[2] *C.J.* iv. 441, 474.

more important question was raised by an ordinance for the general establishment of Presbyterianism throughout England, sent up to the Lords on March 5. Of this ordinance one clause—the 14th—was singled out by the high Presbyterians for animadversion as introducing the authority of the State where they wished to see nothing but the authority of the Church. Whenever the eldership came to the conclusion that a scandalous offence, which ought to exclude the offender from participation in the Communion, had been committed, they were then, if it was not included in the Parliamentary list, to suspend the guilty person for a time, and to report the matter to certain commissioners appointed by Parliament, who were finally to decide upon the case.[1] On the 13th the Lords, though not without strong opposition, passed the impugned clause, and gave their assent to the whole ordinance on the following day,[2] though it had, in consequence of amendments made in it, again to come before the Commons.

The House of Commons which adopted this ordinance was not altogether the same as that which, in the crisis of the war, had stood at the head of Parliamentary England. Not far short of 150 new members had been chosen, and these Recruiters, as they were called, counted amongst them men like Ireton and Fleetwood, Ludlow and Algernon Sidney, not to mention Henry Marten, whose expulsion was thus virtually annulled. By the sheer weight of numbers, if their votes had been thrown on one side or the other, they would have been able to make an entire change in the balance of parties. Yet it is doubtful whether the complexion of the House was much altered. Still, as before, the Presbyterian party was predominant, if by that name it is intended to include those who desired the establishment of Presbyterianism and were unwilling to tolerate the wilder forms of opinion. Still, as before, the Independent party was predominant, if by that name is meant to include those who would hear nothing of a combination with the Scots to come to terms with the

The 14th clause.

Clause on suspension from Communion.

March 13. The clause passed by the Lords,

March 14. and the whole ordinance.

The Recruiters.

---

[1] *C.J.* iv. 464.   [2] *L.J.* viii. 208, 209.

King, and who wished to grant some modified form of toleration to those whose opinions were not in all respects identical
with those which generally prevailed.   The Long Parliament
at this period, like the assemblies of the French Revolution,
contained groups rather than parties.   There was a small
group of members in favour of unlimited, or almost unlimited,
toleration.   There was a somewhat larger group of members
in favour of refusing toleration of any kind.   There was a
powerful group of lawyers, with Selden and Whitelocke at their
head, entirely opposed to any scheme for entrusting the clergy
with secular jurisdiction even in church matters, except under
the permanent control of Parliament.   Between the lawyers
and the Independents in the stricter sense an alliance was
formed, and the general drift of opinion against clerical
power was strong enough for the present to give them the
mastery.

The sentiments of the Assembly in opposition to those of
the Parliament were well expressed by Baillie.   " We find it
necessary," he wrote, " to say that Christ in the New

Baillie's view of the situation.   Testament had instituted a church government distinct from the civil, to be exercised by the officers of
the Church without commission from the magistrate."   The
conduct of the Houses filled him with despair.   "The Pope
and the King," he added, " were never more earnest for the
headship of the Church than the plurality of this Parliament.
However, they are like for a time, by violence, to carry it.   Yet
almost all the ministry are zealous for the prerogative of Christ
against them."   The crisis had now arrived.   The Scottish
commissioners, he hoped, and the Assembly together with the
City ministers would petition against the obnoxious clause,
' but that which, by God's help, may prove most effectual is
the zeal of the City itself.' [1]

On March 14, in fact, the City presented to the Commons

March 14. The City petition.   its objections to the 14th clause, which, as the ordinance was on that day returned with amendments
by the Lords, was still before the House.   It is no
matter for surprise that the City was tenaciously Presbyterian.

[1] *Baillie*, ii. 360.

The fear of ecclesiastical tyranny which was so strong on the benches of the House of Commons had no terrors for the merchants and tradesmen of the City. By filling the elderships those very merchants and tradesmen constituted the Church for purposes of jurisdiction. Whatever ecclesiastical tyranny there was would be exercised by themselves.

In the House of Commons the interference of the citizens was treated as impertinence. The petitioners were told that they had broken the privileges of Parliament, and that they must present no more petitions of the kind.[1]

Answer of the Commons.

After this the Scots were easily able to assure Montreuil that they were secure of the support of the City. The keystone of the arch was, however, the approbation of Charles, and it was to secure this that the French Agent took his way to Oxford. No sooner had he arrived than he discovered that the King was as firmly resolved as ever to give no consent to the establishment of Presbyterianism. In his letters to his wife Charles characterised the efforts made to explain away the promise which he was asked to give as 'Montreuil's juggling.'[2]

Charles's assent to the Presbyterian combination needed.

March 17. Montreuil at Oxford.

March 22. Charles's opinion of Montreuil.

The time had, however, now come when Charles must nerve himself to some decision. He must have known, if not of the actual surrender of Hopton, at least of the heavy blows of misfortune which would soon make surrender inevitable. Now, too, arrived news of fresh disaster. Even after the Western army had been definitively cut off from Oxford, Charles had still entertained hopes of rallying round him soldiers enough to enable him to effect a junction with those French auxiliaries for whose coming he still looked with eager expectation. With this object Astley was already on the march through Worcestershire to Oxford with 3,000 men. On March 21, in the early morning, he was attacked near Stow-on-the-Wold by the combined Parliamentary forces of

A decision necessary.

Charles's military prospects.

March 21. The fight at Stow-on-the-Wold.

---

[1] Whitacre's Diary. *Add. MSS.* 31,116, fol. 259.

[2] The King to the Queen, March 22. *Charles I. in* 1646, p. 27.

Morgan, Birch, and Brereton, the numbers on either side being about equal. After a sharp engagement the Royalists were overpowered. As in Cornwall, the King's soldiers had no heart to prolong the war, and at once surrendered in crowds. Deserted by his men, Astley gave himself up as a prisoner. The white-haired veteran, seated on a drum amongst his captors, frankly acknowledged that the King's defeat was final. "You have now done your work," he said, "and may go play, unless you will fall out amongst yourselves."[1] A few garrisons might still, for honour's sake, bid defiance to the victors for a time, but to gather an army in the field was no longer possible for Charles.

Astley's warning.

If it be asked what were the causes which had led to such a disastrous result, the answer cannot be otherwise than a complex one. Something may be laid to the account of Charles's inferior financial position ; something to the reluctance of the classes which furnished his principal supporters to submit to discipline ; something to the ill-feeling which prevailed between the military and the civilian element in his court. Nor was it of little moment that, although he had succeeded in enlisting on his side commanders like Rupert and Brentford, whose military talents were unquestionable, he had, in England at least, no one to direct his armies who rose, as Cromwell rose, to the rank of those who are possessed of the rare quality of military genius. Yet, after all, these things were but symptoms of causes of evil more profound. Charles's own character was most in fault. His entire want of sympathetic imagination had ruined him in the day of his power by rendering him incapable of understanding the nation which he claimed to govern. It ruined him equally when he was striving to recover the power which he had lost, because he was unable to rouse enthusiasm even in that part of the nation which, through an unexpected concurrence of events, had rallied to his standard. Over those who shared his devotional feelings, especially over such of them as were eyewitnesses of his passive constancy of endurance, his ascen-

Causes of Charles's defeat,

[1] *Rushw.* vi. 140.

dency was complete. A nation looks for the word of command from a leader who is imbued with its virtues, its passions, and its prejudices. Such a word of command Charles never had it in his power to give. He could criticise his opponents, but he was absolutely devoid of constructive power.

Hence it was that in spite of the tendency of a great mercantile community to support the cause of order, Charles was never able to win back the allegiance of the London citizens, and left to his opponents the enormous advantages, military and financial, which the City of London had to offer to them, and which more than any other cause contributed powerfully to their success. Hence, too, it was that on the disastrous field of Naseby, when his gallant and well-disciplined infantry was crushed by superior numbers as well as by superior skill, it was found to be composed almost entirely of Welshmen. It was not for nothing that the nickname of Cavaliers clung to his adherents. The bulk of the gentry made common cause with him ; but the bulk of the middle classes, the tradesmen in the towns, the farmers and yeomen in the country attached themselves to his adversaries, whilst the labourers in town and country stood, for the most part, aloof from the struggle, and after a while could no longer be brought by force or persuasion to fight for a King who knew not how to find the way to their hearts.

Ruinous as were the defects of Charles's character, they were rendered still more fatal by his positive antagonism to the national spirit. Nothing could be more disastrous to him than his constant appeals to Welshmen, Irishmen, Scots, Frenchmen, Lorrainers, and Dutchmen to assist him in arms. Englishmen, without regard to party, felt the affront, and their indignation quickly made itself perceptible to Charles in the slackening of the arms of his defenders and in the strengthening of the arms of his enemies. Charles grew weak in proportion as he sought to make good his claims through combinations outside England. Cromwell grew strong in proportion as he brought the objects at which he aimed into harmony with the grand design of

and of Cromwell's success.

preserving the national unity and independence intact. That Cromwell should have had at his disposal more skilful commanders and more energetic and better disciplined soldiers than Charles could gather round him was no more than the natural result of the moral and intellectual difference between them.

CHAPTER XLI.

THE KING'S FLIGHT TO THE SCOTS.

IT was ever Charles's habit to meet difficulties with neatly arranged phrases, rather than with a prompt recognition of the significance of unpleasant facts. Since he had re- ceived Montreuil's communication, the Scots had been out of favour with him, and on March 23, upon the arrival of the bad news from Stow-on-the-Wold, he despatched a request to the English Parliament for permission to return to Westminster, on the understanding that an act of oblivion was to be passed and all sequestrations taken off the property of his supporters.[1]

1646. March 23. Charles asks to return to Westminster.

Even had this offer been ingenuous, it simply concealed a demand that the whole civil war should go for nothing, and that Charles should be allowed to step back on the throne, free to refuse his assent to any legislation which displeased him. On the 26th the Commons drew up a reply refusing to concede his request until he had given satisfaction for the past and security for the future. In other words, there was to be a mutual understanding on the constitutional changes which were to be accepted by both parties before Charles could be permitted to take up the position which he held to be, by indefeasible right, his own. The proposal of the Commons was accepted by the Lords and by the Scottish commissioners, after which, on April 1, it was despatched to Oxford.[2]

Character of the request.

March 26. Reply of the Houses.

Charles's proposal, in short, had gone far to reconcile the opponents whom he hoped to divide. Already, on March 18, before his message was penned, the Commons had recognised

[1] *L.J.* viii. 235.   [2] *Ibid.* viii. 248.

their mistake in reflecting on the conduct of the City, and had
expunged from their journals the resolution [1] in which they
had embodied their feelings of dissatisfaction.[2]   On
the 24th the arrival of the King's letter completed
the reconciliation.   The citizens were terrified at the
prospect of Charles's return to London before he
had bound himself to the constitutional and ecclesiastical changes which they desired, especially as the
Royalists in London had recently been reinforced
by hundreds of still more pronounced Royalists, who had
flocked into the City to make their compositions with Parliament.

April 1.
It is sent to
Oxford.

Overtures of
the Com-
mons.

March 24.
Alarm in the
City.

On the 26th the Houses urged the City to stand on its
guard.   The sense of a common danger showed
itself in a mutual interchange of civilities.   The
Commons invited the authorities of the City to be
present at their thanksgiving service for the victories
in the West, and the City authorities returned the
compliment by asking the Commons to dinner.[3]

March 26.
The City to
stand on its
guard.

Mutual
civilities.

Baillie's remarks on this sudden revulsion of feeling were
dismal enough.   "The leaders of the people," he moaned,
"seem to be inclined to have no shadow of a king;
to have liberty for all religions; to have but a lame
Erastian Presbytery; to be so injurious to us as to chase us
home by the sword. . . .   Our great hope on earth, the City of
London, has played nip-shot"—in other words, has missed
fire.   ". . . They are speaking of dissolving the Assembly."[4]

Baillie's
complaint.

The sermon on Thanksgiving-day was delivered by that
prince of army chaplains, Hugh Peters.   At times rising into
what, compared with the dull platitudes of most of
the celebrated preachers of the day, almost ascends
into real, if somewhat incoherent, eloquence, he was
entirely without fear of giving offence to any of his
hearers.   "I could wish," he said, "some of my learned

April 2.
Hugh Peters
preaches a
thanks-
giving ser-
mon.

[1] See p. 79.

[2] *C.J.* iv. 479; Whitacre's Diary, *Add. MSS.* 31,116, fol. 259.

[3] *Merc. Civicus.* E. 330, 15.

[4] *Baillie*, ii. 362.

brethren's quarrelling hours were rather spent upon clearing the originals, and so conveying over pure scripture to posterity, than in scratching others with their sharpened pens, and making cockpits of pulpits." In another place he pitilessly represented Charles's court as travailing as a woman with child with its great design for the overthrow of the Parliament. "And then," he continued, "before the birth, what throes and pains! Send to Denmark, run to Holland, fly to France, curse Digby, imprison Hamilton, &c.; and then all help is called in for midwifery—entreat friends here and there, pawn jewels, break and close with Irish even in a breath—anything for help— hazard posterity—engage in marriage,[1] and—as she did—roar out, 'Give me a child, or I die!' and that miscarriage we are this day to praise God for, and wonder at." If their enemy were indeed such a one as this, let those who had opposed him in the field be deaf to his pleadings for an insidious peace. Yet it was not with political considerations alone that Peters was concerned. He had thoughts for the salvation of the profane and the sinner. "Men and brethren," he cried, "whilst we are disputing here, they are perishing there, and going to hell by droves. If I know anything, what you have gotten by the sword must be maintained by the word—I say the word, by which English Christians are made; in other countries discipline makes them so. Drive them into a church together, and then dub them Christians; you will find too much of this abroad, and hence it comes to pass that most of their religion lies in polemics, which is the trade we are likely to drive if God prevent not." What Peters asked for was not stricter discipline but more attractive preaching. Nor were men's bodies to be neglected. Why, he asked, was not the Charterhouse employed in helping the widows and orphans of those who had been slain in the war? Why were there so many beggars in the City? Why could not the courts do justice more quickly? and, as a means thereto, why could not the language of the law be English instead of French—that

[1] Referring, I suppose, to the latest matrimonial project. The Great Mademoiselle, being a Roman Catholic, would if married to the Prince hazard posterity.

badge of conquest? There might even be 'two or three friend-makers set up in every parish, without whose labour and leave none should implead another. Why, he asked again, were poor debtors to be kept in prison? Why, finally, should men's names be exposed to detraction? He did not, indeed, ask for punishment. He had learnt better things from the Lord General. "Let us look to our duties," Fairfax was accustomed to say, "and the Lord will care for our reproaches." [1]

No one who has read this sermon will be at a loss to know why the man who preached it was favoured alike by Fairfax *Character of* and Cromwell. There was no canting fanaticism *the sermon.* here. There was distrust of an intriguing enemy, but, for the rest, there was an appeal to all who came within the influence of the preacher to leave windy disputations for a religion which manifested its reality in abounding well-doing, especially in the direction of social reform.

As a matter of fact Peters's suspicion that Charles was not straightforward in his request to come to London was per-*March 23.* fectly well-founded. On March 23, the very day on *Charles* which his letter to the Houses had been despatched *sends a* *secret* from Oxford, he dictated to Montreuil a secret mes-*message to* *the Scots,* sage to the Scottish commissioners in London, which, though it contained no direct promise that he would do anything they wished him to do, might serve to keep them in hope of his possibly doing it at some future time. "First," so ran the words, "as concerning church government, we do really promise that we shall give full contentment therein as soon as we come to London, so as in the meantime you give us satisfaction—which we shall be willing to receive—that what you desire therein shall not be against our conscience." In case of a refusal of his offer to come to Westminster, he would betake himself to the Scottish army on receiving assurance that he would be there secure in conscience and *March 24.* honour. On the next day he added that as soon as *and offers to* this assurance reached him he would surrender *surrender* *Newark.* Newark into their hands. Nor was London forgotten in Charles's promises. He offered to satisfy the demands which

[1] *God's doings and Man's duty,* 114, e. 15.

the City had made at Uxbridge, especially in respect to the command of the militia.[1]

On the 27th Montreuil, in Charles's name, pressed the Scots for a reply.[2] Though their answer has not been pre-served, there can be little doubt that they gave assurances that if the King placed himself under the protection of their army he should be secure both in conscience and honour ; though it is most unlikely that they allowed anything of the sort to appear in their own hand-writing.[3] The result was that on April 1 engage-ments were exchanged between Montreuil and the King. The French Agent promised in the name of the King of France and of the Queen Regent that, if Charles 'put himself into the Scots' army, he' should 'be there re-ceived as their natural sovereign, and that he' should 'be with them in all freedom of his conscience and honour . . . and that the said Scots shall really and effectually join with the said King . . . and also receive all such persons as shall come in unto him, and join with them for his Majesty's preservation ; . . . and that they shall employ their armies and forces to assist his Majesty in the procuring of a happy and well-grounded peace . . . and in recovery of his Majesty's just rights.' Charles on his part promised to take no companions with him except his two nephews and John Ashburnham. "As for church government," he added, "as I have already said, I now again promise that, as soon as I come into the

March 27. Charles presses for a reply.

April 1. An exchange of engage-ments.

---

[1] The King's messages, March 23, 24. *Clar. St. P.* ii. 218, 219.

[2] The King's message, March 27. *Ibid.* ii. 220.

[3] Clarendon in his History (x. 26) says that Montreuil visited the Scottish army before he made the engagement. This is, however, an evident mistake, first, because there was hardly time to do it between the 27th and the 1st ; and, secondly, because not only had his communications hitherto been with the commissioners in London, but the Frenchman's letter of April 11 shows that up to March 25 the commissioners with the army knew nothing about the affair. Montreuil to Mazarin, April $\frac{11}{21}$. *Arch. des Aff. Étrangères,* lii. fol. 227. Clarendon's account of the Scottish commissioners with the army waiting for Loudoun's arrival shows that he was really thinking of the modification of the Scottish terms made on March 16, after Loudoun's arrival in London. See p. 75.

Scots' army, I shall be very willing to be instructed concerning the Presbyterian government, whereupon they shall see that I shall strive to content them in anything that shall not be against my conscience." [1]

A question might one day arise whether the Scottish commissioners in London had any right to bind their Parliament
Faults on both sides. and nation. However this may have been, there was undoubtedly a want of straightforwardness on both sides. The Scots did not urge the King's acceptance of Presbyterianism as a necessary condition of the help which they were prepared to offer. The King talked of contenting the Scots about church government as far as his conscience would allow, and of being instructed in the Presbyterian system, without stating that he had resolved never to abandon Episcopacy. If we knew all, we should probably come to the conclusion that both parties were trying, perhaps to some extent unconsciously, to outwit one another. Charles was hardly able to conceive it possible that the Scots, when he was once among them, would really insist on the establishment of Presbyterianism in England, and the Scots were hardly able to conceive it possible that, considering all that was at stake, Charles would ultimately refuse to establish it. Neither spoke clearly or openly on the all-important subject. In such a case it is the weakest who goes to the wall ; and Charles was certainly not the strongest.

Of all this Montreuil seems to have had no conception. On April 3 he took the road towards Newark, in full confidence
April 3. Montreuil goes to Newark. that, as had been agreed in London,[2] Leven would despatch a body of cavalry to meet the King. He was to tell the Scottish commanders that Charles would leave Oxford on the 7th, and would expect to meet his convoy at Harborough on the 8th.

When Montreuil reached the army on the 5th he found that all his work must be begun afresh. Balmerino, who was

[1] The King's promise, and Montreuil's engagement, April 1. *Clar. St. P.* ii. 220.

[2] Montreuil to Mazarin, March $\frac{12}{13}$. *Arch. des Aff. Étrangères,* lii, fol. 169.

to have come from London to persuade the commissioners with the army and the officers to receive the King, had not

April 5.
Montreuil's disappoint-ment. arrived. On inquiry, it appeared that, as the day was a Sunday, he had halted thirty miles short of Newark to keep the Sabbath. Montreuil, to whom

Balmerino keeps the Sabbath. the scruples of a Scotchman were inexplicable, rode off to hasten his coming. Balmerino, when at last he appeared, argued but feebly in support of the plan to which he had assented in London. The Scottish officers not only refused to send the required escort, but even hindered Montreuil from despatching a messenger to inform Charles of their refusal.

For some days the French Agent feared that Charles might already have set out from Oxford, and have been cap-

Montreuil's fears. tured by the enemy for want of a convoy. He was finally relieved by a letter from the King telling him

April 12.
The King's journey postponed. that he had postponed his journey. At last, on the 15th, Montreuil was able to forward somewhat better tidings. Loudoun had come down to Royston, and

April 15.
Modified terms offered by the Scots. had there had an interview with Dunfermline and Balcarres,[1] two of the Scottish commissioners with the army. The result was a proposal to receive the King into the army, on the understanding that to avoid giving offence to the English Parliament, he should give out, when he arrived, that he was on his way to Scotland, and had merely halted in the camp. The Scots professed themselves still ready to receive the two Princes and Ashburnham, but only on condition that, if their surrender were demanded, they would leave the country rather than bring their hosts into trouble. If these terms were accepted the Scots would send an escort as far as Burton, and a few horsemen might push on

Presby-terianism to be granted. to Bosworth, but to send men to Harborough was out of the question. "As to the Presbyterian government," they added, "they desire his Majesty to grant it as speedily as he can."[2]

---

[1] The name is inserted from the copy of Montreuil's letter to Nicholas in the *Arch. des Aff. Étrangères,* lii. fol. 216, where Balcarres is called 'Bacara.'

[2] Montreuil to Mazarin, April $\frac{11}{21}$, *Arch. des Aff. Étrangères,* lii. fol.

The situation was now clear.   Whatever inferences Charles
may have drawn from the communications of the London
commissioners, he would be now wilfully blind if he misunder-
stood the peremptory nature of the demand for the establishment of Presbyterianism in England.   Yet it was this which
he had firmly resolved to oppose to the uttermost.   On the

*April 13.
Charles's
vow.*

13th he delivered to his chaplain, Gilbert Sheldon,
a written vow declaring his resolution that if ever he
was restored to power he would give back to the
Church its right to all impropriations and to all Church lands
hitherto in possession of the Crown, and would thereafter hold
them from the Church at such fines and rents as might be
fixed by a conscientious arbitrator.   It is impossible to suppose that Charles intended to restore this property to any
Presbyterian body.[1]   The paper on which this solemn obligation was written was buried by Sheldon, and remained in the
earth till after the Restoration.

Charles's anxiety to retain the services of Montrose was no
less incompatible with an understanding with the Scots than
was his resolution to maintain Episcopacy in

*Montrose
in the
Highlands.*

England.   For some months Montrose had been
hanging about the Highlands with a scanty following.   Now that he had lost the Macdonalds, and that their
war against the Campbells was being carried on under another
leadership than his own, he had done his best to secure the
co-operation of Huntly.   The old difficulty stood in his way.
Huntly was too great a man to put himself under Montrose's
orders, and Montrose could hardly be expected to serve under

*April 18.
Charles
invites him
to join the
Cove-
nanters.*

a nobleman who had never given proof of courage or
capacity.[2]   Charles had thought of smoothing away
the difficulty by appointing Montrose his ambassador
to the French court, but he still hankered after the
idea of uniting him with the Covenanters.   On the 18th he

227 ; Montreuil to Nicholas, April 15 or 16.; Messages to the King,
April 16, *Clar. St. P.* ii. 221, 223.

[1] The King's vow, April 13.   *Clar. MSS.* 2,176.   Printed in the
appendix to *Eachard's History*, p. 5.

[2] *Wishart*, ch. xx. ; *Patrick Gordon*, 177.

wrote to urge him, if Montreuil should send him favourable news, to combine his own forces with those of the Covenanters and to hasten to his relief.[1]

On the following day [2] Charles heard from Montreuil that the Scots expected him to establish Presbyterianism, and that they would not consent even to allow him to send Montrose to Paris. "The Scots," he complained to his wife, "are abominable relapsed rogues."[3] Yet without the help of the Scots his position was well-nigh desperate. Forces under Fleetwood and Whalley were already gathering round Oxford, and they would before long be joined by Fairfax's victorious army from the West. A new project flashed across Charles's mind. On the 22nd he resolved to escape to Lynn. How he expected to make his way into the place there is nothing to show, but he assured the Queen that when he was there he would attempt to procure 'honourable and safe conditions from the rebels.' If that failed he would join Montrose by sea, and if that resource failed also he would escape to Ireland, France, or Denmark. "If thou hearest," he added in a postscript, "that I have put myself into Fairfax's army, be assured it is only to have the fittest opportunity of going to Lynn in a disguise, if not by other ways."[4]

April 19. Charles hears of the Scots' change of front.

His danger.

April 22. He resolves to take refuge in Lynn.

If Charles had tarried much longer at Oxford, he would soon have come into collision with the army against which he was so strongly prejudiced. On March 31 Fairfax returned to the lines round Exeter, and summoned Sir John Berkeley to surrender. Berkeley, cut off as he was from hope of succour, agreed to treat. The articles of surrender were signed on April 9. The little Princess Henrietta and her governess, Lady Dalkeith, were to remain in any place of England which it pleased the King to appoint. Neither the cathedral nor any

March 31. Exeter summoned.

April 9. Articles of surrender signed.

---

[1] The King to Montrose, April 18. *Clar. St. P.* ii. 224.
[2] The King to the Queen, April 22. *Charles I. in* 1646, p. 37.
[3] The King to the Queen, April 21. *Ibid.* p. 36.
[4] The King to the Queen, April 22. *Ibid.* p. 37.

other church was to be defaced. The garrison, which was to march out fully armed with all the honours of war, was permitted to betake itself to Oxford unless it preferred to disband. There were further concessions made to the lords and gentlemen who had taken refuge in the city, amongst whom was the detested Bristol. That which distinguished this capitulation from all others was, however, a provision that ' no oath, covenant, protestation, or subscription ' was to be imposed on any person within the walls. To this article Thomas Fuller, who had been in the city during the siege, owed it that he was able to continue preaching during the rest of the civil troubles, without being required to take the Covenant.

Special exemption from oaths and covenants.

On the 13th the Parliamentary forces entered the capital of the West, Cromwell taking good care that the terms granted were observed. Fairfax had not waited for the completion of the formalities. Hurrying off to Barnstaple, he soon brought its garrison to terms. On the 20th, the fortifications having fallen into the hands of the besiegers, the place surrendered, and on the same day Dunster Castle gave itself up to Blake. St. Michael's Mount had already submitted on the 15th. The little fort of Salcombe held out for about three weeks longer, and then the Castle of Pendennis was the only unconquered stronghold in the West. Fairfax was already on the way to lay siege to Oxford.[1]

April 13.
Surrender of Exeter.

April 20.
Surrender of Barnstaple and Dunster Castle,

April 15.
and of St. Michael's Mount.

If Charles had been in earnest with the schemes of toleration which he from time to time proposed, he would surely have discerned the significance of the article exempting the besieged at Exeter from the obligation of taking the Covenant. That he was not, under such circumstances, attracted to the army is strong evidence that his talk about toleration never went deeper than his lips. Whilst the infatuated King inclined rather to the Scots than to the army, events were occurring in London which drew the Scots towards the King. The temporary withdrawal of the City from its alliance with them [2] had delivered

Charles and the army.

The Scots and the Parliament.

their commissioners over to the mockery of the Independents and Erastians, whose alliance dominated the Commons. Re-

April 7.
The Scots
urge a
speedy
settlement.

solved to stand up in their own defence, on April 7 they presented to the Houses a paper urging the importance of speedily coming to terms with the King, and suggested that a committee might discuss with them each point of the proposed articles. If this were done, the propositions on religion might be agreed to in a few days, and 'a method for a model of uniformity in church govern-

April 11.
The Scots
publish their
papers.

ment' discovered.[1] On the 11th, without waiting for a reply, the Scots not only sent to the press this paper and two others, which they had formerly presented, but added a preface, written by David Buchanan, in which every point which had been raised by them against the

April 13.
The Com-
mons order
t em to be
burnt.

English Parliament was set forth succinctly. On the 13th the Commons ordered the whole publication to be burnt ; and though subsequently the Lords re-

April 18.
On'y the
reface to
be burnt.

stricted the execution of the order to Buchanan's preface, the condemnation of the attitude taken up by the Scots was hardly less complete.[2]

On April 17 the Commons replied to the manifesto of the Scots by a counter-manifesto. They protested their desire to

April 17.
Declaration
of the
Commons.

settle religion in accordance with the Covenant, 'to maintain the ancient and fundamental government of this kingdom, and to lay hold on the first opportunity of procuring a safe and well-grounded peace . . . . and to keep a good understanding between the two kingdoms.'

Then, entering into details, they declared that the future church government was to be Presbyterian 'saving in the point

The Church
to be Presby-
terian,

of commissioners.' It was impossible for them to 'consent to the granting of an arbitrary and unlimited

but under
Parliamen-
tary con-
trol,

power and jurisdiction to near ten thousand judicatories to be erected.' Presbyterian the church was to be, but it was to be Presbyterian in due submismission to the authority of Parliament. If so far satisfaction

---

[1] *L.J.* viii. 256.

[2] *Some Papers of the Commissioners of Scotland,* E. 330, 1 ; *C.J.* iv. 506 ; *L.J.* viii. 277, 281.

was given to the Erastians, satisfaction was given to the Independents by that which followed.   "Nor," continued
the manifesto, in words which were only inserted on
a division of sixty-seven to forty-one, so scanty was
the attendance when even important questions were at issue,
"have we yet resolved how a due regard may be had that
tender consciences, which differ not in any fundamentals of
religion, may be so provided for as may stand with the Word
of God and the peace of the kingdom."

and with a moderate toleration.

In matters of state the House professed its intention of
abiding by the old form of government by King, Lords, and
Commons, and of asking no more of the King than
that he should abandon to Parliament such powers
as were needed to make a recurrence of civil war
impossible.   Justice was to be administered by the courts of
law, and the subject to be, as soon as was possible, eased of
his burdens.   After taking this rosy view of the political situation, the Commons addressed a final defiance to the Scots.
They were still ready, they declared, to observe the
Covenant, but they expected 'that the people of
England should not receive impressions of any forced
constructions of the Covenant, which, in case of any
doubt arising, is only to be expounded by them by whose
authority it was established in this kingdom.'¹

Proposed settlement of the State.

The Covenant to be expounded by Parliament.

Whilst the Commons, falling, in their animosity against the
Scots, under the guidance of the Independents, were thus
carrying on a paper war, they were contemptu-
ously setting their foot upon one of the two but-
tresses of Scottish power in England, the Assembly
of Divines.   In their wrath against the appointment
of commissioners to decide on ecclesiastical offences,
the divines had presented a petition, in which they asserted
that ecclesiastical jurisdiction was, by Divine right,
vested in the Church.   On April 11 the Houses
voted this petition to be a breach of privilege,
and on the 16th appointed a committee to draw
up questions to be submitted to the Assembly.²   Already

The Commons and the Assembly.

Petition of the Assembly.

April 11. The Commons declare it to be a breach of privilege.

¹ *C.J.* iv. 512.   ² *Ibid.* iv. 506, 511.

by the 22nd the questions were prepared, which if we may judge by internal evidence originated in the critical mind of

April 22.
Questions
for the
Assembly. Selden. Did the Assembly mean that 'parochial and congregational elderships appointed by ordinance of Parliament, or any other congregational or presbyterial elderships,' were of Divine right? Then followed a string of similar interrogatories, ending with a request that the answers given might be followed by Scripture proofs.[1]

It is needless to pursue the unequal struggle further. Parliament was as disinclined as the Tudor kings had ever been to allow the establishment in England of a church system claiming to exist by Divine right, or by any right whatever independent of the authority of the State.

On the 23rd, the day after that on which these questions were brought in, Cromwell once more took his place at Westminster, and received the thanks of the House for

April 23.
Cromwell
receives the
thanks of
the House. his extraordinary services.[2] The political situation must have been almost as much to his mind as was the military.

The events of the last few days had strengthened the hands of Parliament in dealing with the King. On the 22nd Charles,

April 22.
Charles
sends a
message to
Ireton. doubtless in pursuance of the project which he had announced to the Queen, of making his escape by throwing Fairfax's army off its guard,[3] sent a message to Ireton through some Royalist officers who had passes to go beyond sea, and were visiting Oxford on their way. The King, they declared, was ready to come in to Fairfax, and to live wherever Parliament might direct, 'if only he might be assured to live and continue king still.' Ireton at once refused either to discuss a political question with the

Ireton
relates the
story to
Cromwell. officers or to allow them to return to Oxford. All that he would do was to acquaint his superior officers with their proposals, and he accordingly wrote to Cromwell telling him all that had passed.[4]

---

[1] *C.J.* iv. 519.   [2] *Ibid.* iv. 520.   [3] See p. 91.
[4] Ireton to Cromwell, April 23. Cary, *Memorials of the Civil War*, i. 1.

It was not much to do, yet even this was more than Cromwell approved of. Hitherto he had been a Parliamentary

April 25.
He is
blamed by
Cromwell.
general in the fullest sense of the word, setting his
face against every attempt to bring political questions
within the cognisance of military authorities, and he
now, from his place in the House, denounced Ireton as worthy

Fairfax not
to listen to
overtures
for peace.
of reproof. It was at his instigation that Fairfax was
instructed to forward to Westminster any letter which
came into his hands with the King's signature, and
to take care that neither he nor anyone under his command
listened to any overture for peace from whatever quarter it
might come.[1]

The close combination which now existed between Parliament and army was by no means to the taste of the English

An overture
from the
English
Presby-
terians,

April 24.
answered
by the
King.
Presbyterians. Some of them had recently besought
Charles to take up his dropped negotiation with the
Scots, and on April 24 Nicholas begged Montreuil
to convey to the Scottish commissioners in London
assurances that the King was still ready to take
refuge in the Scottish army, if only he could be
received on fit conditions.[2]

Charles could not afford leisurely to await the issue of a
lengthy negotiation. Colonel Rainsborough was attacking

April 25.
A fresh
attempt to
negotiate
with the
army.
Woodstock, and on the 25th Charles sent to him the
Earls of Lindsey and Southampton, nominally to
arrange for the surrender of the place, but in reality
to ask him to take the King's person under his protection till Parliament could be applied to, and even to engage
to defend Charles and his servants if the answer of Parliament
should prove unsatisfactory.[3]

Charles waited in vain for a reply from Rainsborough, and
a fresh attempt to win over Ireton proved equally unsuccessful.[4]
A letter from Montreuil turned the hopes of the unhappy King
in another direction. "The disposition of the Scottish com-

---

[1] *C.J.* iv. 523; Whitacre's Diary, *Add. MSS.* 31,116, fol. 266b.
[2] Nicholas to Montreuil, April 24. *Clar. St. P.* ii. 225.
[3] Instructions to Lindsey and others, April 25. *Clar. St. P.* ii. 228.
[4] *Ashburnham's Narrative*, ii. 71.

manders," wrote the French envoy from the camp before
Newark, "was all that could be desired." They had already

A communication from Montreuil. detached some troops towards Burton to look out
for the King.[1] Nothing was said about the Scots
abating their demands for the establishment of
Presbyterianism, but, with Fairfax approaching and a siege
of Oxford imminent, Charles was ready to catch at any straw.

April 26. Charles takes leave of his council. Late in the evening of the 26th he assembled his
council, and assured them that he had made up his
mind to go to London. If they did not hear of him
in a fortnight or three weeks, they had his leave to
make the best conditions they could.[2] Of the Scots he did
not breathe a word, knowing well that he would only rouse
opposition by mentioning the design on which he was really
bent. It is possible, however, that he had not finally made up
his mind as to the course which he was to take.

A direct ride to the Scottish camp was in any case impossible. Dr. Hudson, one of the royal chaplains, who knew
Dr. Hudson's advice. the country well, and had been employed in carrying
letters between Charles and Montreuil, warned the
King that his only chance of reaching Newark without interruption lay in his taking at first the direction of London. At
April 27. Charles leaves Oxford, three in the morning of the 27th Charles, disguised
as a servant, with his beard and hair closely trimmed,
passed over Magdalen bridge in apparent attendance
upon Ashburnham and Hudson. "Farewell, Harry!" called
out Glemham to his sovereign as he performed the Governor's
duty of closing the gates behind him.[3] The little party rode
leisurely on through Dorchester, Henley, and Slough, putting

---

[1] Montreuil to Nicholas, April 20. *Clar. St. F.* ii. 224. Ashburnham in his *Narrative* (ii. 71) says that Montreuil's letter, apparently
received on the 26th, 'did import that all difficulties were reconciled, and
Mr. David Leslie, their Lieutenant-General, had orders to meet his
Majesty with two thousand horse at Gainsborough.' The last word is an
obvious blunder for Harborough. The message appears to have related
to military movements, and does not appear to have touched on religious
concessions.

[2] Narrative of affairs. *Clar. MSS.* 2,240.

[3] Payne to Browne. Cary, *Mem. of the Civil War*, i. 12.

VOL. III.

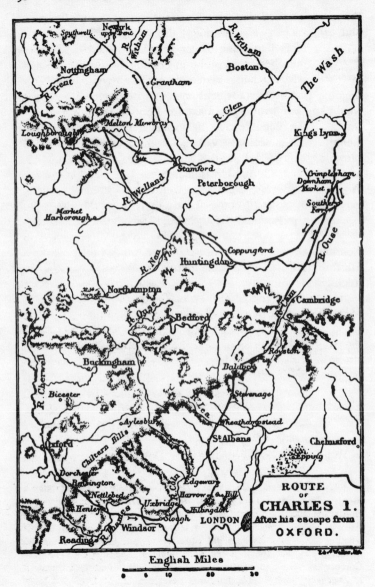

ROUTE
OF
CHARLES 1.
After his escape from
OXFORD.

English Miles

the guards on the road in good humour by small gifts of money, and exhibiting a pass bearing Fairfax's signature, which be-

and takes
the road
towards
London. longed to some officer who had received leave to make his composition in London. Between ten and eleven Charles rested for about three hours at Hillingdon, where time was consumed in a discussion whether it would be more prudent to make for London or to turn northwards. It is possible that he expected some message from London to meet him here, either, according to a rumour which prevailed at Oxford, from the Lord Mayor and Aldermen, or, as Ashburnham afterwards stated, from the Independent leaders. It would only be in consonance with Charles's character if he expected tidings from both. However this may have been, no

He turns
northwards. communication reached him, and, sadly acknowledging that it would be useless to arrive uninvited in London, he turned his horse's head, and riding through Harrow and St. Albans, he halted at Wheathampstead for the night.

On the morning of the 28th Hudson was despatched to Montreuil, whom he found quartered at Southwell, to urge

April 28.
Hudson
sent to
Montreuil. him to demand a written assurance from the Scots that they would receive the King on conditions satisfactory to himself. Charles, meanwhile, rode on towards Norfolk, with the evident intention of throwing himself

April 30.
Charles at
Downham. into Lynn, in order to leave England by sea should the answer of the Scots prove contrary to his wishes. On the 30th he reached Downham and waited for news.[1]

Whilst Charles was making for Downham, Montreuil was

---

[1] Hudson's examination. Peck's *Desiderata Curiosa*, 358. On May 1 Montreuil wrote to Du Bosc (*Arch. des Aff. Étrangères*, lii. fol. 260) in cipher that the King was at *Cois*, 'en lieu d'où il peut aller en France, en Escosse, ou en Dannemarc.' In a letter of May 11 Du Bosc doubts whether the decipher of *Cois* was correct. 'Lynn,' being also composed of four letters, was doubtless the word intended. Compare a letter from Corbet and Walton to Lenthall, in Hearne's edit. of Morin's *Chronicle of Dunstable*, ii. 799. The King was never actually at Lynn, but Montreuil may have thought that he had reached it.

urging the Scots to put their engagements to the King into

writing. To this request the Scots returned a peremptory refusal. All that they would do was to allow Montreuil to draw up a written form to which they verbally expressed their assent. A copy of this form was given by the French Agent to Hudson to carry to the King, and, according to a statement subsequently made by the bearer, it ran as follows :—

" 1. That they should secure the King in his person and in his honour.

" 2. That they should press the King to do nothing contrary to his conscience.

" 3. That Mr. Ashburnham and I should be protected.

" 4. That if the Parliament refused, upon a message from the King, to restore the King to his rights and prerogatives, they should declare for the King, and take all the King's friends into their protection. And if the Parliament did condescend to restore the King, then the Scots should be a means that not above four of them should suffer banishment, and none at all death." [1]

That the Scots were glad to allure the King to come amongst them may be taken for granted, and it may perhaps

be accepted as equally certain that they had no conception how insuperable was Charles's objection to Presbyterianism. Nor was it altogether their fault that they fell into the mistake. Charles had, at all

---

[1] Montreuil's despatch of May $\frac{15}{25}$ (*Arch. des Aff. Étrangères*) gives an account of the paper to which the Scots verbally assented, which agrees with that given by Hudson in his examination, and printed in Peck's *Desiderata Curiosa* 361. Unfortunately the secretary whose duty it was to put Montreuil's letter into cipher omitted a few words, and the important passage relating to the message to be sent by the King was thus left out. We have therefore only Hudson's evidence to fall back on. He himself tells us that the terms as he states them were given him by Montreuil, and it is to be supposed that he had the paper still with him when he was examined. The agreement between his account and that of Montreuil as far as it goes is strongly in favour of the theory of his substantial accuracy.

events, done his best to cherish their delusion. On March 23
he had promised to give them full contentment on church
government if only they could satisfy him that to do so would
not be against his conscience.[1] On April 1 he had declared
his willingness to receive instruction as soon as he reached the
Scottish quarters.[2] Was it strange if the Scots believed that he
was as ready to be converted as Henry IV. of France had
once been? It is likely enough, if this was their belief, that
they cared more for getting the King into their hands than for
the sincerity of their engagements to him. They had not
hitherto shown themselves scrupulous in the matter of veracity
in their dealings with the English Parliament,[3] and they may
very well have been somewhat unscrupulous in their dealings
with the King.

Yet there is a possible explanation of their conduct which
sets it in a fairer light. In the engagement taken by them at

Nature of
Charles's
obligation.

Newark—the terms of which were, after all, drawn
by Montreuil and not by the Scots—all hung on the
meaning of the expression in the fourth clause,
'upon the sending of a message from the King.' Unless this
message was sent, the Scots would be under no obligation to
do anything to restore Charles to the throne. Yet, even if we
have Montreuil's exact words, it is incredible to suppose that
Charles would have satisfied the obligation under which the
French Agent had brought him by sending any message, however little to the point ; by informing Parliament, for instance,
that it had been raining at Oxford, or that his horse had cast a
shoe. In spite of the indefinite article, if it really appeared in
Montreuil's French, a message of a particular kind must surely
have been intended, and what other kind of message could
have been meant than that which had for some weeks been
discussed by both parties? It was not so very long ago since
the Scots in London had urged Charles to write a letter to the
two Parliaments granting the establishment of Presbyterianism ;
and when Loudoun met Dunfermline and Balcarres at Royston,
the demand that Charles should yield about the Church was
formally made, whilst, as late as the 15th, Montreuil had

---

[1] See p. 86.   [2] See p. 87.   [3] See p. 45.

written to him to urge him to hasten his decision.[1]   To this
demand Charles had never returned a positive refusal.   If,
then, both Montreuil and the Scots expected him to grant
Presbyterianism, but expected him only to do it after some
delay and with the appearance of having been vanquished in
argument, it would to some extent account for, though it would
not excuse, their talking about 'a message' in general, when
they really meant a message of a very particular kind.[2]

Charles, in short, if this explanation be correct,[3] was hoist
with his own petard.   Intending to deceive, he became de-

*The King
resolves to
trust the
Scots.*

ceived.   Following Montreuil's advice to trust the
Scots, he determined to make for their camp.   Ash-
burnham indeed wished him to take shipping for
Newcastle, when he would at least be at a distance from any
English army.   This advice was, however, overruled, and on
May 2 Charles set out from Downham.   By a devious route
through Melton Mowbray he arrived at Stamford on the even-
ing of the 3rd.   The next day he kept himself concealed, and

*May 5.
Charles at
Southwell.*

then, after travelling all night,[4] alighted at seven in
the morning of May 5 at Montreuil's lodgings in
Southwell.[5]   He fancied himself to be a guest, but
the days of his captivity had in fact begun.

[1] See p. 89.

[2] That the Scots' commissioners in London still expected the King to
write letters announcing his acceptance of Presbyterianism is shown by a
letter from Moray, written after the King's arrival in the camp, in which
he expresses surprise that the letter has not yet arrived.   Moray to Du
Bosc, May $\frac{7}{17}$.   *Arch. des Aff. Étrangères,* lii. fol. 272.

[3] It is in favour of the view that the message was intended to grant
Presbyterianism that in all his subsequent correspondence Montreuil never
refers to this engagement as having been broken.   His argument always
turns on the engagement made through Sir R. Moray.   (See p. 73 in
which the nature of the message was distinctly expressed.)

[4] Browne's examination.   Peck's *Desiderata Curiosa,* 352.

[5] Montague to the Speaker of the House of Lords, May 5.   *L.J.* viii.
305.   According to tradition, the house in which the King was received
was the Saracen's Head, which boasts, truly or falsely, of having been an
inn in the days of Richard I.   The sitting-room and bedroom are now
thrown into one as the inn parlour, but an oaken beam across the ceiling
still marks the place where the partition was.

CHAPTER XLII.

THE KING IN CAPTIVITY.

WHATEVER may have passed through the minds of the Scottish commissioners when they signified their assent to the terms

1646.
May 5.
The Scots
expect
Charles to
yield. which Montreuil forwarded to the King, there can be little doubt that they expected Charles, as soon as he came amongst them, to yield to their most extreme demands. Lothian, on receiving the news

Lothian's
demands. of his arrival, hurried to Southwell, and imperiously called on him to command the surrender of Newark, to sign the Covenant, to order the establishment of Presbyterianism in England and Ireland, and to direct James Graham to lay down his arms. To all this Charles positively refused his assent. " He that made you an earl," he sternly replied to Lothian, "made James Graham a marquis." He was, there-

Charles re-
moved to
Kelham. fore, removed to Kelham, the headquarters of David Leslie, who was now in command of the army, Leven having withdrawn to Newcastle. He was there treated as a prisoner, sentinels being placed before his windows lest he should communicate with his friends by letter.[1]

Assurances
of the Scots. Before he left Southwell the Scottish commissioners wrote to the Houses at Westminster, assuring them that the King's coming had been entirely unexpected, that it

May 6.
Newark
surrendered. had filled them with amazement and made them like men that dream. On the following day they gave practical evidence of their wish to remain on good terms with the English Parliament. Charles, who knew that Newark was incapable of prolonged resistance, ordered its sur-

[1] *Sir James Turner's Memoirs,* 41.

render to the Scots. They, however, refused to accept it, and insisted that it should be given up to the English commissioners.[1]

Laying aside all question of the personal truthfulness of the Scottish commissioners, it is hard to see how they could have acted otherwise than they did. Charles came amongst them as his grandmother had come to Elizabeth, not merely to seek refuge from imminent ruin, but to rouse them to intervene in arms on his behalf. Whatever this or that Scottish nobleman may have said, or allowed to be said, in his name, it was absolutely impossible to begin war afresh on Charles's conditions. Not only was the Presbyterian feeling too strong in Scotland itself to tolerate the employment of the Scottish army in a war waged for the restoration of Episcopacy, but Leven's soldiers were not prepared to face the New Model without the aid of English allies, and their only possible allies, the English Presbyterians, would to a man refuse to take arms unless Charles made the ecclesiastical concession which they required. If the Scottish commissioners had not seen this before—which there is no reason to suppose—they saw it now. All that they could do in the face of the English Parliament, was to repudiate their past dealings with the King, to deprecate a hasty decision, and to retire to a place less exposed than Newark to the forces which Fairfax might bring against them.

Difficulties of the Scots' position.

Accordingly, on May 7 David Leslie broke up from Newark. On the 13th, with his royal captive, he reached Newcastle. Unable long to withstand the demands of the English Parliament for the surrender of the King's attendants, the Scots allowed both Ashburnham and Hudson to escape. Ashburnham made his way to France, but Hudson was retaken in London, and placed in confinement, in order that he might be subjected to a rigorous examination.[2]

May 7. The Scots march northwards.

May 13. The King at Newcastle.

It was hard to persuade the English Parliament that

---

[1] *L.J.* viii. 305-311; Montreuil to Mazarin, May $\frac{16}{23}$, *Arch. des Aff. Étrangères*, lii. fol. 292.

[2] *Rushw.* v. 271; Peck's *Desiderata Curiosa* 349, 361.

Charles's arrival at Newark had been wholly fortuitous, and they therefore became all the more anxious to rescue his person from a suspected guardianship. On the 6th the Commons resolved that the King's person should be disposed of wherever the English Parliament should appoint, and selected Warwick Castle as his place of residence. The Lords objected, apparently on the ground that Warwick was in the midst of Fairfax's cantonments, upon which the Commons agreed to omit the designation of any particular locality. The Lords, however, refused to concur even with the general proposition, and after much warm language had passed between the Houses the subject was allowed to drop.[1]

May 6.
Resolution of the Commons.

It was probably a strong sense of the necessity of union, in the face of dangers which might arise in the North, which led the Commons on May 21 to propose that some substitute should be found for the commissioners for Church causes, whose appointment had given so much offence to the extreme Presbyterians. Ultimately, on June 5, the power of suspending from communion was placed in the hands of a committee of both Houses, and for some unexplained reason the change was accepted as satisfactory by both parties.[2]

May 21.
The Commissioners for Church causes to be removed.

June 5.
A substitute found.

The Independents, who naturally took the lead in all measures directed against the Scots, had the more need to walk warily because their majority in the House of Lords, which had hitherto depended on a single vote, was now transferred to the Presbyterians by the act of the aged Earl of Mulgrave, who took his proxy away from Say and entrusted it to Essex.[3]

May 18.
The majority in the House of Lords Presbyterian.

---

[1] *C.J.* iv. 535, 540, 547 ; *L.J.* viii. 314.

[2] *C.J.* iv. 552, 562 ; *L.J.* viii. 359.

[3] *L.J.* viii. 319. A list of the Peers on both sides is given by Montreuil (*Arch. des Aff. Étrangères*, lii. fol. 734). It is undated, but as Essex is stated to hold Mulgrave's proxy it must be later than May 18, and earlier than the death of Essex on Sept. 15. It is as follows :—

With the King and the Scots	Against
Manchester	Northumberland
Rutland	Kent
Essex	Pembroke

In the Commons, on the other hand, the majority, in its
hostility to the Scots, was still under the influence of
Independent leadership. On the 19th the House
resolved, without a division, 'that this kingdom hath
no further use of continuing the Scots' army within
the kingdom of England,' and ordered that 100,000*l.*
should be provided to pay it off.[1]

May 19.
Resolution
that the
Scottish
army is no
longer
needed.

If there was a rift between the English parties, Charles
might be trusted to do his best to widen it. His position at
Newcastle was one of increasing discomfort. The
Scots were daily pressing him to declare for Presbyterianism, and, relying apparently on the fact that no
promise in the handwriting of any one of their commissioners was in his possession, refused to recognise the
assurances given by Moray and Montreuil, and boldly averred
that he had come into their camp without any agreement whatever. If the Scots resorted to unblushing falsehood,
Charles fell back upon his old course of raising
hopes which he never intended to fulfil. He asked
that Henderson might come from London to instruct him, and
promised to do his best to receive enlightenment. He also

The King at
Newcastle.

The Scots
deny any
engagement.

Charles asks
for Hender-
son.

With the King and the Scots	Against
Lincoln	Nottingham
Suffolk	Salisbury
Warwick	Denbigh
Bolingbroke	Middlesex
Berkeley	Stamford
Dacres	Say and Sele
Willoughby of Parham	Wharton
Robartes	Howard
Maynard	North
Hunsdon	Grey
Mulgrave (by proxy)	Montagu

Montreuil states that two days before the list was made out, Pembroke
and North had leant towards the King.

It will be observed that the numbers here given are equal. Lord
Bruce is, however, omitted, who was Earl of Elgin in the Scottish peerage, and may be safely added to the Presbyterians, thus giving them a
majority of one when all the peers were present.

[1] *C.J.* iv. 551.

requested that Loudoun might accompany Henderson. To gain time was his real object. He intended to despatch Montreuil to France, hoping to induce the French court to intervene in his behalf.[1]

In much the same spirit Charles drew up a letter to the Houses. If words ever implied anything, those which he

May 18.
Charles's
letter to the
Houses,

selected were fitted to convey an impression that he was on the point of changing his mind. "Since," he wrote, "the settling of religion ought to be the chiefest care of all councils, his Majesty most earnestly and heartily recommends to his two Houses of Parliament all the ways and means possible for the speedy finishing the pious and necessary work, and particularly that they take the advice of the divines of both kingdoms assembled at Westminster." He hoped that the propositions which they were preparing would speedily be sent, 'his Majesty being resolved to comply with his Parliament in everything which shall be for the happiness

to the Scot-
tish Com-
mittee of
Estates,

of his subjects.'[2] A similar letter was despatched to the Committee of Estates at Edinburgh.[3] Charles, having at least caught the watchwords of his subjects,

May 19.
and to the
City.

also wrote to the City declaring his readiness to concur in settling truth and peace.[4] With his packet for Westminster he enclosed a letter to Glemham ordering him to surrender Oxford, which, as he was well aware, could not hold out many days longer.[5]

For the moment Charles succeeded in throwing the apple of discord amongst his enemies. On the 25th the Lords voted

May 25.
Effect of
his letters
at West-
minster.

his letter to be satisfactory.[6] On the 26th the City presented a strongly worded petition calling on the Houses to suppress heresy and schism, to join in union with the Scots, and to despatch propositions to the King with all possible speed.[7] The Lords commended

---

[1] Montreuil to Mazarin, May $\frac{15}{25}$. *Arch. des. Aff. Étrangères*, lii. fol. 292.

[2] The King to the Houses of Parliament. *L.J.* viii. 329.

[3] *Acts of the Parl. of Scotl.* vi. 635.

[4] *L.J.* viii. 334.　　　　[5] *Ibid.* viii. 329.

[6] *Ibid.* viii. 328.　　　　[7] The City Petition. *Ibid.* viii. 332.

the City highly. On the other hand, the Commons were offended with the City authorities for opening a letter from the King without the leave of Parliament. So strong was the feeling of annoyance that the Presbyterians, not venturing to express direct approval of the petition, moved that the citizens should be told that an answer would be given them in convenient time. Yet this very moderate proposal was only accepted by the House after two divisions.[1]

The Presbyterians had still sufficient hold upon the House to hinder an open rupture with the City. In questions involv-

May 29.
The King's letter not to be sent to Glemham.

ing acceptance of the King's overtures they were unable to make head against their rivals. They could only muster 103 votes against 145 in favour of a resolution, which had come down from the Lords, for sending to Glemham the letter in which Charles had commanded him to surrender Oxford.[2]

The capital of the Cavaliers was incapable of prolonging its resistance. On May 9 Banbury Castle submitted to Whalley.[3]

May 9.
Reduction of Banbury.

May 11.
Oxford summoned.

A long negotiation.

On the 11th Fairfax, having drawn his lines round Oxford, summoned the Governor to surrender. Glemham indeed was ready to repeat the efforts which he had made at Carlisle, and to hold out till every horse and rat in the place had been eaten. It was, however, impossible to induce the Royalist lords and ladies who filled the rooms of the departed scholars to take this view of their duty. On the 15th the King's Privy Council declared itself empowered to treat, and at once notified its sense that only one issue was possible by committing to the flames all existing records of the Oxford Parliament, lest they should rise up in judgment against those who had taken part in its proceedings.[4] Negotiations were quickly opened, though in the face of the opposition of the Royalist officers progress was necessarily slow. There was, however, no doubt how matters would end, and Cromwell at least

---

[1] C.J. iv. 555; Whitacre's Diary, Add. MSS. 31,116, fol. 271.
[2] C.J. iv. 558.
[3] Whalley to Lenthall, May 9. Cary's Mem. of the Civil War, i. 28.
[4] Dugdale's Diary.

showed his sense that all danger of a fresh outbreak of hostilities was over by sending for his daughter Bridget, that she might be married at Fairfax's headquarters to his favourite officer, Ireton. On June 15 Ireton became the son-in-law of Cromwell.

June 15.
Ireton's
marriage.

On the day after the wedding it was known in Oxford that a quick surrender was inevitable. The storekeeper announced that he had only provisions for twelve days more, and that there was not powder enough to resist a storm. At the same time the soldiers broke out into mutiny in the streets, clamouring for pay which was not forthcoming. Delay was no longer possible, and on June 20 articles of capitulation were signed. For some time the lords of the council had been in fear of their lives from the mutinous soldiery, and now they only succeeded in stilling the tumult by pawning to a Parliamentary officer the insignia of the Garter which had been left behind by Charles.[1]

June 16.
The store-
keeper's
report.

On the 22nd the two Princes, Rupert and Maurice, rode out of the city, and they were followed on the 23rd by the greater part of the noblemen and gentlemen. The garrison itself marched out on the 24th, when the defences of the city were then given over to the Parliamentary commanders.[2] Of the outlying posts, Boarstall and Radcot had already surrendered. Wallingford held out till July 27.[3]

June 24.
The surren-
der of
Oxford

By the surrender of Oxford the Duke of York fell into the hands of Parliament. The Prince of Wales alone of the King's children was still at liberty. On April 16 he left Scilly for a safer and more pleasant abode in Jersey.[4] No sooner was he there than he was assailed by frequent messages from his mother urging him to take refuge in France. In singularly thoughtful and vigorous language Hyde

The Duke
of York a
prisoner.

---

[1] The official narrative (*Clar. MSS.* 2,240) is the primary authority. With this may be compared *Dugdale's Diary*, 87, and Wood's *History of the Univ. of Oxford*, ii. 480. The latter represents the discontent of those who believed that the place had been unnecessarily abandoned.

[2] *Wood*, ii. 485.   [3] *Sprigg*, 261.

[4] Hyde to Arundell. *Clar. St. P. ii. 229.*

argued for the Prince's stay within his father's dominions, at
least till the approach of actual danger made his position untenable. The letter was in fact one long protest against
the system of dependence on foreign aid, which
had done more to wreck Charles's cause than all
the efforts of Parliament. The one thing needful,
according to Hyde, was 'the resurrection of English
loyalty and courage,' and such a resurrection was
out of the question if the heir to the throne was
found dangling about the court of France, consorting
with Papists, and liable to the accusation of being himself a
Papist. It would be time enough to consider the advantages
to be gained from French aid whenever the French began to
act instead of merely talking.[1]

*April 16.
The Prince
of Wales
leaves
Scilly for
Jersey.*

*May 20.
Hyde
protests
against his
removal to
France.*

Hyde had on his side all the councillors in Jersey except
Culpepper, and he had still sufficient influence with the Prince
to induce him to resist his mother's entreaties. It
would however go hard with him if the Queen
appealed to her husband. Of the strength to be
gained by relying exclusively on English feeling Charles was
absolutely ignorant. All his thoughts since his arrival at Newcastle had been directed, not to the adoption of a policy which
might rally Englishmen round him, but to the making of
meaningless promises which would enable him to gain time to
summon foreign powers to his aid. On May 28 he
despatched Montreuil to lay his case before the
Queen Regent and the Cardinal. Yet though he
was ready to make use of Montreuil as his agent, he turned a
deaf ear to his pleadings for the concession of Presbyterianism.
The Scots, he assured the Queen, cared more for clipping
the royal power in England than for any alteration in the
government of the Church. As Charles did not wish his
power to be clipped, he was ready to turn for help in another
direction. He recommended the Queen to press on Mazarin
the advantage of urging the Pope to support the
restoration of English Episcopacy in consideration of a grant of liberty of conscience to the Catholics.

*The Prince
remains in
Jersey.*

*May 28.
Montreuil
sent to
France.*

*The Pope
to be won,*

[1] Hyde to Jermyn, May 20. *Clar. St. P.* ii. 230.

With this notion in his head he was not likely to lay much
store by considerations such as those which had

**and the
Prince
removed.** weighed heavily with Hyde, and he accordingly
directed the Queen to send for the Prince from
Jersey, as he no longer considered him to be in safety in the
island.

For the time Charles's position at Newcastle was easier
than it had been. Loudoun and Moray had arrived from

**The strict-
ness of
Charles's
captivity
relaxed.** London, and by their influence something had been
done to relax the strictness of his captivity.[1] On
the 29th he finally abandoned all hope of inducing
the Presbyterian Scots to coalesce with Montrose,

**May 29.
Montrose
to leave
Scotland.** and sent orders to the hero of the North to disband
his troops and to go to France.[2] On the same day

**The confer-
ence with
Henderson.** he began a long controversial argument with Henderson, which, if it had no other effect, would serve to
postpone the day when he would have to speak out
on the subject of Presbyterianism. The argument was carried
on in writing in a leisurely fashion, and was spread over seven
weeks. There can be no doubt that Charles thoroughly enjoyed the opportunity of standing forth as the champion of the
Church which he loved. There is evidence in his papers of
a strong devotional piety, of the kind which takes pleasure in
resting on well-defined authority and consistent practice, and
which loves not to embark on overmuch questioning of the
heavenly laws. Henderson's argument, on the other hand,
was of the usual Presbyterian type, in no way calling for special
commendation. The minds of the two men moved in differ-

**Aug. 19.
Death of
Henderson.** ent planes,[3] and, after his part had been played at
Newcastle, Henderson, whose health was broken,
betook himself to Edinburgh, where he died before
many weeks were over.

[1] Montreuil to Mazarin, $\frac{May\ 28}{June\ 7}$, *Arch. des Aff. Étrangères*, lii. fol.
317 ; the King to the Queen, May 28, June 3, *Charles I. in* 1646, 41,
43.

[2] The King to Montrose, May 29. Napier's *Memoirs of Montrose*, ii.
634.

[3] *The Papers which passed at Newcastle.* E. 1,243,

Charles had to endure assaults more difficult to meet than were Henderson's polemics. Twice, on June 5 and 8, the

June 5-8.
Urgency of
the Scottish
commis-
sioners.

Scottish commissioners were on their knees before him urging him to give way. His reply was that he was willing to allow the establishment of Presbyterianism in England, and the suppression of 'all the

June 9?
Charles
proposes a
local tolera-
tion of
Episcopacy.

superstitious sects and Independents,' provided that liberty of conscience might be granted to himself and his co-religionists. For this purpose it would be enough if bishops were retained in the sees of the South-West, namely, in those of 'Oxford, Winchester, Bristol, Bath and Wells, and Exeter.' [1]

It is doubtful whether this extraordinary proposal was made with any serious expectation of its proving acceptable to any-

The
proposal
neglected in
Scotland,

one. Though Charles asked that it might be submitted to the General Assembly, which was then in session, there is no evidence that it was ever laid before the Scottish clergy, and it does not seem to have been

and never
heard of at
Westmin-
ster.

even heard of at Westminster. The House of Commons was indeed in no mood to take into consideration a scheme which began by arranging for an attack on the Independents, and ended by proposing the erection of an Episcopalian fortress from which it would be easy to make assaults upon Puritanism thus divided and weakened.

The leadership of the Independents in the Commons was too firmly established to be easily shaken, especially as it was

Hostility to-
wards the
Scots in the
House of
Commons.

founded on the national detestation of Scottish and French intrigues. On June 1 the Commons urged the Lords to assent to the vote of May 19, to the effect that the Scottish army was no longer needed in England. [2] On the 2nd they passed—it is true, by a small

---

[1] Burnet's *Lives of the Hamiltons*, 369. The true date of this proposal is fixed not only by the reference in it to the General Assembly, which, as Professor Masson has pointed out (*Life of Milton*, iii. 500), was sitting at this time, and not in September, the date assigned by Burnet, but by the direct statement of Montreuil's secretary. Bacon to Montreuil, June $\frac{11}{21}$. *Arch. des Aff. Étrangères*, lii. 348.

[2] See p. 106.

majority—a vote of thanks to a body of Londoners who had presented a petition hostile to the anti-tolerationist petition of the Common Council.[1] Complaints against the cruelty and extortions of the Scottish soldiers were greedily welcomed,[2] whilst no effort was made to supply the needful pay, the want of which went far to palliate any enormities of which the Scots might have been guilty.

If any one member of either House still doubted the complicity of the Scots in the King's escape to Newark, that doubt must have been now removed. On June 8 there was read in Parliament an intercepted letter, written early in April by the King to Ormond, in which Charles expressly acknowledged that he had received good security from the Scots, not only for their hospitality to himself, but for the employment of their armies on his behalf.[3]

On the same day the Houses received information from their agent in Paris, telling them that the accord between the King and the Scots had been arrived at through Montreuil's mediation, and that Digby had just brought tidings from Ireland that the Irish peace had been concluded, and that an Irish army would soon be on its way to join the Scots in an attack upon the English Parliament. The French clergy had at last opened their purses,[4] and had presented the Queen with a sum equivalent to 40,000*l.* Digby, it was said, was to go to Jersey to conduct the Prince to Ireland, where it was hoped that his presence would rally English, Scots, and Irish round the royal standard. A later communication added that there had been some delay in Digby's enterprise, and that Bellièvre, who had been at Charles's court as ambassador in the days of his prosperity, was to return to England in a similar capacity, nominally to mediate a peace between the King and the Parliament, but in reality, as the writer thought, to foster

Marginal notes:
June 8.
An intercepted letter.
Information from Paris.

---

[1] *C.J.* iv. 560, 561. There were between 5,000 and 6,000 signatures to it. Whitacre's Diary, *Add. MSS.* 31,116, fol. 272.

[2] *Ibid.* fol. 272b ; *C.J.* iv. 567.

[3] *L.J.* viii. 366 ; *C.J.* iv. 567.

[4] See p. 62, Note 3.

irritation between the Scots and the Parliament, and thus to weaken both.[1]

By this revelation—substantially true as it was—the Scots were deeply touched.   Their commissioners in London took

The Scots declare their innocence.

refuge in blank denial.   What the King meant by his letter to Ormond, they said, he was himself best able to explain.   As to its contents, they had no hesitation in expressing themselves freely.   "It doth consist in our perfect knowledge," they asserted, "—and we declare it with as much confidence as ever we did or can do anything—that the matter of the papers, so far as concerneth any assurance or capitulation for joining of forces, or for combining against the Houses of Parliament, or any other private or public agreement whatsoever between the King on the one part, and the kingdom of Scotland, their army, or any in their name and having power from them upon the other part, is [2] a most damnable untruth." [3]

False as this was, the Scots were at least aware that nothing had passed in writing except under the hands of Moray and

Falsehood of the declaration.

Montreuil, and it was certain that neither Moray nor Montreuil had been commissioned by the kingdom or the army of Scotland.   At Newcastle the shame of detection drove the Scots there to put fresh pressure

June 10.
Pressure put upon Charles.

on the King, in the hope that the understanding, the existence of which their countrymen were repudiating in London, might at last bear fruit.   "I never knew," wrote Charles to his wife on the 10th, "what it was to be barbarously treated before."   He was told that he must sign the Covenant, and enjoin its signature upon all his subjects. He must, in his own family, abandon the Prayer Book for the Directory, and declare without reserve for a Presbyterian settlement.   If he refused his assent to these demands, the Scots

---

[1] *C.J.* iv. 568 ; the Agent at Paris to the Com. of B. K. May 22 May 29 June 1, June 8, Cary's *Mem. of the Civil War,* i. 56, 72.

[2] Printed 'as.'

[3] The Scots' commissioners to the Speaker of the House of Lords, June 8. *L.J.* viii. 364.

would throw him over and come to terms with the English Parliament.[1]

Charles preferred at least an appearance of coming to terms himself with the English Parliament. On the day on which he described his miseries to the Queen he wrote to the Houses, begging them to hasten the sending of propositions, and to permit him to come to London to co-operate in the work of peace. To inspire confidence in his words he enclosed orders directing the commanders of the scattered fortresses still holding out for him to surrender them at once.[2]

June 11.
He turns to the English Parliament.

The Houses were the less likely to be won over by this overture as, at the time when it reached them, they were engaged in an investigation which promised to reveal to them a part, at least, of his past intrigues. Hudson, the King's guide to Newark, had been for some time under examination, and on the 18th he acknowledged that he had come from Newcastle with the intention of crossing to France, in order to bring about a league between the French and the Scots against the English Parliament.[3] Baillie, who was not in the secrets of the Scottish commissioners, watched the rising storm of English indignation, and, like the partisan he was, threw all the blame upon the Independents. "This people," he wrote, "is very jealous, and the Sectarian party, intending only for private ends to continue the war, entertain their humour : 'Let the Scots do and say what they can, yet certainly they cannot be honest. They have a design with the King and foreign nations to betray and ruin England ; therefore let us be rid of them with diligence ; if they will not immediately be gone, let us drive them home with our armies.' "[4]

June 18.
Hudson's confession.

Blame thrown on the Scots.

The Scots had been more at fault than Baillie was aware. As readers of Montreuil's despatches know, some, at least, of their leaders had been prepared for the outbreak of a fresh

[1] The King to the Queen, June 10. *Charles I. in 1646,* 45.
[2] The King to the Houses, June 10. *L.J.* viii. 374.
[3] Whitacre's Diary. *Add. MSS.* 31,116, fol. 274b.
[4] *Baillie,* ii. 374.

civil war, in which they and the English Presbyterians were to bring to reason the Independents and the New Model.   The knowledge of these dealings, vague as it yet was, was strength-

Growing strength of the Independents.

ening the undoubted preponderance of the Independents in the House of Commons.   They were now the national party, hostile alike to the French, the Irish, and the Scots, and distrustful of any accommodation with a king in league with foreigners.

As an organised opposition the Presbyterians were for the time helpless.   Some of them supported the Independents in

Weakness of the Presbyterians.

their resistance to the Scots, whilst their leaders, baffled in their intrigue by the refusal of the King to accept the one condition on which either the English or the Scottish Presbyterians would assist him, took refuge for the time in sullen silence.   The Scots themselves were aware that they had committed a blunder, and that if Presbyterianism was to be advanced in England, they must work for it in co-operation with Parliament rather than in co-operation with the King.

To give emphasis to this new policy Argyle himself, the real leader of the nation, appeared upon the scene.   Miserable

Argyle at Westminster.

June 25. Argyle's address.

soldier as he was, he had a keen eye for political tendencies, and when, on June 25, he stood up in the Painted Chamber to address the committees of the two Houses which had been appointed to receive him, he was not likely to strike blows at random. After a complimentary exordium he went straight to the point of church government, severing himself both from the sects

His views on toleration,

and from the rigid Presbyterians.   "Upon one part," he said, "we would take heed not to settle lawless liberty in religion, whereby, instead of uniformity, we should set up a thousand heresies and schisms, which is directly contrary and destructive to our Covenant.   Upon the other part," he said, "we are to look that we persecute not piety and peaceable men, who cannot, through scruple of conscience, come up in all things to the common rule." Having thus placed himself in accord with the prevailing sentiment of the House of Commons, he proceeded to lay stress

on the essential unity of the two kingdoms, 'so that in
effect we differ in nothing but in name—as brethren do—
on the union
of the
kingdoms, which I wish were also removed, that we might be
altogether one, if the two kingdoms shall think fit;
for, I dare say, not the greatest kingdom in the
earth can prejudice both so much as one of them can do
the other ' harm.[1]

Having thus cleared the way, Argyle approached the burn-
ing question of the relations between his countrymen and the
and on their
relations
with the
King. King.   The Scots, he said, had always borne affection to his Majesty.   "Yet" as,[2] he said, "experience may tell, their personal regard for him has
never made them forget that common rule, 'The safety of the
people is the supreme law,' so likewise their love to monarchy
makes them very desirous that it may be rather regulated than
destroyed."   In the end he played his commanding card.
He accepts
the peace-
propositions. The peace-propositions, in the elaboration of which
the Houses had spent so many months, had at last
been completed, and had been handed to the Scottish
commissioners two days before.   Argyle now returned them as
accepted without a single alteration.[3]

Hearty co-operation with the English Parliament in the
establishment of a somewhat elastic form of Presbyterianism
Argyle's
policy. in the Church, and the establishment, if possible, of
constitutional monarchy in the State, were the main
lines on which Argyle's policy was drawn.   The weak point in
it was that it could not be realised without the King.   Charles
was, in fact, as uncompromising as ever.   He knew that the
June 24.
Charles's
intentions. propositions would soon be laid before him.   On
June 24, the day before that on which Argyle delivered his speech at Westminster, he disclosed his
intentions to the Queen.   "It is folly," he wrote concerning
the English Parliament, " to think they will go less so long as
they see none to resist them, knowing that the Scots will not ;
so that all my endeavours must be the delaying my answer till

---

[1] 'harm' is not in the original.

[2] ' as ' is not in the original.

[3] Argyle's speech, June 25.   *L.J.* viii. 392.

there be considerable parties visibly formed, to which end I think my proposing to go to London, if I may be there with safety, will be the best put-off, if—which I believe to be better—I cannot find a way to come to thee." [1]

If Charles could not himself go to France, the orders which he had given for transferring his son thither were already in course of execution. Before the end of May the Prince's councillors in Jersey despatched Capel and Culpepper to St. Germains to urge the Queen to desist from her importunate request for the removal of the Prince.[2] Though she failed to persuade Capel of the prudence of her demand, she had no difficulty in winning over Culpepper, who had been a warm advocate of the intrigue with the Scots, and who was easily drawn to support the intrigue with France. On June 20 the pair returned to Jersey, accompanied by Digby and others of the Queen's associates, amongst whom was Jermyn. Jermyn brought with him a pressing letter from the Queen to the Prince, begging him to come to her, and he was also able to produce extracts from letters written by the King in support of her entreaties.[3]

May.
A message to the Queen.

June 20.
The Prince's removal from Jersey demanded.

It was only with difficulty that Hyde and those councillors who agreed with him in opposing the plan obtained an adjournment of its discussion for a single day. In private conversation Digby spoke plainly. All their dependence, he said, was on the French, as the Scots were only to be reached through the French. Unless the Prince were in France nothing could be done. It was to no purpose that Hyde expressed his entire disapprobation of a policy which made the fortunes of England depend upon a foreign government. On the following morning the Prince was asked to declare his mind. He was probably by this time tired of his residence in a narrow island, and he replied that he

Arguments in favour of the plan.

June 21.
The Prince resolves to go.

June 26.
Hyde, Capel, and Hopton remain.

---

[1] The King to the Queen, June 24. *Charles I. in* 1646, 50.

[2] Hyde to Nicholas, June 1. *Clar. St. P.* ii. 236.

[3] The Queen to the Prince of Wales, June $\frac{10}{20}$; Extracts from the King's letters, *Ibid.* ii. 238, 239.

meant to obey his parents. On the 26th he embarked for France. Hyde, Capel, and Hopton refused to accompany him.[1]

These three men represented the honourable royalism which stooped to no intrigue, and would soil itself by no baseness. "Truly," Hyde had written some weeks before, "whoever enough considers the admirable confusion in all three kingdoms, to which in the instant the wisdom of men and angels can hardly find an expedient to apply, will think the station very happy from whence he may without prejudice so long look on, till upon full observation and free counsels such designs may be formed, with all circumstances for prosecution, as good men may confidently undertake and cheerfully persist in."[2]   "I will endeavour," he declared a few days later in a letter to his old friend Nicholas, "to follow your good example . . . and, in spite of what can come, do the part of an honest man, and die by those principles I have lived in ; for truly I would not buy a peace at a dearer price than was offered at Uxbridge ; and I am persuaded in my soul, if ever it shall be purchased at a more dishonourable or impious price, it will be more unpleasant and fatal to those who shall have their hands in making the bargain than the war hath been."[3]

May 20.
Hyde content with his position.

June 1.
His resolution.

It was well and wisely said. No concession to Puritanism, still less any seeming concession to Puritanism, could avail those who in their hearts believed that Puritanism was an evil thing. Little as there was of genial statesmanship in Hyde, and tied down as he was to the pedantries of the constitutional law, he nevertheless represented, as far as religion was concerned, the only living force with which Cromwell had seriously to count. The English Presbyterian members of Parliament, the Scottish Presbyterian lords, nay, even the King himself, were but the weavers of one

Hyde and Cromwell.

[1] Hyde's Memorandum, *Clar. MSS.* 2,249; Capel, Hopton, and Hyde to the Queen, undated, *Clar. St. P.* ii. 239.

[2] Hyde to Jermyn, May 20. *Ibid.* ii. 231.

[3] Hyde to Nicholas, June 1. *Clar. St. P.* ii. 236.

vast intrigue with many faces. Hyde stood firmly upon the ground of a sentiment which would one day, through the errors of his antagonists, gain a hold upon the nation, and he knew how to bide his time till the nation was ready to declare in his favour. It was not Puritanism, but the very opposite of Puritanism—the expansion of the reasoning intelligence— which held the main current of the thought of the seventeenth century. Cromwell, mighty as he was, could but dam back that current for a time, and when he had done his utmost he would have toiled only that Hyde might step into his place.

Political work there would be none for Hyde for many a year to come. Neither with the enemies of Episcopacy and the Prayer Book nor with the enemies of constitu-

Hyde's strong feeling against the Puritans,
tional monarchy could he find anything in common. "For your Presbyterians and Independents," he assured Nicholas, "I am not yet grown learned enough to know which side to be of, nor charitable enough to know which to pray for. . . . The truth is, I take many who think and find it necessary and safe to pretend to be of one side are indeed of neither ; but they who abhor Presbytery in the Church join with the Independents, and they who tremble at Independency in the State join with the Presbyterians, and yet would be as willing to have the heads of their own party hanged as you or I would. But the first form of either party I take to be as devout enemies to Monarchy, at least to the King and his posterity, as the other ; and therefore I expect no great good from either till they have bettered their understandings and reformed their consciences by drinking deep in each other's blood ; and then I shall be of your opinion that whosoever shall by God's blessing be able to preserve his conscience and his courage very few years will find himself wished for again in his country, and may see good days again if the Turk in that time prove not strong enough to send them another Covenant." [1]

Though Hyde's view of the situation was much the same as Charles's, he had none of Charles's restless impatience, and

[1] Hyde to Nicholas, Nov. 15. *Clar. St. P.* ii. 285.

he was too much of an Englishman not to be horrified by Charles's tampering with the Irish Catholics. "Oh, Mr.

and dis-
satisfaction
with the
King. Secretary," he wrote to the same correspondent, "those stratagems have given me more sad hours than all the misfortunes in war which have befallen the King, and look like the effects of God's anger towards us."[1]

Stranded thus for a time on the beach of politics, Hyde could not endure to fold his hands idly before him. No sooner had he reached Scilly, and all thought of active resistance was at an end, than he seized his pen to record, without Hyde begins his History of the Rebellion. hope of influencing the existing generation, the events of which he had been a witness, and amidst which his more energetic years had been spent. The work of which the foundations were thus laid within hearing of the plash of the Atlantic waves was one day, through the stately dignity of its style and its lifelike pourtrayal of character, to be reckoned as one of the masterpieces of English prose. The task taken up in Scilly was carried on in Jersey,[2] and by the middle of August Hyde had completed three books and a part of a fourth, bringing his story down to the unhappy day of the King's flight from Westminster after the failure of his attempt upon the five members.

Under such circumstances minute or even tolerable accuracy was not to be expected. An exile, writing without books Inaccuracy of the early portion. or literary materials of any kind, and trusting merely to a memory the impressions upon which have been blurred by the influences of political strife, must of necessity depart widely from the truth in every page. That Hyde did not depart from it willingly does not appear merely from his own protestation.[3] When writing of the war itself he

[1] Hyde to Nicholas, Feb. 12, 1647. *Clar. St. P.* ii. 336.

[2] The first two books were written in Scilly. See Ranke, *Engl. Geschichte*, viii. 217. Compare the Preface to Mr. Macray's new edition of Clarendon.

[3] "As soon as I came to Scilly, I began, as well as I could, without any papers, upon the stock of my own memory, to set down a narrative of this prosperous rebellion, and have, since I came hither, continued it, to the waste of very much paper, so that I am now come to the King's leaving London; in which, though for want of information and assistance

made use of the documents in his own possession, and it can be shown that when he founded his narrative upon them he adhered to them as closely as can be expected.[1]

That Hyde's work rose above the level of a party pamphlet on a large scale may be freely granted.   If he failed to recog-

Was the History a party pamphlet? nise virtue or largeness of mind on the Puritan side, he was lavish enough in distributing blame amongst the Royalists.   Yet for all that—and it could hardly be otherwise—the book is instinct with party feeling.   Hyde's party, however, was not that of the Royalists as a body, but of a little group amongst them—a church within a church—which maintained its principles with uncompromising severity, and which regarded the wiles of Digby or Jermyn, and even—though Hyde did not venture to speak his mind out here—the shifty weakness of Charles, as evils almost as dangerous as Puritanism itself.   Hyde's opening sentences have none of the

Hyde's exordium. ring of all-weighing justice.   " Though for no other reason," he began in conscious imitation of the first paragraph of the *Ecclesiastical Polity*,[2] " yet lest posterity may be deceived[3] by the prosperous wickedness of these times into an opinion that less than a general combination and universal apostasy in the whole nation from their religion and allegiance could, in so short a time, have produced such a total and pro-

I shall leave many truths unmentioned, upon my word, there shall not be any untruth nor partiality towards persons or sides, which, though it will make the work unfit in this age for communication, yet may be fit for the perusal and comfort of some men, and, being transmitted through good hands, may tell posterity that the whole nation was not so bad as it will be then thought to have been." Hyde to Berkeley, Aug. 14. *Clar. MSS.* 2,280.

[1] This is especially true of his narrative of the Western campaign. In his account of events in London he gives himself up to mere unfounded gossip.

[2] " Though for no other cause, yet for this : that posterity may know we have not loosely through silence permitted things to pass away as in a dream, there shall be for men's information extant thus much concerning the present state of the Church of God established amongst us," &c. *Eccl. Pol.* i. 1.

[3] This is the true reading, as Ranke pointed out, and it is now restored in Mr. Macray's edition.

digious alteration and confusion over the whole kingdom; and so the memory of those few, who out of duty and conscience have opposed and resisted that torrent which hath overwhelmed them, may lose the recompense due to virtue, and, having undergone the injuries and reproaches of this, may not find a vindication in a better age; it will not be unuseful, at least to the curiosity if not the conscience of men, to present to the world a full and clear narrative of the grounds, circumstances, and artifices of this rebellion." [1]

After such an exordium a calm and philosophical narrative is the last thing to be expected. Yet it is not without signifi-

His relation to Hooker.

cance that at the very opening of his work Hyde deliberately attached himself to Hooker. He was engaged on another stage of that conflict against Puritanism in which the great author of the *Ecclesiastical Polity* had couched his lance. The combat was more political now than it had been in the days of Elizabeth, but in the main the issues were the same. The ideas of the organic development of the Church, of the power of the trained human intelligence to grasp the significance of Divine laws, and of the application of the whole of man's complex being to the service of his Creator, were handed down by Hooker to his successors, and, though it can hardly be said that the author of *The Great Rebellion* lived and moved on these ethereal heights, at least something of their influence had fallen upon him. Hyde, in short, was a lawyer

His merits and defects.

who had applied himself to statesmanship, and if he had the defects of his personality, he had also its merits. He could not descry the larger issues to which the work of his generation was tending, and he was bereft of the imaginative power which sometimes enables statesmen to perceive what will be the working of forces not yet called into existence; but he was able to see that in some way or other kingship and Parliamentary institutions must be brought into active co-operation, and that Puritanism was incapable of giving permanent guidance to the nation. His History is chiefly important as a revelation of himself and of the beliefs which outlasted the victory of Puritanism.

[1] *Clarendon,* i. 1.

The causes which ultimately made Hyde successful were already visible. The very earnestness of the Independents, and their craving for the development of the inward and spiritual life at the expense of the laws and traditions of the past, gave rise in unbalanced minds to manifestations which jarred painfully with the feelings of men whose chief guidance was derived from what was outward and customary. On May 5 a deputation of upwards of 2,000 persons from Hertfordshire and Buckinghamshire appeared at the bar of the House with a petition for the abolition of tithes. Their request found no supporter, and the Speaker was directed to inform those who made it, that they were ignorant of the laws both of God and the kingdom, and that they must go home and obey them. Some of the members observed that tenants who wanted to be quit of tithes would soon want to be quit of rent. Nine-tenths were due to the landlord on the same ground that one-tenth was due to the minister.[1]

Offence given by the extreme Independents.

Lilburne, too, had again been making himself heard, and Lilburne always contrived to express himself in the most irritating way. Early in June he published *A Just Man's justification*,[2] in which he assailed a certain Colonel King, who had brought an action for libel against him. Incidentally, he also took opportunity to find fault with the proceedings of the Earl of Manchester, who had given his support to King. On June 10 the Lords summoned him to the bar for speaking ill of a member of their House.[3] Lilburne boldly repudiated the claim of the Lords to take cognisance of his case. "You," he said to them, "being Peers, as you are called, merely made by prerogative, and never entrusted or empowered by the Commons of England, the original and fountain of power; *Magna Carta*, the Englishman's legal birthright and inheritance, so often bought and redeemed with such great seas of blood and mil-

June 6. Lilburne, A Just Man's justification.

June 10. He is summoned before the Lords.

June 11. He repudiates the authority of the Lords.

---

[1] *C.J.* iv. 534 ; Whitacre's Diary, *Add. MSS.* 31,116, fol. 268.

[2] *A Just Man's justification.* E. 340, 12.

[3] Charge against Lilburne. *L.J.* viii. 429.

lions of money, hath justly, rationally, and well provided that
your lordships shall not sit in judgment, or pass sentence in
criminal causes, upon any commoner of England, either for
life, limb, liberty, or estate, but that all commoners in such
cases shall be tried only by their peers or equals."

The Lords at once committed Lilburne to Newgate for
contempt. Lilburne appealed to the Commons; but finding

June 16.
He appeals to the Commons.

that they were not inclined to do anything for him,
he published the whole story of his wrongs in a fresh
pamphlet, called *The Freeman's freedom vindicated*,

The Freeman's freedom vindicated.

in which he deliberately charged Manchester with
causing his arrest, and asserted his belief in the
truth of the charges brought by Cromwell against

June 23.
Lilburne again at the bar.

the Earl after the second battle of Newbury.[1] The
author being again brought to the bar of the Lords,
refused to kneel or in any way to acknowledge their
jurisdiction over him. He was sent back to Newgate, and
orders were given to prepare a charge against him. On July 11,

July 11.
Sentence against him.

when brought up for trial, he again refused to kneel,
and on the reading of the charge against him stopped
his ears with his fingers. He was adjudged to pay
a fine of 2,000*l.*, to be imprisoned in the Tower during the
pleasure of the House, and to be incapable of holding office
during life.[2]

The claim of either House to punish criticism on its members might easily lead to gross abuse. In this case the action
of the Lords, so far as it was not the result of exasperation at
Lilburne's cool defiance of their authority, may be traced to
panic. Lilburne was simply an outspoken exponent of the
spirit of contempt for existing institutions, which appeared the
more dangerous to those interested in their maintenance because they knew that it was not only widely prevalent, but that
it had its strongest support in an important section of the
army.

[1] *L.J.* viii. 368, 370; *The Freeman's freedom vindicated*, E. 341, 12.
[2] *L.J.* viii. 388, 429, 432.

CHAPTER XLIII.

THE NEWCASTLE PROPOSITIONS.

IT was not merely the special circumstances of the time which stood in the way of the complete realisation of the projects of the Independents. Nations, even in time of revolution, take no sudden forward leaps, and the task of the Presbyterians in establishing the authority of Parliament over the King, and the authority of the laity over the clergy, was in itself such an enormous stride in advance as to make it in the highest degree improbable that the Independents would gain the approbation of Parliament, or of the country, for the further reforms upon which their hearts were set.

1646. Character of the influence of the Presbyterians.

The Presbyterians, therefore, in spite of their defeats on all questions relating to war or diplomacy, held their own in the House of Commons on all questions relating to the Church. On June 9 the Commons, without a division, ordered the elections for the eldership to be held in London,[1] and before many weeks were over the capital was actually brought under Presbyterian government. On July 22 the House practically relieved the Assembly from the burden of answering the obnoxious questions on the Divine right of church government, by directing it to proceed at once to the preparation of a catechism and a confession of faith.[2]

June 9. Elders to be elected in London.

If the Independents did not venture to throw obstacles in the way of a Presbyterian settlement, still less did they venture to impede the continuance of the negotiations with the King. On July 6 the Houses announced in a letter to Charles the speedy arrival of their propositions, and they further requested him to direct Ormond to

The propositions to be sent to the King.

[1] *C.J.* iv. 569. [2] *Ibid.* iv. 622.

surrender to them Dublin, Drogheda, and all other garrisons in his keeping.[1] On the 13th Nineteen Propositions—equalling in number those which Charles had rejected in 1642—were despatched to Newcastle under the charge of two lords and four commoners. These commissioners were to demand the King's positive consent, and if it was not obtained within ten days after their arrival, they were to come back without entering into further negotiation.[2]

July 13.
They are despatched.

It is not likely that anything which the Houses could have asked would have been palatable to Charles, but at least nothing was done to make his acceptance easy. He was to take the Covenant himself, and to consent to an Act imposing it on all his subjects ; to accept the abolition of Episcopacy, and 'the reformation of religion according to the Covenant . . . in such manner as both Houses have agreed or shall agree upon, after consultation had with the Assembly of Divines.' Acts were to be passed for the easier conviction of recusants, for the levying of their fines, and for the education of their children in the Protestant religion, as well as for a stricter course in the suppression of the mass. There were also to be Acts against innovations and pluralities, and for correction of divers abuses in the Church. The militia and the fleet were to be controlled by Parliament for no less than twenty years, and even when that long period had come to an end, the Houses were to declare the future conditions of authority over the military and naval forces, and the Bills embodying their resolutions were to become law even if the royal assent were refused. Provision was made for keeping up a good understanding with the Scots. A long list was given of Royalists either entirely or partially exempted from pardon. The Irish Cessation was to be annulled, and the war in Ireland was to be prosecuted in such a manner as both Houses might agree upon.[3]

The propositions not likely to be accepted.

Their main stipulations.

That Charles ought unhesitatingly to have rejected these propositions it is impossible for anyone to doubt who knows what his conscientious belief was. Now, if ever, was the time

[1] *L.J.* viii. 417.   [2] *Ibid.* viii. 423, 433.   [3] *Rushw.* vi. 309.

to speak his mind out plainly, and, whatever might come of his refusal, to reject decisively a scheme to which he could not in honour assent. It was precisely this outspoken as-

Why did not Charles speak out?

sertion of his position which Charles was incapable of making. He was involved in a new phase of his long intrigue with the French Government, and he weakly thought that he could make his answer to Parliament helpful towards the attainment of his object, even though he refused to carry out the policy which the French were urging upon him. When Digby was at Jersey, he boasted in conversing

Bellièvre's mission.

with Hyde of the speedy departure of Bellièvre, who was soon to set out from France as ambassador to England at the instance of Henrietta Maria, carrying with him instructions from Mazarin which had been drawn up by Digby himself and other Englishmen.[1] As often happened, Digby had overreached himself. His own production had, indeed, been committed to Bellièvre's charge, but the real instructions upon which the ambassador was to act had been carefully prepared by the Cardinal himself. Digby's paper is chiefly interesting as revealing the ideas which prevailed at the little court of exiles at St. Germains.

The Queen's memorandum, as it was called, bore unmistakably the impress of Digby's erratic genius. Presbyterianism, it

The Queen's memo-randum.

urged, should be frankly conceded, because that was the surest way to set Presbyterians and Independents by the ears. The militia was to be abandoned to Parliament for a time, to allay the fears of those rebels who dreaded the royal displeasure, but it must eventually be restored to the King. Above all, the Act preventing the dissolution of Parliament without its own consent must be repealed, and the Parliamentary constitution must revert to the principles of the Triennial Act. The government of the country was, in short, to be restored to Charles with the single obligation of meeting a Parliament once in three years, during a session limited at his pleasure to fifty days. Lest the patronage of the Scots should prove oppressive, they were to be persuaded to admit

[1] Hyde's Memorandum, *Clar. MSS.* ; Capel, Hopton, and Hyde to the Queen, undated, *Clar. St. P.* ii. 239.

Montrose to a conjunction with their army at Newcastle, and
to acknowledge Ormond's treaty with the Irish Catholics.   If,
as was probable enough, the Scots objected to this, Bellièvre
was to frighten them by threatening to throw the weight of
France into the scale of the Independents.   No real success
was to be hoped for till the Presbyterians and Independents
had taken arms against one another.   Then France, Ireland,
and the Cavaliers would give victory to that which appeared to
be the weaker side and the King would reign in peace through
the exhaustion of his enemies.[1]

It is unnecessary to point out that this airy scheme was
utterly unpractical.   Hyde, though he can hardly have been
Hyde's
opinion. acquainted with the memorandum itself, pointed out
in his private correspondence the immorality of its
main provision.   "For the propositions," he wrote, "whoever
understands them . . . cannot imagine that, being once consented unto, there are any seeds left for monarchy to spring
out of, and the stratagem of yielding to them to make the
quarrel the more popular, and to divide the Presbyterians and
Independents, is so far above my politics that I am confident
a general horror and infidelity will attend the person that
submits to them after the infamy of such a submission; and if
I know anything of the King's heart or nature, he will not
redeem the lives of his wife and children at the price, though
he were sure they would not be consented unto when he had
done."[2]

Hyde at least knew the rock upon which all the efforts of
Digby and Mazarin would split.   Mazarin indeed had other
Mazarin
hopes to
annex the
Spanish
Nether-
lands. objects in sending Bellièvre than that of exalting the
authority of Charles.   He was now engaged in a
negotiation which, if his hopes were fulfilled, would
lead to the annexation of the Spanish Netherlands,
and he had already sent an army across the frontier to give
emphasis to his diplomacy.[3]   Knowing how readily England,

---

[1] Memorandum by the Queen of England.   Ranke, *Engl. Geschichte*,
viii. 175.

[2] Hyde to Berkeley, Aug. 14.   *Clar. MSS.* 2,280.

[3] Chéruel, *La France pendant la minorité de Luis XIV.*, ii. 267.

if she were free to strike, might be led to resist his enterprise, he was eager to do what he could for Charles by diplomatic means, not because he wanted to make Charles strong, but because he wanted to keep England weak.

Mazarin, therefore, directed Bellièvre to foment dissensions between the two Parliamentary parties. Their union would
Bellièvre's instructions. make a republic possible, and an English republic was the one thing which he wished to avert. It would, he thought, be terribly strong in the strength which grows out of the voluntary effort of its citizens. Even the re-establishment of the King in the plenitude of his power would be less formidable to France.

As a means to the re-establishment of the King, Mazarin looked to the help of the Scots and of the English Presbyterians. He treated Charles's objections to Presbyterianism as a mere passing obstacle, which would be removed by the good advice of his wife. Both from Mazarin's instructions and from Bellièvre's subsequent despatches it is perfectly clear that the ambassador started under a complete misapprehension of the difficulties of the task before him, and that he expected with ease to carry out the undertaking in which Montreuil had failed.[1]

Bellièvre arrived in England early in July. His first report from London was most despondent. Both parties, he found,
July 16. Bellièvre's report. were of opinion that the King was lost if he did not accept the propositions. In case of his refusal the
Plans of the two parties. Independents—the ambassador was probably retailing Presbyterian gossip—would set the little Duke of Gloucester on the throne for a year or two, till they were able to establish a republic. On most points there was a sharp division between the parties. The Presbyterians wanted to disband the army and to dissolve Parliament, on condition— thus anticipating the vote of the French Constituent Assembly—that no member of the existing House of Commons should have a seat in the next. The Independents wanted to keep together both Parliament and army. The Scottish

[1] Instructions to Bellièvre. Ranke, *Engl. Geschichte*, viii. 169.

commissioners, it appeared, were sanguine as to their prospect of obtaining the King's assent to the propositions, if

Expecta-
tions of the
Scottish
commis-
sioners.

they withdrew, as they were prepared to do, the
demand for the signature of the Covenant. They
would then, as they were no longer distracted with
war at home, be able to place twenty thousand men
on the Borders in addition to their army actually at Newcastle.

The English Presbyterians gauged Charles's character more
accurately. Bellièvre reported that they had little expectation

The Eng-
lish Pres-
byterians
despondent.

of a favourable answer from him, and that some of
them even talked of making common cause with the
Independents and of abandoning all hope of coming
to an understanding with the King. It needed all Bellièvre's
assurances that his own appearance in Newcastle would change
the King's resolution to keep them constant to the policy which
they had hitherto adopted.

Having thus fully acquainted himself with the views entertained at Westminster, Bellièvre set out for Newcastle. If

Chances
in favour
of the King.

Charles had been hypocritical enough to play the
game which had been suggested by Digby with
somewhat more of soberness than suited the temper
of that erratic adviser, he would probably have had a fair chance
of recovering his authority. So weary were the people of the
burden of the new taxation, that, if once the existing Parliament were dissolved, the King might possibly regain his power
without much difficulty. So widespread was the impression

Alarm of
the Inde-
pendents.

at Westminster of impending danger, that the Independents were alarmed lest the whole result of the
war should be thrown away. " May God grant,"
said one of them, " that we have nothing worse to fear than to
see the King in as much authority as he had before the war.
It is much to be feared that he will much augment and
strengthen it." [1]

The Independents need not have been alarmed. Already,
on June 28, Charles had received a copy of the propositions.

[1] Bellièvre to Mazarin, July $\frac{16}{20}$, Dec. $\frac{21}{31}$. *R.O. Transcripts.*

On July 1 he informed his wife that he could not accept them,

but 'a flat denial' was 'to be delayed as long as may be.' He quite understood what the consequence would be. He would not be allowed to go to London, and the Scots would refuse to help him.[1]

On the 8th he wrote to Ashburnham that he believed himself to be lost, unless he could escape to France before August.[2]

On July 9 Montreuil returned from France, with friendly messages from the Queen Regent and the Cardinal, and with

assurances of Bellièvre's support. He was also able to cheer the King with tidings relating to Montrose.

On June 15 Charles had repeated his orders to Montrose to disband his army, and again on July 16 he wrote very much in the same strain.[3] The last

letter was, however, accompanied by secret instructions to spin out the operation as long as possible.[4]

It is not improbable that this order was given to Montrose in consequence of a message received from him to the effect that the variable Seaforth had now declared for the King, that he would himself be able to raise 8,000 men, and that an offer of 7,000 more had reached him from the Irish Confederate Catholics.[5]

At the same time that Charles ordered Montrose—at least

in his public despatch—to disband his forces, he sent a similar command to Huntly and Alaster Macdonald.
Huntly was about to obey, but on a countermand from the King prepared to continue the struggle. Macdonald

[1] The King to the Queen, July 1. *Charles I. in* 1646, 51.

[2] The King to Ashburnham, July 8. The letter is in the possession of the Earl of Ashburnham, and has been lent by him to the Stuart Exhibition.

[3] The King to Montrose, June 15, July 16. Napier, *Memoirs of Montrose,* 636, 637.

[4] Montreuil to Mazarin, July $\frac{16}{26}$, $\frac{\text{July 28}}{\text{Aug. 2}}$. *Arch. des Aff. Étrangères,* lii. fol. 438, 467. Montreuil only knew of the secret letter, or did not think the public one worth mentioning.

[5] The message is undated, but a reference to Antrim places it here. *Arch. des Aff. Étrangères,* lii. 517.

had recently been joined by Antrim in person, and was not likely to desist from his attack upon the territory of the Campbells for anything which the King might write.[1]

Fed with empty hopes, Charles prepared himself to receive the Parliamentary commissioners. On July 30 they reached

July 30. Arrival of the Parliamentary commissioners.

Newcastle. At this crisis of the monarchy all who fancied themselves capable of influencing the King's decision gathered round him. Bellièvre was there to counsel acceptance of Presbyterianism in the interests of France. Argyle came to recommend the same in the interests of Scotland, whilst Hamilton, who had been liberated from his captivity by Fairfax, appeared at Newcastle. as lugubrious as of old, denouncing the King's resistance, and

The advice of the Scots.

prophesying all happiness to him if he would only follow the advice of his faithful Scots.[2] Nor was that advice quite as harsh as might have been expected. The Scottish commissioners at Newcastle threw themselves on their knees before him, assuring him that they would venture their lives and all that they possessed on his behalf if only he would accept, not the offensive propositions now laid before him, but those milder ones which had formerly been made through Sir Robert Moray,[3] with some modifications in the clause relating to the militia.[4]

Moderate as Sir Robert Moray's scheme had been on civil matters, its demand for the establishment of Presbyterianism

Aug. 1. Charles replies to the propositions.

in England had been as uncompromising as that of the propositions. It can surprise no one that Charles refused to give way ; but there can hardly be one, even amongst his most devoted admirers, who can approve of the manner in which, after rejecting the offer of the Scots, he replied to the English commissioners. He did not flash out into becoming indignation at the sugges-

[1] *Patrick Gordon*, 194, 198.

[2] *L.J.* viii. 447 ; Montreuil to Mazarin, July 23 / Aug. 2, *Arch. des Aff. Étrangères*, lii. fol. 467.

[3] See p. 73.

[4] Sir R. Moray to Mazarin, Oct. 20/30. *Arch. des Aff. Étrangères*, lii. fol. 630.

tion that he should—as he would himself have expressed it—abandon the Church, his crown, and his friends. Neither did he clearly say what he was himself ready to grant. He merely handed to the commissioners on August 1 a letter in which he complained of the difficulty of giving a decided answer in the short time allowed to him, and pressed once more for leave to come to London to discuss more thoroughly the points which had been raised. He would never, he vaguely added, 'consent to anything destructive to that just power which by the laws of God and the land he is born unto'; but, on the other hand, he was ready to pass all bills 'really for the good and peace of his people.'[1]

It was strange that Charles should think fit to reply to an elaborate demand in such a fashion, but it was still stranger

Charles sanguine of its success.

that he should have been sanguine of the success of his contrivance for spinning out the negotiation whilst Irishmen and Highlanders were preparing to come to his rescue, or whilst parties at Westminster were breaking up under the influence of his personal skill. On

Aug. 3.
Montreuil returns to France.

August 3 he sent Montreuil back to France to inform the Queen of all that had passed, and he assured Bellièvre, who remained at Newcastle, that

A conversation with Bellièvre.

he expected a favourable response from the Houses, and that when he was once in London all difficulties would be at an end.[2] Bellièvre thought it far more likely that the Scots would deliver him up to the English, and that he would either be deposed or allowed to remain on the throne with no more than the name of a king.[3]

In rejecting Presbyterianism Charles was acting in opposition to the advice, not only of all who were in daily intercourse

---

[1] The King's answer, Aug. 1. *L.J.* viii. 460.

[2] "Le Roy de la Grande Bretagne s'imagine que sa response sera bien reçeue du Parlement, qu'il consentira qu'il aille à Londres, et que cela estant, toutes ses affaires se termineront à son avantage." Bellièvre did not think this likely to be the case: "Cependant le dit Roy se flatte de ses imaginations et se nourit d'esperances auxquelles je ne trouve point de fondement solide." Bellièvre to Mazarin, Aug. $\frac{4}{14}$. *R.O. Transcripts.*

[3] *Ibid.*

with him, but also of her from whose judgment he most unwillingly dissented. About the time when Bellièvre left France

Charles acts in opposition to the Queen.

the Queen instructed Jermyn, Culpepper, and Ashburnham to plead with her husband in a joint
letter for an understanding with the Scots based
on the acceptance of Presbyterianism without the Covenant.[1]
In reply Charles denied that the separation was possible. If
he granted Presbyterianism he would be driven to grant the

His views on the influence of Episcopacy on the State.

Covenant. He then proceeded to show the influences which even the concession of simple Presbyterianism would have, not only upon the Church,
but upon the State. Bishops were to him not merely
divinely appointed channels of grace, they were also an effective police for the suppression of anti-monarchical opinions.
" It is not the change of church government," he wrote, " which
is chiefly aimed at—though that were too much—but it is by
that pretext to take away the dependency of the Church from
the Crown ; which, let me tell you, I hold to be of equal
consequence to that of the military, for people are governed
by pulpits more than the sword in times of peace. Nor will
the Scots be content with the alteration of government, except
the Covenant be likewise established, the which doth not only
make good all their former rebellions, but likewise lays a firm
foundation for such pastimes in all times to come. Now for
the theological part, I assure you the change would be no less
and worse than if Popery were brought in, for we should have
neither lawful priests, nor sacraments duly administered, nor
God publicly served, but according to the foolish fancy of every
idle parson ; but we should have the doctrine against kings
fiercelier set up than amongst the Jesuits."

Charles could say all this to his wife and her ministers ;
why could he not say as much openly to the world? It
would have revealed the inward sincerity of his nature,
which lay enveloped in such a cloud of trickery and false-

---

[1] This letter has not been preserved, but its purport can be gathered
from the King's answer on July 22, and from the remainder of the correspondence. *Clar. St. P.* ii. 242.

hood. An agreement between him and either of the parties opposed to him was, in truth, for ever impossible. It was

*An under-
standing
with his
opponents
impossible.*

from no craving after personal aggrandisement that Charles took his stand on the maintenance of the Monarchy and the Church. He believed it in his heart to be contrary to the will of God that he should

*Connection
between
Church and
State in his
mind.*

abandon either. " How," he wrote at a later date, "can I keep my innocency which you, with so much reason oft and earnestly persuade me to preserve, if I should abandon the Church? Believe it, religion is the only firm foundation of all power; that cast loose or depraved, no government can be stable; for when was there ever obedience where religion did not teach it? But, which is most of all, how can we expect God's blessing if we relinquish His Church? And I am most confident that religion will much sooner regain the militia than the militia will religion." [1]

Evidently Charles had in him the stuff of which martyrs are made, and for that very reason, if his opponents had any

*Impossibility
of coming
to terms
with him.*

regard for their own safety, they could be satisfied with no terms which failed to lay him entirely at their feet. Constitutional kingship was unattainable if he was to continue to be the king, because constitutional kingship rests on the idea that, in case of deliberate and prolonged difference of opinion, it is the nation which is to have the last word, and not the king. To this idea, and not merely to the aberrations of the existing Parliament, Charles was strenuously opposed. He gave himself, body and soul, to the maintenance of the Monarchy in Church and State, and the Monarchy, as understood by Charles, had absolutely no future before it. The restored kingship of Charles II. was fettered by Parliament in a way which would have been unendurable to Charles I.; and if, ecclesiastically, the Church of Sheldon and Morley appeared in very truth the Church of Hooker and Laud, there is a sense in which its historical continuity is to be detected in what, in 1646, was known at Westminster as the

---

[1] The King to Jermyn, Culpepper, and Ashburnham, July 22, Aug. 19. *Clar. St. P.* ii. 242, 248. Compare the King's letter to the Prince of Wales, Aug. 26. *Ibid.* ii. 253.

reformed Church of England. When bishops ultimately re-
ascended their ancient thrones, they sat on them because they
were favoured by Parliament rather than because they were
favoured by the king. The supremacy of lay England in its
collective capacity over king and Church was, in reality, the main
object for which the Presbyterians were contending, and their
object, and not Charles's object, was obtained with the full co-
operation of the party of the Cavaliers, when king and bishops
reappeared in 1660 under changed conditions.

The King's procrastinating answer to the propositions—if
answer it can be called—produced far other effects at West

Aug. 12.
The King's
answer
received.
minster than those which he had anticipated. On
August 12, as soon as it had been read in the
House of Lords, a letter from the Scots' commis-

The Scots
offer to go.
sioners was produced, in which they offered to withdraw their forces from England on receiving due
satisfaction for their expenses, and suggested a consultation
between the two kingdoms to decide upon the best way of
disposing of the King.[1] They did not in any way conceal
their resolution not to take him to Scotland.[2]

It was perhaps natural that this overture should be received
in a different spirit by the two parties. It was impossible for

Feeling of
the English
parties about
them.
the Presbyterians to retain the Scots against their
will, but they wished to treat them with every
courtesy, and to keep, as much as possible, the
alliance intact. The Independents, on the other hand, regarded them as detected intriguers, who had attempted, with
the aid of the King and the French, to crush liberty of conscience in England. This time they were unable to rally the

Aug. 14.
Libellers of
the Scots
to be
punished.
House of Commons to their views. Common sense
taught those who had not permanently attached
themselves to either party that it was not well to
irritate the Scots at the moment when they proposed
to free England of their presence, and on August 14 the
House read a second time, by a majority of 130 to 102, an

[1] *L.J.* viii. 461.

[2] *Baillie*, ii. 386-391 ; Grignon to Brienne, Aug. $\frac{10}{20}$, $\frac{13}{23}$, *R. O. Transcripts.*

ordinance inflicting punishment on the printers and writers of all libels against the kingdom and army of Scotland.

On a question of money it was less easy to influence the House in favour of a generous treatment of the Scots. A bare sum of 100,000*l.* was voted without a division as full satisfaction of the outstanding account between the nations.[1] The Scots, on the other hand, reckoned their uncovered expenses in England at 1,800,000*l.*, of which 500,000*l.* was owing to the Englishmen in whose houses their soldiers had lived at free quarter, leaving due to themselves no less than 1,300,000*l.* Nevertheless, they offered to be content with a sum of 500,000*l.* In the end, after a good deal of haggling, and a prolonged party struggle within the House itself, 400,000*l.* was voted on September 1, half to be paid before the Scots left England, and the remainder by instalments at fixed intervals.[2]

100,000l. voted for the Scots,

Aug. 19. who claim 500,000l.

Sept. 1. 400,000l. to be given.

The Scots having consented to this proposal,[3] it only remained to procure the 200,000*l.* needed for the first payment. In the City it was thought that there would be no difficulty in raising a loan upon the security of the excise and the bishops' lands,[4] and this suggestion was supported by the Presbyterians in the House. The Independents, however, carried against them a vote for adding to the security the lands of delinquents,[5] as though they feared that their rivals might bribe Charles to abandon the bishops by offering to restore the property of his followers. The City could hardly take exception to additional security, and the arrangements for paying off the Scots were now likely to take effect without much further delay.

Sept. 9. A loan to be raised.

Strong, however, as, in spite of occasional checks, the hold of the Independents upon the House seemed to be, indications

---

[1] *C.J.* iv. 644.

[2] *Ibid.* iv. 649, 655, 659; Whitacre's Diary, *Add. MSS.* 31,116, fol. 281.

[3] *L.J.* viii. 487.

[4] Whitacre's Diary. *Add. MSS.* 31,116, fol. 283.

[5] *L.J.* viii. 489; *C.J.* iv. 665.

were not wanting that it was only on questions of national policy that they could be secure of a majority, and that when

Character of the influence of the Independents in the House.

at last liberty of conscience came to be seriously discussed, they would have little chance of obtaining the acceptance of their views. On September 2 an ordinance for the suppression of blasphemy and

Sept. 2. Proposed ordinan e to suppress bla phemy and heresy.

heresy was brought in by two members of no great note.[1] Denial of doctrines relating to the Trinity and the Incarnation was to be punished with death ; whilst denial of several other less important doctrines, such as those relating to Presbyterianism and Infant Baptism, was to be punished with imprisonment for life. This monstrous ordinance was read twice without a division, and sent before a committee of the whole House.[2]

It was not only the certainty that prominence would be given to internal and especially to ecclesiastical questions as

Is the English army needed ?

soon as the Scots were fairly gone which boded ill to the predominance of the Independents. The dying down of the flames of war would lead men who had been taught by the Independent leaders to ask whether there was need of a Scottish army in England to ask whether there was any need of an English army. As far as the Royalists were concerned, indeed, it could hardly be pleaded that Fairfax's

Surrender of fortresses.

army was necessary. Worcester had given itself up on July 22, Pendennis on August 17, and Raglan, the last of purely English fortresses to hold out, had surrendered on the 19th. The castles of North Wales took longer to capture, that of Flint surrendering by August 24,[3] that of Denbigh by October 26,[4] and that of Conway by December 18,[5] whilst Holt Castle held out till January 19,[6] Chirk Castle

[1] Bacon and Tate, the latter, however, having been the original suggester of the Self-Denying Ordinance. The proposed ordinance is printed in *A relation of several heresies.* E. 358, 2. See *The Moderate Intelligencer*, E. 353, 18 ; *Some modest and humble queries*, E. 355, 1.

[2] *C.J.* iv. 659.

[3] Mitton to Lenthall, Aug. 24. *Tanner MSS.* lix. fol. 493.

[4] *Perf. Occurrences.* E. 360, 13.

[5] *Perf. Diurnal.* E. 513, 25.

[6] Maurice's Note-Book, *Arch. Cambrensis*, 41, gives Jan. 16, perhaps

till February 28, and Harlech Castle, the last fortified post over
End of the
Civil War. which King Charles's banner waved, till March 13, 1647.[1]

The question of the disbandment of Fairfax's army in consequence of these successes would undoubtedly be raised in the not distant future. As long as the Scots were still quartered at Newcastle it was impossible that it could be entertained.

It was Charles's firm conviction that he was dividing his enemies by his policy. In reality he was unconsciously doing everything in his power to close their ranks. As it
Effect of
Charles's
policy. seemed every day less probable that any concession would be obtained from him, the Scots redoubled their efforts to induce him to give way. In August Hamilton
Aug.
Hamilton's
visit to
Scotland. had visited Scotland, where he had striven to induce his fellow-countrymen to abandon some of their pretensions, but, in face of the King's unbending
Sept. 4.
A Scottish
deputation. resolution, his efforts were of no avail, and early in September he returned to Newcastle as a member of a body of commissioners sent by the Committee of Estates to urge Charles to an unconditional surrender.

Between the two great factions into which the Scottish Covenanting nobility were divided—the Hamiltons and the
The Hamil-
tons and
Argyles. Argyles, as they were called—there was not, from Charles's point of view, much to choose. The only difference between their leaders, as it appeared to Bellièvre, was that, whereas Argyle wished to put an end to the monarchy, Hamilton wished to preserve it, but to be himself the monarch. If this was unfair to Hamilton, who was always ready to serve the King so far as he could so without injuring himself, it hardly did injustice to Argyle. One little knot of
Callander's
party. men indeed there was, of whom Callander was the leading spirit, who were anxious to do what they could to restore the King's authority. These men, who held influential positions in the army, and amongst whom was pro-

the date of the capitulation, while the 19th, given by *Mercurius Diutinus*, is perhaps the date of surrender. E. 372, 9.

[1] *Arch. Cambrensis*, 42.

bably David Leslie himself, assured Charles that they could place at his disposition 4,000 horse and one of the strongest forti-

It offers assistance to Charles.

fications in Scotland. Yet even they acknowledged that the disposition of the Scottish people was such

The deputat on returns to Edinburgh.

that unless he would accept Presbyterianism nothing could be done. Charles rejected their offer without hesitation. What he had refused to Callander he was not likely to grant to Hamilton, and the commissioners of the Committee of Estates went back to Edinburgh

Charles again asks to go to London.

with a negative answer. Before allowing them to return Charles again pressed for permission to go to London. He did not, he said, refuse to sign the propositions. He only asked that his arguments against them might be heard.[1]

To Bellièvre Charles explained that he had no intention of going to London unless he could be received there in honour and safety, or, in other words, unless he could preserve something of the state and influence of a king. He had already, he added, sent Dunfermline there with a message to this effect.

Sept. 7. Charles writes to the Queen.

In writing to the Queen he dwelt more on his annoyance at the continual pressure which was put on him. Not only had he been 'freshly and fiercely assaulted from Scotland,' but Will Murray had been 'let loose upon' him 'from London.' He was even afraid, as he informed his wife, that the Scots would be persuaded by the English to detain him as a prisoner. Meanwhile he assured Bellièvre that he would take no decisive step till he had heard from the Queen, but, as the Frenchman shrewdly remarked, it was very unlikely that he would take her advice when it arrived.[2]

[1] Burnet, *Lives of the Hamiltons*, 366–368 ; *A letter from Scotland*, E. 354, 3 ; *Merc. Civicus*, E. 354, 12 ; Bellièvre to Mazarin, Oct. $\frac{5}{15}$, *R.O. Transcripts*. The ambassador says that the offer of the cavalry was made a month before his letter was written, which would bring it to the beginning of September. Callander's name is not mentioned, but Charles, writing about this time, refers to him as making offers to help him to his liberty. The King to the Queen, Sept. 7. *Charles I. in* 1646, 63.

[2] The King to the Queen, Sept. 7, *Charles I. in* 1646, 63 ; Bellièvre to Mazarin, Sept. $\frac{7}{17}$, $\frac{14}{24}$, *R.O. Transcripts*.

Charles was, in fact, still engaged in replying to the letters in which his wife's ministers, acting by her instructions, were
The Queen urges compliance.
setting forth the advantages which would accrue to him if he grasped the sword and discarded the bishops.
Charles's refusal.
To all their arguments he turned a deaf ear. Taking them on their own ground, he urged, they were utterly worthless. The Scottish religion meant the rule of the clergy. The Westminster religion meant the rule of Parliament. Both were equally anti-monarchical.[1]

Though Charles would never accept Presbyterianism, he had no objection to lead others to think he was
A new scheme.
going to do so, provided that he made no positive
A consultation with Will Murray.
declaration. He easily gained over Will Murray to his view, ' that the Scots ' were ' not to be satisfied without the Covenant,' and that ' the monarchy ' could not ' stand with Presbyterian government.' The two then consulted how ' to find such a present compliance as may stand with conscience and policy.' On the 14th they
Sept. 14.
had not yet succeeded in their task, but Charles thought that there would be no great difficulty in the matter, and proposed to send Murray to London to recommend the scheme which was still in embryo.[2]

One obstacle in the way of Charles, if he wished to come to an understanding with the Scots, had been already removed.
An obstacle removed.
He was, indeed, slow to give up hopes once formed, and the idea of a combination between Montrose's Highlanders and an Irish invasion had been too long familiar to him to pass readily out of his mind. On August 21 he
Aug. 21. Charles asks Montrose to remain.
entreated Montrose to remain in Scotland as long as he could without breaking his word.[3] Montrose was, however, too far advanced in a bargain, upon which he had for some little time been engaged, to wish to hold out longer. Much to the disgust of the Covenanting clergy,

---

[1] The King to Jermyn, Culpepper, and Ashburnham, Sept. 7. *Clar. St. P.* ii. 260.

[2] The King to the Queen, Sept. 7. *Charles I. in* 1646, 64.

[3] The King to Montrose, Aug. 21. Napier's *Memoirs of Montrose,* ii. 641.

Middleton, who commanded the army of the Scottish Parliament in the North, had made him a promise that he, together
Terms
accepted
by him. with Crawford and Hurry, might be allowed to leave Scotland in safety if they would take care to be on shipboard before September 1. One of his followers was allowed to remain in the country with the forfeiture of his estate, while all the others were to be admitted to a complete amnesty.

As the time for his departure approached Montrose found reason to think that Middleton's employers intended to trick
He doubts whether they will be observed. him out of the benefit of the conditions into which their subordinate had entered. The ship which was to carry him away did not make its appearance in Montrose harbour till August 31, the last day on which, according to the agreement, he could be safe in Scotland. Even at this critical moment the captain declared that he would not be ready to sail for some days. Montrose, however, was not to be
Montrose's escape. thus entrapped. Putting on a disguise he flung himself, as the evening darkened, into a small boat, and rowed out to a Norwegian vessel which he had hired to lie off the mouth of the harbour till he appeared. He thus made his way in safety to Bergen.[1] His high enterprise had come to a disastrous end. No skill of warrior or statesmen could deal successfully with a problem the solution of which depended on the one hand upon the wisdom of Charles, and on the other on the discipline of the Gordons and of the Highland clans.

Though Montrose was out of Scotland, the Covenanting government was not yet at its ease. Huntly and the Gordons
State of the Highlands. were still in arms on the East, and Antrim and Alaster Macdonald were still in arms in the West. There was enough to make the Irish peace a special object of alarm to the Scots. It would certainly expose to increased danger their defeated army in Ireland, and it would probably be followed by the sending of reinforcements to their enemies in the Western Highlands. Charles at least was fully alive to

---

[1] Napier's *Memoirs of Montrose*, 639–643; *Wishart*, ch. xxi.

the possibility of a turn in his favour. On September 16 he wrote to Ormond suggesting the seizure and fortification of a spot on the Lancashire coast as a means 'of helping' him 'to make use of the Irish assistance.'[1] Yet even Charles could hardly be very sanguine now. On the day on which his letter to Ormond was written he sent to his daughter in the Netherlands, begging her to persuade the Prince of Orange to send a swift ship to Newcastle, to carry letters between himself and the Queen.[2] Though nothing was said further, it is by no means unlikely that Charles had some thought of using the ship to effect his own escape if he should find it desirable to take that course.[3]

Sept. 16.
Charles asks Ormond to seize a spot on the coast of Lancashire.

The Prince of Orange to send a ship to Newcastle.

At Westminster the Presbyterians now outstripped their rivals in their anxiety to secure Charles's person. On September 18 the Commons, at their instigation, resolved that 'the person of the King shall be disposed of as both Houses of Parliament of England shall see fit.'[4] The Presbyterians had no reason to entertain any further hope of Scottish military assistance. They were at this moment engaged in discussing with Grignon, Bellièvre's brother, who had remained in London to act as his agent, how changes might be effected in the propositions so as to render them more easy of digestion, and they may very well have imagined that they were more likely to win Charles's assent if he were out of the hands of the rigid Scottish Covenanters. The Independents, on the contrary, though they were anxious to separate Charles from the Scots, were unwilling to bring him too near London. "The King," said one of them in the House—was it perhaps Henry Marten?—"could not for the good of England be too far off." On the 22nd the vote was accepted by the Lords,

Sept. 18.
The Commons vote that the Houses are to dispose of the King.

Sept. 22.
The Lords agree.

---

[1] The King to Ormond, Sept. 16. Carte's *Ormond*, v. 17.

[2] The King to the Princess Mary, Sept. 16. MS. letters of the Family of Charles I. *Bodl. Library.*

[3] See his words to the Queen at p. 117. We know from Bellièvre that he was for some time hankering after a scheme of joining his wife in France. See also p. 132.   [4] *C.J.* iv. 672.

though not without difficulty, and a joint committee was appointed to discuss with the Scottish commissioners the best mode in which the King's person could be disposed of. It was, however, to be understood that the negotiation with the Scots was not to affect the right to dispose of the King's person claimed by the English Parliament.[1]

It now remained to carry into effect the proposal which had been previously made [2] for offering the bishops' lands as security for the loan to be raised for the payment of the Scots. On September 29 an ordinance was brought in for the abolition of bishops and for vesting their estates in trustees. The trustees were eight aldermen and sixteen common councillors, who were to hold the lands as security for the repayment of the 200,000*l.* which were immediately wanted for the Scots.[3] On October 9 the ordinance, after some resistance, was accepted by the Lords.[4]

Sept. 29.
Ordinance
for abolish-
ing bishops
and vesting
their estates
in trustees.

Oct. 9.
It is ac-
cepted by
the Lords.

There can be little doubt that the Presbyterians had reconciled themselves to the idea of parting with the Scots, in the expectation that when once they were gone it would be easy to get rid of the New Model as well. They received a warning that the execution of the last part of their plan must at least be delayed. On October 7 the Independents moved that Fairfax's army should be continued in pay for six months longer, urging that it would be treason to the kingdom to disarm when the Scots were still advocating the King's claim, and when there was an imminent risk of invasion by foreign powers. So strongly was the House impressed by this argument, that the Presbyterians did not venture to divide against the motion.[5]

Oct. 7.
Fairfax's
army to be
continued
for six
months.

The Presbyterians, indeed, were undergoing the fate of all parties which at the same time pursue incompatible objects.

---

[1] Grignon to Brienne, Sept. $\frac{19}{20}$; Grignon to Mazarin, Sept. $\frac{10}{20}$, $\frac{\text{Sept. 24}}{\text{Oct. 4}}$; *R.O. Transcripts*; *L.J.* viii. 498, 499.

[2] See p. 138.

[3] *C.J.* iv. 677; Whitacre's Diary, *Add. MSS.* 31,116, fol. 284.

[4] *L.J.* viii. 515.

[5] *C.J.* iv. 686; Grignon to Brienne, Oct. $\frac{8}{18}$. *R.O. Transcripts.*

They wanted both to establish constitutional government and to conciliate Charles. They bitterly complained to Grignon that

Hesitation of the Presbyterians.

in two months they had not had a word from the King which would enable them to advocate his cause with effect. Unless a satisfactory answer should arrive within a week it would be impossible to serve him

The Scots wish the King to come to London,

further.[1] In the meanwhile the Scots, though they urged that the King should be allowed to come to London with honour, safety, and freedom, were entering upon a conflict in which the spirit of Englishmen was roused against them, by declaring that Charles was King of Scotland as well as King of England, and

and themselves to share in the disposal of his person.

that, by the treaties, the English Parliament had no right to dispose of his person unless the Scottish Parliament gave its consent. In this contention the English Presbyterians were unable to support them, and though the controversy was still prolonged for some weeks, there was never any chance that the Scots would win over the House of Commons to their views.[2]

It is impossible to trace definitively Cromwell's action upon Parliament during these stirring discussions. He had returned

Cromwell in the House.

to his place in the House soon after the surrender of Oxford, but though a few not very important letters written during the succeeding months have been preserved, nothing is known of his Parliamentary action at this time. Yet it is not a very hazardous conjecture that he was foremost in holding his party to the policy which it had adopted. The persistence of the Independents in keeping themselves to the one practical object of getting rid of the

Oct. 10. A motion for the introduction of the ballot rejected.

Scots whilst refusing all conflict on wider issues bears the impress of his mind. At last he appears as a teller against a proposal made by the Presbyterians for the introduction of the ballot into the House whenever offices were given away. In a thin House he carried the day against them by a bare majority of two.[3]

---

[1] *C.J.* iv. 686 ; Grignon to Brienne, Oct. $\frac{8}{18}$. *R.O. Transcripts.*

[2] *Rushw.* vi. 329, &c.

[3] *C.J.* iv. 690 ; Whitacre's Diary, *Add. MSS.* 31,116, fol. 285.

Cromwell's objection to the ballot is probably to be explained by his fear lest it might be used to conceal the personal or corrupt motives of the voters in the case of appointment to offices. He held that merit was the sole recommendation of a candidate for promotion or reward, and he had certainly no objection to see rewards conferred on himself. An ordinance

An estate
for Crom-
well. which ultimately passed was now before the House conferring on him an estate taken from the confiscated property of the Marquis of Worcester, and valued at 2,500*l.* a year.

It seemed as if the Independents were to have the mastery in everything. For more than five months they had been

May-Oct.
Question of
disbanding
Massey's
troops. anxious to disband Massey's troops. On the one hand Massey was obnoxious to them as a Presbyterian ; and on the other hand his men had, from want of pay, been guilty of considerable disorders. Obstacles had, however, been thrown in the way, and it was not till the middle of October that Fairfax was in a position to carry out the instructions which he had by that time received from the House of Commons to offer to the men the choice of being paid off or being sent to Ireland. Upon this the Lords

Oct. 16.
The Lords
refuse
consent. took alarm, and on October 16 ordered Fairfax to proceed no further without the commands of both Houses.[1] The Commons insisted on having their way, and Fairfax, without waiting for the consent of the Peers,

Oct. 22.
The regi-
ments dis-
banded. acted according to their wishes. By the 22nd the disbandment was completed. Not a man volunteered to go to Ireland.[2] In order somewhat to lighten the burdens on the country, the same course was pursued with several of the local forces which were no longer needed.

Already the man whose name was most closely connected with the old military order now passed away had ceased to be a witness of the scenes which he deplored. On September 16 the Earl of Essex died. Now that he was no more amongst

---

[1] *C.J.* iv. 537, 548, 577, 581, 615, 630, 638, 640, 652, 658, 670; *L.J.* viii. 530, 531.

[2] *C.J.* iv. 697 ; Ludlow and Allein to Lenthall, Oct. 22, *Tanner MSS.* ix. fol. 566.

them, Presbyterians and Independents combined to do him
honour, and both Houses agreed that his funeral should be cele-

Sept. 16.
Death of
Essex.
brated at the public expense.   Yet even in this
matter the Independents had the upper hand.   It
would only have been in accordance with custom that
his brother-in-law, the Marquis of Hertford, should take a lead-

Oct. 17.
No Royal-
ist to attend
the funeral.
ing part in the ceremony.   On the 17th the Independents carried a vote that neither he nor any others
who had taken arms against Parliament should attend
as mourners.[1]   The credit of the Independents, wrote Grignon,
increases every day.[2]   The Presbyterians, who were coquetting
with a king who would not even vouchsafe them an answer,
could not hope to make head against their rivals as long as the
relations between the Houses and the King formed the main
staple of discussion.

The preacher selected to do honour to the virtues of the
commander who was to lie amongst the mighty dead in the

Oct. 22.
The funeral.

Vines's
sermon.
Abbey Church at Westminster was, as was befitting,
a Presbyterian, Richard Vines.   In the hearing of
both Houses, and of a vast congregation, Vines
dwelt on all that was best in the leader who had
passed away ; on his constancy, his loyalty to his engagements,
and his thoughtfulness for the comfort of his soldiers.   Unless
Essex had stood forth as a rallying-point, he declared, with
scarcely an exaggeration, the Parliamentary army would hardly
have come into existence.   "He was the man," continued the
preacher, with some confusion of metaphor, "to break the ice,
and set his first footing in the Red Sea . . . a man resolved,
when others hung in suspense. . . . No proclamation of treason could cry him down, nor threatening standard daunt him
that, in that misty morning, when men knew not each other,
whether friend or foe, by his arising dispelled the fog, and, by his
very name, commanded thousands into your service.   Such as
were for reformation and groaned under pressures in religion
he took by the hand, and they him.   Such as were patriots
and would stand up for common liberties he took by the hand,

---

[1] *C.J.* iv. 697.

[2] Grignon to Brienne, $\frac{\text{Oct. 22}}{\text{Nov. 1}}$ *R.O. Transcripts.*

and they him, and so became the bond or knot of both, as the axletree of the world, upon which both the poles do move."

It was impossible to express more successfully the services which Essex had rendered at the outbreak of the civil strife.

Essex and Fairfax.

Turning to the present, the preacher could not but remember that a greater, or at least a happier, warrior than Essex was amongst the congregation, and even the very funeral of the Presbyterian Earl was made by a Presbyterian minister to do honour to his successor. "God," said Vines, "had done wonders by the first hand of him that led us through the untrodden paths of the wilderness, and by the second hand of him that had made victory, which Homer calls . . . a Jack on both sides, to change its name ; who, if he shall have but one stone out of each city or stronghold taken by his arms to make his tomb, it will be such a monument that every stone of it will speak a history, and some a miracle ; or, if that cannot be, it will be enough that he lay his head upon an immortal turf taken out of Naseby field. God thought Moses, or rather made him, the fittest man to begin and lead Israel forth, and He honoured Joshua with the completing of the work ; neither doth Joshua eclipse the worth of Moses, nor he the worth of Joshua." [1]

Strangely enough, the effort made to perpetuate the memory of Essex roused the anger of one of those half-crazy fanatics whose existence had exasperated him in life. An effigy of the dead commander ' with his creation robes, his Earl's coronet upon his head, in soldier's apparel,' and the bâton of command in his hand, after being drawn to the Abbey, was brought into

Essex's hearse.

the church, and set up under a hearse, or temporary monument, in the place where the Communion table had once stood. [2] During the days which followed the funeral

His effigy destroyed.

large crowds were attracted by the sight. In the night between November 26 and 27 a certain John White concealed himself in the church, hacked the effigy to pieces,

[1] *The Hearse of the Renowned*, by R. Vines. E. 359, 1. Compare *Perfect Occurrences.* E. 358, 17.

[2] There is a woodcut of the hearse in *The true manner of the funeral of Robert, Earl of Essex.* E. 360, 1.

and then proceeded to mutilate the figure of the antiquary Camden. The next morning he was arrested, and stated that an angel had directed him ' to cut all the said image, hearse, and all that was about it in pieces, and to beat down the rest of the images in the said church.' He defended himself by arguing that it was a dishonour to Christ to introduce the effigy of a man into a sacred building.[1]

[1] *Perfect Diurnal*, E. 513, 26 ; *The whole proceeding of the demolishing of the Earl of Essex's tomb*, E. 264, 2 ; White's examination, *L.J.* viii. 653.

CHAPTER XLIV.

THE FAILURE OF THE IRISH PEACE.

SOONER or later, in the pursuit of an alliance either with the Scots, or with one of the English parties, Charles was certain to be hampered by his long-cherished design of seeking assistance from Ireland. On June 11 he had been forced to direct Ormond to abandon all further negotiations with the rebels,[1] and this letter he allowed to be seen by the Scots around him. Though he did not discover his meaning to Ormond, yet in writing to the Queen he explained that his letter only instructed Ormond 'to stop further treating there after the receipt of it, but meddles nothing with what was done before.'[2] Charles knew that the treaty had been already concluded, and he had no intention of depriving himself of any help which the Irish might be able to give.

*1646.
June 11.
Ormond to abandon his negotiation with the Irish.*

*June 16.
Charles explains that this means nothing.*

Improbable as it was that the Irish would really consent to exert themselves in Charles's behalf, they were at least in a better position to do so than they had been for some time. The fort of Bunratty,[3] indeed, was still untaken, though the Supreme Council, followed by the Nuncio, had migrated to Limerick to strengthen the hands of the besiegers. The principal object of the Confederates, however, had been to gather an army strong enough to bear down opposition in the North. Rinuccini would gladly have seen this army under the command of Owen O'Neill, to whom he wished to assign the

Irish affairs.

---

[1] The King to Ormond, June 11. Carte's *Ormond*, vi. p. 392.
[2] The King to the Queen, June 16. *Charles I. in* 1646, 47.
[3] See p. 54.

money and supplies which he had brought from Italy and France. The Supreme Council asked that part might be given to Clanricarde, who commanded in Connaught and who was on terms of close intimacy with Ormond. To this Rinuccini with difficulty consented, and then only on condition that Preston, the general commanding in Leinster, should accompany Clanricarde as his lieutenant-general. The discord which brought confusion on the counsels of the Confederates was thus reflected in their army. Even in Ulster their power had long been weakened by the personal rivalry of Owen and Phelim O'Neill. Rinuccini now succeeded in effecting a reconciliation between the two, and in launching the Ulster army against Monro and the Scots.[1]

The hostile forces met on June 5 at Benburb, on the Blackwater, the stream on the banks of which Bagenal, the

June 5.
Monro's
defeat at
Benburb. Marshal, had been defeated and slain in 1598. The Irish army, consisting of some 5,000 foot and 500 horse, was drawn up on the western side. Monro, whose following was probably superior in numbers, advanced rapidly from the east. Instead of attempting to cross the stream in face of the enemy, he swerved aside, and, having led his men over by a ford, at some little distance, wheeled round to attack the enemy on his undefended flank, in full confidence that victory was in his hands as soon as he had crossed the river. The Irish, however, were fighting for their race and their faith, and their courage had been raised to the highest pitch of enthusiasm by the confident exhortations of their priests. They resisted with unexpected tenacity, and when, after a combat of four hours' duration, O'Neill gave the word to charge, Monro's horse turned to flight, and the infantry speedily followed the example The slaughter which followed was as unsparing as at Kilsyth. The cruelties of the Scots were returned into their own bosoms, and though a few of the officers were kept alive for ransom, quarter was for the most part refused. When all was over, 3,000 dead bodies were counted on the field. Large stores of provisions and munitions of war fell into the hands of the victors. "The

[1] *Lord Leicester's MS.* fol. 1,161b.

rebels," wrote an English narrator, "had never such a day of the Protestants. The Lord sanctify His heavy hand unto us, and give courage to His people to quit themselves like men till help comes." When the news reached Limerick the Nuncio, attended by the whole population of the city, sang a triumphant *Te Deum* to the Giver of the victory.[1]

The defeat of the Scots at Benburb reduced Ormond to great perplexity. On the one hand the Parliamentary com-

June.
Ormond's
perplexity.

missioners in the North urged him to take arms with them against the triumphant rebels.[2] On the other hand the Supreme Council begged him to proceed to the publication of the peace. They were ready, they declared, to leave Glamorgan's articles for future consideration, and to throw themselves on the King's mercy in regard to their religious independence.[3] On June

June 24.
He receives
orders not to
proceed with
the treaty.

24 Ormond received the letter of June 11,[4] in which Charles forbade him to abstain from further negotiation ; and, as he failed to discover in it the brilliant distinction which Charles drew in his letter to the Queen, between proceeding with a new treaty and acting on an old one, he assumed that he was really intended to put an end to all further communication with the Irish Confederates. In conveying to the King his determination to comply with his

June 29.
Distress of
the garrison
of Dublin.

orders he could not but remind him of the hopeless position of his army in Ireland. If war were to recommence, the situation of Dublin would be desperate. Everything was wanting to the soldiers, and there were but thirteen barrels of powder in store.[5]

On July 4 Ormond's instructions were suddenly changed.

---

[1] *L.J.* viii. 378, 394; *Lord Leicester's MS.* fol. 1,191b; Rinuccini, *Nunziatura*, 136.

[2] Ormond and the Irish Council to the King, June 22. Carte's *Ormond*, vi. 400.

[3] Instructions to Plunket and Browne, June 1. *Carte MSS.* xvii. fol. 492.

[4] See p. 151.

[5] Ormond and the Irish Council to the King, June 29. Carte's *Ormond*, vi. 405.

On that day Digby, having arrived from France, informed him

July 4.
Digby's
arrival.

Ormond to
obey the
Queen and
Prince. that the King had directed that, being himself virtually a prisoner, no respect was to be paid to any commands in ordinary writing bearing his signature. In default of ciphered instructions the Lord Lieutenant was to conform to such directions as he might receive from the Queen and the Prince of Wales, and he was now in particular to carry the Irish peace as soon as possible to its completion.[1]

In acting upon Digby's instructions Ormond would undoubtedly be complying with the King's wishes. A few days

Charles's
explana-
tions. later Charles was explaining to Montreuil that he had already written to Ormond [2] to take no account of his prohibition to negotiate. He could not, he added, send him formal powers to come to terms with the Irish lest he should seem to be guilty not only of inconstancy but in some sort of bad faith.[3] It would be enough that he had bidden him to receive orders in future from the Queen and the Prince.[4]

Charles's notions of bad faith were all his own. On July 20, a few days after he had despatched this communi-

July 20.
A letter to
Glamorgan. cation to Ormond, he wrote to Glamorgan, whose policy in Ireland had crossed Ormond's at every step. He began by expressing a wish to enjoy Glamorgan's conversation, or, in other words, to be set free by an invading Irish army. "If," he added, "you can raise a large sum of money by pawning my kingdoms for that purpose, I am content you should do it, and if I recover them I will fully repay that money. And tell the Nuncio that, if once I can

---

[1] Digby to Ormond, July 4, Carte's *Ormond*, vi. 415 ; Declaration by the Queen and the Prince of Wales, appended to Digby's letter of June 28, *Carte MSS.* fol. 486.

[2] This letter has not been preserved. It may have been carried to Ormond by Digby. If so, we can understand why he accepted the Secretary's directions.

[3] " Puisqu'il ne feroit pas seulement paroître beaucoup d'inconstance dans les actions, mais encore quelque sorte de mauvaise foy."

[4] Montreuil to Mazarin, July $\frac{16}{26}$. *Arch. des Aff. Étrangères,* lii. fol. 438.

come into his and your hands, which ought to be extremely
wished for by you both, as well for the sake of England
as Ireland—since all the rest, as I see, despise me—I will
do it."[1]   Of this letter to Glamorgan Ormond knew nothing.

Whatever Ormond was to do, must be done quickly.   The
Irish forces were already gathering the fruits of O'Neill's
Danger of
an attack on
Dublin. victory at Benburb.   On July 10 Roscommon surrendered to Preston.   On the 14th Bunratty was
given up to its besiegers.   Preston and O'Neill
informed the Nuncio that they were ready to combine in an
attack on Dublin.   The French Agent, Dumoulin, was with
Ormond, pleading with him to seize the opportunity of con-
cluding peace with the Supreme Council.   Mazarin distrusted
Rinuccini as being on too good terms with the Spanish Agent,
French
diplomacy. De la Torre, and he was himself too unfamiliar with
the force of a popular movement to doubt the power
of the Supreme Council to make peace on its own terms.   At
all events a combination between Charles and the Supreme
Council would be likely to lead to the dependence of Ireland
upon France, and would be one more link in the chain which
the French Minister was forging for the purpose of weakening
England.   He therefore supplied Digby with 10,000 pistoles,
a sum amounting to more than 7,000*l.*[2]

Ormond had hardly any choice before him.   The main
obstacle rose in the Privy Council.   Twice did a majority of
Opposition
in the
Council. two-thirds declare against the publication of the
peace without direct orders from the King.   On
July 29 Ormond took upon himself the responsi-
July 29.
Ormond
overcomes it. bility of obeying the orders transmitted by the
Queen and Prince, entering a minute on the Coun-
July 30.
The peace
proclaimed. cil register in which he declared that his authority
was sufficient to enable him to act in the King's
name, and that he expected from the Council nothing

[1] The King to Glamorgan, July 20, *Dircks,* 174.

[2] *Lord Leicester's MS.* fol. 1,220b, 1,228, 1,231b; Rinuccini to Panfilio, July 7, 8, 17, 19, *Nunziatura,* 146, 149, 150; Du Moulin to
Ormond, July $\frac{17}{27}$, *Carte MSS.* xviii. fol. 113.

but obedience.[1] On this the Councillors gave way, and on July 30 the peace was publicly proclaimed in Dublin.[2]

Ormond and the Supreme Council were of one mind, but it remained to be seen whether an agreement exposed to the

The peace precarious.

hostility of the Nuncio on the one hand and of the Protestant councillors at Dublin on the other could possibly be maintained. It was still more unlikely that Charles would derive from it the benefit of an armed intervention in England, for the sake of which he had ordered its

Aug. 6.
A congregation at Waterford.

conclusion. On August 6 a congregation of the clergy was held at Waterford under the presidency of Rinuccini. On the 12th this body utterly con-

Aug. 12.
It condemns the peace.

demned the peace, and pronounced all Catholics who had taken the oath of confederation to be perjured if they accepted it. The objections raised by the clergy were not without weight. The peace had indeed relieved Catholics as individuals from all obligation to take the oath of supremacy, and from all fines and penalties which stood in the way of 'the freedom of the Roman Catholic religion.' Nothing in it, however, gave permission to the Church collectively to possess the property which it now held, or to occupy ecclesiastical buildings, still less to complete its organisation by the exercise of ecclesiastical jurisdiction. The congregation was therefore able to allege, by a somewhat bold stroke of rhetoric, that 'in those articles there is no mention made of the Catholic religion,' and to complain, with greater justice, that the removal of these further grievances was left to the King, from whom, as matters stood, no certain orders could be received, whilst in the meanwhile the government of Ireland, and even the command of the Catholic army, was to be in the hands of the Protestant Council at Dublin, and of 'the Protestant officers of his Majesty.'[3]

---

[1] Digby's declaration, July 28, Carte's *Ormond*; Ormond's declaration, July 29, *Carte MSS.* xviii. fol. 121.

[2] Proclamation of the peace, July 30, *Rushw.* vi. 401 ; Rinuccini to Panfilio, Aug. 3, *Nunziatura*, 151.

[3] Declaration of the congregation, Aug. 2. *Rushw.* vi. 416. The phrase about the King is there printed, 'from whom in this present estate

The clergy had reason to believe that their uncompromising attitude would find support.   On the 9th Ulster King-at-arms

Aug. 9.
The expe-
riences of a
King-at-
arms.

arrived outside the gate of Waterford, and sent in an attendant to inform the mayor that he was come to proclaim the peace.   The attendant found the streets lined with an angry crowd, which scowled at him as he passed, and refused to inform him where the mayor's house was to be found.   At last he bribed a boy by the promise of sixpence to act as his guide.   The mayor's house indeed he found, but not the mayor.   After waiting at the gate for three or four hours the King-at-arms put on his tabard and entered the city.   The mayor, who was not to be found when he was sought for by the servant, at once confronted the master, and told him that he would not be allowed to read the proclamation there till he had read it at Kilkenny.   The discomfited official thought it prudent to withdraw.

At Kilkenny and at Fethard the King-at-arms was at least able to read his proclamation in the presence of the magistrates, but the bulk of the population kept within doors.   At Clonmel he found the gates barred in his face, and at Limerick he was attacked and wounded by a mob.   The mayor, who supported him, was dragged off to prison ; and a vehement partisan of

Aug. 17.
Towns
threatened
with inter-
dict.

the clergy, Dominic Fanning, was installed in his place.   On August 17 the congregation at Waterford threatened to lay an interdict on every town in which the peace was published.[1]   Before the end of the month the greater part of the troops which had served before Bunratty had taken part with the clergy, and, what was of far

Owen
O'Neill de-
clares for the
clergy.

greater importance, O'Neill with his victorious army had declared in their favour.   Preston, who was connected by family ties with the lords of the Pale, advanced, indeed, as far as Birr, but he could not be induced to do more than to make vague promises to either side.[2]

---

we can have nothing settled.' This is more intelligible in the Latin, ' a quo, in præsenti statu, nihil certi potest haberi.' *Lord Leicester's MS.* fol. 1,310.

[1] A relation by W. Kirkby, *Carte MSS.* xviii. fol. 383 ; *Lord Leicester's MS.* fol. 1,315–1,325.

[2] *Lord Leicester's MS.* fol. 1,328, 1,333b, 1,334.

For the present Ormond contented himself with watching the course of events.[1] On August 26 the clergy were sufficiently emboldened to authorise the refusal of taxes to the Supreme Council.[2]

The Supreme Council in the meanwhile had been doing everything in their power to avert the storm. On August 18

Aug. 18.
Action of the Supreme Council.

their secretary, Bellings, assured Rinuccini that he would do his utmost to induce Ormond to give satisfaction to the clergy.[3] Before long they were

A proposition to the Nuncio.

able to propose, apparently with Ormond's assent, that if the Nuncio would accept the peace the Supreme Council should 'privately[4] receive a firm and authentic assurance of the taking away of the penal laws against Catholics, and that their clergy shall not be put out nor molested in their ecclesiastical possessions before a new Parliament called in pursuance of the article of peace ; the said assurance to be . . . severed from the articles of peace to which my Lord Lieutenant hath not power to add anything, his powers being determined.'[5]

[1] *Lord Leicester's MS.* fol. 1,261b, 1,287, 1,328b, 1,332b-1,334, 1,339 ; Clanricarde to Ormond, Sept. 18, Carte's *Ormond,* vi. 429.

[2] *Lord Leicester's MS.* fol. 1,328.

[3] Bellings to Rinuccini, Aug. 18. *Ibid.* fol. 1,312.

[4] There is a curious letter in which Glamorgan sneeringly expresses his pleasure at the scrape into which Ormond had got by having to act against the King's public instructions. He writes of the King's disavowal of his own proceedings, 'which though enforced upon him I esteem it yet a warning from further proceeding therein, and fit only for great persons, who can maintain the same, to go contrary to the intimation of his Majesty's pleasure, though never so compulsatively granted. For, as I never have nor will esteem and be frighted at the contradiction of any others when the intimation of his Majesty's pleasure continues to me in any particular unrevoked, so on the contrary can I never be drawn for any man's pleasure to go immediately contrary to what proceedeth from him, deeming it not my part to enter into dispute which way his Majesty is induced, when I see his positive act extant. Let this, therefore, I beseech your Excellency, give you and the rest of the world satisfaction that I no way countenance the standing upon any articles heretofore treated of by me. . . . In fine, having washed my hands of that business, proving that the child burnt dreads the fire.' Glamorgan to Ormond, Aug. 30. *Carte MSS.* xviii. fol. 370.

[5] Propositions made to the Nuncio. *Ibid.* xviii. fol. 374.

How could the Supreme Council expect to make its way if it had nothing better than this to offer? In vain they sum-

Aug. 31.
Ormond at
Kilkenny. moned Ormond to their aid. Before the end of August [1] the Lord Lieutenant, accompanied by Digby and Clanricarde and a small military force, arrived at Kilkenny. He was here in the centre of the old territory of the Butlers, and his relatives and allies flocked in to meet him. The greater part of the members of the Supreme Council were bound to him by the instincts of self-preservation, and Ormond, thus supported, fancied that he could set at defiance the popular ill-will. So satisfied was he with

An assembly
to meet at
Cashel. his reception, that on September 10 he summoned a general meeting of the nobility, and appointed Cashel as the place of its assembly. To his disap-

Sept. 10.
Ormond
turned back, pointment, the men of Cashel refused to admit him within their walls. Those of Clonmel shut their gates against him, and, what was far more alarming, news arrived that Owen O'Neill was on his march through Leinster

Sept. 14.
and returns
to Dublin. either against Kilkenny or against Dublin itself, and that the wild tribes of Carlow and Wexford were prepared to rise at his approach. To save himself from capture Ormond deemed it prudent to return to Dublin.[2]

The discomfiture of Ormond was the signal of the more

Sept. 18.
The Nuncio
at Kilkenny. assured triumph of the Nuncio. Rinuccini, bringing with him the Spanish Agent, Diego de la Torre,

Sept. 19.
Arrest of the
leaders of the
Supreme
Council. entered Kilkenny on the 18th at the head of an armed force.[3] On the following morning the leaders of the Supreme Council were arrested and imprisoned in the castle. The treaty was declared to be void. Within two days it was known at Kilkenny that Ormond was

---

[1] 'Ad exeuntem Augustum' probably means the 31st, as Ormond's first letter from Kilkenny is dated Sept. 1. *Lord Leicester's MS.* fol. 1,329.

[2] *Lord Leicester's MS.* fol. 1,340b-1342; Lambert to Ormond, Sept. 9, Talbot to Ormond, Sept. 10, Roscommon to Ormond, Sept. 11, *Carte MSS.* xviii. fol. 468, 482, 494.

[3] Rinuccini to Panfilio, Sept. 21. *Nunziatura*, 160. He here speaks of himself as arriving four days ago. *Lord Leicester's MS.* fol. 1,367, no doubt incorrectly, speaks of his leaving Kilkenny on the 19th.

about to take a step which would change the whole state of
affairs. Seeing that the policy which by his master's command
he had pursued for three years had utterly broken down, he
Ormond re- resolved, with the full consent of his council, to place
solves to sub-
mit to the Dublin and the few fortresses which still held out in
English Par-
liament. the hands of the English Parliament rather than
Sept. 26. allow them to fall into the hands of the Nuncio.
New
Supreme Rinuccini, eager to defeat the project, summoned
Council
chosen by O'Neill to bring his armed forces to his aid. On
the clergy. the 26th a new Supreme Council was chosen by the
congregation of the clergy, of which Rinuccini was naturally
appointed president.[1]

One step remained to be taken. Rinuccini must not only
have a Supreme Council, but a Lord Lieutenant of his own.
Glamorgan Glamorgan was ready to his hand. He had brought
to be Lord
Lieutenant. with him to Ireland amongst other papers a document, sealed with Charles's signet, appointing him
Lord Lieutenant in the case of Ormond's death or misconduct.[2] As soon as Dublin was taken—and the Nuncio felt
little doubt that it would soon fall—Glamorgan could possess
himself of the authority which had dropped from Ormond's
hands. It was true that he had not the appointment by
patent, but the Irish were not likely to make a distinction
between one seal and another.[3] The enthusiastic letter in
which Charles had expressed his eagerness to place himself in
the hands of Glamorgan and Rinuccini seemed to leave no
Sept. 28. doubt of his assent.[4] On the 28th Glamorgan
Glamorgan's qualified himself for his high office as the King's
oath to the
Nuncio. representative in Ireland by swearing entire submission to the Nuncio. He would do nothing without his approbation, and would at any time be ready to resign his office
into his hands.[5]

It was not difficult to discover in Ormond misconduct

---

[1] *Lord Leicester's MS.* fol. 1,367, 1,384b.
[2] See vol. ii. p. 165.
[3] Rinuccini to Panfilio, Sept. 21, 25, 29. *Nunziatura,* 160, 162, 166.
[4] See p. 154.
[5] *Lord Leicester's MS.* fol. 1,380.

which in the eyes of Glamorgan and Rinuccini would justify
Ormond at
Dublin. the contemplated change. Ormond had at last
carried out the purpose which he had contemplated
Sept. 26.
Ormond
sends to
Westminster
to ask for aid. ever since his return to Dublin. On the 26th he
despatched commissioners to Westminster to ask for
aid in the defence of Dublin.

Ormond's reluctance to submit to Rinuccini had other
motives than those which weighed with the Supreme Council.
It was not so much the ruin of the Irish-English stock which
he feared, as the loosening of the hold of England upon
Ireland, by the destruction of the English settlements which
formed the Protestant garrison of Ireland. , Those who now
held sway, he declared in his instruction to his commissioners,
aimed, in the first place, at the 'overthrowing of all planta-
tions' which had been made 'for the better strengthening,
civilising, and enriching the kingdom, and establishing it in
due obedience to the crown of England,' and, in the second
place, at 'the setting up of Popery in this kingdom in the
fulness of papal power, jurisdiction, and practice; and both
these aims laboured by the Popish pretended clergy, and by
most of the mere Irish, and others of English extraction too
easily carried away by the seducements of their prelacy and
clergy, and all industriously set on and fomented by two
persons who came into this kingdom, and have a long time
resided here, without any licence from us, his Majesty's Ministers, or any application by them made unto us; namely, the
King of Spain's Agent and the Pope's Nuncio.'

The commissioners were accordingly to inform the Houses
that the Lord Lieutenant was prepared to admit their troops
Ormond's
offer. into his garrisons and to place his remaining forces
at their disposal. He would either carry on the war
with their help as Lord Lieutenant, or would, if they preferred
it, quit his office in favour of some one else. If they adopted
the latter alternative, they must understand that he could not
leave his post without the King's permission, and he therefore
sent a letter in which that permission was asked for, which he
requested the Houses to forward to his Majesty.[1]

[1] Letter of credence and instruction, Sept. 26. *L.J.* viii. 519, 523.

At last the two real combatants stood face to face—the Papal Nuncio and the English Puritan Parliament. The old

The two combatants.

Weakness of the Supreme Council.

Supreme Council had already disappeared and, it must be acknowledged, had deserved to disappear. It had neither a feasible policy of its own nor sympathy with the people whose guidance it had undertaken. It had been voluntarily ignorant, not merely of Charles's inability to support his adherents in Ireland, but of the hopelessness of founding a policy of alliance with any one of the English parties at a time when all English parties were resolutely opposed to every idea which had found favour at Kilkenny. So evident does this appear, that it may well be asked how it

Sept. 3.

Its want of sympathy with Irishmen.

came about that the nobles and gentry of the Supreme Council should have lent themselves to a policy so manifestly futile. The answer is given in a letter in which one of its members, Sir Robert Talbot, implored Preston to range himself on the side of the peace. " I fear," he wrote, " that religion is not the aim of the clergy, but the destruction of the English rule, and of those who derive their origin from England."[1] " If you fail us," he added, "all is at an end for the old Irish-English, who rest especially on your arm."[2]

The man who wrote these words, and those on whose behalf they were written, had not learned that the one unpardonable sin of a conquering aristocracy is to retain its individuality in the midst of the native population of the land which it has invaded. Little more than a century after the Norman invasion of England no one could say of any one of the ruling class that he was of distinctly Norman blood. In less than two centuries the descendants of the conquerors and the conquered,

The Spanish Agent, De la Torre, resided at Waterford, where Rinuccini had lately been for some time, but it is only fair to say that there is no trace of his special influence over the Nuncio in Rinuccini's correspondence.

[1] "Timeo ne Religio non sit scopus sed eversio Regiminis Anglicani, et eorum qui exinde originem trahunt."

[2] "Sin autem actum est de omnibus antiquis Ibernis—Anglis tuo præsertim brachio innitentibus." Talbot to Preston, Sept. 3. *Lord Leicester's MS.* fol. 1,335. The letter only exists in a Latin translation.

without distinction of origin, wrested the Great Charter from a Norman king and faced his son on the hillside at Lewes. Though more than three centuries and a half had passed since Ireland was invaded, the offspring of the invaders still spoke of themselves as Irish-English, and shrank from sharing their authority with the true children of the soil. Community of religion had for a time concealed the cleft separating the races, but at the critical moment the heirs of the conquerors found themselves out of sympathy with the people whose leaders they had professed themselves to be.

It was by no mere accident that the power which had dropped from the hands of the Supreme Council fell into those of Rinuccini and the clergy. Ireland, with national aspirations, was without the elements of a national organisation. Only one organisation—that of the Church—bound together the scattered elements of Irish life for unity of action. That it was so involved a war to the knife with England. The Irish Church, unlike that of Scotland, was not national but cosmopolitan ; and with good reason Englishmen dreaded to allow free scope to an organisation in Ireland the establishment of which would be a standing menace to the development of national life in England. With an Irish nation, it might be possible to come to terms, as it ultimately proved possible to come to terms with Scotland. With the Roman Catholic Church, so long as she thought of making use of an arm of flesh to vindicate her claims, it was not possible. Fear of giving a foothold in Ireland to foreign armies acting in the name of the Church had driven Elizabeth to conquer Ireland, and James to colonise it. Of late years everything had been done to stimulate the terror. Strafford had threatened to coerce England with an Irish army, and even the Supreme Council had followed in the same path. Rinuccini, freed from an alliance with any English party, was ready to walk in it with greater boldness still. Evil—unspeakably evil—as would be the results of a fresh English conquest, it had now become impossible to avert it. There are crises when the spirit of the moss-trooper's cry,

Power of the clergy in Ireland.

The ecclesiastical organisation hostile to England.

Grounds of English resistance.

"Thou shalt want ere I want," becomes the key-note of
national action. It was hardly likely, especially under clerical
guidance, that Ireland would succeed in conquering England ;
but the danger of a combination formed between an independent Ireland and one or other of the Continental monarchies
was sufficiently menacing to rouse in England the bitterest
feelings. England, in short, was making ready to invade Ireland rather because she was resolved to defend her own
national existence than because she was hostile to that of her
neighbour. After all, if the only alternative to an English
conquest of Ireland was to be the weakening and impoverish-
ment of English national life, it may well be doubted whether
the world at large would not have lost more than it would
have gained by the success of the Irish.

On October 12 the attention of the Houses at Westminster
was drawn to the latest phase of the Irish imbroglio.[1] Admirably

Oct. 12.
Reception
of the news
from Ireland
at Westmin-
ster.

as Ormond, by his offer to surrender to them his
authority, was playing into their hands, they could
not overcome their rooted distrust of co-operation
with Charles or of officers who had Charles's confidence. They accordingly agreed to accept Ormond's resignation rather than his services, but they refused to transmit to the
King that letter containing the Lord Lieutenant's demand for
Charles's approval of his conduct which he had declared to be
the necessary condition of his resignation.[2] There can be little
doubt that they were wise in refusing his offer to take service
under them. Upright and loyal as Ormond had in every
circumstance of his life been found, he would have been out
of place as the servant of the English Parliament.

[1] *C.J.* iv. 690.　　　　[2] *C.J.* iv. 693; *L.J.* viii. 530.

CHAPTER XLV.

THE DEPARTURE OF THE SCOTS.

THE complete failure of Charles's Irish policy did not make him any more ready to yield to his English subjects. It was in vain that the Presbyterians at Westminster had cast longing eyes in the direction of Newcastle. About the middle of September Charles received from the Queen's council the draft of a reply which they advised him to give to the propositions. As it contained a more or less open concession of the Presbyterian demands, he summarily rejected it. In time, he answered, they would ask him to submit to the Pope, 'for questionless it is less ill in many respects to submit to one than many popes.'[1]

1646.
Sept. 21.
Charles rejects the Queen's project.

It was about this time that Charles had a fresh overture from the Independents. According to a statement by Sir Robert Moray, they offered him 'his will in religion —that is, moderated Episcopacy—when the Scots' were 'gone, to pass delinquents, and waive Ireland till King and Parliament were agreed.'[2] It can hardly be doubted that, though Moray makes no mention of it, something was also said about liberty of conscience. However that may have been, Charles was, on political grounds, too distrustful of the Independents, to incline him to listen to their proposals, and he was, moreover, at this time entirely absorbed

Fresh offers from the Independents.

---

[1] The King to Jermyn, Culpepper, and Ashburnham, Sept. 21. *Clar. St. P.* ii. 264.

[2] Moray to Hamilton, Sept. 21. *Hamilton Papers* (Camd. Soc.), 115. Mr. Blaize, here and at p. 114, should be Mr. Blair.

in the elaboration of that project of his own which he had
been for some time concocting with Will Murray.[1]

On September 30 this marvellous scheme was at last completed.   The existing church arrangements were to remain in

Sept. 30.
Charles
makes a new
proposal.

force for three years.   During that time a committee
of both Houses was to discuss the future government of the Church with sixty divines, twenty of
whom were to be Presbyterians, twenty Independents, and
twenty chosen by the King.   When their part had been
played—and it could hardly end except in a bitter wrangle—
the King and the two Houses were to pronounce sentence.
In the course of three years of a Restoration government it
was more than probable either that fresh elections would take
place or that the composition of the existing Parliament would
be modified by the readmission of the expelled members, and
there was therefore every reason to expect that Episcopacy
would be brought back without much difficulty.   At all events,

He consults
divines.

this was what Charles in reality expected.   To salve
his conscience he wrote to Juxon for advice, and
bade him consult Bishop Duppa and Dr. Sheldon.   He assured Juxon that he had adopted this plan ' with a resolution
to recover and maintain that doctrine and discipline wherein '
he had ' been bred.'   " My regal authority once settled," he
declared, " I make no question of recovering Episcopal government ; and God is my witness, my chiefest end in regaining
my power is to do the Church service."[2]   The answer of the
divines was favourable,[3] but before it arrived the King had
already decided to act.

Scarcely had Charles's letter left Newcastle when Montreuil returned to press him once more to concede everything

Oct.
Davenant's
mission.

to the Scots.   Montreuil was shortly followed by
the poet Davenant, who was now high in favour
with Jermyn, whose fortunes he had shared in the
days of the Army Plot.   Davenant had been specially instructed by the Queen to urge Charles to give way, but she

See p. 142.
[2] The King to Juxon, Sept. 30.   *Clar. St. P.* ii. 265.
[3] Juxon and Duppa to the King, Oct. 15.   *Clar. St. P.* ii. 267.

could hardly have selected a more unfit agent to charge with
such a commission. He urged Charles to abide by the advice
of his friends. To Charles's inquiry who the friends were, he
named Jermyn and Culpepper, Ashburnham having already
shown that, though he joined these two in signing the joint
letters written to Charles at the Queen's directions, he had
personally no liking for their arguments in favour of Presbyterianism. Jermyn, said Charles, understands nothing about
the Church, and Culpepper has no religion. Davenant then
brought forward an argument which probably seemed to him
conclusive. If the Queen, he said, did not have her way, she
would cease to trouble herself about her husband's affairs and
would retire into a nunnery. After this he spoke slightingly
of the Church, hinting that it was not worth the sacrifice
which the King was making for it. Charles for once lost his
temper, and drove the unlucky disputant from his presence.[1]
Davenant was afterwards readmitted to an audience, but his
mission had plainly failed, and before long he returned to
France.

Davenant's verbal arguments were supported by another
long letter from Jermyn and Culpepper. Episcopacy, they
urged, was an admirable institution, but it was not

Oct. 5.
A case put
to the King. of Divine right. On the other hand, Presbyterianism
was, no doubt, politically dangerous, and as such
was to be avoided as long as possible. The plain fact, however, was that Charles had no longer a choice. " Presbytery,"
they declared, "or something worse will be forced upon you,
whether you will or no. Come, the question is whether you
will choose to be king of Presbytery or no king, and yet
Presbytery or perfect Independency to be."[2] It was plain
common sense, but common sense has no jurisdiction in the
sphere in which Charles's thoughts were moving. He was
resolved to be 'no king' rather than soil his conscience.

If Charles stood alone in his resolve, he also stood alone
in thinking it possible to avoid ruin unless he surrendered to

[1] *Clarendon*, x. 57 ; the King to Jermyn, Culpepper, and Ashburnham,
Oct. 3, *Clar. St. P.* ii. 270.

[2] Jermyn and Culpepper to the King, Sept. 18. *Clar. St. P.* ii. 261.

one party or the other. He had no lack of advisers. Argyle,
anxious, as Montreuil thought, to spare his countrymen the dis-

Charles's
advisers.
grace either of surrendering their king to the English
or of detaining him a prisoner, recommended him
to go to London without permission, throwing himself on the
generosity of the English Parliament. Others pressed him,
through the intervention of Will Murray, to escape to the
Continent. Bellièvre, who needed him as an instrument to
promote the designs of France, urged him to remain in his
own dominions, and if no other course were open to throw
himself into the Highlands, and to seek the support of Huntly
and the Gordons.[1]

Charles listened to none of these suggestions. On
October 12, tired of waiting for the answer of the divines, he

Oct. 12.
He sends
proposals
by Will
Murray,
sent off Will Murray with instructions to show his
scheme for an ecclesiastical settlement, together
with certain political proposals, to the Scottish commissioners in London.[2] He was, in particular,
ready to abandon the militia for ten years, or even, at the last
extremity, for life, if only he could be certain that, at the end
of the appointed term, it would return to its ancient depend-

Oct. 15.
and makes
additional
offers.
ence on the Crown. In a letter which followed
Murray on the 15th he offered to grant Presbyterianism for five years instead of for three, and to
waive his suggestion of a conference, if the leading English
Presbyterians would positively engage that at the end of that
time ' a regulated Episcopacy' would be restored.[3]

As might have been expected, the Scottish commissioners
in London would have nothing to do with offers so

They are
rejected by
the Scots.
illusory, though, in order to cover their own failure
to obtain satisfactory terms, they spread a report that
no answer whatever had reached them.[4]

[1] Montreuil to Mazarin, Oct. $\frac{5}{15}$, *Arch. des Aff. Étrangères*, lii. fol.
610; Bellièvre to Mazarin, Oct. $\frac{5}{15}$, *R.O. Transcripts*.

[2] The King's answers, Oct. 12 and 15. *Clarendon MSS.* 2,333.

[3] The King to Murray, Oct. 15. *Clar. St. P.* ii. 275.

[4] Grignon to Brienne, $\frac{Oct. 29}{Nov. 8}$, *R. O. Transcripts*; the King to the
Queen, Nov. 1, *Charles I. in 1646*, 73.

Before Charles knew that Murray had failed he received a
letter from his wife. Side by side with his conscientious but

Oct. 31.
Charles
hears from
the Queen. tortuous schemes for inveigling his enemies to their
destruction, there is something positively refreshing
in the bold directness with which she broke through
his scrupulosities. " If you are lost," she dashingly wrote,
" the bishops have no resource, but if you can again place
yourself at the head of an army we can restore them to their
sees. . . . Preserve the militia and never abandon it. By that
all will come back to you. God will send you means to your
restoration, and of this there is already some little hope." [1]

It was, as might have been expected, to France that
Henrietta Maria was looking. In the campaign of 1646

French suc-
cesses in the
Nether-
lands. Mazarin had sent Turenne into Germany to out-
manœuvre the Imperialists, but he had thrown the
chief weight of the war upon the Spanish Nether-

Surrender of
Courtrai and
Mardyk. lands. In June the important frontier town of
Courtrai had been captured. Mardyk, the outpost

Siege of
Dunkirk. of Dunkirk, surrendered in August. Then followed
the siege of Dunkirk itself. Enghien, marking his
sense of the hazardous nature of the employment, undertook in person the command of the beleaguering army. It
was all-important to secure the assistance of the Dutch fleet,
and the Prince of Orange, sunk into dotage, was no longer
accessible to argument or persuasion. When the French
ambassador, Grammont, arrived to ask him to send the ships,
he took the astonished Frenchman for a lady, seized him by
the hand, and gravely went through the steps of a German
dance which had caught his fancy. Grammont found a better
reception from Frederick Henry's son than from himself.
Prince William was too ambitious of military fame to share
the unwillingness which was already manifesting itself in the

Dutch ships
sent to aid in
the siege. States General to assist in bringing so powerful a
neighbour as France a step further towards the
frontier of the Republic. He threw all his weight
into the scale in Grammont's favour, and Tromp was ordered,

[1] The Queen to the King, Oct. 9. *Clar. St. P.* ii. 271.

with the assistance of a small French squadron, to seal the entrance of the harbour of Dunkirk.[1]

In their despair the Spanish officers and the Low Countries turned to England. It had been a cardinal principle of Charles's policy, as long as he was in a position to have a policy at all, to keep Dunkirk out of the hands of the French. There is good reason to believe that Cromwell and the Independents would have been ready, if they had had the power, to follow in his steps.[2] They had long been on better terms than their rivals with Cardenas, the Spanish ambassador,[3] and they thoroughly distrusted the French government as the chief accomplice in Charles's intrigues with the English and Scottish Presbyterians. On September 21 it was known in London that Cardenas intended to apply for assistance, and it was believed that he would accompany his request with an offer of liberty of traffic in the Indies. As a matter of fact, he offered, not the trade of the Indies, but a large sum of ready money.

Before an answer could be given, John Taylor, an Englishman residing in the Low Countries, arrived from the Marquis of Castel Rodrigo, the Governor of the Spanish Netherlands, with an offer to place Dunkirk, Ostend, and Nieuport in the hands of the English Parliament, if they would save them from capture by the French.[4] As Cardenas did not venture, without instructions from Spain, to take up Taylor's negotiation, he simply begged the Houses

Marginal notes:
The Independents friendly to Spain.
Sept. 21. Cardenas begs for help.
John Taylor's mission.

---

[1] Chéruel, *Hist. de France pendant la minorité de Louis XIV.* ii. 225-251.

[2] Up to 1654 the *Simancas MSS.* show Cromwell to have been friendly to Spain, and hostile to France.

[3] Cardenas, writing on Sept. $\frac{18}{28}$, speaks of the Independents as less hostile to Spain than the Presbyterians. Consulta of the Council of State, $\frac{\text{Dec. 29}}{\text{Jan. 8}}$, 164$\frac{6}{7}$. *Simancas MSS.* The French ambassadors express themselves more strongly, and I suspect with reason.

[4] Taylor, wrote Cardenas on Oct. $\frac{21}{31}$, 'dijo llevava comision del Marques para poner en manos del Parlamento las plazas de Domquerque, Ostende y Neoport. Con que se desvanecieron las platicas de Don Alonso,' *i.e.* of Cardenas himself, 'no queriendo arrostrar Ingleses á otra cosa si no á la oferta de Teller.'

that 4,000 English soldiers with a suitable naval force might
be sent at once to succour Dunkirk.   Having nothing, as it
would seem, to offer in return, he may have thought that the
natural disinclination of the English to see these places in
French hands would be sufficient to obtain from him a favourable reply.   In any case the Presbyterian members, as allies of
France, would have been against him, and his silence both on
the admission of English traders to the Indies and on the surrender of the Flemish ports put an end to what little chance of
success he might have had.[1]   Even if there had been any disposition to send help—and it is hard to see how, with the Scots

His
demand
rejected.

Oct. $\frac{1}{11}$.
Surrender
of Dun-
kirk.

still at Newcastle, any English party could have been
guilty of the extreme rashness of embarking in a
foreign war—the succour could not possibly have
arrived in time.   On October 1, after a vigorous
defence, Dunkirk passed under the power of

France.[2]

It was upon these successes that Henrietta Maria grounded
her hopes.   Mazarin, she wrote to her husband, had assured

Oct. 9.
The
Queen's
advice.

her that there would be a general peace before
Christmas, and that France would then be at liberty
to give him powerful aid.   It was therefore, continued

the Queen, necessary for him to have the Scots on his side,
though he need not take the Covenant or do anything that was
dishonourable.[3]

To abandon Episcopacy for a time in order to regain that
and everything else was, in short, the advice of the Queen.

Montrose to
take arms
again.

It was not a project likely to commend itself to
Charles ; and even the Queen had just thrown an
obstacle in the way of its realisation by entertaining

another project in direct antagonism with it.   The Earl of

---

[1] It may, I think, be gathered from the quotation in the last note that
the surrender of the ports had no place in 'las platicas de Don Alonso.'
The dissatisfaction of the English with his omission to offer the traffic
of the Indies is noted in the French despatches.   Grignon to Brienne,
Sept. $\frac{17}{27}$, $\frac{\text{Sept. 24}}{\text{Oct. 4}}$, Oct. $\frac{1}{11}$.   *R.O. Transcripts.*

[2] *Chéruel,* ii. 257.

[3] The Queen to the King, Oct. $\frac{9}{19}$.   *Clar. St. P.* ii. 271.

Crawford, Montrose's lieutenant-general, had recently arrived in France, and had given assurances that, what with the loyalty of the Highlanders and what with the zeal of the Irish, Montrose would be able in the spring to take the field at the head of 30,000 men. At this improbable story the Queen eagerly caught. It was true that she knew that there had been differences in Ireland between the Nuncio and the Supreme Council ; but she imagined that by sending a confidential agent to Ireland, she might easily get the better of the difficulty.[1]

It was a sorry policy to revive the plan of combining the Presbyterian Scots with the Catholic Irish in an assault upon

The Channel Islands to be made over to the French.

England. Jermyn was prepared to go further still. He proposed to purchase French aid by the cession of the Channel Islands, as Charles had formerly proposed to purchase Danish aid by the cession of Orkney and Shetland. To the group of exiles at Jersey the proposal appeared to be monstrous. Hyde, Capel, and Hopton were Royalists indeed, but they were Englishmen first. To give up the islands, they thought, was to give up England's mastery in the Channel. They resolved that Capel should carry their united remonstrances to St. Germains, and that, if this step failed, they should apply to Northumberland for help to be sent from England, though they still hoped to be spared the necessity of acknowledging the supremacy of Parliament.[2]

Whether Charles ever heard of this extraordinary proposal or not, he did not share in the Queen's elation at the prospect of help held out to him. It was embittered by her assurance that it would be needful for him to accept Presbyterianism, even if it was to be Presbyterianism without the Covenant. He

Failure of Will Murray's mission.

had just learnt that Will Murray's mission to London[3] had entirely failed, and that the Scottish commissioners there had rejected not only his offer about religion, but his offer about the militia as well. On the latter

---

[1] The Queen to the King, Oct. $\frac{9}{19}$; Jermyn and Culpepper to the King, Oct. $\frac{9}{19}$, *Clar. St. P.* ii. 271.

[2] Articles of association, Oct. 19. *Ibid.* ii. 279. The story rests on information sent by a credible person, and I see no reason to disbelieve it.

[3] See p. 168.

point they adhered to the demand made at Uxbridge for the permanent surrender to the English Parliament of all authority over the armed force of the kingdom. The news does not seem to have been altogether unwelcome to Charles. He had probably felt the difference of opinion between himself and his wife far more than the difference of opinion between himself and his subjects, and he now took the opportunity of removing it. She would not, he seems to have thought, any longer wish him to yield on the question of the Church, now that his offers about the militia, though they went far beyond anything which she would be willing to grant, had been refused. After assuring her on November 1 that he was now in no mood to give way, he added a fresh piece of intelligence. "They tell me from London," he wrote, " that they will neither declare against monarchy nor my posterity, but merely against my person." [1] It was doubtless this news which inspired Charles for the first and last time in his life with the idea of abdicating, in some loose fashion, in favour of the Prince of Wales.

Nov. 2.
He thinks
of tempo-
rarily abdi-
cating.

Not, indeed, that Charles seriously thought of divesting himself of power. His scheme was not intended to remove any obstacles which might stand in the way of the national well-being either in England or in Scotland. It was a mere device to bring home to his wife that not only was her plan of Presbyterianism without the Covenant certain to be rejected by the Scots, but that even the widest ecclesiastical changes would be unacceptable to them unless they were accompanied by political changes to which she, equally with himself, would refuse to submit. He had recently quoted with approval the saying, "No bishop, no king," which he had learned from his father, [2] and, though these words were very far from representing all that he personally believed on the subject of Episcopacy, he placed them in the foreground in his friendly controversy with his wife and her advisers. He now suggested to Bellièvre the idea of allowing the Prince,

His motives.

---

[1] The King to the Queen, Nov. 1. *Charles I. in* 1646, 73.
[2] The King to Jermyn, Culpepper, and Ashburnham, Oct. 10. *Clar. St. p.* ii. 273.

either with or without the name of king, to attempt to satisfy the Scots by a promise of compliance with their desires as far as the Church alone was concerned. He felt no doubt that it would thus be made clear that the Scots aimed at the destruction of monarchy, and he had too much confidence in the affection of his wife and in the respectful obedience of his son to imagine that, when once they had found the Scots as resolute in refusing the control of the militia to a new king as they had been in refusing it to the old one, they would be slow to restore to him the power of which he had temporarily divested himself.[1]

It would be some time before Charles could hear of the reception of this extraordinary scheme by the Queen. In the

Nov. 7.
Will
Murray's
return.

meanwhile he was engaged in pushing forward his fresh plan. Will Murray had returned on November 7, and had told his master that, though nothing was to be gained from the Scots, the English Presbyterians were in

Offers of
the English
Presby-
terians.

a more yielding mood. If they 'might have something to say for religion, and reasonable security concerning the militia . . . a considerable prevailing party' might declare for the King's 'coming to London.'[2] Upon these hopes Charles set to work so to modify his offer of Presbyterianism for three years as to render it palatable to the English Parliament.

To Bellièvre all this senseless intrigue seemed to be the worst of follies. He plainly told Charles that, if he would not

Bellièvre
advises
Charles to
come to
terms with
the Inde-
pendents.

grant the Scottish terms, he had better throw himself boldly into the hands of the Independents. It was true that they did not love him, but if they had liberty of conscience, and their leaders were rewarded with high places, they would allow him to deal with the militia at his pleasure.[3] Charles listened approvingly, but he also listened approvingly to others. The ambassador

---

[1] Bellièvre to Brienne, Nov. $\frac{2}{12}$. Ranke, *Engl. Gesch.* viii. 184.

[2] Moray to Hamilton, Nov. 8, *Hamilton Papers*, 121; the King to the Queen, Nov. 14, *Charles I. in* 1646, 75.

[3] Bellièvre to Mazarin, Nov. $\frac{14}{24}$. *R.O. Transcripts.*

bemoaned the difficulty of serving a prince who never gave
his full confidence to anyone.

Bellièvre was, in fact, aware that Charles had kept to himself an overture which had lately reached him.[1]   The Northern
counties were necessarily subjected to bitter oppres-

Unpopu-
larity of the
Scots in the
North.

sion from the Scottish army, which had been left
without pay for no less than nine months,[2] and their
indignation easily grew into a desire for a return to

Growing
desire in the
North for
the King's
restoration,

that old order of things which, in the North at least,
seemed to be necessarily conjoined with the restoration of the King to his ancient authority.   Nor was
this feeling confined to the North.   In the South and the East
the heavy taxation which had to be borne for the support of
Fairfax's army swayed men's minds in a similar direction,
whatever hope of release from this heavy burden had hitherto
existed being now crushed by the knowledge that the Houses
had voted the reassessment of the tax for another six months.

and in the
Eastern
Association.

Even the Eastern Association, so resolute in the
early days of the war, would have been forward
in supporting an accommodation with the King, if
only he had been ready to make concessions to the Presbyterian feeling which prevailed there.[3]   The causes of this
reaction are, indeed, obscure.   Something, no doubt, was due
to the intensity of local feeling.   The Association was conscious of its own sacrifices, and objected to bear the burden of
military defence outside its own limits.   Something, too, must
have been due to the dislike of militarism natural to a busy
and thriving district.   Nor must it be forgotten that the counties which had produced more than the average number of
Protestants in the days of Mary, and more than the average
number of Puritans in the days of Charles, produced more than
the average number of fanatics in the days of the Long Parliament.   The fanaticism of the few was certain in time to excite
a loathing of fanaticism amongst the many, and the growth of
a strong Presbyterian sentiment, tending even to merge itself
in Royalism, would thus be easily accounted for.

[1] Bellièvre to Mazarin, $\frac{Nov. 22}{Dec. 2}$.   *R.O. Transcripts.*
[2] *L.J.* viii. 555.   [3] See p. 184, note 3.

The feeling against a prolongation of the existing uncertainty was brought before Charles's notice by Dr. Hudson, the

Nov. 18.
Hudson's
escape. guide who had accompanied him to Newark. On November 18 Hudson escaped, or was allowed to escape, from the prison in which he had been confined, and he soon made his appearance at Newcastle as the bearer of proposals which seemed for a moment likely to change the whole state of affairs.[1]

The communication which Hudson was empowered to make announced a general rising in the East, the South, and

Proposed
rising
against
Parliament. the West on behalf of the King. A large force was to be placed in the field to support this design. Charles, on his part, was to issue a general pardon to all who now joined him, even if they had been deeply concerned in the late rebellion. He was to engage to abolish 'the excise and other unlawful taxes, not to bring in foreign forces, not to dispose of delinquents' estates to private uses, nor that the Scots should come over the Trent.' The Prince of Wales was to be the general of the new army. To this last proposal Charles demurred. He wished to take the command in person, but he was ready to give satisfaction in everything else. In the meanwhile Hudson asked the King to despatch Sir Thomas Glemham to Lynn, where he would be ready for all emergencies.[2]

---

[1] *Whitelocke*, 228.

[2] I am aware that Bamfield in his *Apology*, written long after the Restoration, attributes Hudson's mission to the Independent leaders, and that his statement is adopted by Rushworth's editors in the contents to the posthumous fourth part of his Collections. Contemporary evidence, however, seems to me conclusive against this view. In the first place the selection of Lynn as Glemham's landing-place connects the proposed rising with the Eastern Association, and we know that when the Lords proposed that the King should reside at Newmarket, the Commons, under the influence of the Independents, substituted Holmby, because the Eastern Association was too favourable to the King. Moreover, on November 18 a letter was read in the Commons to the effect that Hudson 'intended to go to the King and to get from him commissions to the gentry in Norfolk to raise men, with whom should join the forces in the North and in the West and in Wales, under the command of Colonel Laugharne, who should all declare themselves for the King, and come

Nothing came of this unexpected proposal, nor is it possible to ascertain who were its authors. It is not unlikely that

up to London ' (Whitacre's Diary, *Add. MSS.* 31,116, fol. 290). In 1648 Laugharne took the Royalist-Presbyterian side. The forces in the North referred to seem to be connected with the purely Royalist movement to seize Pontefract Castle, soon afterwards detected by Poyntz (*C.J.* iv. 730). Again, Hudson was taken in December, and soon after his capture Laugharne sent up a letter from him with an enclosed copy of a letter from the King. These were read in the House of Commons on January 5. The only account we have of them is in *Perfect Occurrences* (E. 370, 21). The King's letter is not printed verbatim, but its purport is pretty clear. It is thus given :—

"Hudson, let all my honest friends know that I will grant commissioners [? commissions] as large as I have promised—(And so the said letter went on showing the ends thereof)—to restore his Majesty to his rights, and dissolve the Parliament, that he will not seek foreign help but for money and ammunition, and will either himself or his son be general of the army ; that he shall pardon all the oaths and covenants that formerly they have taken ; that he is resolved to take off the excise and all illegal taxes ; and that his principal aim shall be to restore the Church ; and that he shall endeavour to keep the Scots from coming over Trent.

Dated November 21, 1646.   (Signed)
(Not the King's own hand.)   C. REX."

Hudson's letter to Laugharne is given as follows :—

"Assuring him (by the command of the King) of the great value his Majesty had of him, desiring his assistance, with his other friends, to restore him to his rights, telling him (amongst other passages) that if the Parliament should not bring up the King with honour and safety, before New Year's Day, all his Majesty's friends will declare for him.

(Subscribed) J. HUDSON."

Hudson's name was Michael, and letters abbreviated in this way are not likely to be altogether accurate in other respects besides the signature, but they clearly do not point in the direction of a plot with the Independents. Taking the evidence all together, it looks as if Hudson proposed to the King to appeal to the spirit of dissatisfaction which undoubtedly existed, without much regard for either Independent or Presbyterian. The plan would thus be a predominantly Royalist one, intended to catch weak Presbyterians rather than weak Independents. On the other hand, it seems that at Newcastle (Moray to Hamilton, Dec. 2. *Hamilton Papers*, 132) Hudson was believed to be concerned in proposals made by

some of the Presbyterians were cognisant of it, but on the whole it bears the impress of a spirit totally unlike that which

Question of the author-ship of the scheme. prevailed in either of the Parliamentary parties. It seems to have arisen amongst men who assumed the attitude of the Clubmen of the preceding year, but with better knowledge and greater political experience.

Charles was not likely to neglect an old intrigue because he took part in a new one, and he was still busy over his scheme for granting Presbyterianism for a limited time, even though

Nov. 28. The King hears that the Queen condemns him. his wife in a letter received by him on the 28th expressed her opinion freely that his cherished project was a senseless contrivance. For her part, she wrote, if she had thought of granting for three years something which her conscience forbade her to grant at all, she would go a step further, and grant it altogether to save the throne.[1] Yet in spite of his knowledge that it was impossible to make his wife understand his scruples, Charles was always

Prepares an answer for the Parlia-ment. anxious to have her opinion, and he now submitted to her the answer which he had drawn up for the English Parliament. There was to be a concession of Presbyterianism, for three years, and of the militia for ten. As for Ireland, he would 'give full satisfaction as to the managing of the war, and for religion as in England.'[2] In these

Dec. 5. Boasts of an equivocation in it. words he took especial delight. "I only say," he informed the Queen, "that I will give full satisfaction as to the management of the war, so that if I find reason to make peace there my engagement ends." Bellièvre, to whom he pointed out this excellent contrivance, told Mazarin that he left it to those who knew more English than he did to judge of the force of the equivocation, but that he thought

Independents. Is it possible that Hudson, in order to effect his escape, entered into communications with the Independents, and was believed by them to be their emissary, though he was really working in another direction? I have sometimes thought that Dr. Stewart, who visited Newcastle earlier, may have been the bearer of proposals from the Independents, and that Bamfield, intending to refer to him, gave a description of him which can only apply to Hudson.

[1] The Queen to the King, Nov. $\frac{13}{23}$. *Clar. St. P.* ii. 294.

[2] Proposed message. *Burnet*, 382.

that its interpretation would lie with him that had the longest sword.[1]

For the present, till the Queen's comments arrived, Charles hesitated to send his answer to London; but he fancied that something might be gained by obtaining the preliminary approval of the Scots. Accordingly, on December 4 he sent his scheme to Lanark, that he might test Scottish opinion. Much to his surprise and disgust, Lanark replied that no one in Scotland would have anything to do with it.[2]

Dec. 4.
Charles sends it to Scotland.

Dec. 8.
The Scots reject it.

The days which Charles was thus frittering away were being used to his disadvantage at Westminster. Almost to the end of November, indeed, it seemed possible that the English and the Scots might come to a rupture on their respective claims to the custody of his person. In the press a vigorous paper war was raging on the subject, and on the 28th the Independents carried through the Commons a declaration asserting the right of the English Parliament alone to dispose of the King's person as long as he was in England. They then, by a majority of 110 to 90, obtained a vote that this declaration should be sent to the Scottish commissioners without any previous communication with the Lords.[3] The Scots, however, prudently returned it unopened, on the ground that it only proceeded from a single House.[4]

Nov. 28.
The situation at Westminster.

The Commons assert the claim of the English Parliament to dispose of the King.

Dec. 2.
The Scots return their declaration.

They had probably even stronger reasons for avoiding further controversy. On November 3 the Scottish Parliament had met at Edinburgh, and though it long refrained from touching on so delicate a subject, there was strong reason to believe that it would refuse to afford to Charles a shelter in Scotland.[5]

Nov. 3.
Meeting of the Scottish Parliament.

[1] The King to the Queen, Dec. 5, *Charles I. in 1646*, 82; Bellièvre to Mazarin, Dec. $\frac{6}{16}$, *R.O. Transcripts*.

[2] The King to Lanark, Dec. 4; Lanark to the King, Dec. 8. *Burnet*, 381, 386.

[3] *C.J.* iv. 730; *Rushw.* vi. 341.

[4] *C.J.* iv. 734; Whitacre's Diary, *Add. MSS.* 31,116, fol. 291.

[5] Bellièvre to Mazarin, Dec. $\frac{21}{31}$. *R.O. Transcripts*.

Whatever resolution the Scottish Parliament might take, the English House of Commons pursued its course of making the way of retreat from England easy. There was the more reason to hasten to a conclusion, as on November 30 it was known at Westminster that there had been a Royalist plot to seize Pontefract Castle, which might not unreasonably be thought to be connected with Hudson's mission.[1] The Commons therefore, dropping all reference to their rejected declaration, pressed on, in amicable conference with the Scottish commissioners, the arrangements for the marching away of the Scottish army, and for the payment of the money which would then be due. On the 16th of December the two parties reached an agreement, and twelve thousand pounds was paid over as earnest money to the Scots.[2]

Nov. 30. News of a Royalist attempt on Pontefract Castle.

Arrangements for the departure of the Scots.

Dec. 16. Earnest money paid.

England would rid itself to little purpose of the Scottish army if Charles was to be suffered to retreat with it to Edinburgh, and to make Scotland a centre of intrigue against the English Parliament. Events now showed that no such danger was to be feared. It is true that on the 16th, the day on which the earnest money was paid at Westminster, the Scottish Parliament, under the impulse of Hamilton, resolved 'to press his Majesty's coming to London with honour, safety, and freedom,' and at the same time avowed its own determination 'to maintain monarchical government in his Majesty's person and posterity, and his just title to the crown of England.'[3] The resolution, however, though strictly in accordance with the wishes of the King, would be of little avail until the conditions had been settled on which the promised support was to be given, and there was a powerful party in Scotland which had no wish to make them too easy. Argyle had even been heard to say that a promise to keep the King in honour and safety would be fully observed, even if he were thrown into prison

Is the King to go to Scotland?

Vote in the Scottish Parliament.

---

[1] *C.J.* iv. 730. [2] *L.J.* viii. 603, 614.
[3] Lanark to [? Sir R. Moray], Dec. 17. *Burnet,* 389.

provided that his attendants served him on their knees, and he was carefully guarded against assassination.[1]

Argyle's main support lay elsewhere than in Parliament. When Parliament met on the 17th, it was confronted by a petition from the ministers who formed a standing committee of the General Assembly,[2] protesting against those persons who endeavoured to bring about 'a division and breach between the kingdoms, or the making of any factions or parties contrary to the Covenant under pretence of preserving the King and his authority,' and against those who were remiss in their duty of urging him to subscribe the Covenant and to 'give satisfaction to the just desires of both kingdoms.' To give him shelter in Scotland would 'confirm the suspicions of the English nation' that there had been underhand dealings with him before his coming to the army.[3]

Dec. 17.
Petition of
the minis-
ters.

It is in the highest degree probable that this petition had been drawn up in concert with Argyle. His policy, and that of the ministers, was identical in recognising the cardinal fact of the situation, that Charles did not wish to give satisfaction to the demands of Scotland, but simply to use Scotland as a base of operations against England. The fanatical simplicity of the clergy and the subtle intelligence of Argyle combined to defeat a project so disastrous to Scotland as well as to England.

Argyle and
the clergy.

Under the influence of the clerical petition Parliament addressed itself to the consideration of the conditions under which support was to be given to Charles. All that had been gained for him on the previous day was now swept away. He must accept the propositions made to him by the English Parliament at Newcastle as they stood. If he refused, the government of Scotland was to be settled without him, and he must not think of coming to Scotland to exercise the office of a king. Even if he were deposed in

The Scottish
conditions.

---

[1] Bellièvre to Mazarin, Dec. $\frac{6}{16}$. *R.O. Transcripts.*
[2] *Acts of the Parl. of Scotl.* vi. 634.
[3] *Rushw.* vi. 390.

England, Scotland would do nothing for him unless he took the Covenant and accepted the propositions.[1]

It is hard to find serious fault with the resolution thus taken, except by condemning the whole ecclesiastical and political system which the Scottish nation had deliberately adopted. That Charles was bent upon destroying that system in England if he could get an opportunity is beyond all reasonable doubt, and its supporters were therefore justified in refusing to him the vantage-ground which would be given him by a residence in Edinburgh.

Were the Scots justified?

In every direction Charles's schemes were, as usual, breaking down. On December 16 he learned that his plan of a temporary abdication had been scornfully rejected by Mazarin, as well as his plan for a temporary establishment of Presbyterianism.[2] More trying still must have been the sarcastic comment of the Queen. His proposal to grant the militia for ten years, she told him, was equivalent to a confirmation of the existing Parliament for that time. "As long as the Parliament lasts," she continued, "you are not king. As for me, I will not again set foot in England. With your scheme of granting the militia you have cut your own throat, for when you have given them that power you can refuse them nothing, not even my life, if they ask you for it. You ask my opinion about Ireland. I have often written to you about it. You must not abandon Ireland. . . . I am surprised that the Irish do not give themselves over to a foreign king. You will force them to do so at last, when they see that you are offering them up as a sacrifice." [3]

Dec. 16. Charles learns that Mazarin rejects his proposal to abdicate,

and that his other suggestions are derided by the Queen.

A day or two after the reception of these communications from France came a doleful letter from Lanark, telling Charles how the Scottish Parliament had declared against him. It

---

[1] Lanark to [? Sir R. Moray], Dec. 17. *Burnet,* 389. The instructions founded on this resolution were adopted on the 24th. *Acts of the Parl. of Scotl.* v. 635.

[2] Mazarin to Bellièvre, $\frac{Nov. 30}{Dec. 10}$; Jermyn and Culpepper to the King, Dec. $\frac{1}{11}$, *Clar. St. P.* ii. 301.

[3] The Queen to King, Dec. $\frac{1}{11}$. *Ibid.* ii. 300.

would now be useless to send to Westminster the elaborate

Dec. 20.
Charles
again asks
to come to
London. answer to the propositions which had satisfied no one but himself, and on December 20 he substituted for it a renewed request to be allowed to come to London.[1]

To this request no attention was paid. The policy of the Independents was still in the ascendant, and was likely to remain in the ascendant as long as a Scottish army was quartered at Newcastle. In matters of religion, indeed, the Independents still found it prudent to maintain a discreet silence. The ordinance against blasphemy and heresy was being pushed

Dec. 12.
Books re-
ferred to a
committee. steadily on through committee. On December 12, when the Presbyterians proposed to refer to a committee a sermon in which Dell, one of Fairfax's army chaplains, had denied to the civil magistrate the right of interfering with a gospel reformation, the Independents offered no opposition, but contented themselves with demanding that another book, written in defence of the Divine right of Presbyterianism, should be treated in a similar manner.[2]

Naturally the Royalists sought to turn to account the antagonism which existed on religious matters between the

Dec. 19.
A City peti-
tion. two parties, and they hoped that a fresh City petition, which was ultimately presented on the 19th, would be a further cause of strife. That petition was certainly unfavourable to the Independents. In addition to the usual demand for the suppression of heresy, it asked that the English army might be disbanded in consequence of the favour shown by it to heretics, but it was entirely silent as to the treatment of the King. It contented itself with expressing confidence in the wisdom of Parliament.[3]

Charles had not conciliated anyone, and had not cared to conciliate anyone. To have him in London, fighting for his

---

[1] The King to the Speaker of the House of Lords, Dec. 20. *L.J.* viii. 627.

[2] *C.J.* v. 10; Whitacre's Diary, *Add. MSS.* 31,116, fol. 293; *Right Reformation*, by W. Dell, E. 263, 2.

[3] The City Petition, E. 366, 14; *C.J.* v. 20; Grignon to Brienne, Dec. 23/Jan. 2, *R.O. Transcripts.*

own hand, would be resisted by everyone, whether Presbyterian or Independent, who believed that, in the old sense of

Charles conciliates no one.

the word monarchy, there was no longer room for monarchy in England, and that it must give place to a government founded, in some way or other, upon

Dec. 21. Design to carry off the Duke of York.

the national will. A discovery made on December 21 probably served to knit the parties together for a time. In the preceding July the little Princess Henrietta had been carried off to France by her governess, Lady Dalkeith.[1] It now appeared that a design had been formed to carry the Duke of York, who since the surrender of Oxford had been in Northumberland's custody, either to Newcastle or to France.[2] That such an attempt should have been contemplated was convincing evidence that Charles had no thought of coming to terms with Parliament.

On the 22nd the Lords, taking into consideration the City petition, directed Fairfax to see that all officers and soldiers

Dec. 22. The Lords' resolutions.

under his command took the Covenant, and ordered that all Anabaptists and other sectaries disturbing public worship should be punished according to

They wish the King to come to Newmarket.

law. They then voted that the King should come to Newmarket, there to remain till the two kingdoms had consulted on the ultimate disposal of his

Dec. 24. The Commons declare for Holmby House,

person. On the 24th the Commons substituted Holmby House for Newmarket. Newmarket was in the Eastern Association, and the Eastern Association was now given over to Presbyterian, if not to Royalist views. The revelation of Hudson's plot had plainly not been forgotten.[3]

---

[1] Mrs. Everett Green, *Princesses of England*, vi. 408.

[2] *L.J.* viii. 619. On the effect of this discovery in hardening the House of Lords against the King, see Grignon to Brienne, $\frac{Dec. 28}{Jan. 2}$. *R.O. Transcripts.*

[3] *C.J.* v. 28; Whitacre's Diary, *Add. MSS.* 31,116, fol. 294b. Grignon says plainly what Whitacre only hints at. The Associated Counties, he says, are those 'qui ont toujours tesmoigné beaucoup d'affection pour leur Roy, le presence duquel leur pourroit donner de courage d'entreprendre quelque chose; ce qu'ils craignent d'autant plus que le ministre

The assignment of Newmarket as a residence to the King was not the only part of the Lords' resolution to which the

and object to consulting the Scots.

Commons took exception. They objected to declare that the disposal of the King's person could be a

Dec. 31.
Vote on the King's person.

fitting object of consultation between the two king-doms. The amendments of the Commons were accepted by the Peers, as well as a clause in which the King was called on to give his complete assent to the propositions and to the ordinance for the sale of the bishops' lands, failing which the two Houses would maintain 'the happy union already settled between the kingdoms.'[1]

The King's refusal to come to terms with the Presbyterians had, for the moment, weaned them from their unhappy

Indirect results from the King's action.

policy of seeking to realise their aims in concert with the King, the Scots, and the French.[2] Their rivals, no longer having the credit of being the exclusively national party, lost ground rapidly. The return of the Scottish army to its own country and the bringing up of the King to Holmby House would dispose of the questions which had given the lead to the Independents. Ecclesiastical discussions would then mainly occupy the attention of Parliament, and on ecclesiastical questions the Presbyterians had more of the national feeling behind them than their opponents.

Even now, whilst the Scots were still at Newcastle, the result of the agreement of the two Houses on matters relating to the King was quickly seen. The Lords had prepared

---

Hudson qui s'estoit eschappé dernierement, et que l'on disoit conduire quelque dessein en faveur du Roy de la Grande Bretagne dans ces mesmes Comtés, a esté repris depuis quatre jours sur le chemin de Newcastle, et l'on croit qu'il venoit d'auprès du dit Roy pour cela.' Grignon to Brienne, $\frac{Dec. 23}{Jan. 2}$. *R.O. Transcripts.*

[1] *L.J.* viii. 635, 638.

[2] The King, wrote Grignon, would hardly come to London unless he accepted the propositions, 'voyant que les Presbyteriens qui s'imaginent avoir à present l'avantage sur leurs adversaires, ne se disposent point à porter ses interests, s'il ne consent à ce qu'ils ont desiré de luy.' Grignon to Brienne, $\frac{Dec. 31}{Jan. 10}$. *R.O. Transcripts.*

an ordinance forbidding all who had not been ordained, either in the Church of England or in some foreign reformed Church,

Dec. 31.
Ordinance
against lay
preaching. 'to preach or expound the Scriptures in any church or chapel, or in any other place.' On December 31 this ordinance was taken into consideration in the Commons. The Independents, doubtless knowing that they could not hope to reject it, attempted to amend it so as to permit laymen at least to expound the Scriptures. After a long and stormy debate, lasting well into the night, they were beaten on a division, in which Cromwell himself acted as teller, by 105 to 57. A motion to restrict the prohibition to places 'appointed for public worship' was defeated without The Presby-
terians
regain the
majority. a division.[1] That night's work indicated a shifting of parties, of which there had, no doubt, been clear indications before. It was not that a sufficient number of members had changed their minds to give a majority to the Presbyterians, but that the questions on which the Presbyterians had always had a majority had now become the questions of the day, whilst those on which the Independents had had the majority were now practically solved.

It was impossible that Charles should remain much longer in the hands of the Scots. On the 22nd, when the resolution Dec. 22.
Offers made
by the
Scottish
com-
manders. of the Edinburgh Parliament was known at Newcastle, the commanders of the army made one last effort to bring him over to their side. They assured him that, if he would only promise to establish Presbyterianism when once he was firmly seated on the throne, they would undertake to recover his authority in the teeth of both the Parliaments. Though the French ambas- Dec. 24.
Charles
attempts to
escape. sador added his entreaties to theirs, Charles firmly declined the tempting offer.[2] With no prospect now before him except that of being handed over to the Dec 29.
Precautions
taken. English, he began at last seriously to think of escaping to the Continent, and Will Murray was employed to make the arrangements for his flight.[3] The scheme,

---

[1] *C.J.* v. 34 ; Grignon to Brienne, Jan. $\frac{7}{17}$, *R.O. Transcripts.*

[2] Bellièvre to Mazarin, Jan. $\frac{2}{12}$. *R.O. Transcripts.*

[3] *L.J.* viii. 665. For Murray's denial, which was to be expected, see

however, got wind, and the Scots, redoubling their precautions, treated him as a veritable prisoner.[1]

Dark as the outlook was, there could hardly fail to be a gleam of hope on some quarter of the horizon. This time it was once more from Ireland that Charles looked for help. The attempt of the Confederate generals to seize Dublin had been wrecked, for this season at least, by their own dissensions, and by the diffi-culty of conveying supplies through a devastated country and over streams swollen by the Novem-ber rains.[2] In the meanwhile the Parliamentary commissioners who had been sent to take possession of Dublin found Ormond unwilling to accept the terms which they were empowered to offer. The Lord Lieute-nant had made it a condition of the surrender that the letter in which he had asked leave to surrender his authority should be forwarded to the King for his approval. Parliament having refused to send this letter on, Ormond declared himself no longer bound by his own conditional promise. He would not, he said, give Dublin up without positive directions from his master.[3] On January 5 Charles, having heard what Ormond was doing, gave him his hearty approval,[4] and directed him 'to re-piece' his 'breach with the Irish,' if it could be done 'with honour and a good conscience.'

Charles again looks to Ireland for help.

Nov. Failure of the Con-federates to take Dublin.

*Ormond re*fuses to *surrender it to the English Parliament.*

1647. Jan. 5. The refusal approved by Charles.

Whilst Charles was thus cherishing new imaginations, Bellièvre had made up his mind that nothing could be done for a man who could do nothing for himself. He made one last attempt to win over David Leslie, telling him, evidently with Charles's authority, that if he would restore the King without insisting upon Presby-

Bellièvre attempts to win David Leslie.

ibid. 703. Bellièvre's despatches constantly refer to the thought of escape as being in Charles's mind, so that there is every reason to believe the story. The protestations of the Scots are worth absolutely nothing.

[1] Sir R. Moray to Hamilton, Dec. 29. *Hamilton Papers*, 141.

[2] *Lord Leicester's MS.* 1,411b–1,439.

[3] *Carte MSS.* xix. *passim ; Several passages of the treaty,* E. 378, 4; *Rushw.* vi. 420.

[4] The King to Ormond, Jan. 5. Carte's *Ormond*, v. 18.

terianism he should be created Duke of the Orkneys, and made a Knight of the Garter and Captain of the Guard, with a sum of 8,000 jacobuses[1] paid down, and a yearly revenue of 2,000. It was of no avail. Leslie told the Frenchman plainly that nothing could be done unless the King yielded on the religious question. On January 4 the ambassador turned his back on Newcastle, where he had met with so many disappointments, and made his way to London.[2]

Jah. 4.
Bellièvre leaves Newcastle.

The final catastrophe could not be long deferred. There was, indeed, some delay about the arrangements for counting the money, and it was not till January 26 that the commissioners who had been appointed by the English Parliament to inform the King of the vote of the Houses relegating him to Holmby came into his presence. On the following day Charles despatched another letter to Ormond, again urging him to come to terms with the Irish.[3] On the 28th he informed the commissioners that in a few days he would be ready to accompany them.

Jan. 26.
Charles's interview with the English commissioners.

Jan. 27.
A despatch to Ormond.

Against this arrangement the Scots had nothing to say. On the 30th, the first 100,000*l.* having been duly paid, the Scottish commissioners took their leave of Charles. Their garrison marched out, and their guards were relieved by English soldiers as if nothing more was occurring than an ordinary piece of routine. On February 3 the second instalment of 100,000*l.* was also paid,[4] and by the 11th[5] every garrison had been delivered up, and every Scottish soldier had crossed the Tweed.

Jan. 30.
The Scots leave Newcastle.

Feb.
They cross the Tweed.

Such was the transaction which Royalist partisans were soon to qualify as the act of Judas, who sold his Lord for money. The despatches of Montreuil and Bellièvre tell a very

---

[1] *i.e.* guineas.

[2] Bellièvre to Mazarin, Jan. $\frac{8}{18}$. *R.O. Transcripts.*

[3] The King to Ormond, Jan. 27, Carte's *Ormond,* v. **18.**

[4] *L.J.* viii. 699, 716.

[5] *A most worthy speech.* E. **378, 10.**

different tale. They show, beyond possibility of dispute, that
the Scottish leaders, soldiers and civilians alike, would wil-

Comparison
of the Scots
to Judas.

lingly have renounced the English gold and have
defied the English army to do its worst, if Charles

Evidence of
the French
despatches.

would have complied with the conditions on which
alone—even if they had been personally willing to

What was
the promise
given to
Charles?

come to his help without them—it was possible for
them to raise forces in his defence. It is true,
indeed, that from time to time, in the early stage

of the negotiations, some of their number showed signs of
wavering, and that in the final offer made before the King
arrived at Newark Montreuil was allowed to use words which,
under the most favourable interpretation, must be allowed to
be ambiguous. Yet, at all events, the engagement made
through Sir Robert Moray gave no uncertain sound, and, if
ever the strict demand for the establishment of Presbyterianism was for a moment relaxed, it was almost immediately
renewed.

Apart from the personal question of the truthfulness of the
commissioners—in which, after all, only five or six persons

Were the
Scots to give
him a refuge
in Scotland?

were involved—is it to be seriously argued that the
Scots, as a nation, were in any way bound to give to
Charles a refuge in their own country? It was not

for the sake of a peaceful retreat that Charles thought at one
time of accompanying the army to Scotland. What he wanted,
as Montreuil, who knew him well, declared, was to give encouragement to the Scottish Royalists, and above all to bring
about a quarrel between the two nations.[1]

Were the Scots to be blamed because they refused to

---

[1] " Pour ce qui est de la resolution qu'à ladite Maté de se retirer en
Escosse avec l'armée des Escossois, s'il ne luy est pas permis de se sauver,
il espere en recevoir de differents avantages ; comme d'estre en lieu ou sa
presence pourra donner du cœur à ce qui luy reste d'amys, et les porter à
chercher les moyens de le restablir ; de se pouvoir sauver plus aisement
estant là, que demeurant en Angleterre ; de donner sujet à les deux
nations de se brouiller, puisque les Anglois qui ont arresté que leur Roy
viendroit à Homby auront sujet de le demander à l'Escosse." Montreuil
to Mazarin, Jan $\frac{10}{20}$. *Arch. des Aff. Étrangères,* lvi. fol. 23.

expose themselves to such a danger? Were they even under obligation to allow the King to escape to the Continent? It is probably the course which posterity would be inclined to recommend. Yet, knowing as we do the whole network of Charles's foreign intrigues and his continual expectation of aid from foreign armies, it is not for us to feel surprise if Scots and English alike shrank, as Elizabeth had shrunk in the very similar case of Charles's grandmother, from incurring so evident a danger.

What were the Scots to do?

If in modern times the Scots get less than justice, because the ineffectual wiles of Charles's diplomacy are so hard to bear in mind, they also get less than justice because they attempted, with the assistance of a certain number of Englishmen, to force upon the English nation an ecclesiastical system which was uncongenial to its character and its traditions. It is almost forgotten that bishops were known to that generation as the organs of a system of political despotism, or that Charles supported them, not merely as ecclesiastical functionaries of Divine appointment, but also as the supporters of something very like absolute monarchical authority. He wanted them to ordain a lawful clergy, but he also wanted them to 'tune the pulpits'—that is to say, to prevent the free expression of the only kind of opinion which had in his time any hold upon the masses, lest it should lead to an uprising against monarchy. When he spoke of monarchy he meant the monarchy of Henry VIII. and Elizabeth, not the monarchy of William III. and Victoria. He was hankering after the restoration of the system which Laud had praised and which Strafford had supported.

Could Presbyterianism be forced upon England?

What did Charles want bishops for?

Presbyterianism had many faults, but at least its existence rendered impossible a return to a mode of government which had been tried and found wanting. It rested in the Church on an organisation proceeding out of the nation itself in the form of elderships, classes, and assemblies, rather than on an organisation proceeding from the King. In the State it rested upon the House of Commons, an elective body proceeding from constituencies which were more or less extensive, but

which on the whole fairly represented the mind of the nation.
In the hands of men of expansive genius such a system might
have acquired, at least for a time, a hold upon the nation
itself. Its leaders were, however, by no means men of expansive genius. They could not see that no bridge was strong
enough to cross the gulf which separated them from Charles.
They sought to carry out with his aid changes which, through
motives of interest as well as of principle, he thoroughly detested. What was more fatal still, in seeking to combine with
the King they were driven to combine with the Scots, and
even with the French. They became the anti-national party
when their strength lay in being truly national.

The Presbyterians had done their work. They had overthrown the monarchy, never, in the sense in which Charles
understood the word, to rise again in England.[1] In
accomplishing this they had called forth an army
which had translated their phrases into action, and
the virtual head of that army was a statesman as
well as a soldier. Whether Cromwell and the Independents
would succeed where the Presbyterians had failed, in establishing a government which had the elements of endurance, remained to be seen ; but at least they had recognised that
England was called upon to work out her own destiny without
respect to Scots or Irish or the Continental powers. It had
been the statesmanship of the Independents which had cul-
minated in the departure of the Scots and the surrender of the
King. In gaining the custody of Charles's person England
had in truth entered into possession of herself.

*Weakness
of the
English
Presby-
terianism.*

[1] Since this was written Mr. Frederic Harrison has said much the
same thing (*Oliver Cromwell*, 129) in speaking of Charles's death. "It
is said," he writes, "that the regicides killed Charles I. only to make
Charles II. king. It is not so. They killed the old monarchy ; and the
restored monarch was by no means its heir, but a royal Stadtholder or
hereditary President. In 1649, when Charles I. ceased to live, the true
monarchy of England ceased to reign." If, however, the act was the act
of the Independents, the mental preparation for it was the work of the
Presbyterians, even more than they were themselves aware of.

CHAPTER XLVI.

FINANCIAL AND ADMINISTRATIVE DISORDER.

In the first months of 1647 a cry was raised on all sides for the restoration of peaceful order. In addition to the devasta-

1647. Increase of the public burdens. tions of war there had been an enormous increase of the public burdens, though it is impossible to calculate, even conjecturally, what that increase was.[1] The collection of the revenue was in the hands of separate

Confused finance. committees, and the funds thus acquired were liable to be drawn on, or even to be anticipated by Parliamentary orders issued, not on the recommendation of any official responsible for the financial soundness of the course adopted, but on the spur of the moment, as news arrived that some fortress was hard pressed, or some regiment was clamouring for pay. Under such conditions economy was impossible.

No balance-sheet kept. No general balance-sheet was kept, perhaps because the Houses had no mind to look their liabilities in the face. Recourse was constantly had to loans, and large sums of money were thus obtained from the City, at first

Parliamentary indebtedness. simply on Parliamentary security, or, as the phrase then was, on 'the public faith,' and afterwards, as the value of this security decreased, by mortgaging future revenues, or by pledging confiscated property still unsold.

---

[1] The greater part of the increase was upon the army and navy. It appears from a report from the Committee of Accounts (*C.J.* vi. 63) that before the formation of the New Model Army, the expense of the navy was about 236,000*l.* a year, and that of the army about 444,000*l.*, making together 680,000*l.* This result is, however, far from being complete, as ordnance stores and money spent on local forces are left out of the account, more than 10,000 soldiers, for instance, being employed in garrisons.

Whilst it would be hazardous even to guess at the amount of Parliamentary expenditure, it is not quite impossible to form a conjectural estimate of the revenue of 1647 which may not be very far distant from the truth. The Royal income at this time gathered in by the Parliamentary authorities can hardly have exceeded 450,000*l.*, if, indeed, it reached that amount,[1] though in 1635 it had been estimated at 618,000*l.* Of this revenue the only head on which we have definite information is that of the customs. In 1635 the customs brought in 328,000*l.*; in 1643 they had dropped as low as 165,000*l.*; in 1647, after some fluctuations, they brought in 262,000*l.*[2]

Estimate of the Crown revenue.

The customs.

An income of 450,000*l.* was manifestly inadequate to meet even a peace-expenditure, especially if any considerable part of the army was to be kept on foot. Nothing, therefore, was for the present heard of any proposal to diminish those additional sources of revenue which had been opened by Parliamentary Ordinances since the beginning of

Inadequacy of the revenue.

---

[1] In 1660 (*Parl. Hist.* iv. 118) the revenue which Charles I. had enjoyed just before the Civil War was estimated at 819,000*l.* From this must be deducted, to arrive at the amount of it receivable in 1647, payments which had ceased to be made before that date:—

	£
Casual and dropped payments	45,000
Court of Wards	100,000
Decrease of Customs	138,000
Post Office	21,000
	304,000

leaving 515,000*l.* I have deducted a further 65,000*l.* as a moderate estimate of the general decline of revenue owing to the ravages of the war, thus bringing my estimate down to 450,000*l.*

[2] The receipts from customs were as follows:—

	£
1643	165,000
1644	225,000
1645	192,000
1646	276,000
1647	262,000

R. O. Audit Office Declared Accounts. The drop in 1647, when a large

the war. These were, in the main, three—the excise, the assessment, and Royalist forfeitures and compositions.

The excise, which pressed on all classes alike, was levied not only on food and drink, but on goods of almost every description. In the three years beginning with 1647 it averaged 330,000*l.*[1] The assessment raised by monthly payments from the counties for the support of the New Model Army was estimated at 641,000*l.* a year.[2] The compositions, taking the average of eight years beginning in 1643, yielded an annual revenue of 162,000*l.*[3]

Excise.
Assessment.
Composi-
tions.
General
estimate of
revenue.

Upon these data, therefore, a rough estimate of the revenue of 1647 becomes possible :—

	£
Crown revenue	450,000
Excise	330,000
Assessment	641,000
Compositions	162,000
	1,583,000

The produce of the sale of forfeited lands is not included in this estimate, as it was usually either kept for the payment of debt, or given away to persons who had incurred losses in the service of the State, or were held to be specially deserving of reward. As the assessment money was badly paid, the actual revenue was in all probability far below 1,583,000*l.* This sum, however, even if it had been gathered in, would have been quite inadequate for the maintenance of the existing army and navy in addition to the very large current expenses of government, especially as there can be little doubt that peculation prevailed to a considerable extent.

That this increase of taxation, and especially the imposition of the excise, weighed heavily on the poor does not admit of doubt, though the employment of large numbers of agricultural

increase would naturally be expected, is probably accounted for by the badness of the harvest in 1646 and 1647.

[1] *R. O. Audit Office Declared Accounts.* [2] *L.J.* vii. 204.
[3] Preface to Mrs. Everett Green's *Calendar of S. P. Dom.* 1649-1650, p. ix.

labourers as soldiers no doubt afforded an escape for the more vigorous. The economical position of those who remained The labour- at home cannot be accurately defined. In many ing class. places they suffered from military violence, but, in spite of the disturbed state of the country, wages appear to have remained much at the level at which they had stood before the war, that is to say, at 7*d.* a day, with a tendency to rise to 8*d.*, this sum being, however, supplemented by the produce of the domestic labour of wives and daughters, by pasturage on commons, and by fowling on moor and fen.

Yet the greatest suffering to which the labourer was at this time subjected arose from a cause entirely independent of Bad human agency. The year 1646 was the first of a harvests. series of six years in which the harvest was deplorably bad; wheat, which even in plentiful years seldom fell below 30*s.* a quarter, standing at an average of 58*s.* 7¾*d.*, and for the three years beginning with 1647, even at an average of 65*s.* 3½*d.* It is true that the labourer seldom, if ever, tasted wheaten bread ; but the oats, the rye, and the pease which formed the staple of his diet rose in like proportion. On the other hand, meat did not rise to the same extent, the increase of price being about 50 per cent. in the worst years, whereas the price of bread had more than doubled.[1] In one respect, indeed, the position of the labourer may seem to have been Wages fixed worse than at the present day. A statute was in by the existence which directed that his wages should be justices. fixed by the justices of the peace. Yet the absence of complaint, at a time when every possible grievance found advocates, seems to show that on this score no feeling of resentment was entertained, and indeed there is strong reason to believe that this law was usually if not altogether disregarded. At all events the justices, where they acted in accordance with

---

[1] Rogers, *Hist. of Agriculture and Prices,* v. 205, 623 ; vi. 54, 286. Those who calculate the relative value of money in the seventeenth and nineteenth centuries sometimes forget that, though most commodities were at far lower prices than they are at present, the price of grain was as high or higher. Mutton was ordinarily at 3*d.*, beef at 2*d.* a pound. Did the labourer eat more meat than at present ?

the law, recognised the strength of the labourer's case for
higher wages by raising them gradually, till in 1651 they fixed
The labourer them at 1s. 2d. a day.[1] As a factor in the religious
not a and political disputes of the time the agricultural
political
factor. labourer counted for nothing. No evidence exists
to show that he cared for either King or Parliament. The
party which brought him peace and abolished the excise would
have his good will, whatever that might be worth.

The effect of the war on other classes is more easily traced.
In the spring of 1645 the fall of rents even in the Associated
Burdens Counties which had been untouched by war, was
on other estimated at a seventh, and it is probable that this
classes.
was too low an estimate. One proprietor complained
Falling off
of rents. that a fourth part of his leases in Suffolk had been
returned on his hands, and that from some parts of his estate
he received less than half of the income which he had enjoyed
before the war.[2] In the North, the injury to property had been
exceptionally severe. In the five years ending in 1646, the
Earl of Northumberland had lost either by actual damage or
by the non-payment of rents 42,500l.[3] In Wirral Hundred,
Cheshire, the rental of thirty-one estates dropped, between
1642 and 1647, from 4,142l. to 2,047l.; and in Gloucestershire
the rental of twenty-seven estates was similarly reduced from
6,542l. to 3,241l., the fall to about half the amount being
the same in both cases.[4]

From a modern point of view, the most faulty part of Parliamentary finance was the exaction of the Royalist composi-
Royalist tions. In the case of civil war we feel at once the
composi- injustice of marking off as specially guilty one portions.
tion of the population, and the folly of exasperating
that portion by laying special burdens on its shoulders. To

---

[1] See Cunningham's *Growth of English Industry and Commerce in
Modern Times*, 195–200.

[2] D'Ewes's Diary, *Harl. MSS.* 166, fol. 210b.

[3] Report, Sept. 1646; *Hist. MSS. Com. Reports*, iii. 86.

[4] *Calendar of the Proceedings of the Committee for Compounding*,
part i. pp. 60, 85. In both calculations I have omitted rents given under
only one date.

these considerations the men of the seventeenth century were blind. They had before them the precedents of the sweeping confiscations of estates of traitors by a long line of kings, and of the fines imposed on Catholics by the recusancy laws of the reign of Elizabeth. In their eyes the delinquent was as the traitor or the recusant had been. He had, as they fully believed, broken up the peace and order of the realm without adequate excuse, and with this idea firmly fixed in their minds, it is to their credit that they contented themselves with pecuniary mulcts, and, save in the instances of Strafford and Laud, had abstained from shedding the blood of their political opponents on the scaffold.

It is true that in every treaty with the King it was proposed to except a few of his adherents from pardon, but at the end

Banishment and confiscation.

of the war even these were allowed to leave the realm without hindrance, though the whole of their property was confiscated. Other Royalists were treated with more leniency in accordance with a system which

1643. March 27. Sequestration Ordinance.

had been gradually brought into existence. On March 27, 1643, an Ordinance declared that all who had directly or indirectly assisted the King were to be reckoned as delinquents, and that their property was to be sequestered by the Committee of the county in

Aug. 19. Allowance for wives and children.

which it was situated. Another Ordinance on August 19 mitigated this sentence so far as to set aside a sum, not exceeding a fifth of the sequestered income of the delinquent, for the benefit of his wife and children.[1]

In 1644, by summoning the Oxford Parliament, Charles unwittingly brought about an amelioration in the lot of some

1644. Jan. 30. Exceptional compositions.

who had hitherto supported him. On January 30, in that year, the Houses at Westminster, being anxious to attract deserters, offered pardon to all Royalists who would submit before a certain date. To this offer was affixed the condition that those who took

---

[1] *Husbands' Collection*, 13, 296. For the date of the first Ordinance see *L.J.* v. 672. See also vol. i. 100.

advantage of it should compound for their delinquency by the payment of a sum to be assessed on them towards the relief of the public burdens.[1] Thirteen persons who submitted on these terms were allowed to compound by paying a sum usually equal to two years' purchase of their estates,[2] and after the expiration of the term fixed, special leave was given to others to compound in the same way.[3]

It was not till October 1645, after the capture of Bristol, when the whole of England was falling under the power of the

1645.
Oct. 4.
General
composition. Parliament, that this method of dealing with Royalists was made general. All who would submit before December 1 were to be admitted to composition.[4] This limit of time was subsequently extended, and thus every opportunity given to all desirous of making their peace, save those whose names were on the list of persons exempted from pardon.

Delinquents who wished to free their estates from seques-

The Gold-
smiths' Hall
Committee. tration had accordingly to present themselves before the Committee for compounding which sat at Goldsmiths' Hall. This Committee, which was at first composed only of members of the House of Commons, was

1647.
Feb. 6.
Its recon-
struction. modified by an Ordinance of February 6, 1647, after which date it consisted of members of both Houses, with the addition of a few persons who were not members of either House.[5] The first step required of the

The delin-
quent to
take the
Covenant
and the
Negative
Oath. delinquent appearing before this Committee was the taking of the Covenant and of the Negative Oath, by which he bound himself never again to bear arms against the Parliament. After this he had to declare the full value of his estate, any misstatement rendering him liable to a heavy fine. These prelimina-

Classifica-
tion of
delinquents. ries having been accomplished, delinquents were arranged in classes. Members of Parliament, for instance, might be deprived of half of their estates, whilst undistinguished

---

[1] See vol. i. 501.   [2] *C.J.* iii. 572.
[3] As for instance to Serjeant Glanvile, *id.* iii. 720.
[4] *Husbands' Collection*, 751.   [5] *C.J.* v. 78.

Royalists might escape on payment of a sixth part.   The rates exacted, however, varied from time to time.[1]

Whatever may be thought of the treatment of the Royalist gentry, it was at least better than the treatment of the Royalist

Condition of the delinquent gentry;

clergy.   The gentleman might have to sell or mortgage part of his land, or to cut down the woods which were the pride of his estate, in order to pay his fine, but after this his account with Parliament was closed,

and of the delinquent clergy.

and he was free to enjoy what was left to him.   The clergyman noted either as a Royalist, or as attached to Episcopacy or the Prayer Book, was ejected from his living, and was thus deprived at one sweep of his means of

Fifths paid to wife and children.

livelihood ; excepting so far as he profited by the fifth of his late income, which was payable to his wife and children in the same way as to lay delinquents whose property was sequestered, though in his

Their payment sometimes withheld.

case it was payable not by the committee of sequestration, but by the incumbent who had succeeded him.   That this fifth was grudgingly paid, and sometimes absolutely withheld, has often been asserted, and it is highly probable that the charge was in many cases well founded.   As far, however, as can be judged from the fragmentary evidence which has come down to us, the dispossessed

Action of the Committee for Plundered Ministers;

clergy often obtained their rights from the Committee for Plundered Ministers, which, though it had been originally instituted to provide benefices for the Puritan clergy driven from their livings by the King's forces, ultimately acquired a practical supervision over the financial side of ecclesiastical affairs, and frequently intervened to secure the payment of the fifths.[2]

Another piece of evidence points in the same direction.   In each county there existed a committee charged with the general management of affairs in the Parliamentary interest, and it

---

[1] Preface to Mrs. Everett Green's *Calendar of the Committee for Compounding.*

[2] Proceedings of the Committee of Plundered Ministers, *Add. MSS.* 15, 669-71.

appears from the minute-book of the Dorset Committee, the
only one whose records are now accessible,[1] that in that county

and of the Dorset Committee.
at least the payment of fifths was enforced. In one
instance, in which the Puritan incumbent refused
to pay them to the wife of his predecessor, on the
ground that his conscience would not allow him to support
malignants, the committee promptly placed his living in the
hands of trustees, giving them directions first to pay over the
fifths to the wife, and only after she had been satisfied to make
over the remainder to the actual holder of the benefice.

It is needless to inquire minutely into the numbers of the
ejected clergy. Whether it exceeded or fell short of 2,000 [2] is

Significance of the ejectment.
of no historical importance. The real significance
of the ejectment is that it rendered permanent the
ecclesiastical disruption of the English Church.

At the time of the Reformation that Church had been brought
under two distinct influences. On the one hand, there was a

Two elements of the English Reformation.
conservative reverence for the past, moulded by the
critical spirit of the Renascence ; and, on the other,
a readiness to adopt, first from Zwingli, and afterwards from Calvin, a system built up out of the study
of the Bible itself, without regard to the historical development
of Christianity. During the Elizabethan struggle with Spain
and Rome the latter influence had been preponderant, and
when, in the reigns of James and Charles, a new and rising
school amongst the clergy threw itself back on the teaching of
the more conservative reformers, it suffered from the enormous disadvantage of having very few lay supporters. The
country gentlemen, slow to move, were Calvinists almost to a

Union between the Royalist clergy and laity.
man ; and though time would probably have modified their sentiments, Laud's impatient violence
checked the natural course of intellectual development. What Laud had failed to do the Long Parliament had gone far to accomplish. It had singled out the

---

[1] This book is in the possession of W. R. Bankes, Esq., of Kingston
Lacy, where he kindly allowed me to examine it.

[2] Walker's *Sufferings of the Clergy* ; Calamy's *The Church and the
Dissenters.*

Royalist gentleman and the anti-Calvinist clergyman for special penalties, with the result that every Royalist gentleman became not only a sworn foe to Puritanism, but a reverent admirer of doctrines and practices which ten years before he had pronounced to be detestable. Community of suffering draws friends more closely together than community of enjoyment.

Nor was the work of consolidation amongst the Royalists confined to the healing of the breach between the clergy and the laity. Minor differences no less tended to disappear. Amongst the laity Hyde and Culpepper were in close combination with Charles, whose policy they had long combated ; and amongst the clergy Sheldon and Morley, the friends of Falkland, were at one with Jeremy Taylor, the pupil and disciple of Laud. The whole phalanx of the opposition to the Long Parliament had closed its ranks.

Disappear-nce of minor differences.

It would be some time before this union would tell to the advantage of the losing party. Numerous as were the Royalist gentry, they were defeated and overthrown. Without armed force or political organisation, they had but to receive the law from their conquerors. Moreover the Presbyterian party in Parliament was also mainly composed of country gentlemen, and so long as the gentry were divided amongst themselves, the weight and influence of their class would be unable to tell.

The adoption of Presbyterianism in 1643 had been the result of mixed motives, in which the desire to conciliate the Scots was the dominant factor. Many therefore who voted for its establishment approved in their hearts of a very different kind of Presbyterianism from that of Scotland—a Presbyterianism such as had appeared in the Root and Branch Bill, in which there were no Church courts, and in which all ecclesiastical jurisdiction was exercised by lay commissioners. Even when Parliament authorised the establishment of Presbyterianism its mode of doing so was of the nature of a compromise, as the Church courts although called into existence were subjected to the control of the lay Parliament. In practice the system established was even more remote from the Scottish system. Though the often repeated

Parlia-mentary Presby-terianism.

statement that Presbyterianism was only established in London and Lancashire is very far from the truth,[1] yet it is true that for some little time only London and Lancashire accepted the new scheme :—London because there was there a strong middle class to take possession of the eldership ; Lanca-shire because a strong Puritan organisation was made popular by the presence of a strong Roman Catholic element in the population.

If, however, the Dorset Committee Book may be trusted as an exponent of the system which prevailed in the rest of Eng-

The Church and the county com-mittees. land—and there seems no reason why it should not—the new Church organisation outside London and Lancashire resembled that of the Root and Branch Bill far more than that of the later Parliamentary Ordi-nances.   In place of the lay commissioners of that Bill, there were the county committees.   These committees indeed had no definite authority to govern the Church, and did not inter-fere in any high-handed fashion unless in cases in which the patronage of a living was under sequestration.   Otherwise patrons still presented to the livings in their gift, and when the committee assumed the right of exercising patronage be-longing to delinquents, it appointed the candidate most accept-able to the parishioners, subject to his being able to produce a certificate of orthodoxy and good conduct from three approved ministers.

With the Dorset Committee at least interference with the Church went little farther.   In the course of many years it only

Want of discipline. silenced two ministers, one for using portions of the Book of Common Prayer, and the other a separatist preacher near Weymouth, whom, however, it only ventured to meddle with on the pretext that his sermons attracted the soldiers of the garrison from their duties, and thus exposed the fortifica-tions to an attack from the enemy.   Public worship for the most part followed the rules laid down in the Directory, but of

[1] See especially the introduction to the *Minutes to the Manchester Classes*, edited for the Chetham Society by Mr. W. A. Shaw, who will, I hope, conduct a more exhaustive inquiry into the history of English Presbyterianism than is possible in these pages.

internal discipline in the parishes themselves there is no trace,
a fact which goes far to explain the ease with which the country
The Puritan at large, in spite of occasional ebullitions of feeling
clergy not when maypoles were cut down and Christmas sports
unaccept-
able. prohibited, accepted ecclesiastical changes thorough
enough in other times to set every county in England ablaze.
The notion that Englishmen were at this time ardently craving
for relief from the Puritan teaching is one which receives no
countenance from documentary evidence. If they were ever
driven to revolt, it would be by a desire to throw off the burden
of taxes or to free themselves from military rule, not from any
eagerness to change the Puritan doctrines for those which
found credence amongst the cultivated divines who adhered to
the fortunes of Charles.

Whatever their motives might be, the gentry of both parties
were eventually swept into the current which made for a Re-
A study of storation. Even at the opening of the year 1647
personal influences drawing them in that direction were in
interests
desirable. operation, influences which will be better estimated
by dropping generalities for a time, and by studying the particular career of some personage who was not a violent partisan
of one side or the other.

Happily knowledge of this sort, though rarely attainable, is
offered by the voluminous correspondence of the Verneys of
The Claydon. Since the death of Sir Edmund Verney,
Verneys of
Claydon. who fell at Edgehill with the King's standard in his
Character hands, his eldest son, Sir Ralph Verney, had become
of Sir the head of the family. Sir Ralph was formed after
Ralph
Verney. the best model of an English country gentleman.
Critical by nature, he was, till near the close of a long life, the
opponent of every government in turn. He was alike dissatisfied with Laud, with the Presbyterians and the Independents,
with Charles II. and James II. At last in extreme old age he
died, politically contented as a member of Parliament under
William and Mary. In this Sir Ralph was the type of his class
and age. His own tender and self-reproachful character was
reflected in his melancholy face. In 1650, on the death of his
wife whom he dearly loved, he wrote to an intimate friend that

so solemn a time was a fitting occasion to search into the faults of his past life. Once in his youth, he confessed, he had been A youthful 'fond of a little face,' but the tale which followed escapade. was far from being one of passion or sin. The 'little face' was of painted glass in a church window. Slipping out in the dark from the house in which he was then staying, the young Ralph had mounted a ladder and carried off the prize. Years afterwards his conscience continued to prick him, and gave him no rest till his friend promised to visit the church and to drop two shillings into the poor-box, in atonement for the boyish theft.[1]

So delicate a conscience could ill brook the rough wear and tear of public life. Sir Ralph, who was a member of the 1643. Long Parliament, had remained at Westminster Sir Ralph refuses the when his father joined the King. In 1643, in con-Covenant. sequence of some religious scruple, the exact nature of which is unknown, he refused to take the Covenant. Having no sympathy with Royalism, he also refused to join the King, and betook himself with his wife and two of his three children to Rouen, from which place he afterwards removed to Blois. The rental of his estates might His income. seem to be enough to secure him a comfortable living, as from his Buckinghamshire property alone he received slightly more than 1,000*l.* a year,[2] and he had also property in Oxfordshire and Berkshire, the additional income from which sufficed at a later date, even after some of these lands had been sold, to raise his total income to more than 1,500*l.*[3]

His estates, considerable according to the reckoning of those days, were, however, not only heavily mortgaged to pay

---

[1] Sir R. Verney to Dr. Denton, June 2, 1650, *Verney MSS.* It is characteristic of the artistic weakness of the age that Sir Ralph adds that the glass was but a trifle, and that he could have had a piece of white glass put in for twopence. In letters written during a visit to Italy, he has no admiration to bestow on anything except a certain grotto at Rome. Since these pages were written, the most interesting portions of these letters have been printed in Lady Verney's *Memoirs of the Verney Family during the Civil War.*

[2] *Calendar of the Proceedings of the Committee for Compounding,* 68.

[3] Sir R. Verney to Mrs. Isham, Aug. 22, 1655, *Verney MSS.*

off debts contracted by his father during his life at Court, but
were burdened with rent-charges [1] payable to his three brothers
His estates encumbered. and five unmarried sisters, one sister only having
been married before his father's death. After these
payments had been disbursed, the amount left to himself was
but small even in good times, and when times were hard it
threatened to disappear altogether. What was worse, brothers
and sisters for the most part agreed in considering his purse
inexhaustible, and were constantly applying to him for addi-
tions to their scanty incomes, 40*l.* having been according to
his father's disposal of his property the allowance of each of
the sons, and 20*l.* of each of the daughters.

Accordingly, Sir Ralph had been forced to pawn his plate
to pay the expenses of his journey to France.[2] Before many
He pawns his plate. months passed he is found complaining that he has
had to make up the income of his sister Susan to 40*l.*
"Would to God," he writes, "every one of my children were
sure of 40*l.* a year to keep them from starving, and I should
sleep much the quieter, I assure you. Certainly, if the taxes,
the fall of rents, and other unavoidable losses, together with
how many depend upon me, were well considered, it would
appear a more liberal allowance than I perceive she deems it."[3]

In one respect Sir Ralph was more fortunate than his
neighbours. In the beginning of the war he obtained a letter
He has a double pro-tection. of protection for Claydon from the Earl of Essex on
account of his own adoption of the Parliamentary
cause, and another from Rupert on account of his
father's services to the King and his death at Edgehill.
Hoping, accordingly, that his house would be safe from plun-
derers to whichever side they belonged, Sir Ralph offered it

---

[1] This is not literally accurate, as the income of two sisters was to be
paid out of a pension of 400*l.* on the alnage revenue, payable to the Crown
by the Duke of Lennox (see *Memoirs of the Verney Family*, ii. 431).
As, however, this security was not now available, Sir Ralph paid the
income of his sisters out of his own estate, thus practically converting the
burden into a rent-charge.

[2] Sir R. Verney to Edmund Verney, Nov. 1643. *Verney MSS.*

[3] Sir R. Verney to Dorothy Leke, May $\frac{3}{13}$, 1644. *Ibid.*

as a refuge to any of his five unmarried sisters who might
be unable to find a home with other relatives. It
was but a poor retreat at the best for young girls in
time of war, with no woman of their own rank to
guide their steps.

In the summer of 1644 four of Sir Ralph's sisters were at
Claydon. Two of these, Susan and Penelope—or, to give
them the names by which they were invariably known
amongst their friends, Sue and Pen—were young
women, whilst the other two, Mary and Elizabeth,
were still children. With them was Sir Ralph's youngest son,
John, a child in weak health. The remaining unmarried sister
Margaret, or Peg, had for the time found a home elsewhere.

Sue and Pen at this time kept up a constant correspondence with their brother abroad. In their letters is never to
be found any appreciation of the great issues of the
struggle raging around them, nor is there any sign of
their possessing any kind of intellectual interest. Their minds
are entirely occupied with the everyday affairs of life, and they
fill the sheets which they despatch with querulous complaints
now of one person, now of another. Pen is vexed because the
nurse of her little nephew refuses to act also as lady's maid to
herself and to comb her hair. Sue is out of temper because
Mrs. Alcock, Sir Ralph's housekeeper, expects her to pay 25*l.*
a year out of the 40*l.* which was now her income for her 'diet,
and half a maid's,' besides requiring her to find 'firing, candles,
and soap' at her own expense. Sir Ralph had as little comfort
from his brothers as from his sisters. Tom, the eldest of the
three, was in the course of a long life guilty of every villainy
short of murder, and was constantly dunning Sir Ralph for
money in the most sanctimonious language. The next, the
chivalrous and affectionate Edmund,[1] was fighting on the King's
side, and, by some mischance, his letters, full of the tenderest
feeling, miscarried, leaving Sir Ralph under the impression
that his best-loved brother was as heartless as the rest. Henry,
the youngest, was a cold-hearted man of the world, whose chief
interest lay in horse-racing, and who lived through the civil

[1] See vol. i. 5.

wars in a well-to-do fashion, though there is nothing in the family correspondence to indicate the sources of his income.

The fortune of war played sad havoc amongst the Verney kindred. In the spring of 1644, Hillesdon House, hard by
Losses by Claydon, the residence of Sir Ralph's Royalist cousin,
war. Sir Alexander Denton, was stormed by Cromwell and burnt to the ground, Sir Alexander himself being lodged in the Tower. Later in the year a son of Sir Alexander, John Denton, was killed in a fight near Abingdon. "I think," wrote Mrs. Isham, an aunt of Sir Ralph and Sir Alexander, "if these times hold there will be no men left for women." [1]

Matters, however, had not reached that stage as yet. A Royalist, Colonel Smith, who was one of the Hillesdon
A marriage prisoners transferred to the Tower, employed his
in the Tower. enforced leisure in courting Sir Alexander's daughter. The couple were married, and, soon after the ceremony had been performed, Smith succeeded in effecting his escape. Suspicion of having aided in his evasion fell not only on his young wife, but also on Mrs. Isham, who lived in London, and in this suspicion Sue Verney, who was visiting her aunt at the time, was unfortunately involved. The charge, however, could not be substantiated against any one of the three ladies, and
Sue's im- after a week's imprisonment they were all released.
prisonment. Imprisonment in those days was expensive as well as unpleasant. The houses which had been occupied by persons arrested were usually ransacked by constables in the hope of finding evidence against them, and property was apt to disappear in the process. "I lost," wrote Sue to her brother, "almost all my linen, and the best of it new, so I have not any left that is fit to wear." [2]

Once more Mrs. Isham's melancholy forebodings were falsified. Sue had before long more pleasing tidings to impart.
Sue's en- "My brother Thomas," she wrote in November
gagement. 1644, "has wished me to a gentleman which has a very good fortune for me, for he has at the least 300*l.* a year." All the Verney sisters were Royalists, and Sue, therefore, was

[1] Mrs. Isham to Sir R. Verney, Aug. 15, *Verney MSS.*
[2] Sue Verney to Sir R. Verney, Oct. ? *Ibid.*

careful to add that if the gentleman had not been on the King's side, she would 'not think of it.' He was, it appeared, a widower without children, so that the match was in every way desirable. Unfortunately he was at the time 'a prisoner for his sovereign.' Before long, however, it came out that, as a matter of fact, John Alport, the gentleman in question, was confined as a debtor in the Fleet. Being a good-natured, weak man, he had become security for a friend, who had allowed the burden to rest upon his shoulders rather than on his own.[1]

Tom's activity in match-making was doubtless not unrewarded, and his next achievement was to find a suitor for Pen,

1645.
Pen's engagement.

a certain Mr. Thorne, who was also a widower, but whose estate was worth as much as 500*l.* a year. Henry Verney, who also interested himself in the affair, wrote to Sir Ralph, who was, of course, expected to find portions for the two girls, that Thorne is deeply in love with Pen, and 'presents her daily both with his purse and person.'[2] Then ensued the usual wrangle over the settlements, which, in time of peace, would probably have ended in a compromise. As it was, Thorne stood to his demands. He must have the interest of 1,000*l.* and good security for the capital. Sir Ralph offered an allowance of 50*l.* a year to his sister. Thorne insisted on an engagement to make over land worth 1,000*l.* within three years of the marriage. Sir Ralph, heavily indebted

The engagement broken off.

and harassed by claims on every side, declared this to be impossible, and the ardent lover broke off the engagement. Some years afterwards Pen married one of her Denton cousins without any settlement at all. Her husband, who was given to drink, had before marriage promised to abandon his bad habits if she would accept him, a promise which, it need hardly be said, was not strictly observed.

In Sue's case there were somewhat similar difficulties. She was constantly flinging her poverty and her thriftiness in her brother's face. On March 6, 1645, she wrote that she had

[1] Sue Verney to Sir R. Verney, Nov. 6. *Verney MSS.*

[2] The correspondence on this affair is too voluminous for special quotations.

but one gown, of 'very coarse stuff,' which had cost her 'but forty shillings, tailor's bill and all.' The greater part of her *Sue's corre- spondence.* wardrobe, she again complained, had disappeared at the time of her imprisonment. "I was left," she declared, "so bare in shifts that I was fain to wear my Aunt Isham's, whilst [1] I could make some very coarse ones, for fine I could not buy, and I never ware any so bad in all my life." [2] Then followed long pleadings for money. Sir Ralph did his utmost this time, even offering land as security if a loan could *Difficulty of raising money.* be raised upon it. His father's half-brother, Sir John Leke, wrote in July 1645, just after Naseby had been fought, and when, therefore, the worst stress of the war was at an end, that one of his friends might possibly be induced to lend, but his name was not to be disclosed, 'so jealous are they of discovery, for no man must be known to have money.' [3]

On his side, Sir Ralph pleaded the difficulty of giving security that would be considered satisfactory in the City. *Sir Ralph impover- ished.* "It is true," he wrote, "my estate at present lies . . . in the midst of troubles. I have no remedy for that. Were it in my power to remove it, I would soon place it in the midst of Cheapside to encourage the moneyed citizens to lend upon it." [4] In a little less than two years he had received but 90*l.* out of which to meet his own family expenses. "Losses, taxes, brothers, sisters, and some *1646. Sue's marriage.* little interest hath swallowed up the rest, and yet I am railed at beyond measure." [5] Finally, in August 1646, Sue was married to John Alport, and spent her honeymoon happily in the Fleet prison.

It was not only on the Verney family that the pressure of *An offer refused.* the times fell. "I have lately received your letter," wrote another young lady to her suitor, "by which I perceive you have received mine, wherein I sent you

---

[1] *i.e.* until.
[2] Sue Verney to Sir R. Verney, March 16. *Verney MSS.*
[3] Sir J. Leke to Sir R. Verney, July 3. *Ibid.*
[4] Sir R. Verney to Sir J. Leke, Aug. 11. *Ibid.*
[5] Sir R. Verney to Dr. Denton, Sept. 3. *Ibid.*

my full and instant resolution concerning the disposal of myself. I will never do it without the consent of my mother, by whom I must in duty be advised ; and, though I were never so free and at my own disposing, I will in no sort engage myself in the way of marriage without her free consent. Besides, these distracted times affright me from thinking of marriage, and the rather because I conceive that all men's estates are very desperate, for aught that I can hear ; and whereas you desired me to make inquiry of you and your estate, I cannot hear of any you have at all ; and I would have you know, without an estate I will neither marry you nor no man living, and such as my friends will like of. This is my resolution, and the reason why I deal so plainly with you is this : you have made so great professions of your affections in your letters to me, for which I must needs return you many thanks." [1]

'These distracted times' form the burthen of well nigh every letter in this vast correspondence. On none did the sorrow fall more heavily than Cary, the only one of Ralph's sisters who was married in her father's lifetime. Her husband was Thomas Gardiner, the son of the Sir Thomas Gardiner of Cuddesdon, who had been Recorder of London, and Charles's candidate for the Speakership of the Long Parliament. By an arrangement not uncommon in those days, the young couple were to live in the house of the parents of the bridegroom. Between Cary and her mother-in-law there was constant bickering, but her husband's kindness compensated for the discomfort. When the Civil War broke out he took service in the King's army, and so distinguished himself at the relief of Newark, that Rupert chose him to bear to the King the tidings of victory. Charles knighted him on his arrival, and everything seemed to mark him out for a distinguished career ; but in 1645 he was killed in a skirmish, and his young widow, who was in immediate expectation of becoming a mother, was thrust without a penny upon the house of her father-in-law, and thrown for support on the slender resources of her brother.

Cary Gardiner's marriage.

[1] Mary Villiers to Col. Busbridge, Aug. 23. *Verney MSS.*

Sir Ralph was personally in trouble enough. On September 22, 1645, he was expelled the House for absenting himself from his duties as a member. His sensitive mind felt the sentence as a bitter trial. " I received," he wrote to his friend Sir Roger Burgoyne, who had informed him of his misfortune, "your most sad letter . . . which I confess brought me tidings of one of the greatest and most inexpressible afflictions that ever yet befel me, for which my soul shall mourn in secret."[1] One thing alone was clear to him. He could not soil his conscience by taking the Covenant, even to avoid beggary itself. He soon learnt that beggary was impending. Though his only fault was absence from Parliament, and though he had never even breathed a word in the King's favour, the sequestration of his estate was talked of at Westminster. It was no mere question of a composition which would have compelled him to sell a portion of his estate to save the rest. No one was admitted to compound till he had first taken the Covenant, and the Covenant Sir Ralph would not take. Months, however, passed by without news of the dreaded sentence, and during this long period of suspense, fear alternated with hope. It was not until October 14, 1646, that Claydon was actually sequestered.

Though the story of the Verneys is but the story of a single family, it is a sample of the miseries weighing on many hearts, which combined to produce an ardent longing for peace as the only possible relief.

Side notes:
1645.
Sept. 22.
Sir Ralph
expelled the
House,

and
threatened
with se-
questration.

1646.
Claydon
sequestered.

The story
of the
Verneys
a sample.

---

[1] Sir R. Verney to Sir R. Burgoyne, Oct. 10, *Verney MSS.* ; *C.J.* iv. 283.

CHAPTER XLVII.

THE PRESBYTERIANS AND THE ARMY.

ON February 3, 1647, Charles set out from Newcastle, travelling to Holmby House by easy stages, under the guardianship of Commissioners of the English Parliament. At Ripon he touched for the King's evil. As he approached Leeds, the road, for about two miles, was crowded with persons who had ostensibly come to be restored to health by his wonder-working hands, but who were for the most part attracted by curiosity.[1] Curiosity easily passed into enthusiasm. Royalism had gained favour in the North during the Scottish occupation, and wherever the King passed bells were rung and every sign of rejoicing was shown. When he drew near Nottingham, Fairfax rode out to meet him, alighted from his horse, and kissed his hand. "The General," said Charles to one of the commissioners, "is a man of honour. He hath been faithful to his trust, and kept his word with me."[2] Some thought of the lip-service of the Scottish nobility doubtless rose in Charles's mind as he spoke, but everything that he witnessed on his journey contributed to put him in a good humour. Even in Puritan Northamptonshire hundreds of the gentry appeared to escort him, and in Northampton itself bells were rung and guns fired in his honour. Wherever he

margin notes:
1647
Feb. 3.
The King
sets out for
Holmby.

Feb. 7.
Touching
for the
King's evil.

A hearty
welcome.

Feb. 13.
Fairfax
meets
Charles.

Charles
in North-
amptonshire.

---

[1] The Commissioners to the Speaker of the House of Lords, Feb. 3, 9. *L.J.* viii. 713; ix. 6.
[2] *The King's Majesty's Speech*, E. 377, 12.

showed himself he was greeted with shouts of " God bless your
Majesty ! " When he reached Holmby, though still
practically a captive, he fancied his cause half won,
and was in excellent spirits.[1]

Feb. 16.
He reaches
Holmby.

In truth, the welcome accorded to Charles was very similar
to that which had deluded him on his return from Scotland in
1641. His subjects were sick of heavy taxation, of
the continual existence of an army which made taxation necessary, and of the yoke of the County Committees ; but they were not yet in a mood to cast themselves
unreservedly at his feet. " No man knows," was the burden
of a letter from Northampton, " what a bondage it is to be
under the power of an army, but they that feel it." To settle
the Church—that is to say, to establish Presbyterianism ; to
defend the King from libellers, and to put down the committeemen, were, according to a lively rhymester, all the steps which
it was necessary to take for the consolidation of
peace.[2] It seemed hardly possible to garner in the
results of the war and to secure the permanence of
the religious and political institutions which had grown up
during its course if there was to be a complete change in the
form of government. If the King refused to take his place at
the head of the new order of things, the outlook would indeed
be gloomy. Distractions of every kind would be multiplied as
each section of the community strove to embody in new constitutional forms its own views of that which was necessary or
desirable. It was the reluctance to face this danger of drifting
into anarchy which led each party in turn to make efforts to
win Charles over to its side, whilst Charles's persistency in
abiding by his own ideals was to render every one of these
efforts futile.

Explanation
of the
popular
welcome.

Importance
of gaining
the King.

Already, before Charles set out from Newcastle, the leading
Presbyterian Peers, Warwick, Holland, and Manchester, combined with Northumberland, who represented the less thoroughgoing Independents, to trace
out the lines of a pacification which would, as they hoped,

January.
A fresh
Presbyterian
negotiation.

[1] *The King's Majesty's Propositions*, E. 377, 16.
[2] *The Copy of a Letter*, E. 373, 20 ; *Time's Whirligig*, E. 374, 10.

be less objectionable to the King than the propositions offered
to him in the preceding year. They took for the basis of
their scheme the concession of Presbyterianism for three years
which Charles himself had suggested in September,[1] but which
he had in his private correspondence explained to be a contrivance by which he hoped to gain the ultimate re-establishment
of Episcopacy. According to the proposals now made Charles
was to concede Presbyterianism for three years and the militia
for ten, whilst he would no longer be asked to sign the
Covenant. On his acceptance of these conditions, he was to
be invited to come to Theobalds, or to some other place in the
immediate neighbourhood of London. Bellièvre, who had
been admitted to the consultations in which this plan was
concocted, engaged to forward it to Henrietta Maria, in order
that, if she approved of it, she might transmit it to her
husband.[2]

That the Presbyterian leaders should thus have swallowed
Charles's bait was a matter of capital importance. It was by
their acceptance of his terms that their coalition with
the Royalists, which almost restored him to the
throne in 1648, and which actually restored his son
in 1660, was rendered possible. In so doing they had fallen
back on the natural basis of Parliamentary statesmanship, a
readiness to accept a compromise, and a belief that in the long
run progress is attainable through the higgling of the political
market. They calculated that before the three years had
expired some arrangement would have been come to satisfactory
both to the King and to themselves. Their greatest error was
their failure to realise that in Charles they had to do with a
man who regarded any possible compromise merely as a half-
way house to the complete realisation of his own ideas, and
that as long as they left to him the negative voice, he could
reject any Bills presented to him, and so could by his mere silence
restore Episcopacy, after the lapse of three years, to the legal
position which it held in the summer of 1641.

The Presbyterians swallow the bait.

---

[1] See p. 166.

[2] Bellièvre to Mazarin, $\frac{\text{Jan. 29}}{\text{Feb. 8}}$, *R.O. Transcripts.* Memorandum sent
to Mazarin, *Constitutional Documents,* 226.

There was certainly nothing in the language which at this time escaped Charles's lips to render it probable that he would

Feb. 10.
Charles's
unguarded
language.

yield on any important point. On February 10 a letter from one of the commissioners in attendance upon him was read in the House of Commons, from which it appeared that he had been so indiscreet as to say openly that, if he had but patience for six months, things would be in such confusion that he would obtain his ends without trouble.[1] A letter was intercepted in which Charles himself wrote to an old Cavalier, bidding him to keep himself in readiness and reminding him that there were still many honest men

Feb. 12.
Bellièvre
in the City.

in England. So alarming were these revelations, that when Bellièvre visited the City on the 12th with the object of urging the acceptance of the Presbyterian scheme, with certain modifications contained in a letter which he had received from the Queen, he found all doors closed against him. Peace, he wrote to Mazarin, was desired by the Royalists above all other things, but it was now the general opinion that Charles did not wish for peace.[2]

Nor were the Presbyterians in Parliament more conciliatory than their brethren in the City. On February 9 the Commons

Feb. 9.
The King's
Com-
munion
plate to be
melted.

ordered that the Communion plate of the Chapel Royal should be melted down and transformed into a dinner service for the King's use.[3] On March 2

March 2.
No house-
hold to be
provided.

they declined to provide a household for him, apparently to indicate that he was not to be treated as a King till he had accepted the Parliamentary terms.[4]

March 8.
He is not
allowed
his own
chaplains.

On the 8th the Lords took the initiative in refusing his request to be allowed his own chaplains, a request which Charles had hoped to make palatable by the specious plea that he needed their advice upon any

proposals which might be made to him for the alteration of

---

[1] "Qu'il est certain qu'ayant patience six mois toutes choses se brouilleront, en sorte que ses affaires se feront sans qu'il s'en mesle." Bellièvre ascribes this letter to a brother of Sir Henry Mildmay, but there was no Mildmay amongst the commissioners.

[2] Bellièvre to Mazarin, Feb. $\frac{12}{22}$. *R. O. Transcripts.*

[3] Whitacre's Diary, *Add. MSS.* 31,116, fol. 301.

[4] *C.J.* v. 102.

religion.[1] "I wish," said Marten audaciously, when the vote of the Lords was brought down to the other House, "the King may have two chaplains, as I desire to prepare him for heaven."[2] The Commons, taking no notice of this outrageous argument, concurred with the Lords.

Both Houses, in fact, were now controlled by a Presbyterian majority; a considerable number of members who had previously voted with the Independents in order to be rid of the Scots, swinging round to the Presbyterians as soon as that object had been gained. The new majority, however, had no easy task before it. Its leaders, Holles, Stapleton and the others, were men of no special ability, and were hardly likely to succeed in persuading the King to acknowledge the doctrine of Parliamentary control. The problem with which they were immediately confronted was scarcely less difficult. The nation was crying out for a diminution of taxation, and no diminution of taxation was possible without a complete or partial disbandment of the army.

A Presbyterian majority.

Difficulties before it.

On February 15 there was a demonstration of popular feeling serious enough to startle Parliament into immediate financial action. A man who had purchased an ox at Smithfield refused to pay the excise. The bystanders took his part, and in the tumult which ensued the collectors were cudgelled, their office burnt down, their books torn, and 80*l.* scattered or carried off. It required the personal intervention of the Lord Mayor and Sheriffs to quell the disturbance.[3] The Presbyterians were ready enough to move in the direction indicated by the riot. On the next day they welcomed a petition from Suffolk asking for the establishment of Presbyterianism as the national religion, the suppression of an accursed toleration, and the disbandment of the army.[4] Before long the example of Suffolk was followed by most of the other Associated Counties.

Feb. 15. A riot at Smithfield.

Feb. 16. A Suffolk petition.

On February 18 the Presbyterian scheme for dealing with

---

[1] *L.J.* ix. 68, 69.
[2] Letter of Intelligence, March 18, *Clarendon MSS.* 2,472.
[3] *The Weekly Account*, E. 377, 3.　　　[4] *L.J.* ix. 18.

the aimy was brought forward in the Commons. It was first proposed that 6,600 horse and dragoons should be maintained in England, and as this motion only involved the reduction of the existing force by 400,[1] it was agreed to without a division. The first serious conflict came on the following day, when the Presbyterians, by a majority of only 10,[2] carried a resolution that, except in garrisons, no infantry should be kept in pay in England.[3]

Feb. 18.
Scheme
for the
reduction of
the army.

Feb. 19.

The plan thus adopted was from a constitutional point of view not without its merits. The cavalry, the most difficult part of an army to train and discipline, was to be preserved almost intact. Cavalry, however, without the co-operation of infantry was helpless in a campaign, and the only infantry on which such a force could rely would be the trained bands, which, composed as they were of civilians summoned from their daily occupations for temporary service, would be most unlikely to assist in the establishment of a military despotism. The whole organisation of the country would be of a piece. As in the State Parliament was to act as a check upon the Crown, and in the Church the lay elders were to act as a check on the ministers, so in the army the civilian infantry were to act as a check on the professional cavalry. It is undeniable that a certain unity of idea pervaded the whole plan of the Presbyterian party.

Advan-
tages of the
scheme.

The only difficulty remaining was to dispose of the existing infantry, and on the 20th a letter from Ormond[4] offered a means of bringing the intended disbandment within moderate limits. Ormond, as might have been foreseen, had at last found it necessary to make his choice, between the Papal Nuncio and the English Parliament.[5] On January 16 the citizens of Dublin refused longer to support the 1,425 men who formed the only effective force remaining under his command.[6] For a few days he continued to make head against this

Feb. 20.
A letter
from
Oimond.

Jan. 16.
Dublin
refuses to
support his
soldiers.

---

[1] There were 7,000 horse and dragoons in the New Model.

[2] 158 to 148.   [3] *C.J.* v. 90, 91.   [4] *C.J.* v. 91.   [5] See p. 187.

[6] Lambert to Ormond, Jan. 16; Petition of the Citizens of Dublin, Jan. 16, *Carte MSS.* fol. 145, 149.

sea of troubles, but on February 6 he abandoned hope, and, waiving his former stipulation that he should not be required to leave Dublin till the King's consent had been obtained,[1] he offered to surrender the Lord Lieutenantship to the English Parliament without any other conditions than those necessary to secure his own personal good treatment.[2] From the despatch in which Ormond announced his resolution, the Houses learnt that the burden of the war in Ireland would henceforth fall on their shoulders, and they were thus enabled to offer service in Ireland to those soldiers of the New Model who were unwilling to return to civil life.

Feb. 6.
He offers
to sur-
render his
office.

Prospect of
employment
for the Eng-
lish soldiers.

Before shaping out a plan for the reduction of Ireland, the House completed its scheme for the military establishment in England. It was agreed that, with some stated exceptions, the existing fortifications should be demolished. Walled towns were to be rendered easily accessible, whilst actual fortresses, like Ashby and Donnington, were to be so dealt with as to leave no more than picturesque ruins for the enjoyment of future generations. The fewer the defensible positions left, the less numerous would be the garrisons to be kept in pay, and the more difficult would it be to resist the authority of the central government.

English
fortifications
to be de-
molished.

Whatever merits the plan of the Presbyterians may have had, their mode of dealing with the army was most inopportune. They seem, indeed, to have thought that, with the nation on their side, they could afford to treat the army with contempt. On March 4 the Lords, acting as though it were a light thing to rouse the indignation of every man in the ranks, rejected an Ordinance providing for the continuance of the assessment on which the payment of the troops depended.[3] This vote proved to be only the first of a long series of blunders. On the 6th the Lords followed up their mistake by forbidding Fairfax to quarter his troops in the Eastern Association, as though they were anxious to reserve a space in which a new

March 4.
The Lords
refuse to
continue
the pay of
the army,

March 6.
and inter-
fere with
Fairfax.

---

[1] See p. 161. [2] *L.J.* ix. 29.

[3] *Idem*, ix. 57.

force might be brought into existence to hold head against the existing army.[1]

In the Commons the conduct of the Presbyterian leaders was equally provocative. On the 5th they attempted to oust

March 5.
Attack on Fairfax in the Commons.

Fairfax from the command of the horse and dragoons, which were henceforth to constitute the regular army ; but at this point their followers broke away from them and frustrated their plans. On the 6th a

March 6.
A letter from Fairfax.

letter reached the House in which Fairfax, with every expression of good-will, offered to co-operate with Parliament in despatching troops to Ireland. On this the

Numbers of the proposed Irish army.

Commons proceeded to fix the numbers of the new Irish army. It was to consist of 8,400 foot, 1,200 dragoons, and 3,000 horse, making in all a force of 12,600 men. A further vote decided that this whole body of horse and foot should be formed out of the army under Fairfax.[2] There would thus remain for disbandment about 6,000 foot.[3] As, however, the ambassadors of France and Spain

Effect of the new arrangements on the existing army.

were on the look-out for recruits, and as it was probable that many of the men desired to return to their homes, the number of foot soldiers driven against their inclinations to relinquish a military career could not be large. As far as the horse and dragoons were concerned, there were needed for England and Ireland together, 10,800 men,[4] or 3,800 more than Fairfax's army could produce.

Having thus, as they fondly imagined, provided against any discontent amongst the soldiers, the Presbyterians struck at the higher organisation of the army. On March 8 the House resolved that, with the exception of Fairfax himself, there

---

[1] *L.J.* ix. 66.　　　　　　　[2] *C.J.* v. 107.

[3] The number of foot originally in the New Model was 14,000. As 8,400 were wanted for Ireland, there would remain 5,600. As, however, the army was now slightly increased (Whitacre's Diary, *Add. MSS.* 31,116, fol. 306), the number of foot to be disposed of may be reckoned at about 6,000.

[4] For England 6,600, and for Ireland 4,200 ; the horse and dragoons of the New Model being 7,000.

should be no officer in the new army with rank above that
of a colonel ; that no member of the House of Commons
should hold any command in England, and that no
one who refused to take the Covenant should be an
officer at all. · These resolutions, which were obviously
directed at Cromwell's military position, were all carried without a division. A farther motion that all officers should
conform to the government of the Church established by
Parliament was the first which the Independents ventured to
challenge, but on this.they were beaten by a majority of 136
to 108.[1]

March 8.
An attack on
Cromwell.

It can hardly be doubted that if all England had been
polled the result would have been overwhelmingly in favour of
any scheme which would diminish or set aside the
preponderance of the army. Yet a wise dealing
with minorities is not the least of the arts of government, and in this art the Presbyterians had yet to prove their
skill. On March 10, by their appointment, a long-
announced fast was held with the object of imploring
Divine protection against heresy and schism, and,
unless Cromwell was misinformed, some 200 men
were raised near Covent Garden to prevent the soldiers
'from cutting the Presbyterians' throats.' On the
11th the Houses received a petition from Essex
warning them against the danger of an approach of
the army to the neighbourhood of the City, and imploring
them that the petitioners might not 'be eaten up, enslaved,
and destroyed by an army raised for' their defence.
A few days later Cromwell, writing to Fairfax,
quoted this petition as showing that there wanted
not 'in all places men who have so much malice against
the army as besots them.' "Never," he added, "were the
spirits of men more embittered than now. Surely the devil
hath but a short time !"[2]

*Majorities
and
minorities.*

March 10.
A fast
against
heresy and
schism.

March 11.
A petition
from Essex.

*Cromwell's
comment
on it.*

---

[1] *C.J.* v. 107.

[2] *L.J.* ix. 72. Cromwell to Fairfax, *Carlyle*, Letter xliii. In the
original the letter is undated. Carlyle suggests that it was written on
March 11, but I incline to put it a few days later. The soldiers who were

For the present at least the Presbyterians in the House of Commons refused to adopt this direct defiance of the army to
Reply to the Essex petitioners. which the Essex petitioners had invited them. By the mouth of the Speaker, the House replied that it had 'no cause of jealousy of the army,' and liberty
The army kept at a distance from London. was given to Fairfax to quarter his troops wherever he saw fit.[1] Fairfax accordingly forbade his regiments to approach within twenty-five miles of London, and with this the House professed itself well satisfied.[2] It had already voted, in the teeth of the Lords,[3] that the assessment of 60,000*l.* a month should be continued for the support of the armies of England and Ireland.[4] When on
March 17. A City petition. March 17 the Presbyterians in the City attempted to force the hands of their allies in the House by presenting a petition requiring that the King should take the Covenant and the army be speedily disbanded,[5] no heed was taken of their hasty counsels, and it seemed possible that the Presbyterian majority in the House of Commons might prove itself capable of disposing of the military difficulty in a manner satisfactory to itself and to the country.

Of all men living no one was so deeply touched as Cromwell by the rout of the Independent Parliamentary party.
Cromwell's Parliamentary defeat. Not only was his policy defeated, but he himself was practically excluded from military service in England. It was probably on this occasion that the bitterness of his soul found expression in a conversation with Ludlow. "It is a miserable thing," he is reported to have said, "to serve a Parliament, to which let a man be never so faithful, if one pragmatical fellow amongst them rise and asperse him, he shall never wipe it off, whereas, when one serves a general, he may do as much service, and yet be free from all blame and envy."[6]

to cut the Presbyterians' throats were probably those who were in London absent on leave.

[1] *C.J.* v. 114.   [2] *Ibid.* v. 115.   [3] See p. 218.
[4] *C.J.* v. 114.   [5] *Ibid.* v. 115.
[6] *Ludlow* (ed. 1751) i. 160. The conversation is there placed soon after the death of Essex; but Ludlow's chronology is so loose, that I have

Irritated as Cromwell was, it does not follow that he had any thought of resistance. The army had constantly boasted

He has no thought of resistance.

Declares that the army will obey the Houses,

that it was a Parliamentary army, and the belief that obedience to Parliament was the only safeguard against anarchy had settled itself firmly in Cromwell's mind. "In the presence of Almighty God, before whom I stand," he had recently declared to the House, "I know the army will disband and lay down their arms at your door, whenever you will command them." [1]

How little disposed Cromwell was to stir up a military revolution is shown by his actions. Towards the end of

and proposes to take service in Germany.

March he was weighing, in frequent conferences with the Elector Palatine, a proposal to transfer himself, with as many of the victors of Naseby as he could carry with him, to the battle-fields of Germany. News had arrived that the negotiations at Münster were likely to end in a grant of toleration to the Lutherans and its denial to the Calvinists ; and Cromwell might well have been prepared, if it proved true, to wield his victorious sword in the cause of toleration in Germany now that he was compelled to sheath it in England. [2]

---

ventured to transfer it to a date at which the story can be fitted in with existing conditions. In the autumn of 1646 Cromwell and his friends had a Parliamentary majority.

[1] Walker (*Hist. of Independency*, 31) connects these words with the passing of an Ordinance for disbandment. He probably refers to an Ordinance for raising money for this purpose which was brought in on March 20, and read a second time on March 22. That some such language was used by Cromwell at this time is shown by Lilburne's letter to Cromwell on March 25, in which he says that he had heard the day before that Cromwell was thwarting a petition from the army ' because forsooth you had engaged to the House they shall lay down their arms whensoever they shall command them.' *Jonah's Cry out of the Whale's Belly*, p. 3. E. 400, 4.

[2] This negotiation with the Elector Palatine is only known from Bellièvre's despatch of July $\frac{15}{25}$ (*R. O. Transcripts*). The ambassador states that the Elector had intended to ask Parliament for troops ' et qu'il avait en ce sujet de grandes conferences avec Cromwell . . . qui se croyoit lors necessité de quitter l'Angleterre.' Here there is no date given, but

The project thus entertained by Cromwell was, however, speedily abandoned, possibly because the ripening of events convinced him that he had still a place in England. The Presbyterian leaders, encouraged by Cromwell's opinion that the army was ready to submit to disbandment, had obtained from the Committee for Irish Affairs the appointment of a deputation—of which Clotworthy and Waller were the most distinguished members—to visit Fairfax's headquarters at Saffron Walden in order to engage officers and men as volunteers for service in Ireland. On March 21 a meeting of forty-three officers, with Fairfax in the chair, received the deputation in Saffron Walden church. The officers, after hearing the message brought to them, all promised to do what they could to induce their men to go to Ireland, but not one of them would volunteer personally until a satisfactory answer had been given to four questions : What regiments were to be kept in pay in England? Who was to command the army in Ireland ? What assurance was there for the payment and subsistence of those who went to Ireland ? Finally, what satisfaction was to be given 'in point of arrears and indemnity, for the past service in England?' On the last two demands the meeting was unanimous. On the first there were twelve, and on the

Marginal notes:
Cromwell remains in England.
A deputation to the army.
March 21. A meeting at Saffron Walden.
Four questions asked.

Bellièvre puts the statement just before he refers to another event which took place early in April. We also know that on March 25 the Elector acquainted the House of Lords with news which he had received from Münster (*L.J.* ix. 105). According to *The Moderate Intelligencer* (E. 383, 8), this news related to an attempt of the Lutherans to exclude Calvinists from toleration in the coming peace, and this explanation is confirmed by a paper presented by the Elector on May 4, relating to a proposed confirmation of the Treaty of Prague in which Calvinists were excluded from toleration. Salvetti, too, wrote to Gondi on April $\frac{2}{12}$ (*Add. MSS.* 27, 962 L. fol. 341) that the Elector had asked Parliament to allow him to use its army in the recovery of his states. No doubt the Presbyterians would have been delighted thus to get rid of Cromwell and the sectarians of the army. I may add that Cromwell's conduct on this occasion strengthens my view that he supported the first Self-Denying Ordinance with the real intention of abandoning his position in the army.

second seven, dissentients. On the following day a second

March 22.
A second
meeting. meeting was held; but with a few exceptions all present adhered to their previous resolution, and it was agreed that a petition should be drawn up to give effect to their wishes.

Amongst the supporters of the petition were some of the most notable officers of the New Model: the two Hammonds,

Leaders
of the
movement. Whalley, Robert Lilburne, Okey, Pride, and, above all, Commissary-General Ireton, who wielded the pen as well as the sword. Colonel Rich objected to the first question being put, but was immovable on the other three.[1]

The members of the deputation took offence at the determination of the officers to embody their demands in a petition.

View of the
deputation. They seem to have been of opinion that the officers had no grievances whatever, and that in any case they had no right to question the orders of Parliament. They

They appeal
to Fairfax. accordingly appealed to Fairfax, and Fairfax, giving them good words, disclaimed all knowledge of the existence of a petition, but assured them that whenever it reached him he would take care that nothing was retained in it which could give reasonable offence to Parliament.[2] Private solicitations with particular officers were more effectual than the public appeal to the assembled officers, and by the night

Twenty-nine
officers
volunteer. of the 22nd twenty-nine of them had consented to abandon the demand for information as to the regiments selected for service in England, and to volunteer for Ireland in confidence that Parliament, without urgency on their part, would give satisfaction on the remaining wishes of the meeting.[3]

No doubt many of the officers who still supported the four demands were actuated by other motives besides those which

Motives of
the officers
in oppo-
sition. they ostensibly put forward. They wanted, it may fairly be argued, to oppose Parliament mainly because they hoped to make use of the army to baffle the restrictive policy of the Presbyterians. Yet it was only by

[1] *L.J.* ix. 112. *Waller's Vindication,* 49, 50.
[2] *Id.* 51. [3] *L.J.* ix. 114.

placing the material interests of the soldiers in the foreground that they could hope to keep the army united. On all other matters it was far from homogeneous. Large numbers of the soldiers cared little for politics or religion. On a question of the pocket they were ready to stand up as one man, and the question of the pocket was, in a very real sense, a pressing one. The pay of the foot-soldiers was now eighteen weeks in arrear, and that of the horse and dragoons no less than forty-three.[1] The need of indemnity for injuries to life or property done in time of war was even more important. A soldier named Freeman had recently been subjected to an action on account of his conduct as a soldier ; and though the House of Commons had promptly interposed on his behalf, and had ordered the judges to dismiss all similar actions in future,[2] those who were exposed to danger were well-advised in asking that the question might be settled in their favour in some way more binding on the courts than the order of a single House.

The army not homogeneous.

Long arrears owing.

Need of an indemnity.

Under these circumstances the attitude of the officers was certain to have a powerful effect in the ranks. The soldiers, knowing that they had most to lose if the interests of the army were neglected, drew up a petition of their own, differing in many respects from the petition of the officers, and couched in somewhat violent language. It was with some difficulty that the officers, as soon as they became aware of its existence, induced the men to tone it down, and to address it, not to Parliament, but to Fairfax.

A soldiers' petition.

It is toned down by the officers.

The soldiers' petition, in its final shape, was not unreasonable. Besides a request for indemnity and for the payment of arrears, it contained demands that those soldiers who had formerly volunteered to serve Parliament might be exempted from impressment in any future war ;[3] that the widows and orphans of soldiers killed in service

Its demands.

---

[1] *C.J.* v. 126.   [2] *The Moderate Intelligencer,* E. 386, 3.

[3] This demand would therefore not apply to the pressed men who formed a large part of the infantry.

might receive pensions; that such soldiers as had in any way suffered through their adherence to Parliament might be compensated for their losses; and that, finally, the whole army might, up to the time of its disbandment, be supplied with enough ready money to meet the expenses incurred in the quarters of the soldiers.[1]

Moderate as these demands were, they provoked a storm of indignation at Westminster, where it was held that soldiers Indignation at Westminster. were bound to unquestioning obedience. It is especially noteworthy that even Cromwell looked on the Cromwell dissatisfied. petition[2] with dissatisfaction, as an attempt of soldiers to dictate to Parliament with arms in their hands.[3] Yet Cromwell, if he had had his way, would surely

---

[1] *The Declaration of the Army*, E. 390, 26. Waller in his *Vindication*, p. 51, says that the petition was 'pretended to come from the soldiers, but framed and minted by some of the principal officers.' The account given in the *Declaration*, that it was first drawn up by the soldiers and afterwards put into shape by the officers is probably true.

[2] The officers' petition may be defended on the ground that Parliament by asking them to volunteer for Ireland gave them a right to state the terms on which they were willing to do so. The soldiers' petition was a request for fair treatment whether they volunteered or not; but its being addressed to Fairfax ought to have been accepted as bringing it within the bounds of military discipline.

[3] On this point the evidence of John Lilburne is conclusive. "O dear Cromwell," he wrote to him, "the Lord open thine eyes and make thy heart sensible of those snares that are laid for thee in that vote of the House of Commons of 2,500*l. per annum* (*C.J.* v. 57). . . . As poor Mordecai . . . said unto Queen Esther, so say I to thee . . . Thou great man, Cromwell! Think not with thyself that thou shalt escape in the Parliament House more than all the rest of the Lamb's poor despised redeemed ones, and therefore, O Cromwell, if thou altogether holdest thy peace, or stoppest and underminest, as thou dost our and the army's petitions at this time, then shall enlargement and deliverance arise to us poor afflicted ones, that have hitherto doted too much on thee, O Cromwell, from another place than you silken Independents; . . . and therefore, if thou wilt pluck up thy resolutions, and go on bravely in the fear and name of God, and say with Esther, 'If I perish, I perish'; but if thou would not, know that here before God, I arraign thee at his dreadful bar, and there accuse thee of delusions and false words deceitfully, for betraying us, our wives and children, into the Haman-like tyrannical

have dealt with the offenders in a gentle spirit, and have avoided any word or act which might render them desperate of obtaining justice. The very contrary course was taken by the Presbyterian majority. On the 27th Clotworthy, after making a report of the proceedings of the commissioners, produced a copy of the soldiers' petition, which the House abruptly ordered Fairfax to suppress. The whole matter was then referred to a committee, but beyond a cold acknowledgment 'that, notwithstanding any information this day given to the House, they have a good opinion of the army,' no effort was made to convince the soldiers that the Commons were in any way ready to listen to their complaints.[1]

March 27.
A report from the Commissioners.

The soldiers' petition to be suppressed.

No doubt it was difficult to comply even with the justifiable wishes of the army. The arrears of the New Model amounted to no less than 331,000*l*.,[2] and it would not be easy to raise

clutches of Holles and Stapleton, against whom we are sufficiently able to preserve ourselves if it were not for thee, O Cromwell, that art led by the nose by two unworthy covetous earth-worms, Vane and St. John—I mean, young Sir Henry Vane and solicitor St. John, whose baseness I sufficiently anatomatised unto thee in thy bed above a year ago. . . . O Cromwell, I am informed this day by an officer out of the army and by another knowing man yesterday that came a purpose to me out of the army, that you and your agents are likely to dash in pieces the hopes of our outward preservation—their petition to the House, and will not suffer them to petition till they have laid down their arms whensoever they shall command them, although I say no credit can be given to the House's oaths and engagements to make good what they have promised. And if this be true, as I am too much afraid it is, then I say, Accursed be the day that ever the House of Commons bribed you with a vote of 2,500*l. per annum* to betray and destroy us. Sir, I am jealous over you with the height of godly jealousy."—Lilburne to Cromwell, March 25, *Jonah's Cry out of the Whale's Belly*; E. 400, 5. The ordinary notion that Cromwell said one thing in the House and another thing in the army is thus disposed of, at least up to March 25.

[1] *C.J.* v. 127. In his *Vindication* Waller says that Ireton denied the existence of the petition, and afterwards admitted it on the receipt of a letter from the major of Rossiter's regiment. We have not, however, Ireton's own words before us to enable us to judge how far this charge was true. It does not seem likely that Ireton should have told a gratuitous lie.   [2] *C.J.* v. 126.

so large a sum. Yet it can hardly have been financial difficulties alone which actuated the Presbyterians in their high-
handed contempt of the army. Whatever their
motives may have been, the course which they
adopted was absolutely suicidal. Their one chance
of obtaining the quiet disbandment of the army lay
in a determination to satisfy the demands for arrears
and indemnity, which were all that the greater number of the
soldiers really cared for, in order that the religious enthusiasts
might be left without support. This chance they deliberately
threw away, thus knitting together in a common bond against
themselves all the various elements of which the army was
composed.

Worse was yet to come. If the Presbyterians had acted
unwisely on the 27th, at least they had kept their temper. On
the 29th two letters were read in the House which
fairly drove them off their balance. In these it was
stated that not only was the petition still in circula-
tion amongst the soldiers, but that a committee of officers had
been formed to take it in charge as soon as it had been fully
signed in the ranks, thus establishing a connection between the
soldiers and the officers. It was further alleged that Colonel
Pride had obtained eleven hundred signatures by threatening
to cashier all who refused to sign; and that every regiment at
a distance from head-quarters was, with the single exception of
Skippon's, on the march towards Saffron Walden.[1] Instead of
directing Fairfax to inquire into the truth of these allegations,
the House summoned the two Hammonds, Robert
Lilburne, and Pride—Ireton being already in his
place at Westminster—to attend at the bar.[2] Protests were
even heard against this resolution as too lenient, and it was
asked that the petitioners might be declared traitors,
and that Cromwell might be arrested. The debate
was prolonged into the night, and after many of the Independents had left the House under the impression that nothing
would be done till the following morning, Holles, seizing the

Marginal notes:
Amount of arrears claimed.
Suicidal policy of the Presby-terians.
March 29. Two letters read in the House.
Officers sent for.
Attack on Cromwell.

opportunity, scribbled a declaration on his knee, and at once obtained its acceptance by the House.[1]

This Declaration, to which the Lords gave their adherence on the following day, was issued as the manifesto of the whole

March 30.
The Decla-
ration of the
Houses. Parliament. "The two Houses of Parliament," it announced, "having received information of a dangerous petition with representations annexed, tending to put the army into a distemper and mutiny, to put conditions upon the Parliament, and obstruct the relief of Ireland, which had been contrived and promoted by some persons in the army, they do declare their high dislike of that petition, their approbation and esteem of their good service who first discovered it, and of all such officers and soldiers as have refused to join in it, and that for such as have been abused, and, by the persuasion of others, drawn to subscribe it, if they shall for the future manifest their dislike of what they have done, by forbearing to proceed any farther in it, it shall not be looked upon as any cause to take away the remembrance and sense the Houses have of the good service they have formerly done, ... and, on the other side, ... all those who shall continue in their distempered condition, and go on advancing and promoting that petition, shall be looked upon and proceeded against as enemies of the State and disturbers of the public peace." [2]

Not only did the Houses refrain from giving in this Declaration the slightest hint of a desire to meet the complaints of

No effort to
meet the
complaints
of the peti-
tioners. the petitioners, but in passing a resolution to borrow 200,000*l.*, the Commons expressly announced that the money was to be used 'for the service of England and Ireland.' Not a penny, it seemed, was to be spent in satisfying the arrears of the soldiers' pay. At the

---

[1] Ludlow's story (*Memoirs*, ed. 1751, i. 164) evidently fits in here, though he jumbles it up with Cromwell's leaving the House, which really took place on June 3. Another observation ascribed by Ludlow to Cromwell : "These men will not leave till the army pull them out by the ears"—was really spoken under very different circumstances, in the following August ; see p. 350.

[2] Declaration, March 30, *L.J.* ix. 115.

same time Skippon was to be summoned from the North to resume his duties as major general in Fairfax's army, where, as was hoped, the influence of that sturdy and honest soldier would be put forth on the side of Parliament. The Presbyterian leaders were as lacking in imagination as Charles himself. They had no conception of the effect which their stinging words would produce on an already discontented soldiery.

Skippon summoned.

CHAPTER XLVIII.

THE AGITATORS.

BEFORE the Declaration of the Houses had time to work mischief, a letter from Fairfax [1] informed the Commons that *1647.* in one respect at least they had been deceived. The *March 30.* *A letter from* report of a general rendezvous at Saffron Walden, *Fairfax.* it appeared, was without foundation. On April 1, the day on which this letter was read, the incriminated officers appeared at Westminster fully prepared to justify themselves.

April 1. Pride, who was the first to be called to the bar of the *Pride clears* House of Commons, declared that the special charge *himself.* brought against him of having obtained signatures to the petition by threats was also without foundation. After this *The officers* there was nothing to be done but to send the officers *sent back.* back to their posts, with directions to do everything in their power to suppress the obnoxious petition ; [2] but so hot *Quarrel* was the temper of the members that Ireton, having *between* justified the petition, was bitterly attacked by Holles, *Holles and* *Ireton.* and a challenge passed between the two. Other members, however, intervened in time to prevent the duel from taking place, and ultimately the House itself ordered the disputants to lay aside their quarrel. [3]

---

[1] Fairfax to Lenthall, March 30, *Rushw.* vi. 445.

[2] *C.J.* v. 132 ; *Rushw.* vi. 444.

[3] *C.J.* v. 133. " Mr. Holles and Major (*sic*) Ireton going over the water to fight, were hindered by Sir William Waller and some others who observed Mr. Holles to deride Ireton's arguments in justification of the army's petition, which was the occasion of the quarrel." Letter of Intelligence, *Clarendon MSS.* 2,748. A later news-letter gives a story that Holles went out prepared to fight, but that Ireton came without a

At Westminster there was no conception of the gravity of the situation created by the refusal of the Commons to listen to the complaints of the soldiers.   The House lightly turned to the consideration of the future government of Ireland, as if the troops now in England would without difficulty be available for the summer campaign.   In 1646 Parliament had appointed Lord Lisle, the eldest son of the Earl of Leicester, Lord Lieutenant for a single year.[1]   Ireland, however, offered few attractions, and it was not till the end of January 1647 that Lisle set forth.   He had scarcely landed at Cork before he gave deep offence to Inchiquin, the Lord President of Munster, by taking out of his hands the command of the troops in his own province.[2]

Arrangements for the government of Ireland.

1646.
Lord Lisle
Lord Lieutenant.

1647.
January.

March.
He quarrels with Inchiquin.

After this Parliament was not disposed to prolong Lisle's term of office.   The retirement of Ormond[3] had by this time given hope of access to Dublin, and the Houses accordingly appointed Colonel Michael Jones, who had distinguished himself at Rowton Heath and in the siege of Chester,[4] to take the command in Dublin, though he could not leave England till Ormond had actually surrendered the sword of office.   At the same time, Lisle's recall restored Inchiquin's supremacy in Munster. Parliament was resolved that in future the civil and military authority should no longer be combined in one person, and, with the intention of entrusting the former to commissioners of its own, it appointed Skippon to command the army with the title of Field Marshal, and Massey to serve under him as his

Michael Jones to command in Dublin, and Inchiquin in Munster.

sword, pretending that it was against his conscience to take part in a duel, which, according to the writer, confirmed ' the general opinion that the Independents are deadly cowards,' *Id.* 2,495.   On this, with some further embellishment, is built Clarendon's statement that Holles pulled Ireton's nose, *Clarendon*, x. 104.

[1] *L.J.* viii. 127, 261.

[2] Inchiquin to Manchester, March 10 ; Lisle to Manchester, March 13, *L.J.* ix. 108 ; x. 94.

[3] See p. 218.   [4] See vol. ii. 344.

lieutenant-general.[1] Both these officers had done good service
Skippon and
Massey to
command
the whole
force in
Ireland. in the war, but their military careers had not been
sufficiently distinguished to rouse enthusiasm in the
army, especially as they were both disposed to
support the policy of the Presbyterians.

The soldiers, indeed, were in no complying mood. Though
they do not seem as yet to have thought of resistance, they
Temper of
the army. were working themselves up into a temper which
might ultimately lead to it. Why, they asked, when
all other men were allowed to petition Parliament itself, were
they forbidden to make their complaints known even to their
own general?[2]

For such mutterings the Houses had no ear. In their
anxiety to hasten the formation of the new army destined for
April 15.
Parlia-
mentary
commis-
sioners at
Saffron
Walden. Ireland, they despatched to Saffron Walden a new
body of commissioners, amongst whom were War-
wick, Waller, and Massey, to persuade as many as
possible to volunteer for the service. On April 15,
soon after their arrival at head-quarters, the commissioners urged Fairfax to threaten with penal consequences all
who attempted to obstruct their proceedings. Fairfax briefly
answered that, as the men were asked to volunteer, it would be
unreasonable to prohibit freedom of discussion amongst them.
Fairfax undoubtedly resented the harsh language of the recent
Declaration, but he was not the man openly to resist the
authority of Parliament, and he contented himself with refusing
to co-operate with the commissioners whenever he thought it
prudent to hold aloof.[3]

In the afternoon the commissioners, after an address to a
meeting of two hundred officers in the church, were at once
An officers'
meeting. met with a demand for an answer to the four queries
put to the former deputation.[4] On their refusal to
comply with this request, the conversation turned on the names
of the new commanders. There was a general impression that
Skippon would refuse to serve in Ireland, and he had in fact

[1] *L.J.* ix. 122 ; *C.J.* v. 131, 133.
[2] Letters from Saffron Walden, *Rushw.* vi. 446.
[3] *Rushw.* vi. 457. [4] See p. 223.

already sent a letter of excuse to the House of Lords.[1] Why,
called out one of the officers, might they not go under their old
generals? This suggestion was at once caught up. Cries of
"All! All! Fairfax and Cromwell and we all go!" rang round
the church. The commissioners, finding that no better answer
was to be got, hereupon dissolved the meeting, inviting such as
were inclined to volunteer to give in their names personally.

With this invitation a few complied. The larger number
appointed a committee to draw up a representation to Parliament asking for an answer to the four queries, and
urging that if the old generals were named, 'it would
conduce much to their encouragement and personal
engagement.' This proposal was supported by the
signatures of about a hundred infantry officers, and
most of the cavalry officers added their signatures on the
following day.

*A repre-
sentation to
Parliament
to be pre-
pared.*

April 16.

The commissioners were not slow in taking steps to
counteract this alarming demonstration. They extracted from
Fairfax a letter requesting the officers to forward the
Irish service, though they failed to induce him to
put his request in the form of a command. They
also appealed to the interests of the officers, offering
certificates of arrears to those who volunteered, and
dealing out promotions with a lavish hand. These
overtures were not without effect. A fair number of
officers as well as of private soldiers expressed their readiness
to go to Ireland.[2] Amongst these officers was Kempson,
Robert Lilburne's lieutenant-colonel. In order to
save him from temptation he was directed to move
off, with 520 of his men who had volunteered with
him, in the direction of Chester.

*April 17.
The com-
missioners
appeal to
Fairfax,
and try to
gain the
volunteers
by their
interests.*

*Kempson
starts for
Chester.*

At this the soldiers who had refused to volunteer took
umbrage. Every possible effort was made to induce Kempson's men to change their minds, and a considerable
number turned back. On the 21st a certain ensign
Nichols was caught circulating the soldiers' petition
amongst those who held firm, and urging them to return to

*April 21.
Nichols
circulates
the petition.*

[1] *L.J.* ix. 138.   [2] Waller's *Vindication*, 85.

their old quarters. On the same day Lilburne intervened in
person. Regarding himself as still the colonel of the
whole regiment, he ordered Kempson and his followers to march into Suffolk. This at least the
commissioners were able to hinder, but they were unable to
recover the men who had been enticed away. Fairfax was
not eager to abet their proceedings, and as he
was really suffering from ill-health, he chose this
moment to set off for London for medical advice.
Without him the commissioners were powerless.[1]

Lilburne orders Kempson into Suffolk.

Failure of the commissioners.

In all this the Presbyterians saw the hand of the 'Godly
party,' which had caused anxiety in Baxter's mind two years
before,[2] when he had accused some of its members
of being eager to use the army for the enforcement
of a system of toleration, and others of regarding it
as a spiritual aristocracy set apart by God Himself to lead an
enslaved nation through the wilderness into the promised land
of righteousness and freedom. John Lilburne, who,
though still a prisoner in the Tower, was in constant
communication with the hotter spirits in the army,
and was, if not the writer, at least the inspirer of an anonymous
pamphlet entitled *A new-found Stratagem*, in which
the hopes of the 'Godly party' were clearly revealed. It was a reply to an invitation circulated by
the Essex clergy in which they called on their parishioners
to join in petitioning Parliament for the disbandment of the
army. Its main argument was that the resolution of the Commons to raise 60,000*l.* a month for the armies in England and
Ireland[3] showed that the Presbyterians had no real intention
of lessening taxation, and that as an army was in any case to
be kept up, it would be better to put up with the old one
which, except when the Presbyterians stopped its supplies, had
always paid its way, than to submit to a new one which would
probably be less well behaved.

The 'Godly party in the army.

John Lilburne's influence.

A new-found Stratagem.

"Whose poultry," asked the anonymous writer, "hath this

---

[1] Waller's *Vindication*, 88; *L.J.* ix. 152; Narrative of the Proceedings at Saffron Walden. *Clarke Papers*, i. 5.

[2] See vol. ii. 327.   [3] See p. 221.

army destroyed ? Whose goods have they spoiled, or whose sheep or calves have they stolen ?" The way was thus cleared for the assertion that the army was needed to protect law and liberty, that so, in case 'their just demands be denied contrary to duty, oath, and covenant, the poor Commons may have a shelter and defence to secure them from oppression and violence ; and his excellency and every soldier under him by the duty of his place and virtue of the Protestation [1] is bound thereunto.' [2]

The army, in short, was to be the organ of political progress. No wonder that the Presbyterians, with their respect for Parliamentary procedure, were anxious to be rid of it. What is strange is that they did not perceive that their unsympathetic handling of the soldiers' complaints was welding into one forces which they might easily have kept apart, and even throwing power into the hands of men whom they most cordially detested. If arrears had been paid, and indemnity granted, the 'Godly party' would have been isolated. No doubt the country, impatient as it was of taxation, would not easily have been induced to supply the necessary funds ; but it is hard to believe that the City would not have found the money required, if it were once plainly understood that only in this way could the army be broken up.

The Presbyterians distrust the army.

The process by which the soldiers who cared only for their pay were being thrown into the arms of the political and religious enthusiasts is well illustrated by the letter of a Suffolk Presbyterian. He tells us that at a meeting held by Ireton's regiment, which was at that time quartered at Ipswich, the men were of one mind in crying out " All disband, or none !" The writer of the letter had not far to seek for the cause of this unanimity. "Though the army," he assures his correspondent, " differ in religion, they all agree in their discontented speeches against the Parliament. The soldiers conclude that they who have been so badly paid in England shall be wholly neglected if they go to Ireland. As for the petition, they now speak it openly that

April 15. A military gathering at Ipswich.

Unanimity of the soldiers.

---

[1] *i.e.* the Declaration or Petition of the soldiers.

[2] *A new-found Stratagem*, E. 384, 11.

they will send it up with two out of every troop." [1] If their
deputies were imprisoned, the whole army would follow and
Their starve out its enemies in London. It was thought
feelings that there were many discontented men in the City,
towards
Parliament, ready to side with the soldiers. In Essex most people
were dissatisfied because Parliament had not proclaimed an
immediate reduction of taxation. The levy of 60,000*l.* a
month was in everyone's mouth. "The people here grow very
discontented, and the very report of the continuance of taxes
doth so gall the country as it makes them too apt to listen to
the discontented speeches of the soldiers." The growing distrust of a Parliament unsound on the question of arrears was
turning the thoughts of the soldiers in an unexpected direction.
"The soldiers both in Norfolk and Suffolk sing one note,
and to- namely, that they have fought all this time to bring
wards the the King to London, and to London they will bring
King. the King—some of the soldiers do not stick to call
the Parliament men tyrants. Lilburne's books are quoted by
them as statute law." [2]

The suggestion of an understanding between the army and
the King was nothing new. The Independents had been
pressing for it ever since the surrender of Bristol. They may
now have thought that Charles would by this time be sick of
the treatment accorded to him by the Presbyterians, and be at
last ready to come to terms with themselves. His seclusion at
Charles at Holmby was not at all to his taste. He was indeed
Holmby. permitted to ride about the country with an escort,
and to play at bowls in the gardens of the neighbouring gentry,
April 8. but he was not allowed to communicate with anyone
His corre- approaching him without the authority of the Houses.
spondence
stopped. A gentleman attempting to convey to him a letter
from the Queen had lately been arrested. [3] About the middle
of April, however, fortune favoured Charles better. A certain
Colonel Bamfield, a Royalist intriguer, contrived to corrupt
his barber, and by this channel he for the first time heard of

---

[1] This is the first hint of the choice of Agitators.

[2] A letter from Suffolk, April 20, *The Duke of Portland's MSS.*

[3] *L.J.* ix. 131.

the scheme [1] which the Presbyterian lords had endeavoured to

transmit to him through the Queen more than two months before. [2]

Other news, no doubt, reached Charles in the same way. He may have heard how his wife was

instructing the Prince of Wales, now a tall youth in his seventeenth year with dark hair and a swarthy complexion, in the art of making love. The object of this courtship was to a day three years older than the Prince, the daughter of the Duke of Orleans, the Great Mademoiselle, as she was called, whose large dowry would make up for the disproportion in years. The lad, who was already the father of an illegitimate son, [3] showed himself an apt pupil enough, but the young lady merely flirted with her youthful admirer, having set her heart on marrying the emperor, and Charles's perfunctory love-making therefore did not prosper. [4]

The Queen's political schemes proved as ineffectual as her matrimonial. On March 1 Mazarin, hoping to concentrate the

French armies for a final attack on the Spanish Netherlands, had brought the Elector of Bavaria to sign a truce for a year. To Henrietta Maria it was all important that the continental wars of France should be brought to a close in order that when once the military drain on the resources of the country had been lightened, the French Government might be able to turn its attention to the restoration of the King of England. Accordingly, towards the middle of April, backed by a fervid clerical coterie, she urged the Queen Mother, Anne of Austria, to restore peace to Christendom. Ultimately, however, the influence of Mazarin proved too strong for her, but at the time when she wrote the letter

---

[1] Bamfield's *Apology*, p. 20. Bamfield's evidence is to be received with caution, but so much as is given above may, I think, be accepted, as Bellièvre writes about this time that he was now again able to send letters to the King, and Lady Anne Halkett, in her autobiography, speaks of Bamfield as actually receiving letters from Charles.　　[2] See p. 214.

[3] His mother was a lady of good family, whose name is unknown. He was born after Charles's visit to Jersey in 1646, at the age of sixteen. Boero, *Istoria della conversione di . . . Carlo II.*

[4] *Mémoires de Mademoiselle de Montpensier* (ed. Chéruel), i. 126, 138.

which Bamfield conveyed to Charles, the hope of success must have filled her mind.[1]

Charles, therefore, was once more sanguine. He now knew not only that France seemed likely to interfere in his Charles hopeful. favour, but also that influential persons at Westminster had proposed in February to come to an understanding with him on terms not very different from those which he had himself offered to accept. While he was meditating on the favourable prospects thus opening before him, he April 21. A message purporting to come from the army. received a message purporting to be an invitation from the army to take refuge in its ranks, in order that it might restore him to his honours, his crown, and his dignity. "We will not," he replied, "engage our people in another war. Too much blood hath been shed already. The Lord be merciful to my distracted kingdoms when He accounts with them for rebellion and blood ; but let the army know that we highly respect their expressions, and when we shall, by the blessing of God, be restored to our throne in peace, we shall auspiciously look upon their loyal affections towards us."[2]

As soon as the substance of this invitation to the King was The message repudiated at headquarters. published abroad, all knowledge of the matter was stoutly repudiated by officers and soldiers at headquarters. If conjecture may be hazarded as to the authorship of the proposal, what little evidence there Ireton its probable author. is seems to point to Ireton. It was in his regiment at Ipswich that the notion of opposing the King to the Parliament was first heard of,[3] and this notion spread

---

[1] Chéruel, *Hist. de France pendant la minorité de Louis XIV.* ii. 278. The Queen-Mother was being urged by Henrietta Maria to make peace about the end of Lent, Easter-day according to the new style following on April $\frac{11}{21}$.

[2] His Majesty's answer, *Carte MSS.* xx. fol. 630. The petition of the army got abroad and was mentioned in several of the newspapers. Ormond's informant—for the Carte Papers are in reality, as far as this part of them is concerned, Ormond Papers—was concerned only with the King's answer. That it is found in this collection is strong evidence of its genuineness.

[3] *The Moderate Intelligencer*, E. 386, 2. See p. 236.

ιapidly in other parts of the eastern counties. On May 5 it

was reported at Saffron Walden that 'some of the foot about Cambridgeshire give out that they will go for Holmby and fetch the King, which gives much offence and scandal.'[1]

Nor was Ireton himself an unlikely man to take the initiative in such a project. Though he was a good and steady
officer, he had at no time shown signs of military genius, and his failure to cope with Rupert at Naseby had raised a suspicion that his promotion to the high post of Commissary-General was due to the fact that he was Cromwell's son-in-law. Yet, apart from the domestic bond, Ireton was possessed of qualities sufficiently similar and sufficiently dissimilar to those of Cromwell to lay the basis of a lifelong friendship. There was in Ireton a deep, and at the same time tolerant, religious earnestness which early drew him into the ranks of the Independents. Yet, if his convictions were as strong as Cromwell's, they were far more definite. Spiritually he stood on a lower level. It is most unlikely that Ireton ever went through those mental struggles which preceded Cromwell's conversion. He was not one to see visions, or to dream dreams, or in the midst of active work to pour forth outbursts of religious rapture. Neither had he that all-embracing hospitality of soul which made Cromwell so marvellously tender to fanatics and fools. His strong sense of the value of form made him the constitutional authority of his party. What he said was always clearly thought out and clearly expressed, but it gave no glimpses into the immensity of the spiritual horizon such as those which brighten so many of Cromwell's utterances. .Hence, whilst Cromwell provoked enmities, Ireton provoked quarrels. Men distrusted Cromwell because he was to them incomprehensible. They disliked Ireton because they understood him only too well as the author of sayings and actions in direct opposition to those favoured by themselves.

When such a man as Ireton shifts his ground, he shifts it without much warning. If Ireton made up his mind that he

[1] Relation from Walden, May 5, *Clarke Papers*, i. 25.

could no longer trust Parliament as the central authority in the kingdom, he would be likely to leap rapidly to the con-

Ireton shifts his ground.

clusion that the King must be conciliated, just as, rather more than six months later, upon his discovery that the King could no longer be trusted, he leapt rapidly to the conclusion that terms could be kept with him no longer. To such a nature suspension of judgment is intolerable. There is, on the other hand, reason to believe that Cromwell was now passing through one of those long periods

Cromwell's hesitation.

of hesitation which with him always preceded important action. He had come to see that good results were not likely to be attained by devotion to Parliament; but his belief in the necessity of accepting Parliamentary supremacy was too deep-rooted to be hastily shaken, because in his case loyalty to Parliament sprang from long habit and from the craving of an orderly mind for authority which, once shattered, would be difficult to replace. It was observed that

He absents himself from the House.

during the latter part of April both Cromwell and Vane absented themselves except on rare occasions from the House ;[1] but there is no reason to suppose that either of them took any steps to bring its authority into contempt. No doubt their dislike of the course which Parliament was taking was balanced by a rooted distrust of the King.[2]

Whilst Cromwell and Vane doubted, that chartered libertine Henry Marten was giving full licence to his bitter

---

[1] Letter of Intelligence, April 29, *Clarendon MSS.* 2,504.

[2] Earlier in the month Bellièvre had written of the feeling of the Parliamentary Independents about opening negotiations with the King : "Les Independans," he says, "sont desunis ; la plus part manquent de cœur, et ceux d'entre eux qui pourroyent entreprendre quelque chose de grand à l'avantage du Roy de la Grande Bretagne en sont retenus par l'opinion qu'ils ont que l'on ne se peut fier audit Roy, qui ne garde point de secret, et qui n'a point eu de constance dans toutes les resolutions importantes qu'il sembloit avoir pris, jusques icy, près des uns et des autres." Bellièvre to Mazarin, April $\frac{8}{18}$, *R.O. Transcripts.* In a despatch of $\frac{April\ 26}{May\ 6}$ the ambassador speaks of Charles as being in communication with both parties.

tongue. "I know not," he said, when complaints were made

Marten's saying about the King's evil.

of the flocking of multitudes to˙ Holmby House in the hope of being cured by Charles's touch of the King's evil, "but the Parliament's great seal might

April 21. The New-castle Propositions to be sent.

do it if there were an ordinance for it." The majority of the House of Commons were of a different mind. On April 21 it was resolved to send the Newcastle Propositions once more to the King. "The man,"

An audacious proposal.

declared Marten audaciously, "to whom these propositions shall be sent ought rather to come to the bar himself than to be sent to any more."[1]

Whatever might be Charles's answer—and there could be little doubt that it would be an evasive one—the Houses had

April 25. More volunteers for Ireland desert.

more reason to concern themselves with the army than with the King. Other soldiers besides those who followed Kempson for a time had volunteered for Ireland, and had gone some part of the way towards a port of embarkation ; but they slipped back in batches to their old comrades, many declaring, truly or falsely, that their officers 'had first made them drunk, and had then extorted from them a promise to go to Ireland when they were in that condition.' Out of 21,480 men only 2,320 were

Return of the com-missioners.

available for the Irish service.[2] All efforts to increase the number were unsuccessful,[3] and the commissioners, baffled in their task, returned to

April 27. Their report.

Westminster, bringing with them Ensign Nichols as a prisoner. On April 27 they made their report to the House of Commons.

Not to be behindhand, the malcontent officers despatched seven of their number to lay before the House of Commons a

The officers' vindication.

vindication of their own conduct in supporting the soldiers' petition. Though this vindication was signed by 151 commissioned officers,[4] the Commons did not even allow it to be read in the House. After listening to the

[1] Letter of Intelligence, April 26, *Clarendon MSS.* 2,502.

[2] Letter from Saffron Walden, April 25, *Clarke Papers,* i. 16.

[3] *Idem* i. 17.

[4] *The Petition and Vindication of the Officers,* E. 385, 19.

report of the commissioners, they committed Nichols [1] to
Strong prison, and sent for Robert Lilburne and three
measures. other officers to give an account of their conduct
in drawing off soldiers from the Irish service.

In the meanwhile the Lords, having tardily come to the
conclusion that some part of the soldiers' arrears ought to be
Six weeks' paid on disbandment, voted that six weeks' pay
arrears should be the amount offered. The Commons,
voted. though formally protesting against the breach of
their privileges committed by the Lords in meddling with a
grant of money, confirmed the vote. [2] It remained to be seen
whether so inadequate a concession would satisfy the army.
There are no signs that any Presbyterian member of either
April 29. House thought it insufficient. Two days later the
News of confidence in the future which still prevailed in
Skippon's
readiness to Parliament was increased by the news that Skippon
go to
Ireland. had been prevailed on, though most unwillingly, to
accept the command in Ireland. [3]

The Presbyterians were destined to a rude awakening.
Early in April there had been a talk in Ireton's regiment of
sending the soldiers' petition to Westminster in charge of two
deputies from each troop. [4] The contempt with which the
soldiers' grievances were treated now led to the adoption of
this plan in a slightly different form. Eight of the ten cavalry
regiments came to an understanding with one another, and
each chose two representatives, to whom was at first given the
name of Commissioners, a name which was soon afterwards
changed into that of Agitators, or Agents of the Army. [5]

---

[1] See p. 234.   [2] *L.J.* ix. 152; *C.J.* v. 155.
[3] *L.J.* ix. 158.   [4] See p. 237.

[5] "Careful investigation," writes Dr. Murray in *The New English
Dictionary, s. v.* Agitators, "satisfies me that Agitator was the actual
title, and *Adjutator* only a bad spelling of soldiers familiar with *Adjutants*
and the *Adjutors* of 1642. *Adjutator* has naturally seemed more plausible
to recent writers unfamiliar with this old sense of 'to agitate,' and the
functions of the *Agitators* of 1647." The old sense referred to is ' To do
the actual work of (the affairs of) another, to manage, or act as agent.'

The chronology of the word is as follows : At the first appearance of
these representatives of the soldiers they call themselves, in signing a

Instead of carrying the condemned petition to Westminster,
the sixteen Agitators in the name of the regiments
drew up identical letters addressed to the three
generals, Fairfax, Cromwell, and Skippon.[1]

April 28.
Letters to
the generals.

The composers of these letters for the first time answered
the attack of their assailants by a counter-attack. After complaining of the delay in granting an indemnity, though their
fellow-soldiers suffered 'at every assize for acts merely relating
to the war,' they asserted that the proposal to send them to
Ireland was 'nothing else than a design to ruin and break
this army in pieces ; . . . otherwise, why are not those who
have been made instruments in our country's deliverance
again thought worthy to be employed.' It was therefore 'but
a mere cloak for some who have lately tasted of sovereignty,
and being lifted beyond their ordinary sphere of servants, seek
to become masters and degenerate into tyrants.'[2] This letter,
after being read before the regiments and accepted by them,
was entrusted to three Agitators, Sexby, Allen, and Shephard,
to be carried to the generals in London.

letter dated April 28, Commissioners ; in the *Declaration of the Army*
(E. 390, 26), presented to the Parliamentary Commissioners on or about
May 15, it is stated that they have been chosen 'to agitate for those ends
in behalf of them all,' and they are themselves styled 'Agents' of those
who chose them. The noun appears in a petition to Fairfax of May 29,
which is subscribed by 'your Excellency's and the Kingdom's innocent
and faithful servants . . . being Agitators on behalf of the several regiments.' In the next page we have 'Adjutators,' which is thus shown to
be a mere variation of spelling, though this form appears on the title-page.
Two Letters, E. 391, 2. Adjutator, in short, occurs as soon as Agitator,
but it has no meaning, whilst Agitator has, as will appear by the following quotation : "When I wrote last to you, I had been with Sir John
Berkeley, one of his Majesty's Agitators, for that is now the word."
N. Hobart to J. Hobart, Oct. 15, Cary's *Mem. of the Civil War*, i. 354.
The verb also occurs in the sense of 'to act.' "It is our unhappiness
that we are so far distant . . . from the eight regiments . . . by reason
whereof timely notice cannot be given us to agitate according to our real
intentions, which are to add ourselves to them entirely as one man."
Letter from Sir R. Pye's regiment, May 13, *Clarke Papers*, i. 44.

[1] The Agitators' Letter, April 28, *L.J.* ix. 164.
[2] *Ibid.*

On April 30 the vindication of the officers, which had been brought into the House of Commons on the 27th,[1] was at last allowed to be read. Before any step was taken in connection with it, the letters to the three generals were produced, and were also read.[2] As might have been expected, the House was beyond measure indignant at the latter. The Presbyterian majority would indeed have changed its nature if they had condescended to ask whether their own refusal of bare justice had not had something to do with the readiness with which whole regiments applauded a criticism on the conduct of their employers. They could see nothing but sheer fanaticism at the bottom of the attack made on them. The whole army it seemed—to use the words of a report which had just been made from Saffron Walden—was 'one Lilburne throughout, and more likely to give than to receive laws.'[3]

April 30. The officers' vindication and the Agitators' letter in the House.

Indignation of the Presbyterians.

For the present all that could be done was to call to the bar the Agitators who had brought the letters. The three men had convenient memories. They were quite unable to recall the circumstances under which they had been signed. They were then asked to explain the paragraph relating to the members who had tasted sovereignty. The letters, they curtly replied, were the work of the regiments, and it was for the regiments to explain their meaning.[4]

Three Agitators at the bar.

The House, in short, had to deal, not with the three men before it, but with eight regiments —perhaps with the whole army—and this knowledge had a sobering effect. Instead of meting out punishment to offenders, the Commons directed its military members, Skippon, Cromwell, Ireton, and Fleetwood, to go down to their charges in the army, and to employ their

The House sobered.

Cromwell, Ireton, and Skippon to go to the army.

---

[1] See p. 242.

[2] *L.J.* ix. 163 ; *C.J.* v. 158 ; Whitacre's Diary, *Add. MSS.* 31, 116, fol. 308b.

[3] Letter of Intelligence, April 26, *Clarendon MSS.* 2,502.

[4] Examination of the Agitators, *Clarke Papers*, i. App. B.

endeavours to quiet all distempers. They were to inform the
soldiers that an Ordinance for their indemnity would be brought
in at once ; that a considerable portion of their arrears would
be paid immediately ; and that for the remainder there should
be signed debentures, payable in cash as soon as the necessities
of the State would allow.[1]

It was a humiliating capitulation, but humiliating as it was,
there was no other course by which disaster could be avoided.
It was perhaps still possible, if Cromwell's influence
could be secured on the side of Parliamentary
authority, to stave off the religious and political
demands of the majority in the army by redressing the
material grievances of the whole force.[2] At all events it
cannot be seriously doubted that Cromwell left Westminster
with the full purpose of carrying out his instructions honestly,
and that he was still under the influence of those
feelings which had hitherto led him to distrust the
intervention of soldiers in politics.[3]

A humiliating capitulation.

Cromwell's intentions.

---

[1] *C.J.* v. 158.

[2] We have an example in English history of a government taking
successfully the course here suggested. When in 1797 the sailors mutinied
at Spithead because their petition for the removal of material grievances
had been rejected, Pitt met them by conceding all the reasonable wishes
of the mutineers, and was thus strengthened to refuse the slightest concessions to the political demands of the sailors in the fleet at the Nore.

[3] The strongest evidence in such a case is the silence of a hostile
witness thoroughly acquainted with the facts. Such a witness is Major
Huntington, an officer of Cromwell's own regiment, in confidential communication with him, though he afterwards turned against him. In
August 1648, when Huntington tried to damage Cromwell as much as
possible, he drew up a narrative in which he vehemently assailed his past
conduct. In dealing with this employment, however, all that Huntington
could say against Cromwell was that he had declared, after reaching the
army, that he and his fellow-commissioners had come in the double
capacity of commissioners and soldiers, and that he acknowledged that
there had ' lately been much cruelty and injustice in the Parliament.' Of
any secret encouragement to the soldiers to make conditions with Parliament in favour of any political or religious object Huntington has not a
word to say. He states, indeed, that Ireton drew up the Declaration of
the Army, which will be shortly mentioned (p. 247), and that he had told

On May 7 a meeting of officers was held once more in Saffron Walden church, this time in the presence of the new

May 7.
A meeting
of officers.

military commissioners, but it soon appeared that it would be useless to consult officers alone on questions which touched the rank and file so nearly. The officers were therefore directed to collect the views of the

General
election of
Agitators.

private soldiers. By this time the whole army was thoroughly organised. After the example which had been set by the cavalry, each troop or company elected representatives. As, however, a body composed of all these representatives would be too numerous for efficient action, it was now arranged that the combined representatives of each regiment should elect two or more to whom alone the name of Agitators [1] was now given. These Agitators, when collected, could speak in the name of the whole army, and were capable of impressing, in turn, their own views upon their military constituency. In troublous times the most decided and energetic come to the front ; and, little as it was intended at the time, nothing was more calculated than the existence of this elected body of Agitators to give to the army that distinctive political and religious character which it ultimately bore.

On May 15, after long conferences with the Agitators, the

May 15.
A second
meeting of
officers.

officers had a second interview with the commissioners, and on the following day they gave in a *Declaration of the Army*, which bore the signatures of 223 commissioned officers. The Declaration opened with

the Agitators 'that it was then lawful and fit to deny disbanding till we had received equal and full satisfaction for our past service.' Even this, however, relates only to the material grievances which the commissioners were sent to allay, and Huntington, with all his anxiety to make out a case against Cromwell, does not attribute any similar language to him. *Sundry reasons inducing Major Huntington to lay down his Commission,* E. 458, 3.

[1] In *The Declaration of the Army* (E. 390, 26) we are told that the soldiers chose 'a certain number of every regiment or troop or company.' This is vague, but there is a clearer statement in *A Solemn Engagement of the Army,* p. 6 (E. 392, 9) : "The soldiers . . . were forced . . . to choose out of the several troops and companies, several men, and those out of their whole numbers to choose two or more for each regiment."

a narrative of the late proceedings of the soldiers, with whom the officers avowed themselves to be fully in accord. The

May 16.
A *Declara-*
tion of the
Army.

men, they said, had resolved to send to Parliament that petition which had been so summarily condemned,[1] but had been dissuaded by the officers from doing so, as well as from listening to anyone attempting to induce them to take part in politics.[2] The practical proposal made by the officers was that the vote for paying ' a considerable part' of the arrears should be made more definite. It was generally understood, as the officers declared, to mean no more than the six weeks' pay already offered ;[3] an offer which was ' generally looked upon as very inconsiderable,' most of the horse and many of the foot having large arrears due to them for service in former armies, in addition to arrears due to them for service in the New Model.

This very reasonable demand was followed by complaints of the imprisonment of Ensign Nichols by the former commissioners without Fairfax's concurrence ; of the toleration by Parliament of calumnies uttered against the soldiers in the press and in the pulpit ; and also of the thanks which had been given by the Houses to petitioners who had reviled the army. Finally the Declaration asked that Parliament should acknowledge that the soldiers had a right to petition their general on military matters ; should take into consideration their original petition, and should allow them to publish a sober vindication of their own conduct.[4]

With the spirit of this Declaration Cromwell appears to have been entirely satisfied. He and his fellow-commissioners were able to announce that the Indemnity Ordinance had already passed the Commons, and that the six weeks of arrears

---

[1] See pp. 225, 227.

[2] "We perceive there have not wanted some in all quarters, upon their dissatisfaction in those things," *i.e.* their pay, &c., "ready to engage them in an implication of things of another nature, which, though not evil in themselves, yet did not concern them properly as soldiers." The authors of the *Declaration*, perhaps, had their eye on such papers as *A Second Apology*, E. 385, 18.

[3] By the vote of April 27 ; see p. 243.

[4] *Declaration of the Army*, E. 390, 26.

were to be extended to eight.[1] "Truly, gentlemen," said Cromwell to the officers, "it will be very fit for you to have a

May 17.
Cromwell's
reply. very great care in the making the best use and improvement that you can both of the votes and of this that hath been last told you, and of the interest which all of you or any of you may have in your several respective regiments—namely, to work in them a good opinion of that authority that is over both us and them. If that authority falls to nothing, nothing can follow but confusion."[2]

So far Cromwell had prevailed by his strong sympathy with the soldiers, and his equally strong desire to hinder them from

Language of
Cromwell
and Ireton. bringing the kingdom into anarchy through their efforts to obtain justice for themselves. Ireton, indeed, had in private told the soldiers that till justice had been obtained they ought not to disband, but there is no reason to believe that Cromwell used any words of the kind.[3]

The work of the commissioners was now accomplished. In a joint letter to the Speaker they contented themselves with

The Com-
missioners
give account
of their
proceedings. painting the situation in general terms. "We must acknowledge," they wrote, "we found the army under a deep sense of some sufferings, and the common soldiers much unsettled." They therefore suggested that it would be well for Parliament to recall them in order that they might give a verbal report of all that they had learnt.[4]

Will the
Presby-
terians
accept the
Declaration? There could be little doubt that Cromwell would plead energetically for justice to the soldiers ; but all that he could say would be of little avail unless the Presbyterians at Westminster were prepared to meet the Declaration in a spirit of conciliation.

[1] The Commissioners to Lenthall, May 17, Cary's *Memorials of the Civil War*, i. 214.

[2] *Clarke Papers*, i. 72.

[3] See p. 246, note 3.

[4] The Commissioners to Lenthall, May 17, Cary's *Mem. of the Civil War*, i. 214.

CHAPTER XLIX.

THE ABDUCTION OF THE KING.

THE action of the commissioners had at least so far cleared the situation that it could no longer be doubted that Parliament

1647.
May 17.
The situation cleared.

must either redress the material grievances of the army or be prepared to fight it ; and for some time there had been signs that the Presbyterians were ready to venture on the latter and more desperate course. In March the City had asked that a new Militia Committee of its

A new
Militia
Committee
demanded
by the City.

own choosing might be substituted for the existing Committee which had been named by Parliament, and which contained many Independents.[1] Though an Ordinance authorising the City to choose a new Committee was passed by the Lords, it had received no support from the Commons till the dispute with the army opened the eyes of the Presbyterian leaders to the advantage of having the military force of the City entirely at the disposal of their

April 16.
Ordinance
giving the
City power
to appoint
a Militia
Committee.

own party. The Lords' Ordinance was therefore at last taken in hand, and on April 16 it passed both Houses.[2] The Common Council, taking advantage of the permission thus obtained, at once nominated a new committee, consisting exclusively of Presbyterians. On May 4, in Cromwell's absence, another Ordinance was passed giving Parliamentary authority to the nominees of the City.[3]

No immediate objection was raised on any side to intrust-

The Militia
purged of
Independents.

ing the municipal authority with the control of the City trained bands, but the manner in which the new committee exercised its powers soon gave offence. Every officer tainted with Independency was excluded from

[1] *L.J.* ix. 82.   [2] *Idem*, ix. 143.   [3] *Idem*, ix. 143.

the service.[1] It looked as if the Presbyterians were to have

A Parlia-
mentary
army. an army of their own. The London militia, which numbered 18,000 men,[2] was not to be despised as a military force, even if its quality was not equal to that of the tried warriors who had served under Fairfax and Cromwell.

This remodelling of the City force was certain to rouse an angry spirit in the army, and the difficulty of keeping this anger Ill-feeling in within bounds would be much increased if it once the army. came to be known that the Presbyterians were seeking for military support in Scotland as well as in the City. In The Scottish Scotland, too, there was a new-model army formed army under out of the larger force which had returned from David Leslie. England in February, and this army, consisting of 5,000 foot and 1,200 horse, had been placed under David Leslie, who was a warm partisan of Argyle and the extreme Huntly's Presbyterians. In the course of the spring David strongholds Leslie had captured all Huntly's strongholds,[3] and taken. as soon as he had accomplished the not very difficult task of crushing Alaster Macdonald in the West, he and the force which he commanded would be available for a campaign in England.

For the present there was room for diplomacy, and Argyle, Scottish reflecting the sentiments of every Scottish politi- jealousy of cian, watched with jealousy the growth of a strong the English army. military power in England.[4] In April, with his ap- proval, the Committee of Estates despatched to London four

---

[1] *Perfect Occurrences*, E. 390, 7.

[2] List of the London Trained Bands, communicated by the Hon. H. A. Dillon, *Archæologia*, vol. lii.

[3] *Patrick Gordon*, 199.

[4] Much information on the state of Scottish parties at this time is to be derived from the despatches of Montreuil, of which there are copies amongst the *Carte MSS.* (vol. lxxxiii.). Montreuil was, after the King's removal from Newcastle, transferred to Edinburgh, and remained there till the Scottish invasion of England in 1648. His opinion of Scottish statesmen must, however, be received with caution, as he is too prone to ascribe to them far-reaching intrigues which probably originated in his own lively imagination.

commissioners, of whom Lauderdale was the ablest. Though
these commissioners were ostensibly to support the English

April.
Commis-
sioners to
England.

Parliament in urging Charles to accept the Propositions of Newcastle, Lauderdale brought with him secret
instructions to be content if the King would accept

Lauder-
dale's secret
instructions.

the four propositions forwarded to him through
Bellièvre and the Queen at the end of January.[1]

He is accom-
panied by
Dunferm-
line,

Lauderdale was accompanied by the Earl of Dunfermline, who had been won over by Charles at
Newcastle, and had been made a gentleman of the
bedchamber in order to secure for him the right of approaching
the King at any moment.[2] Dunfermline was now selected to
go with the commissioners, in order that by availing himself

May 13.
who is al-
lowed to go
to the King.

of this right he might open a communication between Charles and the Scots. On May 13 the
English Parliament gave him a somewhat reluctant
permission to visit the King at Holmby.[3]

Charles, who had not been left in ignorance of this movement in his favour, had already on May 12 sent to the Houses

May 12.
Charles re-
plies to the
Proposi-
tions.

a letter which was, to all appearance, a reply to the
Newcastle Propositions, though in reality based on
the lines of the scheme suggested in January.[4] This
scheme Charles accepted with some modifications.
Presbyterianism was to be granted for three years, during which
there were to be consultations with the Westminster Assembly,
to which were to be added twenty divines of the King's choosing,
with the object of arranging a permanent settlement, and the
militia was to be granted for ten. Documents to which the
Parliamentary Great Seal had been affixed were to be held
valid, and satisfaction was to be given about Ireland. Finally,
Charles asked to be allowed to come to Westminster as a
sovereign in order that the Bills needed to give legal force to
these conditions might receive the Royal assent.[5]

[1] See p. 214.

[2] The date of his appointment was Jan. 13. *Dunfermline Papers* in
the possession of Dr. Milne of Fyvie.

[3] *C.J.* v. 170.   [4] Bellièvre to Mazarin, May $\frac{17}{27}$, *R.O. Transcripts.*

[5] The King to the Speaker of the House of Lords, May 12, *L.J.* ix.
193. The King to Bamfield, May 16, Bamfield's *Apology*, 24.

On May 18 the King's reply was read at Westminster, and
was at once accepted not only by the English Presbyterians
but even by the Scottish commissioners as a fitting
basis of accommodation, though more clear-sighted
observers might well have doubted whether Charles's
acceptance of a three years' Presbyterianism was
anything more than a prelude to the restoration of
Episcopacy.   The real importance of the agreement
was that it laid the foundations of an alliance which
gave birth to a second Civil War in which Scots and
Presbyterians allied themselves with English Cavaliers.

*May 18.
The King's
offer read.*

*Coalition be-
tween the
Scots and
the English
Presby-
terians in
favour of the
King.*

The immediate difficulty of the new coalition lay in the
necessity of concealing its plans till the army had been disbanded.   How unlikely it was that the army would
suffer itself to be broken up before its grievances
were redressed ought to have been made clear to the
Houses by the letter of their own commissioners, which, written
on the 17th,[1] reached Westminster on the 18th, the day on
which the King's reply was read.   The Commons
at once voted that Fairfax should return to head-
quarters if his health permitted, that one or two of
their commissioners should return to give an account of their
employment, and that a committee should be appointed to
consider the time and manner of the disbandment 'of all such
forces as shall not go for Ireland.'[2]

*Difficulty of
concealing
their plans.*

*May 19.
Circular of
the Agita-
tors.*

At these votes the Agitators took alarm.   On the 19th,
only three days after the presentation of the conciliatory
Declaration of the Army to the commissioners,[3] they issued a
circular letter to the regiments based partly on a rumour that
the Houses intended to offer to the privates the whole of their
arrears and to take vengeance on the officers.[4]   "This is now,"
wrote the Agitators, "the thing in hand to divide between you
and them, and that is either propounding or giving you your
arrears and so take you from your officers, thereby to destroy
them, and then to work about their designs with you also,
which will make your money to be but little useful to you.

---

[1] See p. 249.   [2] *C.J.* v. 176.   [3] See p. 247.
[4] Letter to the Agitators, May 18, *Clarke Papers*, i. 85.

As soon as you have it, and you disbanded, you may be pressed away for Ireland or hanged in England for prosecuting the petition, or refusing to go for Ireland, which we question not but many of us shall be found guilty of, some already saying if you be but disbanded, if you will not go they will draw you along like dogs. Fellow-soldiers, the sum of all is, if you do but stand and not accept of anything nor do anything without the consent of the whole army, you will do good to yourselves, your officers, and the whole kingdom." [1]

All the ground which had been won by Cromwell was now lost. The Agitators were deeply suspicious of the Houses, and the Houses were equally suspicious of the Agitators. On the 20th, instead of attempting to smooth away difficulties, the Lords published to the world their good understanding with the King, by voting that he should be invited to Oatlands, in close proximity to London. [2] Though the Commons were too prudent to support the Lords in their indiscretion, enough had been done to lay bare the drift of the Presbyterian policy. The Independents in the army were stirred to exasperation, and opinions were freely expressed that the politicians who were prepared to sacrifice the liberties of the country should be called to account for their misdeeds. [3]

Mutual suspicion.

May 20. The Lords invite the King to Oatlands.

The army Independents exasperated.

The Houses were the more anxious to be rid of an army which they believed to be pervaded with fanaticism, as they had been vehemently taken to task by a body of political fanatics, who may fairly be regarded as the disciples of John Lilburne. In March a petition had been drawn up by these men for presentation to the House of Commons, which they addressed as the 'supreme authority of the nation,' and on the 15th a copy surreptitiously obtained whilst it was in course of signature was brought to the notice of the House.

March. A Lilburnian movement in London.

A Lilburnian petition.

The petition itself was the work of men who committed the

---

[1] Letter from the Agitators, May 19, *Clarke Papers*, i. 87.

[2] *L.J.* ix. 199.

[3] Joachimi to the States General, May $\frac{21}{31}$, *Add. MSS.* 17, 677 S, fol. 454.

common mistake of persons of strong opinions, in thinking that
it is merely necessary to propose reforms to obtain their general
Grievances　acceptance. They asked the Commons to secure
alleged in it.　themselves against 'a negative voice in any person or
persons whomsoever,' in other words in the King or the House
of Lords; to take off all sentences, fines, and imprisonments
imposed on Commoners . . . without due course of law;[1] to
put an end to the administration of interrogatories by which
accused persons might be forced to inculpate themselves; to
'repeal all statutes, oaths and covenants' by which 'religious,
peaceable, well-affected people' were molested 'for nonconformity, or different opinion, or practice in religion;' to take
care 'that no one was punished for preaching or publishing his
opinion in religion in a peaceable way;' to dissolve mono-
polising trading companies; to settle an easy way for deciding
controversies by 'reducing all laws to the nearest agreement
with Christianity,' and by ordering pleadings to be conducted
in English so as to be generally intelligible; to prescribe the
duties and limit the fees of magistrates; to enact that no life
should be taken without the testimony of two credible witnesses; to see that prisoners had 'a speedy trial,' and be
'neither starved nor their families ruined by long and lingering
imprisonment, and that imprisonment' might 'be used only
for safe custody until time of trial, and not as a punishment for
offences;' to abolish tithes and leave all ministers to be 'paid
only by those who voluntarily choose them and contract with
them for their labours;' to set free insolvent debtors, and, on
the other hand, to hinder debtors who had wherewithal to pay
their debts from sheltering themselves in prison against their
creditors; to regulate the conduct of the keepers of prisons;
to provide some means of keeping the poor from beggary and
vice; and to restrain impious persons from reproaching the
well-affected with the ignominious titles of roundheads, factious,
seditious, and the like; and, finally, to exclude no one 'of
approved fidelity from bearing office of trust in the commonwealth for nonconformity.'[2]

[1] This was directed against the imprisonment of Lilburne by the House
of Lords; see p. 125.　　　[2] *Gold Tried in the Fire,* p. 1, E. 392, 19.

The programme was one for three centuries rather than for a single Parliament. It menaced the habits and interests of

Vastness of the pro-gramme. thousands who belonged to the influential classes. The lawyers, the city traders, and the clergy were all affected by it, and all these found support in the Parliamentary majority, which was necessarily hostile to sweeping reforms. There was, moreover, no democratic wave behind

Danger of its obtaining military sup-port. the petition, and but for the danger of its finding a support in the hotter spirits in the army, the House of Commons might safely have treated it with contempt. The danger of conjunction between the political fanatics ot the City and the religious fanatics of the army was of sufficient weight with the Commons to induce them to refer

The petition referred to a committee. the petition to a committee, the usual function of which was to collect evidence against unlicensed preachers. Neither Colonel Leigh, the chairman of this committee, nor the other members of it bore any goodwill to the petitioners.[1] A certain Lambe being summoned to give evidence was attended by a crowd of well-wishers. Amongst these was Nicholas Tew, who, finding that the petition was being treated as a libel, called on those around him to sign a certificate declaring the petition to be seriously intended for presentation to Parliament. "If we cannot," said

Tew and Tu-lidah impri-soned. Tew, "be allowed to petition, we must take some other course." The committee at once sent him to prison, and a violent altercation between the committee and the petitioners was the result. In the end the committee ordered the room to be cleared. Finding its orders

March 19. Approval of the House. disobeyed, one of its members, Sir Philip Stapleton, seized Major Tulidah by the throat and dragged him to the door. On March 19 the House approved of the commital of Tew, and sent Tulidah to keep him company in prison.[2]

On the 20th the petitioners laid before the House of Commons their original petition together with the certificate

[1] *C.J.* v. 112.
[2] *C.J.* v. 118; *Gold Tried in the Fire*, pp. 6-10, E. 392, 19.

which had been proposed by Tew, and a second petition
asking that the right of petitioning Parliament might
be recognised as essential to freedom. No notice
was taken of this request, but on the 26th Tulidah
was liberated on bail. The offence of Tew was
held to be greater, and he was suffered to remain
in prison.[1]

March 20. A second petition.

March 26. Tulidah liberated.

For some weeks the names of Tew and Tulidah are of
constant occurrence in the various petitions and declarations
of the soldiers, who appear to have taken alarm at
their treatment, as if it were a warning of the fate
likely to befall themselves if they were once disbanded. In the middle of May the petitioners drew
up a third petition, which, perhaps, by way of bravado,
they placed in the hands of Holles, their chief opponent, for
presentation to the House. This time they assumed a more
peremptory tone, demanding the liberation of Tew, whilst they
asked for inquiry into the conduct of the committee and that
restrictions might be placed on the power of committal vested
in committees.[2] The House was in no mood to put up with
interference which it regarded as unauthorised, and
on May 20, the day on which the Lords invited the
King to Oatlands, it ordered, without a division, that
this third petition should be burnt by the hangman, and, by a
majority of 94 to 86, that the original petition should also be
burnt, on the ground that, being addressed to the House of
Commons as the supreme authority of the nation, it called in
question the existing constitution.[3]

The soldiers interest themselves in the affair.

May. A third petition.

May 20. The petitions to be burnt.

It was on the following day, May 21, that Cromwell stood
up in the House to read the joint report of the commissioners
to the army. That report justified the Declaration
of the Army[4] as being more moderate than anything
which would have emanated directly from the private
soldiers. The interference of the officers in drawing it up had

May 21. The report of the com- missioners.

---

[1] *Gold Tried in the Fire*, p. 6, E. 392, 19; *C.J.* v. 119, 125.

[2] *Gold Tried in the Fire*, p. 9, E. 392, 19.

[3] *C.J.* v. 179.

[4] See p. 247. It is styled a Summary in the Report.

'hitherto proved for the best,' and might 'through the good-
ness of God, with the wisdom of the Parliament,' be turned to
a good issue.[1]   Speaking in his own name, Cromwell
declared that the army would 'without doubt disband, but' would not by any means hear of going
to Ireland.   'The greatest difficulty would be to
satisfy the demands of some whom he had persuaded as much
as he could possibly : but a great part of the army' would
'remit themselves entirely to be ordered by Parliament.'[2]

Cromwell again declares the army will disband.

Cromwell's announcement, so different from what was expected at Westminster, could not fail to produce at least a
temporary effect.   The House directed that 'a real
and visible security' should be given to the soldiers
for all arrears left unpaid.   An Ordinance was passed
granting indemnity to soldiers for things done in the war,
whilst others in favour of apprentices who had joined the
ranks before working out their time, and for securing all who
had voluntarily enlisted from being 'pressed to serve beyond
the seas' passed rapidly through the Commons, and
were as rapidly accepted by the Lords.   Moreover,
the pay to be given on disbandment in ready-money
was according to promise raised from six weeks to eight.[3]

Effect of this announcement.

Ordinances favourable to the soldiers.

Those who negotiated with Charles always laid themselves
open to unpleasant surprises, and whilst the Commons were
listening to Cromwell, the Lords were giving their attention to
an intercepted letter from Ashburnham to the King.
In this letter Ashburnham exhorted his master to
hold out.   Peace, he asserted, would soon be signed
between the Spaniards and the Dutch, and after that Prince
William would start for England to relieve his father-in-law at
the head of a foreign force, hoping to find himself supported

An intercepted letter.

[1] Report of the commissioners, May 20, *Clarke Papers*, i. 94-99.

[2] Letter of Intelligence, May 24, *Clarendon MSS.* 2,520.   It is well
to have the date at which these words were spoken.   Cromwell's enemies
quoted them without a date, and held them to be an audacious falsehood.
The question of Cromwell's change of opinion about the disbandment
will be discussed later.

[3] *C.J.* v. 181 ; *L.J.* ix. 201.   See p. 248.

by another army from Ireland.[1] Charles, indeed, had not seen this letter, but it showed what kind of news his agents abroad believed him to be likely to welcome.

The minds of the Presbyterian leaders, however, were too fully occupied with their distrust of the army either to draw

The Presbyterians will not be warned.

back from their understanding with Charles, or to carry out the straightforward policy in dealing with the army to which they had betaken themselves under the influence of Cromwell's pleadings. It is possible indeed that their votes in favour of the soldiers were a mere

May 23.
Their negotiation with the Scots.

expedient to gain time. At all events, on the 23rd, they opened a discussion with Bellièvre and Lauderdale in which a scheme for bringing a Scottish army into England was fully debated. They had little faith in Cromwell's assurances that the army, if fairly treated, would readily disband, and believing that the soldiers intended to get possession of the King's person, they resolved to be beforehand with them, and talked of bringing Charles to Northampton or Windsor.[2] The majority, however, appears

The King to be carried to Scotland.

ultimately to have declared in favour of removing him to Scotland. Colonel Graves, who commanded the guard at Holmby, was a Presbyterian, and could probably be depended on to carry out any directions that might be sent to him to this effect.[3]

---

[1] *L.J.* ix. 203.

[2] Joachimi to the States General, $\frac{\text{May 28}}{\text{June 7}}$, *Add. MSS.* 17, 667, S., fol. 456.

[3] " I have gathered many scraps and looked as far into the clouds as I can, and the result I make to myself is this (but I have only several collections for my grounds and those not very authentic), that the Scots and a Presbyterian party here of some members, not without the counsel of the Queen or some French party, had a design of carrying the King into Scotland, and to set him in the head of an army there, and to bring him up to London, and so to quell the Independent party ; but if I rightly guess, a false Presbyterian father betrayed them to his Independent son, and so the army, to prevent them, seized the King. Dunfermline is gone into France, and, as is thought, to get the Prince into Scotland, and so to play the game the better by that means." Dr. Denton to Sir R. Verney, June 14, *Verney MSS.* Denton does not, it is true, express himself positively, but

Councils are proverbially slow in coming to a decision, and none of the Presbyterians had the promptness of resolution without which no plot is ever successful. "Accord-

Long delibera-tions.

ing to the inveterate custom of England," wrote Bellièvre some time later, " we have been deliberating for ten days without coming to a conclusion. We are trying to prevent the King of England from falling into the hands of the army. . . . Of a dozen propositions—the worst of which would have been better than doing nothing—we have been unable to engage those members of Parliament who were in the design to carry any one into execution." [1]

Parliament and army in short were watching one another with deep-seated suspicion, as Parliament and King had watched

Mutual distrust.

one another five years before. Whether it was true or not [2]—and it is likely enough to have been true—that the idea of bringing the King to the army was ripening amongst the Agitators, the Presbyterians were the first to make a false move. On the 21st they had been all for conciliation. On the 25th, instead of pushing on an

May 25.
The dis-
bandment
to be pro-
ceeded with.

Ordinance giving the promised 'real and visible security' for the arrears,[3] they resolved to proceed at once to the long-threatened disbandment. It was to commence on June 1 with the infantry.[4] Each regiment was to be taken to a separate rendezvous, in order to hinder concerted action, and the choice between service in Ireland and instant disbandment was to be peremptorily offered to every

he was a physician in good practice, and as such had excellent means of ascertaining the truth. What he says about Dunfermline's mission is, as will be seen, confirmed by Bellièvre, and the rest of his story fits in very well with what we know from the despatches of Joachimi and Bellièvre. The father and son referred to may be conjectured to have been the two Vanes.

[1] Bellièvre to Mazarin, June $\frac{3}{13}$, *R.O. Transcripts.*

[2] That the plan of carrying off the King to the army had been sug-gested some weeks before there can be no doubt. See p. 237.

[3] See p. 258.

[4] Waller, in his *Vindication*, 125, writes as if the soldiers ought to have been satisfied, omitting to take into account their distrust of unsecured promises of the future payment of arrears after disbandment.

soldier. This scheme, having been accepted by the Commons on the 25th, was on the 27th adopted by the Lords.[1]

As might have been expected the Agitators at once determined to resist. One of their number, probably Sexby,

The Agitators determine to resist.

wrote from London urging them to stir up the soldiers against all inducements to go to Ireland, and to seize on the persons of those officers who were prepared to lead them thither.[2] On the 27th a

May 27. Ireton expresses the dissatisfaction of the soldiers.

letter, probably from Ireton to Cromwell, expressed in plain words the dissatisfaction of the soldiers at the smallness of the sum offered them, and at the postponement of any vindication of the army from

the charges unjustly brought against them. "Truly, sir," the writer proceeds, "I am loath to express what their sense is of this; 'tis in vain to say anything on their behalf. I only dread the consequences, and desire that on all sides there may be more moderation and temper. I doubt the disobliging of so faithful an army will be repented of; provocation and exasperation makes men think of what they never intended. They are possessed as far as I can discern with this opinion, that if they be thus scornfully dealt with for their faithful services whilst the sword is in their hands, what shall their usage be when they are dissolved? I assure you that passionate and violent counsel which is given thus to provoke the army will in time be apprehended to be destructive, or my observation fails me. It shall be my endeavour to keep things as right as I can, but how long I shall be able I know not. Unless you proceed upon better principles, and more moderate terms than I observed when I was in London in the bitterness of spirit in some Parliament men, citizens, and clergy, and by what I perceive in the resolution of the soldiers to defend themselves in just things as they pretend, . . . I cannot but imagine a storm."[3]

---

[1] *C.J.* v. 183; *L.J.* ix. 207.

[2] Sexby (?) to the Agitators, May 25 (?), *Clarke Papers*, i. 100.

[3] Ireton (?) to Cromwell (?), *Clarke Papers*, i. 101. In the text the letter is dated on the 25th, but Mr. Firth shows that the date was almost certainly the 27th. If Ireton was the writer, it may be taken as strong evidence that neither he nor Cromwell was engaged in a scheme to stir

The storm was already gathering.   In response to Sexby's call,[1] the Agitators drew up a petition in which they complained

An Agitators' petition.

of the order for disbandment, not merely because the soldiers' grievances were still unredressed, but also because the 'intenders, contrivers, and promoters of the destruction of the army,' had not been called to account.[2]

Little hope of an understanding now remained.   On the 28th the House vainly offered security for the arrears, and

May 28. The Houses offer security.

promised redress of grievances after the disbandment.[3]   On the 29th, a council of war which had been called by Fairfax recommended that a general

May 29. A council of war.

rendezvous should be held, ostensibly as a means of keeping the soldiers under better control,[4] but in reality to make it more easy to resist the disband-

A general rendezvous demanded.

ment.   "A committee," wrote someone from Bury St. Edmunds, where the head-quarters now were,

The disbandment to be resisted.

"is appointed . . . to come down on Tuesday next to disband the general's regiment.   They may as well send them among so many bears to take away their whelps."[5]

The army was now thoroughly out of hand.   On the 31st,

The Commissioners for disbandment at Chelmsford.

when the commissioners appointed by Parliament to carry out the disbandment arrived at Chelmsford to make a beginning with Fairfax's own regiment of foot, they found everything in confusion.   The

Mutiny in Fairfax's regiment.

soldiers of one company having broken open their lieutenant's door, pointed a musket at his breast, and compelled him to surrender their colours.   After this exploit

up the soldiers to mutiny. This letter is followed (p. 103) by one from Col. White, member for Pontefract, to Fairfax, dated May 28, in which the writer says that if the army refuses to disband, there will 'follow the ruin and desolation of the Commonwealth.' He then argues that 'the Parliament being disobeyed, and the kingdom burdened with an army voted unnecessary and to be disbanded, a force must be raised to compel obedience, and, rather than fail, the Scots speedily called in.' Here is confirmation enough of Dr. Denton's story ; see p. 259, note 3.

[1] See p. 261.   [2] *Two Letters*, E. 391, 2.   [3] *L.J.* ix. 222.
[4] *Idem* ix. 226; *Clarke Papers*, i. 108.   [5] *Idem*, i. 111.

they marched off towards Newmarket, the place fixed by Fairfax
for the general rendezvous ; and all the other companies of the
regiment soon followed in their steps.　On June 1
the commissioners, hearing that the mutineers were
likely to halt at Braintree, sent Colonel Jackson to
address them.　The men, after professing their willingness to
hear what he had to say, greeted him and his companions with
cries of "Here come our enemies !"　When Jackson proceeded to read the votes of Parliament in their hearing, a soldier shouted out the question, "What do
you bringing your twopenny pamphlets to us?"　The
whole regiment then marched off towards Newmarket.　On the
way, some of the soldiers, unless the commissioners were misinformed, betook themselves to plunder.　At Braintree a house
was broken open, and 50*l.* carried off.　It is true that the
offenders were placed under arrest, but they were soon liberated
by their comrades.　The commissioners made the discovery,
which it would have been well for those who sent them to have
found out two months before, that the whole army was not
yearning for spiritual liberty alone.　"Many of the soldiers,"
they wrote, "being dealt with profess that money is the only
thing they insist upon, and that four months' pay would have
given satisfaction." [1]　It was evidently useless for
the commissioners to attempt to carry out their instructions farther, and on June 2 the Houses recalled
them to Westminster. [2]

Amongst the outlying regiments was one which had been
despatched to Portsmouth with a view to its embarkation for
the reduction of Jersey.　Its colonel, Thomas Rainsborough, was a son of the Rainsborough who, in the
reign of James I., had been employed against the
pirates of Sallee. [3]　At one time he served as a sailor, but soon
after the outbreak of the Civil War had transferred himself to

Marginal notes:
June 1.
An up-
roarious
review.

Misconduct
of some of
the soldiers.

June 2.
Recall of
the commis-
sioners.

Rains-
borough
and his
regiment.

----

[1] The Commissioners for Disbandment to the Committee for Irish
Affairs, May 31, Cary's *Mem. of the Civil War,* i. 219 ; the same to the
same, June 1, *Tanner MSS.* lviii. fol. 129.

[2] *L.J.* ix. 230.

[3] See *Hist. of Engl.* 1603–1642, viii. 270.

the land service of the Parliament, and had recently been elected a member of the House of Commons. On the 28th news

Mutiny of the regiment.

reached Westminster that his regiment had mutinied in Hampshire and was marching towards Oxford. In fact the regiment was acting in accordance with orders from the Agitators, who were aware that Parliament wished to deprive the army of all military coherence by seizing its train of artillery, the greater part of which was stored at Oxford.

May 28.
May 30.
Rains-borough at Abingdon.

On the 28th the House, hearing of the mutiny, sent Rainsborough off to quell it. On the 30th he found his men at Abingdon, and succeeded, though not without difficulty, in maintaining his authority and in hindering the regiment from pursuing its march to Oxford.[1]

May 31.
Order to seize the artillery at Oxford.

On May 31, probably encouraged by their knowledge of Rainsborough's arrival at Abingdon, the Committee for Irish Affairs gave orders for the transportation of the train of artillery to London. It was certain that the Agitators would do their utmost to hinder its removal, and that, unless a strong hand intervened to restore discipline, military anarchy would be the result. Fairfax had

Fairfax and Cromwell.

been drawn both ways, on the one hand by his sympathy with his men who were suffering from undoubted grievances, and on the other hand by his reverence for Parliamentary authority. Up to this time Crom-

Cromwell face to face with military anarchy,

well, actuated by the same motives, had refrained from action. His appearance at head-quarters as a commissioner had been a last attempt to reconcile two contradictory policies, and to secure the disbandment of the army on fair terms.[2] The vote of May 25 for immediate

---

[1] *Clarke Papers*, 105, note e; Rainsborough to Lenthall, June 1. *Archæol.* xlvi. 22.

[2] Mr. Firth has called my attention to the following passage in a letter written to Cromwell on Dec. 3, 1656 (*Thurloe*, v. 674). "Sir Gilbert Pickering was pleased in his garden privately to give me to understand with how much unwillingness you were at last drawn to head that violent and rash part of the army at Triploe Heath, when they would not disband. He did tell me you rode it out until the third letter came to you from them, wherein they peremptorily told you that, if you would not forthwith, nay presently, come and head them, they would go their own

disbandment had flung his mediation to the winds, and he found himself face to face with military anarchy as the only alternative to injustice.

Whether the course taken by Parliament in dealing with the army would alone have been sufficient to change Cromwell's attitude it is impossible to say.   There is every probability that his strongest motive for abandoning his professions of obedience to Parliament was to be found in another quarter.   Great as was Cromwell's dread of military anarchy, he dreaded still

and with a threatened foreign invasion.   more a renewal of the war, especially if it was to involve the invasion of England by a Scottish army.   Towards the end of May, at the very time when the London militia was being reorganised and the army threatened with the loss of its artillery, Cromwell learnt that the leading Presbyterians were negotiating with the French ambassadors and the Scottish commissioners for a Scottish intervention in England, and for carrying off the King from Holmby.[1]   There is no need to seek further for motives to explain his abandonment of the position which he had maintained for the last three months in spite of all temptation.

To meet these designs it was not enough to maintain a hold on the artillery.   The immediate source of danger lay in the

Danger of a Presbyterian seizure of the King.   intention of the Presbyterians to possess themselves of the person of the King.   As far as can be gathered from obscure hints which are all that have been handed down, a counter-move had for some days been projected by the Agitators.[2]   There is, in fact, reason to

way without you.   They were resolved to do so, for they did see Presbytery, London, and the Scots go in such ways as would beget a new war and very fatal also."

[1] See p. 259, note 3.   We may be sure that if Vane knew the secret, Cromwell knew it too.   The betrayal of the plan for a Scottish invasion is corroborated by Joyce's narrative (*Rushw.* vi. 517), where it is said that one Scotch lord had been sent to France, and another to Scotland, 'and all this to bring another army into England.'

[2] In a letter of the 29th (*Clarke Papers*, i. 112) we are told that 'Oxford, where our magazine is, we have well secured.   I wish things at Holmby were as secure.'   A passage from another letter, probably from Sexby, on the 28th, seems to point to the employment of someone who

believe that a certain Cornet Joyce, who had formerly been a tailor, had been directed by them to lead a picked body of horse to Oxford, and to take measures for the security of the artillery there. Possibly he had also orders to proceed to Holmby and to ward off any attempt to carry away the King.

If this plan was discussed amongst the Agitators, it must have reached the ears of Cromwell. Though he had hitherto

Cromwell and the Agitators.

refused to commit himself to the adoption of their projects, he led no isolated life, and he had given them every reason to treat him with confidence. With the knowledge that he had recently acquired, he could no longer regard the situation as he had hitherto done. To keep England out of the hands of the Scots must have seemed to him a purely defensive measure. Yet, though it was no longer possible or even desirable to suffer the disbandment of the army, it was still both possible and desirable that a stop should be put to the military disorganisation now setting in, and that the irregular activities of the soldiers should be directed to the establishment of order on some new basis.

Accordingly, on May 31, the day on which the order of the Presbyterian Committee for Irish Affairs for seizing the artillery

A meeting at Cromwell's house.

at Oxford left London, a meeting was held at Cromwell's house in Drury Lane, at which Joyce received instructions from Cromwell to carry out the double mission with which, in all probability, he had already been entrusted by the Agitators. The official sanction of the Lieutenant-General was thus given to what had hitherto been merely a disorderly and mutinous suggestion.[1]   Joyce was first to

was to be sent at least to Oxford if not farther. 'Let two horsemen go presently to Colonel Rainsborough to Oxford, and be very careful you be not overwitted. Now break the neck of this design, and you will do it well, and you must now do to make a bolt or a shot, and not to dally, but a good party of horse of 1,000, and to have spies with them before to bring you intelligence, and to quarter your horse overnight, and to march in the night.' *Idem* 106.

[1] Our knowledge of these proceedings comes from two witnesses : the first, John Harris, a printer who subsequently printed pamphlets for the army at Oxford and London, and afterwards both printed and wrote pam-

betake himself to Oxford to take measures for the security of
the military stores, and then, placing himself at the head of a

phlets in the interests of the levellers.   In one of those written by himself
under the pseudonym of 'Sirrahniho,' issued on Dec. 8, 1647, he attacked
Cromwell, having had through his communications with the soldiers good
opportunities of knowing the truth, whilst he had a strong desire to say
everything to Cromwell's disadvantage.   The title of this pamphlet was
The Grand Design (E. 419, 5), the substance of which is incorporated in
Holles's Memoirs, which cannot therefore be here regarded as an original
authority.   " The army and council therefore," writes Harris, " did agree
and enter into an engagement . . . to endeavour and employ all their force
to break and prevent that design of raising another army, and to defend,
and to maintain and vindicate the liberties and native birthrights of all the
free Commons of England. . . . In pursuance whereof it was by some
persons at L.-Gen. Cromwell's, he himself being present upon Monday at
night before Whitsunday, 1647," *i.e.* May 31, " resolved that forasmuch
as it was probable that the said Holles and his party had a determination
privately to remove the King to some place of strength, or else to set him
at the head of another army, that therefore Cornet Joyce should with as
much speed and secrecy as might be, repair to Oxford, to give instructions
for the securing the garrison, magazine, and train therein from the said
party then endeavouring to get the same, and then forthwith to gather such
a party of horse as he could conveniently get to his assistance, and either
secure the person of the King from being removed by any other, or, if occasion were, to remove him to some place of better security for the prevention of the design of the aforesaid pretended traitorous party, which was
accordingly done, both with the knowledge and approbation of L.-Gen.
Cromwell, though he afterwards, like a subtle fox, would not be pleased
to take notice of it."

The second witness is Major Huntington, also a witness with intimate
knowledge of Cromwell's proceedings, and, when his evidence was given,
bitterly hostile to him.   In his *Sundry Reasons*, laid before the House of
Lords on August 2, 1648, he mentions a letter written by Joyce to Fairfax
shortly after the seizure of the King.   " The General," he proceeds,
" being troubled thereat, told Commissary General Ireton that he did not
like it, demanding who gave those orders.   He replied that he gave orders
only for securing the King there, and not for taking him away from thence.
Lieut.-Gen. Cromwell, coming then from London, said that if this had not
been done, the King would have been fetched away by order of Parliament,
or else Col. Graves, by the advice of the Commissioners, would have
carried him to London, throwing themselves upon the favour of the Parliament for that service.   The same day Cornet Joyce being told that the
General was displeased with him for bringing the King from Holmby ; he

body of 500 horse, furnished out of several regiments, he was to ride to Holmby and to secure the person of the King against any attempt to carry him off in order to place him at the head either of a new Presbyterian army in England or of a Scottish invading force. It is moreover possible that Joyce was also instructed by Cromwell to carry Charles to some place of greater security in case of any attempt being made to rescue him.

When, on June 1, Joyce reached Oxford, he found the disposition of the garrison all that could be desired. Not only did the soldiers refuse to part with the artillery entrusted to their care,[1] but when on the following day orders arrived from the committee for disband- ment that 3,500*l.* which had been brought down to pay them off should be sent back to London, they resolutely refused to part with the money. Gathering in the High Street, in front of All Souls' College where the treasure

June 1.
Joyce at Oxford.

June 2.
Seizure of money by the garrison.

answered that Lieut.-Gen. Cromwell gave him orders in London to do what he had done, both there and in Oxford."

The two stories, it will be seen, corroborate one another. Harris knows only what passed in Drury Lane, Huntington only what passed at Newmarket. There is further evidence that the plan did not originate with Cromwell. In *A Back Blow to Major Huntington*, E. 461, 34, Hunting- ton is charged with being active in promoting the scheme before either Cromwell or Ireton knew of it. " For the King's remove by Cornet Joyce," the author tells us, "those private instructions he," *i.e.* Huntington, "gave to some troopers can witness how far he was engaged in it, before they knew it." The only question arising from the extracts given above, is whether Cromwell ordered Joyce simply to secure the King, or also to carry him off if necessary. I suspect that Harris's account is correct on this point ; namely, that Cromwell's main instruction was to secure the King from being carried off, but that he also said something about remov- ing him to a place of greater security if a rescue were attempted with any probability of success. This would account both for Joyce's persistence in alleging that he had only obeyed orders, and for Cromwell's refusal to accept Joyce's action as emanating from himself, on the ground that there was no immediate danger of a forcible rescue whilst Joyce was at Holmby. On the other hand, Mr. Firth suggests to me that Harris may have derived his information from Joyce, and that it is thus tainted at its source.

[1] Waller's *Vindication*, 136.

was stored, they beat off a party of dragoons which attempted to reclaim it.[1]

By this time Joyce was far on his way to Holmby at the head of some 500 horse,[2] which had joined him from various regiments. Towards the evening of the 2nd he found Charles in a bowling-green near Holmby, and afterwards followed him to Althorp, whither the King betook himself in the company of Dunfermline and Colonel Graves, the commander of the garrison of Holmby House. Joyce, being in advance of his main body, was, however, accompanied by too small a party to do more than watch the movements of Graves, who, as he knew, was a warm adherent of the Presbyterian party. By ten at night, long after Charles had ridden off from Althorp, Joyce collected his whole force about two miles from Holmby.[3]

Joyce goes on towards Holmby,

and finds the King.

The little garrison of Holmby consisted at this time of no more than fifty or sixty men[4] who had already been gained over by the Agitators.[5] Graves, therefore, prudently fled as soon as he learnt his danger. In the early morning Joyce's followers surrounded the house. No resistance was made, but the back door was thrown open, and, in an instant, the soldiers on both sides flung themselves into one another's arms. The Parliamentary commissioners demanded of Joyce the reason of his intrusion. He had come, he stated quietly, 'with authority from the soldiers to seize Colonel Graves that he might be tried before a council of war,' in order to prevent the execution of a plot 'to convey the King to London without directions of the Parliament.' Being asked to put his statement into writing, he

Flight of Graves.

June 3. Joyce effects an entry,

and explains that he was ordered to seize Graves,

---

[1] Wood's *Annals of the University,* ii. 508 ; see *Clarke Papers,* i. 119.

[2] This is the number given by Joyce himself. *Idem,* i. 119.

[3] A True and Impartial Narrative, *Rushw.* vi. 513. This was no doubt, as Professor Masson has pointed out, Joyce's own account of the affair. See also Montague to Manchester, June 3, *L.J.* ix. 237.

[4] *Idem,* ix. 235.

[5] *Clarke Papers,* i. 113.

handed in a paper in which he reiterated his belief that the
who was in soldiers were 'endeavouring to prevent a second
league with war discovered by the design of some men privately
the pro-
moters of a to take away the King, to the end he might side
second war. with that intended army to be raised, which, if
effected, would be to the utter undoing of the kingdom.'[1]

During the greater part of the day Joyce kept quiet,
seemingly content with watching the King and preventing his
flight.   There is, indeed, reason to believe that on the 2nd,
the day on which Joyce was still on the march, Dunfermline
Joyce keeps had laid before Charles, on behalf of the English
quiet all day. Presbyterians, a recommendation that he should ask
the commissioners to connive at his escape, and that Charles,
having made the request, had been thwarted by the refusal of
two of them to give their consent without an express order
from Parliament.[2]

It is improbable that any word of this project reached
Joyce's ears ; yet, as the day wore on, the suspicions of his
men were aroused.   A few soldiers of the garrison
Suspicions
of Joyce's who had attached themselves to Graves were heard
soldiers. to say that 'they would fetch a party,' and as it was
known that some soldiers who had volunteered for Ireland
were in the neighbourhood, the idea spread that Graves would
return with them to rescue the King.   During the afternoon
there was much discussion amongst the new-comers, and in
the end they resolved that Charles must be removed to a place
of greater security.   At ten at night they despatched Joyce to
the commissioners with a request that he might be allowed to
speak to the King himself.   For half an hour the commis-

---

[1] True and Impartial Narrative, *Rushw.* vi. 513.   This language con-
firms the accuracy of Dr. Denton's story.

[2] The authority for this statement is a letter from the King, printed in
Bamfield's *Apology*, 25.   Bamfield's authority is usually thought to be
questionable, and the letter is dated June 4—an impossible date.   It has,
however, all the appearance of being genuine, and if we suppose June 4 to
be a misprint for June 2, there would be everything in favour of its acceptance.   Bamfield's narrative seems to place it on the 3rd, which can hardly
be right, as in that case it would have contained some notice of Joyce's
arrival and the flight of Graves.

sioners held him off; but he was not to be gainsaid, and made
Joyce forces his way into the King's chamber, his way to the room in which Charles was, by that time, asleep. The attendants attempted to bar his passage, till Charles, roused by the noise of the dispute, commanded them to admit him.

Joyce, once in Charles's presence, was all civility. He had come, he said, for the good of his Majesty and the kingdom. He then asked Charles to accompany him to some other place. After considerable hesitation Charles showed signs of giving way. Would Joyce, he asked, promise three things—to do no harm to his person, to force him to nothing against his conscience, and to allow his servants to accompany *and obtains his promise to accompany him.* him? These questions having been answered in the affirmative, Charles promised to leave Holmby in the morning on condition that the soldiers confirmed the assurances of their commander. On this Joyce quitted the room, and Charles was left to find what rest he could.[1] Voluntarily or involuntarily—it is impossible to say which—Charles had given his word. He did not so love either the army or the Presbyterians as to care much in whose custody he was, and was always well pleased when anything occurred—to use his own language—to set his opponents by the ears.

At six in the morning of the 4th, Charles, according to promise, stepped out on the lawn in front of the house, where *June 4. Joyce shows his commission.* he found himself face to face with Joyce, behind whom were the troopers drawn up in ordered ranks. At his demand the men at once shouted their adhesion to the promises given by their commander. The King then turned inquiringly to Joyce. "What commission," he asked, "have you to secure my person?" Joyce tried hard to evade the question, but Charles fixed him to the point. "Have you nothing," he said, "in writing from Sir Thomas

---

[1] True and Impartial Narrative, *Rushw.* vi. 513; compare Herbert's *Memoirs*, 20. Where the two authorities differ, I have preferred the narrative in Rushworth, which is Joyce's own, to a story told many years after the events, especially as Herbert is demonstrably loose about facts.

Fairfax, your general, to do what you do?" Again Joyce attempted to avoid giving a direct answer, but Charles was not to be put off. "I pray you, Mr. Joyce," he again demanded, "deal ingenuously with me, and tell me what commission you have." "Here," replied Joyce, in desperation, "is my commission." "Where?" said Charles, puzzled for the time. Then Joyce turned in his saddle and pointed to the disciplined ranks of the soldiers who had fought at Naseby. "It is behind me," was all the explanation he had to give. Charles could no longer misunderstand him. "It is as fair a commission," he said—doubtless with a smile—"and as well written as I have seen a commission written in my life : a company of hardsome, proper gentlemen as I have seen a great while."

After some further conversation, Charles asked Joyce whither he was to accompany him. To Oxford, replied Joyce. Charles thought the air of Oxford unhealthy, on which Joyce suggested Cambridge. Charles answered that he preferred Newmarket, and it was at once arranged that to Newmarket he was to go. After a formal protest from the Parliamentary commissioners, Charles went into the house to prepare for his journey, and, before the morning was far advanced, was on his way, under Joyce's escort, to the place which he had selected.[1]

Charles leaves Holmby.

[1] True and Impartial Narrative, *Rushw.* vi. 513. In addition to the evidence given at p. 266, note 1, to establish the complicity between Cromwell and Joyce may be added a story which appears in its most authentic form in Whitacre's Diary (*Add. MSS.* 31, 116, fol. 312ᵇ), under the date of June 4 : "Also the House was informed by Mr. Hoiles of a letter was come to his hands written from Holmby by Cornet Joyce, with direction that it should be delivered to Lieut.-Gen. Cromwell, or in his absence to Sir Arthur Hazlerigg or Colonel Fleetwood, whereby Mr. Holles would have inferred that those three gentlemen held correspondence with that cornet, and so had intelligence of that party's carrying away the King and the commissioners from Holmby. But Sir Arthur Hazlerigg denied any knowledge he had thereof, and the names of none of those gentlemen did appear upon the superscription of that letter ; so there was no further proceeding upon it at that time."

There can hardly be any doubt that Mr. Firth is right in supposing that the letter in question is the one now printed in the *Clarke Papers,* i. 118: "Sir,—We have secured the King. Graves is run away; he

The abduction of the King was the answer to the Presbyterian attempt to raise a force to overpower the army and to break it up in concert with the Scots. That the dispute between Parliament and army should have come to such a pitch was the result of Presbyterian bungling in the early stages of the conflict. When the army had been once estranged, mutual distrust rose so high that the supporters of Parliamentary authority easily convinced themselves that it was better to

(marginal notes:) Result of the dispute between the army and Parliament.

The case of the Presbyterians.

got out about one o'clock in the morning, and so went his way. It is suspected he has gone to London ; you may imagine what he will do there. You must hasten an answer to us, and let us know what we shall do. We are resolved to obey no orders but the General's. We shall follow the Commissioners' directions while we are here if just in our eyes. I humbly entreat you to consider what is done, and act accordingly with all the haste you can. We shall not rest night nor day till we hear from you." This letter, which is dated June 4, evidently by mistake for June 3, completes the evidence in favour of the view that Cromwell sent Joyce not to remove the King, but merely to secure him from a Presbyterian attempt to carry him off. That Joyce took no steps even to suggest a removal during the whole of the 3rd till ten at night is sufficient proof, and there is certainly no hint in the letter of any intention at the time when it was written to move the King from Holmby. According to Joyce's own story, given above, the removal was the result of suspicion of a rescue entertained by the soldiers. Joyce's suggestion of Oxford as the place to which Charles was to be taken looks as if he thought rather of placing him in security than of bringing him to the army, and so falls in with Harris's story, that Cromwell ordered Joyce either to 'secure the person of the King from being removed by any other ; or, if occasion were, to remove him to some place of better security for the prevention of the design of the aforesaid . . . party' (see p. 266, note 1). It may, I think, be gathered from the complete silence of any contemporary writer that no attempt whatever was made to rescue Charles, and Cromwell may very well have found fault with Joyce for doing that which he was only conditionally ordered to do, and that too when the condition did not exist. The idea of bringing the King to the army had emanated from the soldiers (see p. 240), and Joyce's action would appear to Cromwell as having been done in obedience to the wishes of the Agitators rather than to his own directions, and he might thus have fairly joined in the declaration made by the general officers to the King that ' he was removed from Holmby without their privity, knowledge, or consent,' even if he had suggested the removal conditionally upon an event taking place which, in fact, did not occur. Newsletter, June 7, *Clarke Papers,* i. 125.

accept the aid of the Scots than to allow English opinion to be crushed even by an English army. "It's now come to this," Sir Walter Erle had been heard to say of the soldiers, "that they must sink us, or we sink them."[1] The real weakness of the Presbyterians was that they had neither a policy which would conciliate nor a leader in whom they could repose confidence. They could not uphold civilian against military organisation without replacing the King in at least some part of his old authority, and the King was prepared to outwit them as soon as he regained power. Charles was an ally who never failed to ruin any man or party that trusted in him.

[1] *Rushw.* vi. 515.

CHAPTER L.

THE MANIFESTOES OF THE ARMY.

On June 2, the day on which Joyce was riding towards Holmby, the framers of the three Lilburnian petitions, the last of which had been burnt by the Commons,[1] laid before the House a fourth petition, couched in more violent language than was to be found in the other three. It asked, as the Agitators had asked not long before,[2] that the leaders of the majority might be called to account; that a committee might be appointed to dismiss untrustworthy officials; that the grievances of the soldiers might be heard and redressed; and that the old City Militia Committee[3] might be restored.[4]

1647.
June 2.
A fourth
Lilburnian
petition.

The Presbyterian majority was by this time somewhat cowed. Though nothing was yet known at Westminster of Joyce's movements, it was at least suspected that trouble was impending, and the manifest understanding between the petitioners and the Agitators was not calculated to allay the prevailing sense of danger. Consequently the House did not venture to burn the fourth petition as it had burnt the third, and only by a majority of 128 to 112 voted that its immediate consideration should be postponed.[5]

An answer
postponed.

The House was perhaps the more irresolute as old soldiers

---

[1] See pp. 254, 257.   [2] See p. 262.   [3] See p. 250.
[4] *Gold Tried in the Fire*, p. 11, E. 392, 19.
[5] *C.J.* v. 195.

of the armies disbanded when the New Model was formed in
Disbanded
soldiers. 1645 had been crowding into London, to press their
claims.   On the morning of the 2nd some of them
posted up on the door of the House of Commons, a reminder
to

> " All gentlemen commoners that enter therein
> To do justice to all men ; who will then begin
> To pay all those that have for you fought :
> If long you delay, sure all will be naught." ·

These lines were followed by a summons to 'all gentlemen
soldiers that are justly behind in their arrears ' to meet in the
churchyard of Westminster Abbey on the following day.[1]

Assailed by these threats, the House awoke to the necessity
of regaining confidence.   On the 3rd it reappointed
June 3.
Resolutions
against
bribery,
and for
meeting
arrears. a committee which had been instructed to receive
complaints against members or their servants charged
with bribery.   It also passed resolutions to expedite the taking of soldiers' accounts, and to find a
security for the eventual payment of arrears.   Scarcely had
this been done when the House was startled by news that
News from
Holmby, Joyce's party had arrived in the neighbourhood of
Holmby on the preceding evening, and that one of
his men had been heard to say that their design was to carry
and from
Chelmsford. off the King.[2]   The reception of this news was followed by the reading of a letter from the commis-
sioners for disbandment, announcing their complete failure at
Chelmsford.[3]

Under this pressure the Presbyterian majority took a step
which three months before might have averted disaster.   They
Steps taken
in the
House. moved that ' the consideration of money for the
common soldiers be proceeded with in the first
place,' and this resolution they carried by 154 to 123.
Full arrears, it was agreed, and no beggarly instalment of six

---

[1] *MS.* E. 390, 14.

[2] *L.J.* ix. 232.   The time of the reception of the message is not given
in the *Commons Journal,* and is only indicated by the order dismissing
Harris, the bearer of the message.

[3] *C.J.* v. 196.   See p. 262.

or eight weeks, should be given to every soldier. As a counter-

A move of the Independents.

stroke the Independents asked that the Declaration of March 30,[1] in which those soldiers who held firmly by their first petition of grievances were quali-fied as 'enemies of the State,' should be expunged from the

June 4.
The Declaration expunged.

journals. The Presbyterians resisted, keeping up the debate till two in the morning of the 4th, when in a House already thinned and weary the Independents carried their point by a majority of 96 to 79.[2]

When after a brief rest the House met again, it was to hear

News that Joyce has occupied Holmby.

that Holmby was actually occupied by Joyce. It was one more reason for giving tardy satisfaction to the material grievances of the soldiers, and the House

Measures of of the Commons.

resolved to reconsider the Ordinance of Indemnity,[3] and to render it more complete. On the other hand, in order to win over a body of men who might be useful if the army still held out, a resolution was adopted for satisfying the disbanded soldiers of the old armies who had lately been

June 5.
Fairfax to gain the army.

clamouring for their arrears.[4] On the 5th it was known at Westminster that Charles was actually on his way to Newmarket, and the Houses, making a virtue of necessity, directed Fairfax to appoint for the 9th a general rendezvous on Newmarket Heath, when the votes which Parliament had recently passed in favour of the soldiers might be laid before them.[5] In the afternoon Dunfermline

Dunferm-line's mes-sage from the King.

appeared, bearing a message in which the King stated that he had left Holmby against his will, and that he expected Parliament to preserve its own honour and the established laws of the land.[6] Charles was evidently anxious to hinder a good understanding between Parliament and army by every means in his power.

---

[1] The Declaration is in the motion called the Declaration of March 29. It passed the Lords on the 30th, but the date on which it passed the Commons was the 29th. See p. 229.

[2] *C.J.* v. 197 ; Whitacre's Diary, *Add. MSS.* 31, 116, fol. 311b.

[3] See p. 258.   [4] *C.J.* v. 198.

[5] The Houses to Fairfax, June 5, *L.J.* ix. 241.

[6] *L.J.* ix. 242.

What backing the Scots could give to the English Presbyterians was now given. On the 6th, Lauderdale and his fellow-commissioners presented a strong remonstrance against the abduction of the King, and called on Parliament to bring Charles up to the neighbourhood of London. On this the Lords reminded the Commons of the vote sent down to them some days before for bringing the King to Oatlands.[1] The Commons, less rash than the other House, contented themselves with writing to Fairfax to send him back to Holmby.[2]

June 6.
The Scots remonstrate.

June 7.
Proposals of the Houses.

As far as the Presbyterian leaders were concerned, the conciliatory votes of Parliament were a mere blind. On the 6th Massey, on whose military support they were able to count, rode through the City, calling on the citizens to defend themselves against the madmen of the army, whose aim was the beheading of the best men in the Parliament and the City.[3] The Presbyterians in combination with the Scottish commissioners had already despatched Dunfermline across the Channel. When he arrived in France he was to urge Henrietta Maria to send the Prince of Wales to Scotland in order that he might head the projected army of invasion,[4] and to assure the Queen that as soon as her son had crossed the Border every Presbyterian in England would join him in arms.[5] Cromwell's assertion that the Presbyterians were prepared to plunge England

June 6.
Attitude of the Presbyterians.

Dunfermline sent to France.

---

[1] *L.J.* ix. 243, 244.   [2] *C.J.* v. 201.

[3] Letter of Intelligence, June $\frac{7}{17}$, *Clarendon MSS.* 2,528.

[4] Montreuil, who had been at Edinburgh since the beginning of February, wrote in May that this plan had already been adopted. Montreuil to Brienne, $\frac{May 29}{June 8}$, *Carte MSS.* lxxxiii. fol. 176.

[5] According to Bellièvre, Dunfermline was instructed by the English Presbyterians and the Scottish Commissioners to dispose the Queen 'à faire aller le Prince de Galles en Escosse pour, avec toutes les forces de ce Royaume là, venir en Angleterre se joindre aux Presbytériens, que les principaux asseurent se devoir tous déclarer pour les interests dudit Roy.' Bellièvre to Mazarin, June $\frac{7}{17}$, *R.O. Transcripts.* In a Royalist letter of Intelligence, of June 10, it is said, with far less probability, that the Prince was to come to London, *Clarendon MSS.* 2,53ᶜ

into a fresh war rather than miss their aim needs no farther justification.

The Presbyterians, on the other hand, believed, without any real foundation, that the army leaders had plotted a mutiny from the very beginning of the troubles with the soldiers. On June 3, when the first news of Joyce's march reached Westminster, they instinctively picked out Cromwell as the main contriver of the plot. They whispered to one another of impeaching and even of arresting him; but there was no promptitude of action in them, and Cromwell slipped out of the House before they were prepared to act. Either on that evening, or on the morning of the 4th, he left London, reaching Newmarket in the evening.[1] Earlier in the day the appointed rendezvous was held on Kentford Heath, about four miles from Newmarket. Loud shouts from the assembled soldiers testified their welcome to Fairfax as he rode up to take his place amongst them. In their name the Agitators placed in the hands of the General a *Humble Representation of the dissatisfactions of the Army*, criticising the terms formerly offered to the soldiers, claiming the right of petition, and bitterly attacking the Declaration which had been re-

June 3.
The Presbyterians and Cromwell.

They talk of arresting him.

June 5.
He rides to Newmarket.

The rendezvous on Kentford Heath.

A Humble Representation.

---

[1] Ludlow (*Memoirs*, ed. 1751, i. 164) puts Cromwell's flight in connection with the events which led to the Declaration of March 30 (see p. 229), which is obviously absurd. Wildman, in *Putney Projects*, p. 7 (E. 421, 19), says that Cromwell was forced to fly to the army the day after the first rendezvous, which would be on the 5th. This, however, does not fit in with the Parliamentary occurrences of the time, as if Cromwell had remained in London till the 5th he could hardly have escaped arrest, and, unless it is a mere mistake, it may perhaps be taken to mean that Cromwell made his first public appearance at the second rendezvous on Kentford Heath, which took place on the 5th. *Seria exercitûs series* (E. 419, 6) makes him arrive during the rendezvous without stating whether the first or second is meant. Judging by the internal evidence of the *Solemn Engagement*, I feel no doubt that Cromwell had a hand in it; and as that was presented on the 5th, he can hardly have reached Newmarket later than the evening of the 4th. As this date fits in with the course of events at Westminster, I have felt justified in assuming its correctness, but it is a matter of inference, not of evidence.

scinded at Westminster early on that very morning.[1] If, it was further alleged, the men who could frame such a libel upon the army were still in credit, there would be no safety for individual soldiers after disbandment. There was, as far as words went, no actual dictation to the Houses, but no room was left for doubt that the soldiers wished the Presbyterian leaders to be excluded from power. "Having," they said, "in this particular expressed both the case and the consequence very plainly, we leave it at the Parliament's door until they shall be pleased to fix the blame on those particular persons."[2]

It is not improbable that this appeal was penned some days before it was placed in the hands of Fairfax. Another, named

June 5.
*A Solemn
Engagement
of the Army.* *A Solemn Engagement of the Army,* which was produced and subscribed by the soldiers at a second rendezvous held on Kentford Heath on the 5th, was instinct with the fears and passions of the hour. It charged the Presbyterian leaders not merely with hostility to the army, as evinced by their public acts, but with a secret determination to light the flames of a new war. In the face of this danger officers and soldiers agreed that they would not disband before they had received satisfaction for their complaints, and also security that neither they nor 'other the free born people of England' should be subjected to the injustice from which they had suffered in the past. They further demanded that they should themselves be secured—by the cessation of the authority of the men now in power—from liability to punishment for the part which they had taken in resisting disbandment.

Thus far there was little to distinguish the *Solemn Engagement* from the *Humble Representation* except that it was rather

The latter
portion writ-
ten under
Cromwell's
influence. more outspoken. As far as there is any internal evidence of authorship in its earlier paragraphs it points to those Agitators who had come under the influence of Lilburne. The later portion of the document, however, contains two practical declarations which

<hr>

[1] See p. 277.

[2] A Humble Representation, *Rushw.* vi. 505. As appears from a letter in *Rushw.* vi. 504, it was delivered to Fairfax on the 4th, though it received additional signatures on the 5th.

can hardly have been inserted excepting under the influence of Cromwell, whose arrival at Newmarket on the evening before *The Solemn Engagement* was finally put into shape converted a protest into a declaration of policy. It must have been evident to Cromwell that if the army was to refuse obedience to Parliament, except under certain conditions, it must not be left to the Agitators alone to pronounce what those conditions were

A Council of the Army to be erected. to be. Accordingly the *Solemn Engagement* proceeded to demand the erection of a Council of the Army, to be composed in the first place of those general officers who had hitherto sided with the soldiers, and in the second place of two commissioned officers and two private soldiers 'to be chosen for each regiment.' No offer of security or satisfaction was to be held adequate till it had been

No attack on the Presbyterians intended. accepted by this council. Further, there was to be no attack made on the Presbyterians as Presbyterians. "And whereas," continues this remarkable State paper, "we find many strange things suggested or suspected to our great prejudice concerning . . . designs in this army, as to the overthrow of magistracy, the suppression or hindering of Presbytery, the establishment of Independent government, or upholding of a general licentiousness in religion under pretence of liberty of conscience, and many such things ; we shall very shortly tender to the Parliament a vindication of the army from all such scandals." The army, in short, would not support any particular party, but rather 'study to promote such an establishment of common and equal right and freedom to the whole, as all might equally partake of, but those that do, by denying the same to others or otherwise, render themselves incapable thereof.' [1]

To organise the army while weakening the power of the Agitators by bringing them into close contact with the officers,

Cromwell's services. and at the same time to obtain from the soldiers themselves authority for the pursuance of a policy of

His change of front. moderation, was a service worthy of Cromwell's intervention. His change of front in abandoning his strong objection to any military resistance to the authority of

---

[1] A Solemn Engagement, *Rushw.* vi. 510.

Parliament was evident to all, though it was not likely that
those who had hitherto relied on his assurances would ascribe
it to its true cause—his discovery of the intention of his
opponents to use armed force for the accomplishment of their
ends.[1]

[1] The widely accepted view that Cromwell had all through been acting hypocritically finds strong expression in Waller's *Vindication* (p. 139),
where it is said that he stole away 'after he had publicly in the House of
Commons disclaimed all intelligence with the army as to their mutinous
proceedings, and invoked the curse of God upon himself and his posterity
if ever he should join or combine with them in any actings or attempts
contrary to the orders of the House.' No date is given for these asservera-
tions, and Waller was doubtless quite unaware of the importance of dis-
tinguishing between words spoken before Cromwell knew of the Presbyterian negotiation with the Scots, and words spoken after that discovery.
It is at least curious that Holles, Cromwell's bitter opponent, tells a
similar story, but places the event in his *Memoirs*, pp. 84-86, before, and
not after, the mission to Saffron Walden, which was authorised by the
Commons on April 30. He says that the other officers then disclaimed
any sympathy with the resistance of the soldiers, 'as Cromwell did openly
in the House, protesting, for his part, he would stick to Parliament, whilst
underhand they sent their encouragements and directions.' When Cromwell returned, according to Holles, 'he who had made those solemn
protestations with some great imprecations on himself if he failed in his
performance, did notwithstanding privily convey thence his goods (which
many of the Independents likewise did), leaving City and Parliament as
marked out for destruction, and then without leave of the House (after
some members missing him and fearing him gone ; and having notice of
it came and showed himself a little in the House), did steal away that
evening.' I believe that neither Waller nor Holles is correct as to dates.
We can fix on two protestations made by Cromwell, one on March 20 or
22 (see p. 222, note 1) ; the other on May 21 (see p. 258). Cromwell may,
as Holles says, have also protested shortly before April 30, but it is more
likely that Holles was thinking of one or the other of the two protestations for which there is actual evidence. Waller's story no doubt refers
to the protestation of May 21, which was made before he heard of the
Presbyterian plot. That there was no dishonesty in Cromwell's earlier
protestation we know, from Wildman's *Putney Projects*, p. 7 (E. 421, 19),
in which he asserts that Cromwell and Ireton 'were willing at least by
their creatures to suppress the soldiers' first most innocent and modest
petition ; and Colonel Rich sent several orders to some of his officers to
prevent subscriptions to that petition, and the constant importunity and
solicitation of many friends could not prevail with Cromwell to appear

It was difficult even for Cromwell to keep under strict discipline a soldiery which had been so long out of hand.

until the danger of imprisonment forced him to fly to the army.' Wild-man was in close contact with the most violent Agitators, and is therefore a far better witness as to Cromwell's alleged secret communications with them than Holles can possibly be. His words may, therefore, be taken as conclusive against the theory that Cromwell was pursuing a double game, especially as they are corroborated by those of Lilburne (see p. 226, note 3).

There is a story which Burnet (*Hist. of his Own Time*, ed. 1823, i. 25) states that he heard from Grimston, which was adopted without criticism by M. Guizot (*Charles I*. ii. 32). Grimston, according to Bur-net, told him that 'when the House of Commons and the army were a quarrelling at a meeting of officers, it was proposed to purge the army, that they might know better whom to depend on. Cromwell upon that said he was sure of the army; but there was another body that had more need of purging, namely, the House of Commons, and he thought the army only could do that.' Grimston further said that he heard of this from two officers who were present at the meeting, that he produced them in the House, where they re-affirmed their statement, and that 'when they withdrew Cromwell fell down on his knees and made a solemn prayer to God, attesting his innocence, and his zeal for the service of the House; he submitted himself to the providence of God, who, it seems, thought fit to exercise him with calumny and slander, but he committed his cause to Him; this he did with great vehemence and many tears.'

In the first place, Grimston told this story 'a few weeks before his death,' which took place in ~~1683,~~ or more than thirty-five years after the event referred to, nothing of the kind appearing in any of the numerous attacks on Cromwell published in 1647. In the second place there is a passage in Wildman's *Putney Projects*, p. 45, which throws some light on the subject. Cromwell and Ireton, he writes, 'professed themselves to be pained to the very hearts, because their way was not clear to purge the House from these unworthy men,' but when 'seventy or eighty usurped a Parliamentary power, and complotted the imbruing the people in blood, they rejoiced that God had cleared their way to purge the House,' saying, 'the Lord hath justified our cause, and hath suffered the enemies of our peace and freedom to dig pits of destruction for themselves, they have written their wickedness in their foreheads, and made the way plain for their own ejection from the House.'

Purging here means not such action as led to the expulsion of the eleven members, but the clearing away of large numbers, as was done in December 1648 by Pride's purge. Cromwell, as far as we know, first talked of purging the House in this sense in the latter part of August 1647,

Before the rendezvous came to an end, some of the regiments called out that the officers who had not stood by them in their

Some officers expelled.
troubles ought to be cashiered, whilst Robert Lilburne's men, taking the law into their own hands, drove off the heath the objects of their dislike.[1]

The army had all but broken with the Houses, but as yet it had not entered into any direct relations with the King. On

June 4. Whalley sent to guard the King.
June 4, the day of the first rendezvous, Fairfax heard of the arrival of Joyce at Holmby. He at once despatched Whalley with his regiment to protect Charles from insult. On the 5th he ordered the

June 5. Fairfax orders that the King shall be taken back.
removal of head-quarters to Cambridge, and on his way thither, having received news that the King had been actually carried off by Joyce, sent two more regiments as a reinforcement to Whalley, at the same time ordering him to halt at Huntingdon, and, on the arrival of Joyce's party, to liberate Charles and conduct him back to Holmby. To this Cromwell added instructions to Whalley 'to use anything but force to cause His Majesty to return.'[2]

It was by Charles himself that Fairfax's orders were frustrated. He took up his quarters at Sir John Cutts' house at

June 6. Charles refuses to return.
Childerley, not far from Cambridge, and absolutely refused to go back to Holmby. On the 7th, Fairfax, accompanied by Cromwell and other officers, rode over to Childerley, hoping to be able to persuade the King to

which is about the time at which Wildman puts it in his reference to the 'seventy or eighty,' that is to say, to the Presbyterians sitting in the absence of the Speakers at the end of July. If we accept Wildman's whole statement, the earlier profession of being 'pained in their hearts' would seem to indicate some language publicly used in the army to that effect, and this may have been the origin of the alleged information of the two officers in Grimston's story. If Cromwell's protestations were made at all, they may have been directed against a statement that he had actually advised the purge, which, according to Wildman, he had not done.

[1] *Perfect Diurnal*, E. 519, 17.

[2] Sir J. Berkeley's *Memoirs*, 13. Berkeley was on sufficiently friendly terms with the officers to obtain accurate information on this point; and unless he is mistaken we have an additional reason for believing that Cromwell gave no orders to Joyce for the King's removal.

return to Holmby. Charles, who appeared to be in good spirits, rallied Joyce on his liability to be hanged as a traitor,

June 7.
Charles visited by Fairfax and Cromwell.

and begged to be allowed to continue his journey to Newmarket. Fairfax consented, though he refused to allow him to pass through Cambridge, lest the members of the university and the townsmen should

June 8.
Charles arrives at Newmarket.

give him too enthusiastic a reception. On the 8th Charles made his way by country lanes to his own house at Newmarket, and was received by the villagers on his route with open demonstrations of loyalty.

After his return from Childerley, Fairfax addressed a letter to the Houses, giving an account of what had passed, and

June 7.
A letter from Fairfax.

expressly stating that the army wished to leave the settlement of all ecclesiastical questions 'to the wisdom of Parliament.' For the present, under pretext of want of time, he kept back both the *Humble Representation* and the *Solemn Engagement*, no doubt because he still entertained a feeble hope that Parliament might even now be induced of itself to give satisfaction to the soldiers.[1]

The Commons were indeed discovering that others besides the soldiers of Fairfax's army could importunately demand

June 7.
The House beset by Reformadoes.

their due. On the 7th their House was beset, not by Independents or the friends of Independents, but by a mob of Reformadoes,[2] who had formerly served under Essex, Waller, or Massey. These men clamoured for their arrears, and refused to go away till 10,000*l.* had been voted for them. The House knew that it might soon have need of the services of the Reformadoes. Not only was no farther step taken to conciliate the army, but the majority was

June 8.
A separate force to be quartered at Worcester.

settling down into a fixed determination to meet force by force. On the 8th the Commons, hoping to form the nucleus of a Parliamentary army on which they could rely, resolved that those soldiers who had volunteered for Ireland should be quartered at Wor-

---

[1] Fairfax to Manchester, June 7; Montagu to Manchester, June 7, *L.J.* ix. 248, 249; Fairfax to Lenthall, June 8, *Rushw.* vi. 550; *A Perfect Declaration*, E. 392, 11.

[2] Reformadoes were disbanded soldiers.

cester, and at once voted 10,000*l.* for their pay.[1] The main dependence of Parliament, however, was on the City. In the

A petition from the City. course of the day, the sheriffs presented a petition asking that the army might be paid off as soon as possible, and the King's person disposed of in such a way that the two·Parliaments of England and Scotland might have access to him. The authors of this petition, conscious that it could only be carried into execution by force, further demanded the revival of an old Ordinance which permitted the City to raise cavalry in its own defence.[2] The proposal was excused on the ground that it would enable the City to deal more easily with mutinous Reformadoes, but it can hardly be doubted that its real object was to enable the City trained bands to take the field as a complete army. The Commons at once ordered that an Ordinance should be brought in to give effect to the desire of the petitioners.[3]

As often happens when bodies of men are swayed by their impulses towards an irremediable appeal to force, Parliament

Pacificatory tendencies. for a time abandoned itself in a half-hearted way to pacificatory tendencies, though the House of Commons rejected by a bare majority of one a proposal to take into consideration the real grievances of the soldiers.[4] Both Houses concurred in a final effort to persuade the army to disband by offering a complete indemnity for acts done in the war, the actual repeal of the offensive Declaration of March 30,[5] and an engagement to add 10,000*l.* to the sum already voted for the speedy payment of arrears after disbandment. No such offers would now be of any avail unless an attempt was also made to put an end to the army's deep distrust of those who had Parliamentary authority in their hands.[6]

On the morning of the 10th the army was drawn up on Triploe Heath to receive this communication from Westmin-

---

[1] Whitacre's Diary, *Add. MSS.* 31, 116, fol. 312.

[2] *C.J.* v. 203; *L.J.* ix. 251.

[3] *C.J.* v. 206.   [4] *Idem*, v. 202.

[5] The House of Commons alone had already ordered it to be expunged from its Journals (see p. 97).   Now it was repealed by Ordinance.

[6] *L.J.* ix 246, 247 ; *C.J.* v. 202.

ster. Before the arrival of the commissioners each regiment
was warned [1] 'to be very silent and civil towards them,' whilst it

June 10.
Rendezvous
on Triploe
Heath.

was at the same time suggested 'that a way be forthwith consulted for the speedy prevention of the Scotch
invasion to disturb the kingdom.' [2] As soon as the
last votes of Parliament had been read out, Skippon, speaking
in the name of the commissioners, asked Fairfax's regiment of

The Parlia-
mentary
commis-
sioners
rebuffed.

horse whether it was willing to accept the offers now
made. By an evidently preconcerted arrangement,
one of the officers asked, in the name of the regiment, that they might be referred to a select body of
officers and Agitators—in other words, to the newly-erected
Council of the Army. To a demand whether the whole regiment agreed to this, the men replied with shouts of "All!
All!" and when the commissioners retired discomfited, cries
of "Justice! Justice!" followed them as they rode away.
All the other regiments made the same answer. [3]

The position of Triploe Heath, seven miles from Cambridge
in the direction of London, was a significant indication of the

Designs of
the Army
Council.

intention of the new Army Council to abandon a
merely passive attitude. As soon as the appeal of
the commissioners had been made, and made in
vain, the whole army marched forward to Royston. The

A letter to
the City.

request of the City to levy horse gave an excuse for
addressing a remonstrance to the City rather than to
Parliament, and in the evening of the 10th a letter signed by
Fairfax, Cromwell, Ireton, and ten other officers, was written
to the City authorities.

There can be little doubt that this letter was in great part
the work of Cromwell. Not only is most of it written in his
style, but it is redolent of his ideas. [4] It displays Cromwell

[1] Probably by its Agitators, but this is not stated.

[2] The regiments were also recommended to seize the Cinque Ports
in order to prevent treasure going out of the kingdom, and to secure all
committeemen and excisemen that they might render their accounts.
Clarke Papers, i. 127.

[3] *Perfect Diurnal*, E. 515, 19.

[4] Carlyle fixed on it as Cromwell's production from its style. The
evidence of its ideas is quite as striking. It is apparently in reference

as concealing from himself that he was really executing a change of front, and tenaciously holding to his old doctrine

Cromwell
the chief
author of it.

that the intervention of an army in affairs of State is a grave evil, whilst in reality he was furthering a course which he had long condemned. By a strange self-delusion he refused to admit that he was giving

Distinction
between
Englishmen
and soldiers.

his approval to an enterprise in which soldiers were attempting to bend the course of politics by the employment of their swords. What they required to be done was required by them not as soldiers but as Englishmen,[1] and their being soldiers could not strip them of their interest in the welfare of their country. "We desire," continued this noteworthy remonstrance, in a passage which may possibly have come from another pen than Cromwell's,

A happy
settlement
demanded.

'a settlement of the kingdom, and of the liberties of the subject, according to the votes and declarations of Parliament which, before we took up arms, were by the Parliament used as arguments and inducements to invite us and divers of our dear friends out—some of whom have lost their lives in this war, which being by God's blessing finished, we think we have as much right to demand and see a happy settlement, as we have to our money, or the other common interest of soldiers that we have insisted upon."

The army, it was further declared, had no wish to establish a licentious liberty, or to alter the Civil Government. "We

No violent
revolution
intended.

profess, as ever in these things," wrote—this time surely Cromwell himself, "when the State has once made a settlement, we have nothing to say but submit or suffer. Only we could wish that every good citizen and every man that walks peacefully in a blameless conversation may have liberties and encouragements, it being according to the just policy of all States, even to justice itself."

to Cromwell's language in proposing this letter that we are told that ' O. Cromwell spake as gallantly and as heroic as if he had been charging his enemies in the field.'—*Clarke Papers*, i. 134.

[1] Compare his language about coming to the army in the double capacity of commissioner and soldier, see p. 246, note 2. See, too, **Waller's** *Vindication*, p. 145, from which it appears that the distinction between soldiers and Englishmen originated with Cromwell.

The writer of these words would not have been Cromwell if he had forborne to draw a practical conclusion. "These things," he continued, "are our desires, and the things for which we stand, beyond which we shall not go, and for the obtaining these things, we are drawing near your City, professing sincerely from our hearts we intend not evil towards you; declaring with all confidence and assurance that, if you appear not against us in these our just desires, to assist that wicked party that would embroil us and the kingdom, nor we or our soldiers shall give you the least offence." The other alternative, however, must be faced. "If, after all this, you, or a considerable number of you, be seduced to take up arms in opposition to, or hindrance of, these our just undertakings, we hope, by this brotherly premonition, we have freed ourselves from all that ruin which may befall that great and populous City; having hereby washed our hands thereof." [1]

The army will approach the City.

The letter thus drawn up may at least serve as an explanation of the charge of hypocrisy which was from this time persistently brought against Cromwell. [2] Instead of announcing plainly that he had changed his opinion in consequence of new circumstances which had come to his knowledge, he tried to persuade himself and others that he had not changed it at all. Put into straightforward language Cromwell's doctrine was sufficiently intelligible. He held, in a somewhat hazy way, that it was in all ordinary matters the duty of Englishmen to submit to the authority of Parliament; but that if Parliament, after refusing to do an act of justice to soldiers, roused a portion of the community to take arms against those whom it had wronged, and even invited a foreign nation to assist it in the work of compulsion, the soldiers were justified,

The charge of hypocrisy against Cromwell.

Cromwell's doctrine about the limits of State authority.

[1] Fairfax and others to the Lord Mayor, &c. June 10, *L.J.* ix. 257.

[2] "Here," wrote Holles afterwards, "they first take upon them openly to intermeddle with the business of the kingdom contrary to all the former declarations and their protestations; but their words, nor yet their vows were never any rule to know their meaning by." *Memoirs* (ed. 1699), p. 103.

not as soldiers, but as Englishmen, in averting so dire a calamity. It was not in Cromwell's nature to look far into the future, or he might have asked himself how, if once an army, under any pretence, interfered in affairs of State, it could be induced to draw back again when its first object has been

The use of force. attained. In 1647 as in 1642 force had been called forth to resist misgovernment, and the habit of using force would never cease till the sword had been broken in the hands of those who wielded it. Those who blame the army may well be called on to blame still more the blundering incapacity of the King at one time, and of the Presbyterian

Fairfax's part in the matter. majority at another ; whilst those who have no words too strong in their condemnation of Cromwell's action, may do well to remember that the first signature to the letter was that of Fairfax. It is impossible to regard Fairfax as a mere satellite of Cromwell, obediently fulfilling the commands of a masterful subordinate. The most rational interpretation of his conduct is that he, like Cromwell, had been shaken by the discovery of the Presbyterian intrigue, and that, not being resourceful himself, he readily acquiesced in the employment of resources offered by others.

The day on which the letter was written was occupied by the House of Commons in angling for the good-will of the

The temper of the House of Commons. City, of which, as the *Humble Representation* and the *Solemn Engagement* had at last reached Westminster, their need had become pressingly evident. The House offered to abolish the excise on bread and meat,

Overtures to the City. to decree that no member should henceforward derive profit from any office, grant, or sequestration, or receive recompense for his services until the public debt had been paid. Moreover, a committee was to be appointed to consider the abandonment of that privilege covering the goods of a member which had, in 1629, been strenuously upheld against the King.[1]

On the 11th, having received intelligence of the failure of their commissioners on Triploe Heath, the Houses took up the

[1] *C.J.* v. 204 ; Whitacre's Diary, *Add. MSS.* 31, 116, 312b.

challenge there thrown down. They voted that all officers and soldiers deserting from the army should have the benefit of the late votes, and that 10,000*l*. should be set aside for the satisfaction of the expected deserters. An Ordinance was then rapidly passed empowering the Committee for Irish Affairs, on which the Presbyterians were strongly represented, to raise horse and foot ; and at the same time the Ordinance—voted by the Commons three days before [1]—by which the City was empowered to raise cavalry, was issued to the world. To give effect to these measures a new Committee of Safety, composed of members of the two Houses, was appointed to join the reformed City Committee of Militia,[2] in taking all necessary steps to defend 'the Kingdom, Parliament, and City.' An army, in short, was to be constituted in London to oppose the army at Royston.[3]

June 11.
Warlike
resolutions.

A Com-
mittee of
Safety.

It soon appeared that it was more easy to give warlike orders than to execute them. Many of the disbanded officers and some private soldiers gave in their names for enlistment, but, on the whole, the result was not encouraging. An army hurriedly brought together would hardly be able to meet Fairfax's veterans in the open field, and though the Presbyterian leaders counted on a Scottish force to come to their relief,[4] the City would, in all probability, be starved out long before assistance could reach it from the North.

Coldness
of the City.

In the afternoon the arrival of the letter from the officers to the City, accompanied by the knowledge that the army had moved forward to Royston, gave further pause to the warlike spirits. The first thought of the Houses was to forbid Fairfax to approach within forty miles of London. On the 12th, however, the effect of the letter from

Arrival of
the letter
of the
officers.

---

[1] See p. 286. [2] See p. 250.

[3] *L.J.* ix. 255 ; *C.J.* v. 207.

[4] " La fazione Presbiteriale anche ella parla assai alto, et di volere richiamare gli Scozzesi in questo Regno in suo aiuto, più presto che di suffrire l' Independente d' havere il suo intento," Salvetti's despatch, June 11/21, *Add. MSS.* 17, 962, L. fol. 385b.

the army was more clearly seen. New commissioners were appointed to go to Fairfax's head-quarters to find out the extent of the demands of the soldiers, and to assure them that Parliament was 'in a way of settling the peace of the kingdom.' The Common Council, too, drew up a temporising answer to the summons from Royston, in which they repudiated any intention of resisting the just demands of the soldiers, and requested the army to remain at a distance of at least thirty miles, on the ground that, by coming nearer, it would enhance the price of provisions in London.[1] This answer was to be conveyed to head-quarters by a deputation of citizens.

*June 12.
A fresh
message to
the army.*

*Answer of
the City.*

Later in the morning news arrived that the army had left Royston and was marching southwards. At once the Presbyterian Militia Committee ordered the trained bands to turn out on pain of death, and the shops to be closed. The Westminster regiment was the only one which appeared in strength. In the City regiments the attendance was exceedingly thin. Some companies were represented by no more than ten men ; in others the officers found themselves alone. Drummers were sent round to summon the laggards to their duty, but their call to come in on pain of death met with no response except in the jeers of the boys in the streets. The personal intervention of the Presbyterian Lord Mayor—Sir John Gayer—was required to induce the tradesmen round the Exchange and Cornhill to close their shops. In every other part of the City men bought and sold as usual. After a while it was discovered that an army leaving Royston in the morning could hardly reach London in a single day. A strong force was kept on the lines of the fortification, but the remainder of the trained band were suffered to go home and the closed shops to be opened.[2]

*News that
the army is
marching.*

*Difficulty
of rousing
the City.*

In the new Committee of Safety, on the other hand, on which the more fiery spirits of the Presbyterian party were fully represented, there was no drawing back. This committee

[1] *Rushw.* vi. 557, 558.
[2] Newsletter from London, June 13, *Clarke Papers*, i. 132.

was now established at Guildhall, and busied in preparing lists of disbanded officers willing to serve the Parliament.[1]

Action of the Committee of Safety.

It is possible that even in the governing circles of the City umbrage was taken at the attempt to organise the City defence under this purely Parliamentary committee. At all events, when on the 13th the deputation of the citizens, charged with the answer to the army, reached St. Albans, where Fairfax had established his head-quarters, its members were soon on the best of terms with the soldiers. The Council of the Army thus found itself at leisure to reply to the request made by the latest Parliamentary commissioners [2] for a statement of the whole of the demands of the army. The result was a paper styled *The Declaration of the Army*, which was placed in the hands of the commissioners on the morning of the 15th.[3] It was the first deliberate attempt of the army to set forth a political programme.

June 13. A deputation from the City at St. Albans.

June 15. The Declaration of the Army.

Passing lightly over the military grievances brought forward on previous occasions, the Declaration sought to establish the right of the army to speak in the name of the English people, on the ground that it was not 'a mere mercenary army, hired to serve any arbitrary power of a State, but called forth and conjured by the several declarations of Parliament to the defence of their own and the people's just rights and liberties.'[4] These declarations had pointed them 'to the equitable sense of all laws and constitutions as dispensing with the very letter of the same and being supreme to it, when the safety and preservation of all is concerned, and giving assurance that all authority is fundamentally seated in the office, and but ministerially in the persons.' In other words,

The army not merely mercenary.

---

[1] Order of the Committee of Safety, June 12, *L.J.* ix. 275.

[2] See p. 292.

[3] The Commissioners to Manchester, June 15, *L.J.* ix. 269.

[4] This does not mean that all the soldiers were volunteers, but that in whatever way they had entered the army they had been brought into it on the ground of certain declarations of Parliament, and had fought for these, and not only for their pay.

the army argued that erring members of Parliament should be resisted as well as erring kings.   To give effect to this doctrine the authors of the declaration went on to ask that The House the House should be purged of those members who to be purged. by corrupt actions or abuse of their powers, or by any other delinquency, had made themselves unfit to retain their seats, as well as of those who had been unduly elected. To this was added a further demand that those who had defamed the army might be incapacitated from doing further harm by exclusion from the power which they now possessed.

So violent an interference with the existing basis of the Constitution naturally led to an inquiry into the best method Constitu- of averting similar catastrophes in the future.   The tional Declaration, therefore, proceeded to refer to an argu-demands. ment which might possibly be adduced in favour of placing authority in the hands of men 'approved at least for Shall moral righteousness,' and more especially of men religious actuated 'by a principle of conscience and reli-govern? gion.' [1]   Yet, excellent as such an arrangement might appear, the conclusion reached was that there was great force in the objection that it was in any case undesirable to sanction 'absolute and arbitrary power settled for continuance in any persons whatsoever.'

The old way was therefore the best.   Let Parliaments be trusted still, yet without any superstitious belief that Parliaments Parlia- would be always in the right.   Even the dissolution ments to be of a corrupt and factious Parliament gave no security trusted, but not that the next Parliament would not be still more cor-supersti-tiously. rupt and factious.   All that could be done was to The dura- shorten the duration of Parliaments, so that the peo-tion of Parliaments ple might be enabled 'if they have made an ill to be choice one time to mend it in another.'   For the shortened. first time the modern political doctrine that the people themselves are the source of power, and that there is no appeal from their decision when expressed through Parliaments recently chosen, was publicly set forth in England.

[1] This anticipates the ideas of those who summoned the so-called Barebones' Parliament.

To give effect to these principles the soldiers laid down a series of definite requirements. The House of Commons was asked to fix a date for its own dissolution. A certain period was to be fixed for the duration of future Parliaments, which Proposed measures. were not to be adjourned nor dissolved without their own consent. The right of petitioning Parliament was to be clearly acknowledged. Offences were to be punished by law and not by Parliament. The powers of the county committees were to be restricted and the accounts of the nation published. After public justice had been satisfied by a few examples, and delinquents had been admitted to compound, there was to be a general act of oblivion. Finally, after repeating their demand for toleration within the limitations set down in the *Solemn Engagement*, the authors of this remarkable State paper concluded by asking all men to judge whether the army sought anything for itself, or for any party in the nation, 'to the prejudice of the whole.'[1]

As the closing paragraphs of the *Solemn Engagement* bear unmistakably the impress of Cromwell's mind, *The Declaration of the Army* bears no less unmistakably the impress Ireton the principal author. of Ireton's. Cromwell thought first of safeguarding religious liberty with the least possible injury to existing institutions. Ireton, while keeping before him the object of establishing religious liberty, was mainly inspired by a desire to remodel the institutions of the country in order to safeguard popular government from royal or Parliamentary usurpation. Cromwell cared little for constitutional forms, whilst Ireton thoroughly realised their importance.

It was not speculative thought which brought Ireton to anticipate much of the political thought of the closing years of Ireton not an idealist. the nineteenth century. That which weighed with him was mainly the necessity of providing against the arbitrary power of a king whom no one might dethrone, His practical aims. and the arbitrary power of a Parliament which no one might dissolve. There had to be found an arbitrator between the two, and no one who, like Ireton, had

[1] *Rushw.* vi. 564.

imbibed the democratic spirit of the Independent congregations was likely to select any other than the English people, because, though the nation itself might often be mistaken and careless, it alone was interested in coming to a right decision. Ireton seemed to have provided for everything, but there was one thing which he had not foreseen, the absolute refusal of the English people, for many a long year, to take up the high position which he had marked out for it.

CHAPTER LI.

THE ELEVEN MEMBERS.

THERE was little chance that the Houses would pay attention to a scheme so radical and so humiliating to themselves as that which Ireton had sketched out in the army's name. On June 14, whilst that scheme was still under discussion at St. Albans, the Lords asked the Commons to agree to a manifesto setting forth the benefits which Parliament had conferred and still intended to confer on the kingdom. In order to indicate that peace was included amongst the latter, it was proposed to fix upon a place to which the King should be brought with a view to the re-opening of negotiations.[1] Stapleton at once urged that Charles should be invited to come to some place south of the river. As every Independent firmly believed that his opponents aimed at securing peace by means of a Scottish invasion, this proposal to remove Charles from the custody of the army was hotly contested. There was, wrote one of them, 'great talk of a design to bring the Scots in again, and that Lauderdale is gone with a letter from his Majesty for the Prince, who is to come in at the head of that army.'[2] On the 15th, however, both Houses voted that Charles should be removed to Richmond, where he was to be guarded by a regiment which had been raised in Lincolnshire, and which formed no part of the New Model army. This regiment was the more fit to carry

Marginal notes:
1647.
June 14.
Temper of the Houses.

A Parliamentary manifesto proposed.

The King to come to the south of the Thames.

A Scottish invasion feared.

June 15.
Charles to come to Richmond.

[1] *C.J.* v. 210.
[2] Newsletter from London, June 14, *Clarke Papers*, i. 136.

out the designs of the Parliament, as its commander, Rossiter, was himself a staunch Presbyterian.[1]

On the following morning the Houses learnt, even more plainly than they had learnt before, that they could place no dependence on the City. The Common Council would not hear of 'a new war.' Municipal jealousy came to the aid of the tradesmen's love of peace, and even the new Presbyterian Committee of the Militia declared against the levy of soldiers within the limits of the City by the Parliamentary Committee of Safety. The Houses were driven to repudiate the action of their own committee,[2] and also at the urgent request of the City to send a month's pay to Fairfax's army, lest its necessities should compel it to advance on London.[3]

June 16. Attitude of the City.

The Committee of Safety repudiated.

Later in the course of the same day *The Declaration of the Army* reached Westminster ; and it was promptly followed by a charge made in the name of the army against eleven members of the House of Commons: Holles, Stapleton, Lewis, Clotworthy, Waller, Maynard, Massey, Glyn, Long, Harley, and Nichols. The eleven were accused of endeavouring to overthrow the rights and liberties of the subjects ; of delaying and obstructing justice; of misrepresenting the army in order to obtain the authority of Parliament for acts calculated to irritate the army and thereby cause the failure of the proposed relief of Ireland ; of attempting to raise forces in order to throw the kingdom into another war ; and finally of encouraging the violence of the Reformadoes at Westminster. The army, in conclusion, alleged that in due time it would bring forward sufficient proof of these accusations.[4]

The Declaration of the Army before the House.

Charge against eleven members.

An army is particularly ill-qualified to serve as a jury of

[1] *L.J.* ix. 267 ; *C.J.* v. 210.

[2] Act of the Common Council, June 15 ; Order of the Militia Committee, July 16, *L.J.* ix. 274. [3] *C.J.* v. 214.

[4] The heads of a charge, *Rushw.* vi. 570. Speculation had been rife as to the number of those to be accused. According to one statement it was thought that it would reach twenty-eight, namely ten members of the House of Commons, ten citizens, four peers, and four members of the

presentment, and it might have been expected that a charge

State of feeling in the country. brought in such a fashion would have roused considerable indignation in the country. So poorly, however, had the Presbyterians played their cards that, though four months before they had been generally regarded as the party of peace, they were now beginning to be regarded even in friendly quarters as the party of war. It is indeed undesirable to lay much stress on the petitions which now reached Westminster in defence of the proceedings of the soldiers. The signatures to them were probably not numerous, and it was alleged, probably with truth, that they were carefully prepared at head-quarters. The remarkable thing is that there was no counter-demonstration on the other

The Presbyterians without support. side. At a time when the Presbyterians should have had a nation behind them, they had nothing but an intrigue with the King and the Scots. Charles, as might be expected, was most friendly in words, taking care to let his supporters know how well-disposed he was towards them, and to assure them that he passionately desired to be

The King to be sent to Richmond. with his Parliament. On this the Houses took heart of grace, and ordered Fairfax to send the King to Richmond and to remove his army to a distance of forty miles from London. At the same time they gave Lauderdale a pass to travel to Newmarket, doubtless with the intention that he should concert operations with Charles.[1]

Whatever might be the ultimate decision of the authorities in Scotland, their power to intervene in England was greater

State of affairs in Scotland. than it had been when they marched out of Newcastle. Before the end of March David Leslie, having overrun the whole of Huntly's country, left

March. Middleton behind him to pursue the fugitive Marquis, and then made his way across the mountains to put an end to the ravages of Alaster Macdonald in the territory of the Campbells. In the middle of May Leslie was joined by Argyle, and their united forces bursting into Kintyre fell upon the redoubted chief who had accomplished marvels under the

Assembly of Divines. Joachimi to the States General, June $\frac{18}{28}$, *Add MSS.* 17, 677, S. fol. 462.   [1] *L.J.* ix. 272, 273, 276.

leadership of Montrose. Alone, Alaster Macdonald was unable to hold his own, and taking to his boats he sailed for Islay.

His deserted followers surrendered at discretion.

May.

Argyle, however, is said, though on doubtful evidence, to have urged Leslie to make short work with the enemies of the Campbells, and a minister, John Nevoy, who accompanied the army, persistently urged Leslie to put the Amalekites to the sword. To his pleading Leslie somewhat reluctantly yielded, and the whole number of the captives were slaughtered almost to a man.[1] "Now, Mr. John," Leslie is reported to have said to the minister, when the butchery was at an end, "have you not once gotten your fill of blood?"[2] Two forts in Islay held out for a time, but Macdonald ultimately returned to Ireland, and the war in Scotland was practically at an end.

By the beginning of June, therefore, Scotland had it in her power to send an invading army into England, and soon after

June.
A Scottish army offered to Charles.

Charles arrived at Newmarket he received from Argyle and the dominant party[3] an offer of such an army to be sent to his assistance. This offer, however, Charles peremptorily declined.[4] He probably considered that a Scottish army coming to his help under the influence of Argyle would insist upon a complete surrender to the Presbyterians.

A few days later, on June 19, Charles turned somewhat dubiously to the Presbyterians.[5] On that day Lauderdale had

---

[1] Leslie to the Commissioners, March 27; April 8, *Thurloe*, i. 89, 90; Sir James Turner's *Memoirs*, 45, 47; Montreuil to Mazarin, June 8/18, *Arch. des Aff. Étrangères*, lvi. fol. 145, 163.

[2] Guthry's *Memoirs*, 128. As Sir James Turner was actually present on this occasion, I have preferred his authority to that of Guthry, but the saying attributed to Leslie by the latter is probable in itself.

[3] Hamilton was at this time opposed to intervention. See Montreuil's despatches to Brienne for May and June, *Carte MSS.* vol. lxxxiii.

[4] Bellièvre to Mazarin, July, *R.O. Transcripts*. That the army offered to dissolve Parliament is also stated on the Queen's authority, in a letter written at Rome on July 4/14 by Sir K. Digby to the Pope. *Roman Transcripts, R.O.*

[5] It is possible that Charles had already heard of some proposals from

an interview with him at Newmarket, and though Charles's
answers appear to have been considered unsatisfactory in point of religion, he showed his anxiety to
be on good terms with the Presbyterians by expressing, on the following day, his readiness to remove to
Richmond.[1] Charles's decision would have been of
little moment unless Fairfax's approbation could be
secured, but Fairfax, as well as the other officers in
the army, were at this time anxious to conciliate him as far as
possible. They had favourably received an application from
him to be allowed the society of the Duke of Richmond, Sir William Fleetwood, as well as that of two
of his chaplains, Sheldon and Hammond;[2] and
Fairfax now instructed Whalley to attend him to Richmond,
though he was not to allow him to find his way to London.[3]

June 19.
Lauder-
dale's inter-
view with
Charles.

June 20.
Charles
offers to go
to Rich-
mond.

The King to
have his
chaplains.

To the Houses Fairfax showed himself less compliant
Not only did he refuse to obey their order to retire beyond the
radius of forty miles from London, but he had rallied
to his army six companies which had left him for
service in Ireland.[4] Further north, Poyntz's soldiers
in Yorkshire, on whose services the majority was
counting, had been giving ear to some Agitators
sent to them from Fairfax's army, and now showed
a disposition to mutiny.[5]

June 22.
News from
Fairfax.

Signs of
mutiny
amongst
Poyntz's
soldiers.

the army. According to a paper in the *Clarendon MSS.* 2,532, eight heads
were presented to the King, June 19. Another, in the *Rawlinson MSS.* D.
399, No. 33, gives nine, the additional one being ' That his Majesty will be
pleased to consent to the dissolution of this Parliament, and that by August
1 new writs be issued out for the calling of a new.' These seem to be the
same as those referred to by the Roman Newswriter. " E se il Rè havesse
voluto acconsentire al loro desiderio un mese fa, S. M. sarebbe stata reinte-
grata nel suo trono." Newsletter, July $\frac{9}{19}$, *Roman Transcripts, R.O.*
They were, however, denounced by the army on July 1 (*Rushw.* vi.
602), but they may have been some unauthorised draft which had got
abroad.

[1] Montagu to Manchester, June 20, *L.J.* ix. 283.
[2] The King to Fairfax, June 17, *Clarke Papers*, i. 137.
[3] Fairfax to Whalley, June 21 (?), *Clarke Papers*, i. 138.
[4] Nottingham to Manchester, June 21, *L.J.* ix. 286.
[5] Poyntz to Lenthall, undated, Cary's *Mem. of the Civil War*, i. 233.

Powerless as it was, the House of Commons had no mind to submit. On the 21st, indeed, it took into consideration

June 21.
The Declaration of the Army considered,

The Declaration of the Army, and authorised an inquiry into the alleged delinquency of some of its members. On the 23rd, on the other hand, it refused even to discuss the soldiers' demand that a

June 23, but its constitutional proposals rejected.

date should be fixed for a dissolution, or that future Parliaments should be limited in duration, and protested against dissolution without their own consent. Its utmost concession was to express a readiness to consider the question of the right of petition. The army was then required to furnish proofs of the misconduct of the eleven members if it wished the promised investigation into their case to proceed.[1]

In the army the irritation caused by these resolutions was intense. It was there firmly believed that the Houses were

The army ir. itated.

only seeking to gain time till an opportunity occurred for using force. It was remarked that the men enlisted in the City by the Committee of Safety were still under arms, and that attempts had been made—not entirely without success—to encourage desertions from the army itself by the offer of a full payment of arrears. Whilst the danger from the Reformadoes of the City was still dreaded, there was another danger from the side of Worcester, where was collected a considerable body of those soldiers who had volunteered for Ireland, and were now, as was believed at St. Albans, prepared to act against their old comrades. It was possible also that Poyntz's army farther north might be won over to the side of Parliament by a recent order to send down 10,000*l.* in payment of its arrears.[2]

The suspicions of the soldiers did not outrun the facts. According to the plan adopted in the councils of the Presby

Presbyterian designs.

terians, the forces at York and Worcester were to combine with those now gathering in London—which were formed, not, as had been the case earlier in the month, of mere citizen soldiers, but of men who had known the stress of actual war—and were to fall upon Fairfax and

[1] *C.J.* v. 208, 221.   [2] *Ibid.* v. 219.

rescue the King from his grasp.[1] Moreover, the negotiation for transferring the Prince of Wales to Scotland was still on foot.[2]

The danger was, perhaps, not quite as great as the Independents imagined, as the forces on which the Presbyterians could count were far from being in complete agreement, and were widely scattered ; whereas the army was of one mind, and was gathered in one place. Its leaders now spoke plainly out. In a new and lengthy remonstrance presented to the Parliamentary Commissioners on June 23, the Army Council declared that it would have been ready to see the impeachment of the eleven members postponed if their continuance in authority did not increase the risk of a new war. Until they were deprived of the means of doing harm that danger would never be at an end. It was therefore necessary to insist on the suspension of the eleven members from sitting in the House, the expulsion of the Reformadoes from London, the disbandment of the soldiers recently enlisted, and the postponement of the King's removal to Richmond.[3]

The Lords were the first to yield.[4] On the 24th they voted that the King, who was now with the army at St. Albans, should be requested to draw back to Royston or Newmarket,

The Presbyterian forces scattered.

A new remonstrance from the army.

---

[1] Bellièvre, who was deep in the secrets of the Presbyterians, states that if the King is not allowed to go to Richmond, ' l'armée que commande au Nord le General Poyntz, assistée des levées que l'on tient prestes dans les provinces, aussy bien que dans ceste ville, marcheroit contre celle de Fairfax.' Bellièvre to Mazarin, $\frac{\text{June 24}}{\text{July 4}}$, *R.O. Transcripts.*

[2] " Les Independents qui croyent sçavoir les affaires tiennent pour constant que les Presbyteriens ont un traité avec la Royne de la Grande Bretagne, en suite duquel elle et le Prince de Galles doivent sortir de France au premier jour," $\frac{\text{June 21}}{\text{July 1}}$, *Ibid.* Though this is merely put as a belief of the Independents, Bellièvre does not express any doubt of its correctness. As far as the Prince is concerned there is no doubt that Dunfermline had gone to invite him to Scotland (see p. 278). Compare a Letter of Intelligence of June 21, in the *Clarendon MSS.* 2,534.

[3] A Humble Remonstrance, June 23, *Rushw.* vi. 585.

[4] Bellièvre complains bitterly of their weakness. Bellièvre to Mazarin, $\frac{\text{June 24}}{\text{July 4}}$, *R O. Transcripts.*

and the Commons had nothing for it but to give their assent. The Common Council, too, being in a yielding mood, asked leave of the Commons to send a deputation to Fairfax to keep him in good humour with the City, and supporting the demands of the army for the expulsion of the Reformadoes, and the disbandment of the new levies. Before the House broke up a fresh message arrived from St. Albans, reiterating the demand for the suspension of the eleven members.[1]

June 24.
The Houses
give way.

To give point to its message, the army on the 25th shifted its head-quarters to Uxbridge, where, as its posts were scattered over a line reaching from Staines to Watford,[2] it was admirably placed for the purpose of cutting off supplies from London. Special care was taken to keep Charles in the power of the army. Rossiter, who had been appointed by the Houses to take charge of the King's person, was now directed by Fairfax to march together with his regiment to head-quarters.[3]

June 25.
The army
removes to
Uxbridge.

For a time the Houses persuaded themselves that it was possible to stand firm. On the 25th, whilst the army was still on the march towards Uxbridge, the Commons declared 'that it doth not appear that anything hath been said or done within this House by any of the members in question, touching any matters contained in the papers sent from the army, for which this House can in justice suspend them.'[4] The next morning brought from the army letters so menacing in their tone that the eleven members themselves found their position untenable. At their own request they received leave of absence and withdrew from the House.[5]

The Commons refuse
to suspend
the eleven
members.

June 26.
Withdrawal
of the eleven
members.

No one at the present day would be inclined to deny that military intervention to redress the balance of Parliamentary

<hr>

[1] *C.J.* v. 222. Fairfax and the Council of War to the Commissioners at St. Albans, June 24, Cary's *Mem. of the Civil War*, i. 255.

[2] *Perfect Occurrences*, E. 515, 24.

[3] Montague to Manchester, June 25; Nottingham to Manchester, June 25, *L.J.* ix. 296.

[4] *C.J.* v. 223.   [5] *Idem*, v. 225.

parties is an enormous evil. What can be said on behalf of
Undisguised military intervention. the army is that the country was passing through a crisis in which the foundations of government had become unsettled ; and that the existing Parliament was an oligarchy protected by statute against dissolution.

The injustice with which the material grievances of the soldiers had been met by Parliament was no doubt the main
The knot cut, not disentangled. cause which banded the army against the Presbyterian leaders, but it is impossible to leave out of sight the fact that the best men in the army were convinced that in coming to an understanding with the Scottish commissioners, and in agreeing to accept from the King terms which would have left everything in a condition of uncertainty, the Presbyterians were as blind to the true interests of the State as they were to the fairness of the original demands of the soldiery. It had been Ireton's opinion, embodied in the great remonstrance of the army, that if the nation deliberately chose a Parliament which worked evil, it was the duty of all men to submit in the hope that the nation would change its mind at the next election. The power held by the Presbyterians was exempt from the chances of an election, and the army, having the sword in its hands, cut the knot in a rough and ready way. How, having once employed force, the army could step back into the domain of legality was a question not easy to answer, and it would become still more difficult as time went on, bringing temptations to solve fresh difficulties in the same way as it had solved its difficulties now.

Even before the withdrawal of its members, the House of Commons had shown its consciousness of weakness by asking
A question to the army. the army to signify what were the least concessions which would be deemed satisfactory.[1] On the 28th
June 28. The army's demands. the answer of the army was received. Parliament must discourage the desertions which it had before invited, must pay the soldiers who were constant to their duty as much as had been offered to the deserters, must send the Reformadoes out of London, must abandon all warlike preparations and all invitations to armies from Scotland or the

[1] *C.J.* v. 224.

Continent, must pay the army till a settlement of the kingdom was reached, and must consent not to bring the King nearer London than the place where the quarters of the army might be at any given time. If these requests were granted the army would retire to Reading. As for the eleven members, the proceedings against them might be postponed till the business of the kingdom had received its due attention. In other words, there was no disposition to bring them to punishment now that they had ceased to be dangerous.[1]

Whilst the army was engaged in its dispute with the Houses, it had taken care to facilitate a future good under-

The King's treatment. standing with the King by granting his reasonable requests. On June 25 he was allowed to receive a

June 25. He is visited by Richmond and by his chaplains, visit from the ever-faithful Duke of Richmond, and his chaplains, Sheldon and Hammond, reached him at the same time.[2] A letter from Cromwell and Hewson instructed Whalley, who was still in command of the guard placed over the King, that, in the event of the Parliamentary commissioners directing him to dismiss the chaplains, he was to refuse to obey their orders.[3] On Sunday,

June 27, who officiate before him. June 27, Charles, who had by that time removed to Hatfield, for the first time since he left Oxford, more than a year before, joined in divine service conducted in accordance with the Prayer Book of the English Church.[4]

In spite of the withdrawal of the eleven members, the

June 28. The Houses order the dismissal of Richmond and the chaplains, and the removal of the King. Houses were still controlled by a Presbyterian majority, and, on the 28th, flaming up in indignation, they sent orders to their commissioners to drive Richmond and the two chaplains from the King's presence.[5] The next day they voted that Charles should return to Holmby, hoping in this way to remove him from the influence of the army.[6] These, however,

[1] Nottingham and Wharton to Manchester, June 27, *L.J.* ix. 299. Certain Independent articles said to have been presented by the army to the King (*MS.* E. 393, 11) were no doubt forged. See *Rushw.* vi. 602.

[2] See p. 301.

[3] Cromwell and Hewson to Whalley, June 25, *Clarke Papers,* i. 140.

[4] Letter of Intelligence, June 28, *Clarendon MSS.* 2,538.

[5] *L.J.* ix. 302.   [6] *Idem,* ix 304.

were but counsels of despair, and on the 30th, the day of the
monthly fast, the preacher who addressed the Commons gave

June 30.
A preacher's
remark.

vent somewhat profanely to what was doubtless the
general feeling. "If the wheels turn thus," he said,
"I know not whether Jesus Christ or Sir Thomas
Fairfax be the better driver." [1]

The Houses were soon brought to a sense of their impo-
tence. They learnt that Whalley had opposed a passive

The Houses
powerless.

resistance to their orders for the dismissal of Richmond and the chaplains, and, what was still worse,
that even the King had given way before the seductions of the
army. He had made up his mind, he said, when he was told
of the vote for his return to Holmby, to go to Windsor and to

July 1.
The chap-
lains sum-
moned to the
Commons'
bar.

Windsor he would go. On this the Commons
summoned Sheldon and Hammond to their bar,
to answer for having used the Book of Common
Prayer 'with divers superstitious gestures contrary
to the Directory as prescribed by ordinance of Parliament.' [2]
The chaplains, however, as well as the King, were already at
Windsor, and when the messengers arrived to carry out the
orders of the House the soldiers took good care that neither
Sheldon nor Hammond should be found. [3]

With all their desire to take Charles's actions in good part,
the soldiers could hardly feel satisfied with his bearing. He

Charles at
Windsor.

talked as if he could summon both Parliament and
army before him to accept their judgment at his
hands. "Sir," said Ireton in reply to some such language,
"you have an intention to be the arbitrator between the Parliament and us ; and we mean to be it between your Majesty
and the Parliament." [4]

On July 3, Parliament having assented to some at least
of the demands of the army, head-quarters were removed to
Reading, whilst the King was established at Lord Craven's

[1] Newsletter from London, July 3, *Clarke Papers*, i. 150.
[2] *L.J.* ix. 305, 307.
[3] *Id.* ix. 313 ; Letter of Intelligence, July 5, *Clarendon MSS.* 2, 547.
[4] Sir J. Berkeley's *Memoirs*, 15.

house at Caversham on the opposite bank of the Thames.

July 3.
Head-
quarters
removed to
Reading,
and the
King at
Caversham.

On the 4th Charles had an interview with Cromwell, and it was observed that they both appeared well satisfied with the result. The leading personages of the army openly expressed their belief that an understanding with the King would be arrived at in a fortnight, and with Parliament even sooner,

July 4.
Charles's
interview
with
Cromwell.

a body of commissioners having been already appointed to represent the army in discussing with the Parliamentary commissioners the terms of a definite settlement.[1]

Though it is untrue that Fairfax allowed himself to be a mere puppet in Cromwell's hands, he undoubtedly allowed his energetic Lieutenant-General to take the lead in the negotiation which was now opened.[2] Fairfax,

Fairfax
and
Cromwell.

like Cromwell, whilst deeply sympathising with his soldiers in their grievances, had been anxious to cling as long as possible to Parliamentary supremacy as the surest means of averting military anarchy or military despotism. Fairfax, like Cromwell, had seen in the attempt of the Presbyterian leaders to raise 'a new war' in England, the point at which patience must end, and it may fairly be concluded that they both hoped to find in the authority of the King that basis of a reasonable constitutional settlement which they had failed to obtain from Parliament. It is true that Charles had hitherto proved impracticable, but those who were now about to negotiate with him can hardly be blamed if they believed the source of the mischief to be not in Charles's own character, but in the unreasonable demands of their rivals. That their own

---

[1] Letter of Intelligence, July 4, *Clarendon MSS.* 2,544; Joachimi to the States General, July $\frac{9}{19}$, *Add. MSS.* 17,677, S, fol. 471; *Clarke Papers*, i. 148.

[2] In his article on Fairfax in the *Dict. of Nat. Biography*, Mr. Firth has shown that Fairfax's statement in *The Short Memorial*, that he was obliged to sign papers which he disliked, cannot be literally true, as the State-papers of the army were signed by Rushworth and not by Fairfax. Still weightier evidence of Fairfax's general concurrence in the proceedings of the army is to be found in Rushworth's letters printed in the Fairfax Correspondence, Bell's *Memorials of the Civil War*, i. 343–371.

demands would appear to him no less unreasonable was hardly likely to occur to them.

The chance of gaining the good-will of the King was not to be lightly thrown away. That Charles was still a force in
Importance of gaining the King. the kingdom had been recently shown by the popular welcome accorded to him in his progress to Holmby in February, and in his progress to New-market in June. After his removal from Holmby pamphlets
Royalist pamphlets. undisguisedly Royalist in tone were, for the first time since the beginning of the Civil War, openly sold in London. A Welsh judge named Jenkins boldly
Judge Jenkins. asserted that the rule of the law was inseparable from the rule of the King, and though Parliament cast him into prison, his arguments were greedily devoured. The instinctive feeling which causes every community to shrink from throwing all its ancient institutions into the melting-pot made for the restoration of the monarchy, and this feeling was now reinforced by a sentiment of pity for a captive King, whose patience under personal hardships made more impression on the world than the untrustworthiness of his engagements.

To all this tide of pity swelling into indignation a voice was given by a parody of George Herbert's *Sacrifice*, which
June 25. A parody on George Herbert's *Sacrifice*. struck the keynote of thousands of subsequent inflammatory appeals to the popular temper. It audaciously compared the sufferings of Charles with the sufferings of Jesus. Yet, blasphemous as the comparison was, few could listen unmoved to such lines as these, halting as they were :—

> " I have been trucked and bought and sold, yet I
> Am king (though prisoner) ; pray tell me why
> I am removèd now from Holdenby :
> Never was grief like mine.

> " To Newmarket now I am by your army led ;
> They'll sell me better than your brethren did,
> Else seek to make me shorter by the head :
> Never was grief like mine.

" For my wronged kingdom's sake, my very grief
   Doth break my heart.   Until I find relief
   I'll sue to heaven mercy from God, my chief:
               Never was grief like mine.

" Causeless they like a bird have chasèd me ;
   Behold, O Lord, look down from heaven and see,
   Thou that hearest prisoners' prayers, hear me !
               Never was grief like mine." [1]

The idea of attempting to come to terms with the King had been familiar to Cromwell ever since the fall of Bristol.   He may well have thought that by scrupulously respecting Charles's conscience, he might succeed where the Presbyterians had failed.

Cromwell for an understanding with the King.

In pleading, as he would certainly do, for liberty of conscience, Cromwell would not be without the support of some of Charles's most attached followers.   Persecution had called forth amongst his clerical adherents a growing attachment to the principle of toleration, which had found expression in the recommendations of the Oxford clergy at the time of the Treaty of Uxbridge.[2]   The principle which was then enunciated in brief and dry propositions was now set forth at length in a sustained argument by the most eloquent of the Caroline divines, who on June 28,[3] a few days before the negotiation between Charles and the army was opened, sent forth to the world *The Liberty of Prophesying.*

Growth of the idea of toleration amongst the Royalists.

June 28. The Liberty of Prophesying.

The author of the work, Jeremy Taylor, had been in his youth in high favour with Laud, and had zealously adopted his principles.   He had recently been reduced to poverty by the events of the Civil War, but his misfortunes had only served to mellow his sweet and harmonious temper.   Though Taylor was distinctly more emotional and less severely logical than the

Jeremy Taylor.

Comparison between Taylor and Chillingworth.

---

[1] *His Majesty's Complaint*, E. 393, 38.   Thomason's date of publication is June 25.   [2] See vol. ii. **125.**

[3] This is Thomason's date of the publication of the first edition, E. 395, 2.

author of *The Religion of Protestants*, three-fourths of his argument were written under the influence of Chillingworth's great work. Taylor condemns intolerance as uncharitable rather than as unreasonable, but his leading idea is much the same as that of the elder writer, that of a Church in which everyone is allowed to profess his own opinion as long as it does not affect the bases of religion and morality, though he is not without hope that even in minor matters, free and charitable discussion will ultimately lead to substantial agreement.

It was, however, impossible for Taylor to leave the matter here. Since *The Religion of Protestants* had appeared, the Separatist claims had been pushed more fully home, and arguments which, like those of Chillingworth, had been originally directed against the Church of Rome, and which therefore laid special stress on the importance of giving free scope to intellectual divergences, could not be expected to satisfy men who claimed full liberty of sectarian worship. In face of an attack from a new quarter must of necessity come a change in the defence. With Milton's belief in the positive advantages of sectarianism Taylor had no sympathy whatever. Instead of rejoicing in the assistance which it gave in the development of strong characters, and in fostering salutary ideas which were in danger of neglect, he fixed his eyes on its uglier aspect, its tendency to exaggerate differences of opinion, to encourage intellectual narrowness, and to extinguish the fire of charity. So much the more praiseworthy is it in Taylor that he recognises that these evils are not to be combated by force, and 'that matters spiritual should not be restrained by punishments corporal.'[1]

Taylor's own contribution to the toleration controversy.

Yet even Taylor, advanced as he was, does not, any more than Cromwell, uphold that standard of perfectly unlimited toleration which had been raised by Roger Williams. "But then," he argues, "because toleration of opinions is not properly a question of religion, it may be a question of policy, and although a man may be a good Christian, though he believe an error not fundamental, and not

Limits to his approval of toleration.

[1] *Liberty of Prophesying*, § 16.

directly or evidently impious ; yet his opinion may accidentally disturb the public peace, through the over-activeness of the persons and the confidence of their belief, and the appearance of their appendent necessity ; and therefore toleration of differing persuasions in these cases is to be considered upon political grounds, and is just so to be admitted or denied as the opinions or toleration of them may consist with the public and necessary ends of government." [1]   Taylor indeed was careful not to give a handle to those who would use his admission to establish a right of constant interference.   " As," he proceeded, " Christian Princes must look to the interests of their government, so especially must they consider the interests of Christianity, and not call every redargution or modest discovery of an established error by the name of disturbance of the peace." Yet for all his warnings it was probable that those who had power in their hands would fix the limits of State interference in accordance with their fears.

Only those governments which have a sense of their own security will grant liberty of association as well as liberty of opinion, and it was the want of this sense of security which made complete toleration impossible in the crisis through which the nation was passing. Charles, it is said, expressed his dissatisfaction with Taylor's argument,[2] and though his own mind was constitutionally hostile to the very notion of toleration, some of his dislike of the reasoning by which it was supported may fairly be attributed to his knowledge that those who had been most hostile to his religious belief had also been most hostile to his method of government.

Want of a sense of security.

Charles disapproves of Taylor's argument.

It was not Charles alone who hesitated to abandon control over opinions which might shake the foundations of the State. Up to this time, at least, Parliament had shown no indication of a desire to tolerate religious opinions similar to those which were professed by Taylor. It had hunted out from the parishes every clergyman who opposed the Puritan teaching, and early in the war it had hunted them

Intolerance of Parliament.

---

[1] *Liberty of Prophesying,* § 16.
[2] Warwick's *Memoirs* (ed. 1702), 301.

out from the University of Cambridge. If England was to be kept steady to the Puritan cause, her religious teachers must be Puritan, and that which had been done in Cambridge must be done in Oxford as well.

Yet for nearly a year after the capitulation of Oxford the University had been left to recover itself as best it might from

1646-1647.
The University of Oxford after the capitulation. the distractions of the evil days when the colleges had been crowded with soldiers and courtiers, and when the few scholars who remained thought more of the drill-sergeant than of their books. The time

1647.
May 1.
Ordinance for its visitation. of Parliament was fully occupied with other matters, and it was not till May 1, 1647, that an Ordinance was issued appointing twenty-four persons to visit and reform the University in which the principles instilled into it by Laud were completely predominant, though a Puritan minority was still to be found in the Colleges.[1] The chairman

Sir Nathaniel Brent. of the visiting commissioners was Sir Nathaniel Brent, Warden of Merton, who after conducting, as Laud's Vicar-General, the Archbishop's Metropolitical Visitation, had changed his principles with the change of times, and now stood forward to destroy what he had once built up, and to build up what he had once destroyed. Those of his

Francis Cheynell. colleagues who interested themselves personally in the visitation were mostly Presbyterian clergymen,

Committee of Lords and Commons. amongst whom Francis Cheynell, the fanatical antagonist of Chillingworth,[2] was perhaps the most conspicuous. The Visitors were to act under the direction of a large committee of Lords and Commons, of which Francis Rous, a Puritan of the Puritans, was the chairman.

Before long the Visitors gave notice to the University to meet them in the Convocation House, between the

A day fixed for the visitation. hours of nine and eleven on June 4, probably expecting that the Vice-Chancellor and the Convocation would make no difficulty in submitting to their authority.

---

[1] The story of this visitation is told in a spirit hostile to the Visitors in Wood's *Annals*, and has been retold with admirable impartiality by Professor Burrows in his introduction to *The Visitors' Register* (Camd. Soc.).   [2] See vol. i. 282.

They little knew the temper which prevailed at Oxford. A Convocation, held on June 1, resolved to hold out against the Visitors to the uttermost. A delegacy was appointed to guard the interests of the University, and a statement of reasons in defence of the course adopted was accepted with unanimity. This statement, afterwards known as *The Judgment of the University of Oxford*, had been drawn up by Robert Sanderson, and it argumentatively condemned the Covenant, the Negative Oath, and the Ordinances for Church discipline and worship. Its importance lay in the firmness with which it connected the monarchical system in the State with the ecclesiastical system which had, before the late convulsions, prevailed in the Church of England.[1]

June 1. The University declares for resistance.

The Judgment of the University of Oxford.

Before the day fixed for the meeting of Convocation to receive the Puritan intruders, events took place which delayed their arrival. On the 1st Joyce passed through Oxford on his way to Holmby, and on the next day there was a fight in the High Street over the treasure which had been sent for the soldiers' pay.[2] Accordingly the Visitors, fearing to trust themselves amongst a mutinous garrison, delayed their arrival in Oxford till the morning of the 4th. They proceeded to St. Mary's, where one of the number preached at so inordinate a length, that before they could reach the Convocation House the last stroke of eleven had sounded. The time mentioned in their summons having thus elapsed, the Vice-Chancellor, Dr. Samuel Fell, Dean of Christchurch, dissolved the House in literal obedience to their orders. As the throng poured out the two processions met face to face. "Room for Mr. Vice-Chancellor!" shouted the Bedell, and the Visitors, as was long remembered with glee in the University, shrank aside to allow those very men whose conduct they had come to arraign to pass in triumph. "Good morrow, gentlemen!" said Fell, with polite sarcasm, as he swept by, "'tis past eleven o'clock."

Disturbances in Oxford.

June 4. Arrival of the Visitors.

Their visitation abortive.

[1] *Judicium Universitatis Oxoniensis.*   [2] See p. 268.

In face of a determined opposition the Visitors were left without Parliamentary support. The day on which they were baffled by Fell was that on which the King was removed from Holmby, and for nearly three months nothing was done at Westminster to enable them to resist the successful efforts of the University authorities to obstruct their proceedings. It is most improbable that the neglect of the Houses to supply their Visitors with additional powers was purely accidental, and it can hardly be wrong to trace the cause of it to the growing influence of the army, and to the hope which the military leaders entertained of settling the institutions of Church and State on some basis which would not involve the complete submission of either religious party. They knew that the task they had undertaken was difficult, but how difficult it was they could not know. They had not merely to draw up a constitutional scheme which both King and Parliament could accept, they had to introduce the spirit of compromise into the hearts of King and Parliament alike, and that spirit was not likely to be found in men who were still angrily battling for their rights. It needed a complete victory on one side or the other to give that sense of established strength to the conquerors which would alone permit them to concede freedom to the vanquished.

July–Aug. Parliamentary support withheld.

CHAPTER LII.

THE HEADS OF THE PROPOSALS.

ON July 6, when Charles was first settled at Caversham, Bellièvre, naturally anxious to contribute to his restoration, set out
to learn his intentions and those of the army. On
the 8th he had a long conference with Charles. On
the 9th he received a visit from Fairfax and Cromwell, and saw the King again on the 10th. On the 11th he
returned the visits of the officers, going back to London on the
following day.[1] It was doubtless on this occasion
that Bellièvre, apparently after sounding Cromwell
as to his ambitious aims, received the memorable
reply: " No one rises so high as he who knows not whither he
is going." [2] In these words Cromwell revealed the secret of
his life, the refusal to adopt any definitely premeditated plan
of action, and the resolution to treat each occurrence as it arose
in the light vouchsafed to him when the need of action was
felt.

To Bellièvre, Fairfax and Cromwell gave assurances that
they were not only in favour of a restricted toleration for Protestants, but were even ready to tolerate the Roman
Catholic worship, no doubt—though our informant
in writing to Rome does no more than state the bare fact—

1647.
July 8-11.
Bellièvre's
conferences.

His conver-
sation with
Cromwell.

Offers of
toleration.

---

[1] Newsletter, July $\frac{16}{26}$, *Roman Transcripts, R.O.*

[2] De Retz (*Mémoires*, ed. 1859, iii. 242), who heard this from Bellièvre,
characteristically added that he then knew Cromwell to have been a fool.
No date is given to the story, but this is by far the most likely time for
the occurrence to have taken place. Bellièvre's despatches only mention
one other possible meeting with Cromwell. At all events, it cannot have
taken place earlier than July 9, or later than October in this year when
Bellièvre left England.

under conditions of privacy such as had been agreed upon in former engagements by James and Charles.[1]

If Bellièvre was somewhat puzzled as to the sincerity of those who showed such unexpected liberality,[2] he was staggered at the apparent hopelessness of fixing the King to any decided policy. In his correspondence with Mazarin, he remarked that Charles might have had the English army on his side if he had frankly accepted its proposal ; and that he might have had the Scottish army on his side if he had only allowed it to act.[3] No word spoken by Charles reveals his inherent incapacity for understanding the characters and feelings of the men with whom he was dealing more than his request that Bellièvre should convey to Parliament his wish that Ormond and Digby should retain their authority in Ireland till he had come to terms with the army.[4]

Bellièvre's judgment of the King.

A message about Ireland.

Neither Fairfax nor Cromwell had as yet had experience of Charles's peculiar qualities as a negotiator, but they felt their need of an intermediary, who had more of the King's confidence than they could possibly gain, and their thoughts fell on Sir John Berkeley, who had been governor of Exeter in the war time, and had honourably stood aloof from the misdeeds of the Gorings and the Grenvilles by whom the name of Royalist had been disgraced in the west.   Cromwell no doubt remembered that when Exeter surrendered, Berkeley had expressed to Lambert an opinion that the Independents were better qualified than the Presbyterians to restore ' both King and people to their just and ancient rights.'   Singularly enough Berkeley had already, before Cromwell's communication could reach him, been despatched by the Queen to

Fairfax and Cromwell send for Sir John Berkeley,

who is already on the way.

---

[1] Bellièvre on his return told the writer of the Newsletters sent to Rome to assure his Holiness ' che quanto al punto della nostra religione, i capi dell' armata li hanno dato parola che consentiranno al libero esercitio di quella per tutti li stati.'   Newsletter, July $\frac{16}{26}$, *Roman Transcripts, R.O.*   [2] *Ibid.*

[3] Bellièvre to Mazarin, July $\frac{12}{22}$, $\frac{15}{25}$, $\frac{19}{29}$, *R.O. Transcripts.*

[4] Newsletter, $\frac{July\ 28}{Aug.\ 2}$, *Ibid.*

England to ascertain the real intentions of the army towards her husband.[1]

Thus doubly qualified for the part of mediator, Berkeley arrived in England. In the second week in July he was at the head-quarters at Reading, where Cromwell promptly assured him that the army wished for no more 'than to have leave to live as subjects ought to do and to preserve their consciences,' and more than this, 'that they thought no man could enjoy their estates quietly without the King had his rights.' On the following day Berkeley saw Charles, who, much to his surprise, told him that he distrusted the whole army, with the single exception of Major Huntington, an officer who had lately been deep in Cromwell's confidence. The reason given by Charles for his distrust of all the other officers was that they had been backward in asking him for personal favours.[2] The whole secret of the failure of the negotiations on which Cromwell was about to enter is written in these words.

July 12.
Berkeley at Reading.

Cromwell's declaration to him.

Berkeley's interview with Charles.

In vain Berkeley urged Charles to keep on good terms with the officers, if only with the object of discovering their intentions. Charles would have none of his advice, and Berkeley, modestly attributing this rebuff to his own insufficiency, expressed a hope that Ashburnham, who, as he knew, was soon to follow in his footsteps, might succeed better than himself.[3]

Berkeley's advice.

Meanwhile Berkeley was engaged in probing the reality of Cromwell's friendliness. From all that he heard he came to the conclusion that both Cromwell and Ireton were genuinely desirous of coming to an agreement with the King, and that even those of the Agitators who distrusted Cromwell professed their willingness to support him as long as he was honestly striving to lay the foundations of a peaceful settlement.[4]

Berkeley convinced of the honesty of Cromwell's intentions.

---

[1] Berkeley's *Memoirs*, 3–10. These have, as is well known, been incorporated in Ludlow's *Memoirs*, which are, therefore, not to be quoted in these matters as an original authority.

[2] *Idem*, 16.   [3] *Idem*, 17.

[4] *Idem*, 24.

Nothing, in fact, which the army could do to create a favourable impression in Charles's mind was left undone. He had been already allowed to avail himself of the ministrations

July 15. Charles sees his children.

of his chaplains, and, on July 15, the insistency of Fairfax wrung from the reluctant Houses an order permitting him to receive a visit from those of his children who were still in the custody of Parliament, James, Elizabeth, and Henry. According to the terms of the permission given, Charles was to have the children with him at Caversham for two days. He rode over to Maidenhead to meet

Cromwell witnesses the meeting,

them on their way. Cromwell, who was himself a father, afterwards recounted to Berkeley, with tears flowing from his eyes, the particulars of the affecting scene of which he had been a witness. His estimate of Charles as a politician was, for the time at least, raised by the sight of

and speaks highly of the King.

his tenderness as a father. The king, he assured Berkeley, 'was the uprightest and most conscientious man of his three kingdoms.' The Independents, added Cromwell, were under infinite obligations to him for having rejected 'the Scots' propositions at Newcastle, which his Majesty's interest seemed to invite him to.'

Cromwell had thus singled out the higher side of Charles's character, his adherence to his convictions even when they

His judgment of Charles's character.

came into collision with his interests. Yet he was not blind to his weakness. He wished, he said, that the King would be 'more frank,' and it was to be regretted that he had tied himself 'so strictly to narrow

He hopes that the terms offered will soon be ready.

maxims.' Cromwell then proceeded to express a hope that Ireton, upon whom had fallen the duty of preparing the terms which were to be offered to the King in the name of the army, would be as conciliatory as possible, and that no time would be lost, lest the army should change its mind and let slip the chance of an accommodation.[1]

In revealing these conversations Berkeley unconsciously gives the key to the charge of hypocrisy which was already

[1] Berkeley's *Memoirs*, 26.

coiling round Cromwell.   One of the Agitators assured
Berkeley that 'Cromwell resolved to prosecute his ambitious
ends through all means whatsoever, and did not only
dissemble, but really change his way to those ends ;
and when he thought the Parliament would make
his fortune, resigned himself totally to them, even
to the disbanding of the army, before it was paid.[1]
When the Presbyterians prevailed, he took the Covenant.
When he quitted the Parliament, his chief dependence was on
the army, which he endeavoured by all means to keep in unity,
and if he could nót bring it to his sense, rather than suffer any
division, went over himself and carried his friends with him
into that very way the army did choose, and that faster than
any in it.'[2]

Charges of hypocrisy against Cromwell.
Opinion of an Agitator.

The charge brought against Cromwell by the Presbyterians
was precisely the same.   "Did not Cromwell," asks one of
them in an appeal to the army, "your great ringleader into disobedience, solemnly protest and
promise upon his life and honour, many times and
oft in the House of Commons, that the army should disband
and lay down their arms at their door whenever the House
demanded them?   Now, whether your papers agree with his
promise the world will witness.   It seems he can take that
liberty of conscience with the Papists to promote the Catholic
cause . . . by right means or wrong, by truth or falsehood.
This palpable breach of Cromwell's engagement makes all
indifferent men believe that this promise of obedience was
only made that your purpose of disobedience might be the
less suspected, and the practice of it the more easily promoted.
Is not this like the practice of Garnet the Jesuit, who . . . did
lay his commands on the Papists to obey their king and keep
themselves quiet ; and all was that the plot might not be suspected?   If Cromwell follow Garnet's steps, I would have him
take heed of Garnet's end."[3]

Opinion of a Presby- terian.

[1] Another piece of incidental evidence against the theory that Cromwell had been working underhand with the Agitators in April and May.

[2] Berkeley's *Memoirs*, 25.

[3] *Works of Darkness brought to Light*, E. 399, 36.   Thomason's date

There is nothing surprising in the readiness of men, on
the evidence before them, to come to the conclusion that
Cromwell, in the sudden change of front which he had
undoubtedly made, had been actuated simply by regard to his
personal interests. The only way in which he could meet the
charge was to tell the whole truth, and to explain publicly the
effect which his discovery of the Presbyterians' intrigue with
the Scots had had on his course of action. It was the very
last thing that Cromwell was likely to do. "If," he said a few
days later of an officer's complaint that libels had been printed
against the army, "upon his apprehensions, or any man's else,
we shall quarrel with every dog in the street that barks at us,
and suffer the kingdom to be lost with such a fantastical
thing!"[1] It is possible, too, that on this occasion Cromwell's
silence is to some extent accounted for by a reluctance to
irritate the Scots and the French by revealing their intrigues.

It was not merely on the forces which the eleven members
had attempted to raise in London that Cromwell and his

Danger from Poyntz.
associates kept a watchful eye in the first week of
July. They had then strong reason to believe that

Determination to remove him.
Poyntz was prepared to place the army of the
Northern Association at the disposal of the Scottish
invaders, and it was certain that he was himself
strongly hostile to their own proceedings.[2] His soldiers, however, were still dissatisfied, as, although the Houses had voted
10,000*l.* in payment of their arrears,[3] the money had never
been sent. Emissaries from Fairfax's army were again busy

July 3. Poyntz's complaints.
amongst them, and on July 3 Poyntz wrote that his
men were following the example of the main army
by choosing Agitators, and were clamouring to be
incorporated with it, in the hope that they would thereby
receive their pay more punctually.[4] On the 5th the soldiers

of publication is July 23. The writer's capacity as a judge of Cromwell's
character may be gathered from the fact that he charges him with 'las-
civiousness.'　　　　　　　　　　　　　　　　[1] *Clarke Papers*, i. 205.

　　[2] Articles against Poyntz, *ibid.* i. 167.　　　　　[3] See p. 302
　　[4] Poyntz to Lenthall, July 3, Cary's *Memorials of the Civil War*, i.
282.

held a meeting at Pontefract, at which they addressed a message to Fairfax, begging him to mediate with Parliament on

July 5.
A meeting at Pontefract.

their behalf.[1] On the 8th the troops quartered at York broke into mutiny, dragged Poyntz out of his lodgings without giving him time to put on his boots,

July 8.
Poyntz captured and sent to Reading.

set him on horseback, and carried him off to Pontefract.[2] From Pontefract he was sent to Reading,[3] and though Fairfax liberated him almost as soon as he arrived,[4] he had no longer an army at his command, and he therefore ceased to be dangerous.

The news of Poyntz's capture was the more welcome at Reading as the army was still anxious about the course of

Attitude of the eleven members.

events in London. The eleven members had objected to allow the charges brought against them to be suspended over their heads till a settlement of public affairs had been reached,[5] and had called for an imme-

July 6.
Articles against them.

diate trial. Accordingly on July 6 the accusation against them was presented to the House of Commons. It consisted of twenty-five articles, of which the most important alleged that they had constantly met at 'Lady Carlisle's lodgings at Whitehall and in other places, with divers other persons disaffected to the State, for holding correspondence with the Queen . . . with intent to put conditions on the Parliament, and to bring in the King on their own terms.' They had further 'assured the Queen 40,000*l.* per annum,' as the price of her assistance. Moreover, six of them, Holles, Stapleton, Lewis, Clotworthy, Waller, and Massey, had 'invited the Scots and other foreign forces to come into the kingdom in a hostile manner,' and had also advised the Queen to send her son to Scotland, 'to march

---

[1] *Rushw.* vi. 622.

[2] Poyntz to Lenthall, July 9 ; Elizabeth Poyntz to Lenthall, July 9, Cary's *Mem. of the Civil War,* i. 298, 300. The lady complained that her husband was ' carried away in his slippers, not suffered to express any conjugal comfort or courtesy to me his wife, and what will be the doom they will pass on him, I cannot tell.'

[3] Poyntz arrived at Reading on the 15th, *Perf. Diurnal,* E. 518, 6.

[4] Bell's *Mem. of the Civil War,* i. 370.

[5] See p. 306.

into this kingdom at the head of an army.' In pursuance of this design, all the eleven had listed soldiers in order 'to levy and raise a new war in this kingdom,' and had encouraged the Reformadoes to raise tumults round the Parliament House.[1]

The truth of the whole charge was categorically denied by those who were most concerned to establish its falsehood, but though it is likely enough that, if an independent investigation had taken place, many inaccuracies would have been detected in it, its substantial truth hardly admits of question.[2] Nor can the army be fairly accused of ripping up old sores to destroy a fallen enemy. Truly or falsely, the soldiers believed that the danger of a conjunction between an army from Scotland and the levies in the City had not altogether passed away. On July 6, the day on which the articles against the eleven members were handed in, a member of the House of Commons sent information to Reading that there were at least 16,000 men enlisted in and about the City, and that there was a talk of sending some of them into Kent to receive a Scottish army expected by sea, as well as of the apprentices coming to Westminster to declare their resolution to have the King in London whether the army consented or not.[3] Much of this information was doubtless mere gossip, but it was gossip founded on knowledge of existing danger, and it can hardly be a matter of surprise that, on the receipt of this intelligence, the army forwarded to Westminster a peremptory demand for the actual disbandment of the Reformadoes.[4]

The Houses, as far as lay in their power, complied with this demand, which, indeed, they were too weak to resist.

Their substantial truth.

The danger not past.

Information from London.

---

[1] *C.J.* v. 236 ; *A Particular Charge*, E. 399, 17.

[2] *A Full Vindication and Answer*, E. 398, 17. The story about the invitation to the Scots, for instance, was not invented, and that Dunfermline was sent to open communications with the Queen is also beyond doubt.

[3] Information by Sir F. Pile, July 6, *Clarke Papers*, i. 152.

[4] *L.J.* ix. 320.

On the 9th they passed an Ordinance for the expulsion

July 9.
An Ordinance for the expulsion of the Reformadoes.

of the Reformadoes from London, and on the 13th the Commons, in accordance with another requirement of the army, voted that those of its members who had in any way favoured the King's cause since the beginning of the war should be

July 13.
Members to be expelled.

expelled.[1]

It was more easy to pass an Ordinance against the Reformadoes than to carry it into execution. On the 13th

The London apprentices hostile to the Independents.

the London apprentices appeared on the scene. They were hostile to the Independents, partly because they resented their interference with the municipal control of the militia, partly also because, in the heyday of vigorous youth, they regarded the eccentricities of the tub-preacher as a fair object of derision. Of late, too, they were beginning to feel themselves bound to the

Feb. 9.
Their petition for holidays.

Presbyterians by the tie of self-interest. In February they had petitioned for the establishment of public holidays for 'lawful recreations for the needful refreshments of their spirits, without which life itself is unpleasant and an intolerable burden,' in lieu of the festivals of the Church recently abolished.[2]   For some time no notice

April 20.
An Ordinance to be brought in.

had been taken of their demands, and though, on April 20, the Commons directed the preparation of an Ordinance to give effect to them,[3] weeks were allowed to pass without anything being done.

It was not indeed till the Presbyterians were preparing to measure swords with the army that they recognised the danger of alienating the apprentices.   On July 8 an Ordi-

July 8.
Ordinance for a monthly holiday.

nance was passed appointing a holiday to be held on the second Tuesday in each month, on which 'all scholars, apprentices, and servants' were to have such time for recreation as their masters could 'conveniently spare from their extraordinary and necessary services and occasions.'   In the case of dispute arising out of the vague wording of this part of the Ordinance, appeal was to be made to the

---

[1] *L.J.* ix. 322 ; *C.J.* v. 238, 244.   [2] *L.J.* viii. 715.

[3] *C.J.* v. 148.

nearest justice of the peace. It is to be supposed that the apprentices complained of the requirement to obtain their masters' permission before exercising their new rights, as a new Ordinance was issued on the 11th, in which it entirely disappeared. The apprentices were still liable to be kept at home in cases of urgent necessity, but the burden of proof that this existed was to be thrown on the master, who would no longer be entitled simply to refuse leave without giving a reason.[1]

July 11.
A second
Ordinance.

The first of these monthly holidays fell on July 13, and the lads, grateful for the concession, celebrated it by presenting to the Houses a petition calling for the suppression of conventicles, the restoration of the King, the maintenance of the Covenant, and the disbandment of the army.[2] It is possible that this ill-timed support was not altogether welcome to the Presbyterians, and it undoubtedly roused the indignation of the army, especially as, in spite of the Parliamentary Ordinance, the Reformadoes still swarmed in the City. At the same time the expectation of a Scottish invasion took so firm a hold on the minds of the soldiers that on July 16 Fairfax spoke of it to the King.[3] Moreover, it was known that Colonel Doyley, who had formerly commanded Fairfax's lifeguard, had presented himself at Bristol without any authorisation from the commander-in-chief, and had demanded the submission of the garrison.[4]

July 13.
The first
holiday.

An apprentices' petition.

Irritation in the army.

July 16.
Expectation of a Scottish invasion.

The first result of these alarming rumours was that the Agitators appeared on the 16th before the Army Council with a demand for an immediate march on London.[5] They found much support amongst the officers, but they were strenuously opposed by Cromwell and Ireton. Cromwell, indeed, was ready to admit that obedience to

The Agitators wish to march on London.

[1] *L.J.* ix. 248–255; *C.J.* v. 202, 206.
[2] *L.J.* ix. 330; *C.J.* v. 243.
[3] Letter of Intelligence, July 19, *Clarendon MSS.* 2,556.
[4] Fairfax to Lenthall, July 16, *Clarke Papers*, i. 162.
[5] Representation of the Agitators, July 16, *id.* i. 170.

Parliament had its limits, but he argued strongly that force ought only to be employed in the last resort, and that the time for

Opposition of Cromwell and Ireton.

employing it had not yet arrived. There was, he thought, still room for amicable negotiation.[1] Ireton, to whom, together with Lambert, had been entrusted the preparation of the proposals to be presented to the King,[2] as it was hoped, with the good-will of Parliament, was against the use of force lest it should hinder a good understanding with the Houses. "Whatsoever we get by a treaty," said Cromwell, "it will be firm and durable, it will be conveyed over to posterity as that that will be the greatest honour to us that ever poor creatures had, that we may obtain such things as these are that we are now about : and it will have this in it too, that whatsoever is granted in that way, it will have firmness in it. We shall avoid that great objection that will lie against us that we have got things of the Parliament by force, and we know what it is to have that stain lie upon us."[3]

"For my own part," said Cromwell, "perhaps I have as few extravagant thoughts . . . . of obtaining great things from

Cromwell not sanguine,

Parliament as most men ; yet it hath been in most of our thoughts that this Parliament might be a re-formed and purged Parliament, that we might see men looking at public and common interests only."[4]   Now

but has hopes.

that the eleven had left their seats, the friends of the army had been gaining ground, and it would be doing them an ill service to bring an armed soldiery to their aid. "That which you have by force," he added, later in the course of the discussion, "I look upon it as nothing. I do not know that force is to be used except we cannot get what is for the good of the kingdom without force . . . . I wish we may respite our determination till . . . . four or five days be over ; till we see how things will be"[5]   At last Cromwell closed the

A final argument.

discussion by an argument which admitted no reply. "If," he said, decidedly, "you be in the right, and I in the wrong ; if we be divided, I doubt we shall all be in the

---

[1] *Clarke Papers*, i. 184.   [2] *Idem*, i. 197, 202.

[3] *Idem*, i. 185.   [4] *Idem*, i. 192.

[5] *Idem*, i. 202, 203.

wrong . . . . The question is singly this : whether or no we shall not in a positive way desire the answer to those things before we march towards London, when perhaps we may have the same things in the time that we can march.   Here is the strictness of the question." [1]   Cromwell, as might be expected, had his way, and the demands of the soldiers were transmitted to Westminster, unaccompanied by any threatening demonstration.

Cromwell
has his way.

As Cromwell had judged, enough had been done to secure the acceptance of the requirements of the army.   On the 16th and on the following days a considerable number of Presbyterian members asked for leave of absence and abandoned the struggle. [2]   On the 19th the Houses placed under Fairfax's command all the forces in their pay in England and Wales, and on the 21st they ordered the disbandment of all deserters from his army. [3]   By the final disappearance of these men the army lost those disintegrating elements which had prevented its cohesion as a thoroughly Independent body.

Presby-
terians
abandon the
struggle.

July 19.
Fairfax to
command all
the forces.

July 21.
Deserters
disbanded.

The first result of the vote which placed all military authority in the hands of Fairfax, was that the eleven members, perceiving that their designs were now incapable

[1] *Clarke Papers*, i. 209.   The body in which this discussion took place is in this report spoken of as a Council of War.   It was, however, properly a full army council, as Agitators were present.   The phrase council of war was used indiscriminately.   "Yesterday," we are told of this very council, "there was a great Council of War called . . . consisting of officers besides Agitators ; who now, in prudence we admit to debate, and it is not more than necessary they should be, considering the influence they have upon the soldiers, and the officers we hope have such an interest in them, as if any of more fierce disposition amongst them moderate not their reason, the officers can command it ; and I can assure you it is the singularest part of wisdom in the General and the officers so to carry themselves considering the present temper of the army."   Letter from the army, July 17, *ibid.* i. 214.

[2] *C.J.* v. 245; Letter of Intelligence, July 22, *Clarendon MSS.* 2,559.

[3] *L.J.* ix. 338, 342.

of accomplishment, asked and obtained leave to go beyond

July 20.
The eleven
members
ask leave
to go
abroad.

sea, and also permission to postpone their defence for six months, although, on the 28th, they had sent in a preliminary answer to the charges against them.[1]

In the army the news that the Houses were in a more conciliatory temper gave lively satisfaction. On the 18th the

Satisfaction
in the army.

Parliamentary commissioners at Reading were informed that the proposed terms of accommodation would be completed in a few days. On the 19th the army forwarded to the Parliament four requests accompanied with an announcement that, if these were granted, nothing more

July 19.
Four re-
quests.

would be asked. Prisoners held in captivity without having been subjected to a lawful trial were to be set at liberty; a declaration was to be issued against the invitation of foreign troops; the army was to be constantly paid; and the old Parliamentary Committee was to take the place of the new City Committee in the command of the London militia.[2] So satisfied was Fairfax that all

July 22.
Removal of
head quar-
ters.

danger was at an end, that on the 22nd, when he removed the head-quarters to Bedford, he suffered his cavalry to be scattered over a stretch of country which reached from Bristol to Newark.[3]

Cromwell had done his best, even when violating a constitution which had been equally disregarded by his opponents,

Cromwell's
attitude.

to preserve at least an outward respect for Parliamentary forms. Both he and the Presbyterians were anxious to substitute government by discussion for government by the sword; but the way to that consummation was blocked by Charles, with whom government by discussion was impossible. Cromwell and his military allies perceived clearly that the securities with which the Presbyterians thought to bind Charles were utterly inadequate. He was now seeking, with scant prospect of success, to devise other securities which

---

[1] *C.J.* v. 251; *Rushw.* vi. 628; *A Full Vindication and Answer*, E. 398, 17. This is said to have been drawn up by Prynne. Burgoyne to Sir R. Verney, July 25, *Verney MSS.*

[2] *L.J.* ix. 339.   [3] *A Diary*, E. 400, 22.

might prove more satisfactory. To gain standing ground for this he had used force to repel threatened force. Unfortunately those who once appeal to force have a tendency to appeal to it again, and it comes to be regarded first as a necessary evil and ultimately as a salutary remedy for public mischiefs. The constitution as it stood in Elizabeth's day had long been broken up, and there was no general agreement as to the principles on which it was to be reconstructed. Every man craved for a peaceful settlement, but, in the midst of the general distraction, they who had the longest swords were most able to make their voices heard.

It was now Ireton's turn to try whether he could in reality win the King's assent to some form of real constitutional government. On July 17 his scheme was laid be-

July 17.
Ireton's constitutional scheme before the Council of the Army.

fore the Council of the Army, and on the 18th a committee consisting of twelve officers and twelve Agitators, with leave for Cromwell to be present 'when he can,' was named by Fairfax to put it into shape.[1] Though Parliament had not yet been consulted, the King appears to have been allowed to have an inkling of the terms about to be offered to him, and a few changes had been made—too readily as some of the Agitators thought—in consequence of his suggestions.[2] As the scheme was now prepared, it did not claim to be the draft of a final agreement

---

[1] *Clarke Papers,* i. 211, 216.

[2] According to *Putney Projects,* p. 14 (E. 421, 19), the first draft deprived the King of that negative voice—the right of refusing the royal assent to bills—to which he was so much attached; and had also excluded Royalists from office for ten instead of for five years; whilst it asked Charles to pass two Acts, one abolishing Episcopacy, and the other confirming the sale of the bishops' lands. Some of these things may have been mere suggestions made in the Council of the Army. At all events they had disappeared before the draft was submitted to Berkeley to be shown to the King, as he represents Charles as objecting only to three points. "The first was the exception of seven," so it then stood, "not named from pardon; the second, the excluding his party being eligible in the next ensuing Parliament; and the third, that, though there was nothing against the Church government established, yet there was nothing done to assert it." Berkeley's *Memoirs,* 31.

covering all details. The paper which contained it bore the
The Heads of the Proposals. name of *The Heads of the Proposals*, as if to indicate that it was a mere sketch which was to be
filled up in detail hereafter.

The plan laid down in this paper for the settlement of
Church disputes had at least the merit of originality. The
Their scheme of Church government. existence of Episcopacy was indirectly admitted, but
an Act was to be passed to take away from bishops
and all other ecclesiastical officers all coercive jurisdiction extending to any civil penalties, and also to repeal all
laws by which the civil magistrate was bound to inflict punishment upon those who lay under ecclesiastical censure. Moreover, there was to be a repeal of all Acts 'enjoying the use of
the Book of Common Prayer, and imposing any penalties for
neglect thereof,' as well as of all Acts enforcing attendance at
church, or forbidding the holding of religious meetings elsewhere, some fresh provision being made, in lieu of the Recusancy Acts, for the discovery of ' Papists and Popish recusants,'
Jesuits and priests. The Covenant, too, was no longer to be
enacted.

The scheme of Ireton was virtually that which was adopted
in the Toleration Act of 1689. In 1647 it was too far in
It is in advance of the time. advance of the time to be generally acceptable, even
if it had secured the approbation of the King, for
whose benefit it had been prepared.

The political concessions demanded were based on principles entirely different from those which pervaded the
The political scheme. Propositions of Newcastle. The Presbyterian idea
had been to force the Crown to submit to the exist-
ing Parliamentary system. The Independent idea was to
bring Parliament itself under popular control. Parliament was
to indicate a date for its own dissolution, after which it was to
be succeeded by biennial parliaments, elected by a reformed
constituency in which the franchise was to be exercised by
populous towns and districts hitherto unrepresented or under-
represented, whilst it was to be taken away from the villages
and hamlets, which had been the main strength of the Crown
and its Cavalier supporters. These biennial parliaments were

not to be dissolved without their own consent till the session had lasted one hundred and twenty days : on the other hand, in no case was the session to continue more than two hundred and forty in the course of the two years of its existence.

In this new constitution a prominent place was to be given to the Council of State, of which the members were, in the first instance, to be named by agreement, and were to continue in office for a term not exceeding seven years. As nothing was said about the way in which their successors were to be appointed, it is to be presumed that they were to be nominated by the King. However this may have been, the Council of State was to occupy a more important constitutional position than the old Privy Council, from which every member could be dismissed at the King's pleasure, and by which no business could be transacted except by his permission. The Council of State, of which the idea was probably taken from the Committee of Both Kingdoms, was to carry on negotiations with foreign Powers, and, subject to the approval of Parliament, to conclude peace or declare war ; to superintend the militia during ten years with the approval of Parliament itself when sitting, or of a Parliamentary committee appointed for the purpose in the intervals between the sessions. In case of necessity the King might summon an extraordinary Parliament after one Parliament had been dissolved, and when the obligatory election to another was not yet imminent, but he was only to do this with the consent of the Council of State. Though the direction of the militia was to be for ten years in the hands of the Council of State, its commanders were for the same time to be appointed by Parliament. After that time, if Charles were still living, he might make the appointments with the approval of Parliament or of its committee. The next king was, apparently, both to superintend the militia and to appoint its officers without reference to Parliament, provided that he could obtain the consent of the Council of State.

The domestic government was to be carried on, as it had been before the war, by royal officials, but those officials were for ten years to be appointed by Parliament and, after that

A Council of State.

The militia.

time, by the King out of three candidates nominated by Parliament for every vacancy.   To preserve the independence of
Domestic   Parliament, no peer created since May 21, 1642, or
government. created hereafter, was to sit in Parliament without the
consent of both Houses, whilst the judicial power of the House
of Lords was to be limited by requiring the assent of the
House of Commons to its judgments whenever they affected a
commoner.   Each member of the House of Commons was to
have the right of protest.

If Charles accepted these proposals, his partisans were to
be dealt with more leniently than in any of the propositions
Treatment   made by the Houses.   Not more than five were to
of Royalists. be left to the judgment of Parliament, and the
compositions enacted from the remainder were to be lowered.
No Royalist, however, was either to hold office during the next
five years without the consent of Parliament or the Council of
State, or to sit in either House till the second biennial Parliament had come to an end.   Other clauses there were, but of
less importance, and a list of desirable reforms was added in
the hope that the existing Parliament might find time to pass
them without prolonging its sittings unreasonably.[1]

In their main lines *The Heads of the Proposals* anticipated
later constitutional developments.   They substituted the in-
Constitu-   fluence of the Crown for its direct authority, and
tional de-   they brought the House of Commons more under
velopments
anticipated. the control of the constituencies than it had been
hitherto.   In other words, they were pervaded with jealousy of
the reigning King, and with jealousy of the existing Parliament,
though it was on the approval of the reigning King and of the
existing Parliament that those who framed them counted to give
legal authority to their project.   Unless, however, the consent
they required were willingly given they would have laboured in
vain.   The first requisite of successful government is confidence
between the ruler and the ruled.   Such confidence could never
be replaced by a series of restrictions which were well enough
on paper, but which Charles, if he ever consented to be bound
by them, would seek every opportunity to explain away.

[1] The Heads of the Proposals, *Const. Doc.* 232.

That Charles would be hostile to *The Heads of the Proposals*
might easily be foreseen.   Not only did they impose perma-
Charles
hostile to
them. nent restrictions on that authority which he still
believed it possible to preserve intact, but there was
a marked contrast between their elaborate stipulations and the vague conditions which had been offered to him
upon his arrival at Newmarket.[1]   The change, no doubt,
might be accounted for in part by the necessary contrast
between terms verbally expressed and terms set down in
writing; but it was also owing to the lesson taught by Charles's
refusal to accept the original proposal.   The army now knew
that it had an opponent to bind down, and not a friend with
whom it might co-operate.   Suspicion, absent in June, had
entered in July into the minds of the framers of the present
scheme.   Unfortunately Charles sought the cause of this suspicion in others rather than in himself.   In combating the
proposals of the army he had no difficulty in persuading
himself that they were supported not by the army at large, but
simply by a few ambitious chiefs.

[1] " Pendendo queste negotiationi secretamente l' armata dava al Rè
propositioni contrarie alla sua autorità, et alla libertà del popolo, pregiudi-
tialissime a se medesimo et a' suoi successori, le quali S. M., se bene nelle
loro mano, non ha mai voluto passare, non le desiderando ancora tutti
quelli dell' armata, ma solamente li capi di quella come ancora li Capi
degli Independenti." Newsletter, $\frac{\text{July 30}}{\text{Aug. 9}}$, *Roman Transcripts, R.O.*

CHAPTER LIII.

THE MILITARY OCCUPATION OF LONDON.

CHARLES'S usual habit when dissatisfied with one party was to turn to another, and on July 22, being not well pleased with *The Heads of the Proposals*, he graciously received Lauderdale at Latimers, where he was resting for the night on his way to Woburn. The interview resulted in Charles offering to write a letter which was to be carried to Edinburgh by Cheisley, the secretary of the Scottish commissioners in London. Consequently, Lauderdale returned in good spirits under the impression that this letter would open the way to the long-talked-of invasion of England by a Scottish army.[1] Lauderdale, strongly as from political motives he had hitherto sided with the Presbyterian party, had little sympathy with the Presbyterian zealots of his own country, and it is likely enough that he under-estimated the difficulty of obtaining the acceptance in Scotland of such half-hearted concessions as Charles was likely to make in matters of religion.

1647.
July 22.
Charles's interview with Lauderdale.

[1] " Par les nouvelles que j'eus avant-hyer, du Roy de la Grande Bretagne, et par celles que j'en ay encores aujourdhuy receues, il commence à s'appercevoir de ce dont nous l'advertissons il y a bien longtemps, que les Independants establissant leur pouvoir, non seulement mesprisent le sien, mais aussy s'efforcent de le ruyner absolument : si plustost il eust reconnu ceste vérité, plus aysement il y auroit pourveu qu'il ne pourra cy après. Par le retour du Comte de Lauderdale . . . qui le doibt aujourdhuy veoir à Latimer, nous sçaurons demain comment il aura receu les offres qu'il a ordre de luy faire de la part du dict Royaulme." Bellièvre to Mazarin, $\frac{\text{July 22}}{\text{Aug. 1}}$, *R.O. Transcripts.*

" Le Comte de Lauderdale est revenu d'auprez de luy assez satisfait de ce qu'il luy a promis de donner une lettre de creance à Chisley . . . pour

If, as can hardly be doubted, Lauderdale was acting in combination with the eleven members,[1] who, in spite of leave of absence asked and obtained, were still lingering in England, it would have been prudent in the Presbyterian leaders to await the reception of Charles's letter in Scotland before raising a fresh agitation in London. Either, however, their impatience was too great, or the turbulent elements in the City were no longer under their control. On the 21st, the day before Lauderdale's interview with the King, a crowd of apprentices, watermen, reformadoes, and others streamed into Skinners' Hall, where they signed a Solemn Engagement, in virtue of which they were to maintain the Covenant, and to procure the King's restoration to power on the basis of the letter of May 12,[2] in which Charles had abandoned Episcopacy for three years and the militia for ten.[3]

The Presbyterians and the City.

*July 21.
The Solemn Engagement of the City.*

It was doubtless on the municipal independence of the City that the hearts of the supporters of this Engagement were mainly set, but after the withdrawal of the eleven members, they could no longer count on the support of the Commons. On the 22nd the proposal of the army that the control of the City militia should be restored to the old Parliamentary Committee was accepted in a thin House by a majority of 77 to 46, and on the following day this vote was confirmed by the Lords. On the 24th both Houses joined in denouncing the Solemn Engagement of the City.[4]

*July 22.
The Commons side with the army,*

*July 23.
as do the Lords.*

*July 24.
The Solemn Engagement denounced.*

In appearance at least Parliament and army were of one

---

aller dire de sa part tant au conseil d'Escosse qu'à l'Assemblée des ministres qui se tiendra à Edimburg le 15me de ce mois," *i.e.* Aug. $\frac{5}{15}$, "beaucoup de choses qui donneront aux Escossais le pretexte qu'ils cherchent avec tant d'ardeur d'entrer encore en Angleterre." Bellièvre to Mazarin, $\frac{July\ 29}{Aug.\ 8}$, *R.O. Transcripts.*

[1] For his connection with them, see Bamfield's *Apology*, 31.

[2] See p. 252.

[3] A solemn engagement, *L.J.* ix. 354.

[4] *C.J.* v. 254, 256 ; *L.J.* ix. 346, 354.

mind. On July 23 the army assured the Commons of its
readiness to support them in any measures they might take
Feeling in   to provide fitting security for the kingdom. The
the army.   acceptance of the terms indicated in the King's
letter of May 12 meant to the soldiers the abandonment of all
the principles at issue in the great struggle.

Whether those who organised the movement in the City
were supported by any of the eleven members or not,[1] it is quite
                     certain that they had the municipal authorities at
July 26.
A City   their backs. On the 26th a petition was presented
petition.   to both Houses by the Common Council, asking for
the repeal of the Ordinance by which the old Parliamentary
Committee of Militia had been re-established in the City.[2]
                     The deputation bringing it was followed by an ex-
A mob at
West-   cited crowd of apprentices and others, clamouring
minster.   for a favourable answer. The Lords—only nine
peers were in attendance—replied evasively, but being roughly
                     told that unless they recalled the recent Militia
Submission
of the   Ordinance and the declaration against the Engage-
Lords.   ment 'they should never come out,' did as they
were bidden, and were then allowed, after adjourning to the
30th, to depart unhurt.

The turn of the Commons came next. They, too, in vain
attempted to take refuge in a dilatory answer. The rioters

---

[1] "Whereupon the Earls of Manchester, Holland, Lauderdale—who,
though not of the Parliament, but one of the Scots' commissioners, had
great credit in the City—my Lord Willoughby of Parham, my Lord
Holles" (this title was borne by him when this was written), "Sir Philip
Stapleton, Sir William Waller, Major General Massey, Major General
Browne, all which, and divers more who had great influence in the
City, judged it now the critical season to engage it to petition Parliament
for the continuance of their militia under the establishment it was."
Bamfield's *Apology*. Bamfield, as perhaps was to be expected in a book
written so long after the event, is loose as to dates, and goes on to include
in the demands made in the City Petition some which were subsequently
made by the mob. Waller (*Vindication*, 101-106) admits that he knew
of the petition, but says that had nothing to do with the tumults. Holles
(*Memoirs*, 153) disclaims knowing anything about either.

[2] *L.J.* ix. 356; *C.J.* v. 258.

poured into the lobby, burst open the doors, and from the
entrance called upon the members to do as the Lords had

Attack
on the
Commons.

done. For six hours the House held out in spite
of threats and shouts of "Vote! Vote!" from
the boisterous crowd. Outside, men who were discovered to be servants of officers of the army were roughly
handled. Their ears and noses were pulled, and they were
dragged about amidst mocking cries. Hostile as the City
was, the House had no means of restoring order without its
aid. Message after message was accordingly despatched to
Guildhall, but the Lord Mayor and Aldermen were in no
hurry to shorten the troubles of the members, and when at
last one of the sheriffs appeared on the scene he was followed
by no more than forty halberdiers. Gathering courage from
the smallness of this force, the mob pushed on over the floor
of the House itself, telling the members, as they had told the
peers earlier in the day, that none should stir till the Ordinance
and declaration had been repealed. It was eight o'clock in

Forced
votes.

the evening when the members, worn out and ex-
hausted, at last gave way, yielding to pressure which
they were no longer able to resist. Having passed the repealing votes, they voted an adjournment, and at last rose to
leave the House.

The intruders, however, were still unsatisfied. Thrusting
Lenthall back into the chair, as Finch had been thrust eighteen
years before, they insisted he should put to the vote a resolution inviting the King to London. The terrorised House

July 27.
The House
adjourned.

again obeyed orders, after which some members of
the Common Council tardily arrived. Finding that
all had been done that they desired, they dismissed
the mob. The next morning the House, taking example from
the Lords, adjourned to the 30th.[1]

The independence of a Parliament which had long ceased
to represent the nation was by this time a thing of the

---

[1] *L.J.* ix. 356; *C.J.* v. 258; *Whitelocke*, 260; Rushworth to Lord
Fairfax, July 27, Bell's *Mem. of the Civil War*, ii. 379; Lenthall's *Declaration*, E. 400, 32; Mabbot (?) to ——, July 26, *Clarke Papers*, i.
217.

past. Pressure from the army had been succeeded by pressure from the mob, and moderate men might be
excused for thinking that, of the two, the former was
to be preferred.

*Pressure
and counter-
pressure.*

For the present the City stood firm. On the 28th, after
attending a course of sermons which lasted from ten o'clock
in the morning till five in the afternoon, the Common
Council wrote to Fairfax urging him to keep back
his forces, and intimating that their own preparation
for placing the City in a state of defence 'was no just cause to
provoke the soldier.' On the 29th it was known in
London that Fairfax had on that morning broken
up from Bedford and was marching towards the
City. The trained bands were at once sent to man
the walls, and orders were given for a general levy
of the whole male population capable of bearing arms.[1]
Poyntz had for some time been at liberty,[2] and it was now
suggested that either he or Massey should be placed in command of the whole of the forces of London and Westminster,
which were calculated as amounting to no less than 30,000
foot and 10,000 horse. To give to this armament a basis of
legality, it was proposed that when the Houses met on the
30th, the Commons should recall their absent members, in-
cluding the impeached eleven, and enter upon a negotiation
with the King.[3] In Independent circles it was believed that,
in order to ensure the acceptance of these proposals, a far
larger mob than that which had broken into the House on the
26th would appear at Westminster on the 30th.[4] On the
other hand, there were rumours abroad amongst the Presbyterians, that when the Houses met they would under the
influence of the Independents adjourn themselves for a
month,[5] in which case it would be impossible to give Parliamentary sanction to the projected armament.

*July 28.
Prepara-
tions in
the City.*

*July 29.
Fairfax
leaves
Bedford.*

*An alarm
in the City.*

[1] *Rushw.* vi. 645, 646.   [2] See p. 322.
[3] *A continuation of certain . . . passages,* E. 400, 25 ; *The Perfect
Weekly Account,* E. 401, 1 ; Dr. Denton to Sir R. Verney, July 27, *Verney MSS.*
[4] Lenthall's *Declaration,* E. 400, 32.   [5] *L.J.* ix. 377.

The Independents, at least, had no intention of carrying
out the project attributed to them.   When the morning of the

July 30.
Retreat
of the
Speakers
and the
Indepen-
dent
members.

30th arrived it was found that the two Speakers,
Manchester and Lenthall, together with eight Independent. peers and fifty-seven Independent members of the House of Commons, were missing.[1]
That Manchester, who had strong reasons for
bearing a grudge against the Independents, should have been
amongst the absentees was significative of the disgust which
mob-violence is apt to rouse.   For the moment, however, the

Proceedings
at West-
minster.

Presbyterians were masters of both Houses.   They
chose new Speakers, Lord Willoughby of Parham in
the Lords and Pelham in the Commons, recalled the
eleven members, and reconstituted the Committee of Safety,
placing Waller and Massey upon it.   They also put themselves
under the protection of the militia of the City, now once more
under the authority of the new Presbyterian committee, to
which they gave power to appoint a commander-in-chief.   Finally,
they sent orders to Fairfax to abstain from coming within thirty
miles of London.   These orders they accompanied with an
assurance that the City authorities would keep the apprentices
under restraint, and that, so far as the apprentices themselves
were concerned, it was not to be doubted 'but the sense of so
great an offence' as the violation of the privileges of Parliament
would 'at last strike their breasts . . . with a detestation of
any practices of the like nature for the future.'[2]

There could be no doubt that the Presbyterians intended
to fight now, if they had the chance.   After most of the eleven

The Houses
prepare for
defence.

Fairfax at
Colnbrook.

members had taken their places at Westminster,
the Militia Committee named Massey commander
of all the forces raised by the City.   Time was,
however, running short.   On the 30th Fairfax esta-
tablished his own head-quarters at Colnbrook.   Some of his
regiments seized on Tilbury Fort, whilst others crossed the

---

[1] The evidence on the story that Cromwell and Ireton persuaded
Lenthall to go to the army is collected in a note of Mr. Firth's to p. 219
of vol. i. of the *Clarke Papers.*

[2] *L.J.* ix. 358; *C.J.* v. 259.

Thames above Westminster, and threatened to march on Gravesend,[1] and thus to starve out the commerce of London by occupying both banks of the Thames. They actually pushed on to Deptford, where they came to blows with the deserters, four of the latter being slain.[2] The strategy which had failed in Charles's hands seemed likely to succeed in the hands of Fairfax.

It may well be believed that neither Fairfax nor Cromwell desired to enter London as conquerors. They were coming,

The army and the expelled members.
they alleged, not as enemies, but as protectors of the true Parliament, expelled by the violence of the mob. On their side was peace and order ; on the side of their opponents was riot in the streets, and a New Civil War in the land. Yet it was not merely on a restored Parliament that they had based their hopes of a restoration of order.

Continuance of the negotiation with the King.
During the days in which their eyes appeared to be exclusively fixed on Westminster, they had not neglected to push on their negotiations with the King, in the hope that they might be able, with no long delay, to announce that a general reconciliation had been effected.

It was on July 23, before troubles had occurred at Westminster, that *The Heads of the Proposals* in their amended

July 23. The Heads of the Proposals before Charles, in an amended form.
shape[3] were placed in Berkeley's hands to be communicated unofficially to the King. It is probable that the insistence of the army on binding him in constitutional fetters outweighed all gratitude, if indeed he felt any, for their greater tolerance in matters of religion. If the army, said Charles to Berkeley, had had a mind to close with him, they would not have insisted on such hard conditions. Berkeley sensibly replied that he should have had more cause to suspect them if they had asked for less. Charles would not listen to such an argument. The army, he said, 'could not subsist without him.' "I shall see them glad ere long," he added, "to accept more equal terms."[4]

---

[1] *The Perfect Weekly Account*, E. 401, 1.   [2] *Rushw.* vii. 741.
[3] See p. 329.   [4] Berkeley's *Memoirs*, 30–32.

Berkeley could no longer conceal from himself the failure of his mission. With characteristic modesty he expressed a hope

Berkeley and Ash-burnham. that Ashburnham, when he arrived,[1] would be more successful. Ashburnham, when he arrived, proved himself to have no more insight into the situation than the King himself. Charles actually fancied that he was furthering his own ends by directing Ashburnham and Berkeley

An appeal to the cupidity of the generals. to join in appealing to the cupidity of the heads of the army. Fairfax and Cromwell, forsooth, were to be urged 'to fasten their affections to his Majesty's perfect restoration by proffers of advantages to themselves, and by fulfilling their utmost expectations in anything relating to their own interest, or that of any of their friends whom they would involve in the work of his Majesty's re-establishment.'[2]

So were the precious hours in which the army had most need of Charles's concurrence allowed to slip away. When, on

July 28 (?). *Formal presentation of The Heads of the Proposals.* or about July 28,[3] *The Heads of the Proposals* were formally presented to him at Woburn by a deputation from the army, he answered peremptorily that he would not have one of his followers exempted from pardon, and that the Church must not only be allowed freedom, but must be positively established by law.

Charles's rash talk. The burden of his discourse was "You cannot do without me ! You will fall to ruin if I do not sustain you." Berkeley, amazed at his master's indiscretion, attempted to stop the torrent. "Sir," he whispered into Charles's ear, "your Majesty speaks as if you had some secret strength and power that I do not know of ; and since your Majesty hath concealed it from me, I wish you had concealed it from these men also."[4] The fact was that Charles had lately received encouraging messages from Lauderdale, and was filled with expectation of a triumphant movement in his favour in the City.[5]

---

[1] See p. 318.   [2] Ashburnham's *Narrative*, ii. 90.
[3] It was whilst the army was still at Bedford, and therefore before July 29.
[4] Berkeley's *Memoirs*, 33–35.   [5] Bamfield's *Apology*, 32.

At Berkeley's hint, Charles moderated his language; but the effect of his intemperate speech was beyond recall. Rainsborough, the leader of that section of the army which was most adverse to an understanding with the King, hastened from his presence to Bedford, where he spread the news of his rash sayings amongst the soldiers. On the 29th the army broke up from Bedford, in consequence of the serious news from Westminster, and on the following day its irritation was further increased by the intelligence that Lauderdale had arrived at Woburn, and had brought Cheisley with him. As a matter of fact, he had come to receive Charles's last instructions before despatching Cheisley to Scotland on a mission, the object of which was to hasten an invasion of England by the Scots. Though the soldiers knew little of Lauderdale's plans, they suspected much, and on the morning of the 31st some of them broke into his lodging, before he had risen. In order to prevent him from seeing the King, they ordered him to leave his bed and to quit the place at once without visiting the Abbey. In vain Lauderdale, probably hoping to melt the hearts of his assailants, asked for a short delay in which to say his prayers; but the soldiers inexorably hurried him off as soon as he was dressed.[1] The fears of the soldiers were justifiable enough, but as the views of Charles and the Committee of Estates at Edinburgh were still widely apart, there was little likelihood of an immediate invasion. In a letter written by the King on the 27th, he forbade Lanark 'to mention—as to England—either Covenant or Presbyterial government.'[2]

Whilst Lauderdale was in vain attempting to reach the Abbey, Charles was preparing, after long consultations with his lawyers and divines, an answer to *The Heads of the Proposals.* In the opinion of Berkeley, who had himself a share in

The officers dissatisfied.

*July 30.
Lauderdale at Woburn.*

*July 31.
Lauderdale sent off by the soldiers.*

---

[1] Complaint of the Scottish Commissioners, Aug. 1, *L.J.* ix. 367; Lellièvre to Mazarin, $\frac{\text{July 30}}{\text{Aug. 9}}$, *R.O. Transcripts*; Whalley's Narrative printed in *A Declaration from his Excellency*, E. 407, 36.

[2] *Burnet*, v. 110.

drawing it up, it was absolutely conclusive. "We easily," he wrote, "answered the proposals both in law and reason ; but we had to do with what was stronger than both." The army leaders, on the other hand, being well aware of the general nature of the King's reply, answered it in advance on August 1, by publishing *The Heads of the Proposals* themselves, whilst they, at the same time, urged Berkeley, if he could not persuade the King to assent to their terms, to obtain from him 'at least a kind letter to the army,' before the submission of London, which they knew to be impending, deprived the courtesy of all its grace. A letter to Fairfax repudiating the enemies of the army and declaring himself in the main satisfied with *The Heads of the Proposals* was indeed prepared for Charles's signature, but he refused to sign it, and before he consented to sign any letter at all, events had occurred which robbed it of both 'grace and efficacy.'[1] Yet at the very time when he was so sparing of any public demonstration of good-will, he was sending private messages to Ireton, assuring him of his readiness to confide in the army, and to entrust it with the settlement of the kingdom.[2]

Charles prepares an answer to The Heads of the Proposals.

Aug. 1. Their publication.

Charles's double dealing.

By this time the citizens were growing weary of the anarchy which they had fostered in their midst. The Reformadoes were beginning to talk of plundering the City.[3] The Independents, who, after all, constituted a not inconsiderable minority amongst the Londoners, were emboldened by Fairfax's arrival at Colnbrook to appear on August 2 at Guildhall with a petition for an accommodation. They were there attacked by Poyntz and his officers, and some of them were wounded mortally. The arrival of a deputation from Southwark, where there had long been a jealousy of the City's claim

Danger of anarchy in the City.

Aug. 2. Independent petitioners attacked.

[1] Berkeley's *Memoirs*, 38, 39. Draft of a letter, Aug. 3, *Clar. St. P.* ii. 371.

[2] Major Huntington's *Sundry Reasons*, p. 7. E. 458, 3.

[3] "Il n'y a pas un soldat qui veuille sortir d'icy maintenant : ils croyent tour avoir bonne part dans le butin de ceste ville qu'ils imaginent pouvoir piller." Bellièvre to Mazarin, $\frac{\text{July 29}}{\text{Aug. 8}}$, *R.O. Transcripts.*

to command the militia of the suburbs, was even more ominous of danger. Southwark required from the Common Council

A demand from Southwark. that an agreement should be made with the army, and that the disposal of its militia should ·be conceded to it.[1] Even in the seventeenth century the City was weakened by the growth of a greater London beyond the limits of its jurisdiction.

Before nightfall on the 2nd, the Common Council made up its mind to yield ; and the next morning despatched a letter

Aug. 3.
A deputation from the City to Fairfax. to Fairfax, disclaiming any wish to enter upon a new war. The deputation which carried the letter found the army drawn up on Hounslow Heath, 20,000 strong, and, for a reply, had to be content with a

A declaration by the army. long declaration, drawn up on the preceding day, in which was set forth the intention of the army to march on London, as well as its expectation that the eleven members would be either delivered up, or kept in custody till they could be tried according to law. Then followed a scene which had no doubt been carefully pre-arranged. The fugitive

Reception of the fugitive members. members of the two Houses headed by their Speakers, and accompanied by Fairfax himself, rode along the front of the regiments. Their reception could not have been more enthusiastic. The soldiers threw their hats into the air with cries of " Lords and Commons and a free Parliament." The Elector Palatine, who always took care to attach himself to the stronger party, then rode up and received a greeting equally warm.[2] If the soldiers shouted for Lords and Commons, they shouted for themselves as well. There could be few amongst them who were not glad to discover that their purposed intervention was strictly constitutional.

Fairfax was by this time assured of success. A message had come from Southwark imploring his aid. Four regiments

Southwark sends for help. were rapidly pushed forward on the south side of the Thames, and at two in the morning they entered Southwark through a gate opened to them by their friends inside. Even before this the City had surrendered at dis-

<hr>

[1] *Rushw.* vii. 741. [2] *Idem*, vii. 743-751.

cretion. The letter announcing its resolution to submit, written on the afternoon of the 3rd, reached Fairfax at Hammersmith on the morning of the 4th. Later in the day another letter arrived from Charles, who now briefly disclaimed all intention of making war against Parliament, without even attempting to meet the charge, to which he was really open, of having sympathised with the attempt of the Presbyterians to make war against the army.[1]

Surrender of the City.
Aug. 4. A letter from the King.

On August 6 the army, escorting the returning members, tramped along the road to Westminster. The march resembled a triumphal procession rather than the occupation of a hostile city. Every soldier had placed a leaf of laurel in his hat. When Hyde Park was reached the Lord Mayor and Aldermen welcomed the General, and the distasteful ceremony was repeated by the Common Council at Charing Cross.[2]

Aug. 6. The army enters London.

In Parliament opposition, for the moment, died away. Manchester and Lenthall returned to their chairs, and the fugitive members were once more seen in their respective Houses. Fairfax having been duly thanked by Lords and Commons, received the appointment of Constable of the Tower, which was no longer to be entrusted to the citizens. The Reformadoes were at last to be actually ejected from London, and a Committee consisting of members of both Houses was appointed to inquire into the violence recently offered to Parliament.[3]

Restoration of the members.
Fairfax Constable of the Tower.

On the following day a display of force was made of which the citizens could hardly fail to appreciate the significance. The bulk of the army, some 18,000 strong, marched through the streets of the City, and passed over London Bridge on the way to Croydon. Cromwell rode at the head of the Cavalry, but Fairfax, whose health was not yet completely restored, was seated in a carriage with Cromwell's wife and his own. A Royalist spectator,

Aug. 7. The army marches through the City.

---

[1] The King to Fairfax, Aug. 4, *Rushw.* vii. 753.

[2] *Rushw.* vii. 756.

[3] *L.J.* ix. 374; *C.J.* v. 268.

indeed, declared that the troops were 'neither well-horsed nor well-armed,' but their martial vigour and their orderly discipline were beyond dispute.[1]   A sufficient force remained behind at Westminster and the Tower to guard the Houses against a fresh incursion of the City mob.   In the eyes of Fairfax this military occupation of London was but a necessary prelimin-

The army hopes for an understanding with the King.

ary to an understanding with the King, and there is every reason to believe that the majority of the officers and men under his command shared his hopes.   With their full knowledge, the General had declared, in a letter recently addressed to the City, that the army had 'no other design but the quiet and happy settlement of a firm and lasting peace.'[2]   When, upon his entry into the

Fairfax and the Great Charter.

Tower, the records of the kingdom were shown to him, he called for the Great Charter. "This is that," he said, "which we have fought for, and by God's help we must maintain."[3]

To maintain the principles of the Great Charter under the changed conditions of the seventeenth century was indeed the

Comparison between the times of John and of Charles.

work in hand.   Neither Fairfax nor anyone then living was likely to remember that it was only after the struggles of two generations that the benefits of the Great Charter had been more than nominally secured.

The first difficulty of the army after its day of triumph was, however, not with Charles but with Parliament.   The House

Independent majority in the House of Lords.

of Lords, indeed, gave little trouble.   With the exception of Pembroke, who always sided with the party which happened for the moment to be upper-most, none of the Lords who had voted Willoughby of Parham into the chair reappeared after the restoration of Manchester. The attendance of a little knot of twelve or thirteen peers, who

---

[1] Letter of Intelligence, Aug. 9, *Clarendon MSS.* 2,572 ; Newsletter, Aug. $\frac{9}{19}$, Aug. $\frac{13}{23}$, *Roman Transcripts, R.O.*   The latter writes that the soldiers 'passerent sy modestement, et en sy bon ordre, que je ne crois pas que l'on puisse voir une armée mieux disciplinée."

[2] Fairfax to the Lord Mayor and Aldermen, Aug. 5, *Rushw.* vii. 756.

[3] Sanderson's *Life of King Charles*, 1,002.

occupied a corner of the empty chamber, now converted the House of Lords into an Independent stronghold.

It was far otherwise with the House of Commons. On August 9 a large number of those members who had prudently asked leave of absence during the recent troubles returned to the House, where their presence seriously imperilled the mastery of the Independent party. Both Presbyterians and Independents, indeed, were now ready to protest against the violence of the mob, but whilst the Independents urged the House to affirm that all votes passed in the absence of the legitimate Speakers were null and void, the Presbyterians merely wished to expunge them from the journals, on the ground that if they were once admitted to have been without force from the beginning, the members who had assented to them might be called in question for having taken part in an unconstitutional action.[1]

Aug. 9.
Struggle in the House of Commons.

When at the close of the debate the question was put for declaring the votes to have been null and void, the Ayes rang loudly out, whilst the Noes of the Presbyterians were few and feeble. In the insolence of victory an Independent member called for a division, for no other reason, it would seem, than to reveal the weakness of the other party. If the Presbyterians were too depressed to shout, they were not too depressed to vote, and to the astonishment of all present the division gave to the Independents a bare majority of one, the votes being 95 to 94. A worse disappointment was in store for the Independents. Three members who had retired into a committee-room to avoid voting with either side were discovered and brought into the House. As they had been present when the question was put, they were ordered to vote, and all three gave their voices for the rejection of the Independent resolution, which was therefore lost by a majority of two.[2] On the following day the Presbyterians rejected, by a largely increased majority of 34, another resolution which implied approbation of the recent proceedings of the army.[3]

A bare majority for the Independents.

---

[1] *A Perfect Summary*, E. 518, 19.

[2] *C.J.* v. 270 ; Dr. Denton to Sir R. Verney, Aug. 12, *Verney MSS.*

[3] *C.J.* v. 271.

In less than a week after the entry of the army into London, the instrument which it chose to call a free Parliament had broken in its hands.   The last vote left officers and soldiers exposed to the penalties of the law, and it was therefore followed by a cry for a fresh and more stringent application of force.   " If things are current thus," said an Independent member, "it is high time for us to betake ourselves to the strongest power and the longest sword."[1]   A party in the army was ready to resort to extreme measures.   A few days before Berkeley had asked Rainsborough what would happen if *The Heads of the Proposals* were accepted by the King and rejected by the Houses.   "If they will not agree," answered Rainsborough, "we will make them," and of this all the officers present at the time signified their approval.[2]

Aug. 10. Increase of the Presbyterian majority.

A fresh appeal to force demanded.

Rainsborough's view of the situation.

It soon appeared that the Commons had no intention of abandoning their hostile attitude.   On the 13th a resolution sent down from the Lords, for making the Presbyterian Militia Committee answerable for its recent action, was rejected by a majority of 25, on the ground that it had no legal existence after its re-establishment by the mutilated Parliament, whilst on the same day they passed, by a still larger majority of 40, an Ordinance for repealing, not annulling, the votes of the Houses in the absence of the Speakers.[3]

Aug. 13. The Commons persist.

On the following day, to counteract the effect of these proceedings, the Agitators presented a petition to Fairfax.   The attempt of the army, they asserted, 'to secure to the honourable members of Parliament that discharged their trust' the possibility of sitting as 'a free and legal Parliament' had failed 'through the unexpected intrusion of those usurpers' who had formerly taken part in the mischievous proceedings of a pretended Parliament.   As a remedy they proposed 'that all and every person that have sat in

Aug. 14. The Agitators call for a purge.

---

[1] Dr. Denton to Sir R. Verney, Aug. 12, *Verney MSS.*

[2] Berkeley's *Memoirs*, 36.

[3] *C.J.* v. 273.

that pretended Parliament, or adhered to them or their votes when the free legal Parliament was by violence suspended, might immediately be declared against as persons incapable of sitting or voting in this Parliament.'[1] The House, in short, to employ a phrase at this time coming into vogue, was to be purged of those members who hindered the views of the army from prevailing.

The petition of the Agitators had, at least, the effect of finally convincing most of the eleven members of the hope-
Aug. 16. Flight of six of the eleven members. lessness of their position. On August 16 five of them—Stapleton, Lewis, Waller, Clotworthy, and Long—availed themselves of passports given them by the Speaker to take shipping for France. They were, how-ever, stopped by a frigate, and brought before Batten, who, as Vice-Admiral, commanded the fleet in the Downs. Batten, who was notoriously friendly to the Presbyterians, readily left them at liberty to go where they would. They therefore pur sued their voyage to Calais, where Stapleton died, as some thought, of the plague. A few days later Holles made his way safely to St. Malo.[2] Of the other five, Nichols was under arrest ; Glyn, Harley, and Sir John Maynard preferred to face the worst in England ; whilst Massey, who was specially in-culpated as having been concerned in raising and disciplining the City forces, had escaped with Poyntz to Holland as soon as he discovered that resistance was hopeless.[3]

In the House of Commons itself, the threats of the Agita-
Aug. 17. The Commons show signs of giving way, but continue to resist. tors produced an irritation which stiffened the resist-ance of the Presbyterian majority. On the 17th, a proposal of the Independents to declare that the House had been under coercion from July 26 to August 6 was rejected, though it is true that it was only rejected by a majority of three. During the next day or two the

---

[1] *The humble address of the Agitators*, Aug. 14, E. 402, 8.

[2] *A Perfect Diurnal*, E. 518, 21 ; *Perfect Occurrences*, E. 518, 23. See, however, *A true relation of Captain Batten*, E. 404, 38 ; *A short and true Narrative*, E. 409, 3.

[3] He and Poyntz left behind them a *Declaration* (E. 401, 12), pub-lished on Aug. 9.

majorities fluctuated in a surprising manner.[1] By this time
the impatience of the army was growing beyond restraint. On

Impatience
of the army.

Aug. 18.
The Army
Council
supports the
Agitators.

Cromwell
eager to
purge the
House.

the 18th the Army Council met at Kingston, where
they drew up a declaration fully supporting the petition of the Agitators,[2] and even gave orders for a
forward movement of the army towards Westminster
to support the demand for the purging of the
House. Those who cried loudest for immediate
action found a warm supporter in Cromwell,[3] who
had been driven out of all regard for constitutional
propriety by the recent proceedings of the Presbyterians in the
House. "These men," he said, "will never leave till the
army pull them out by the ears,"[4] and on another occasion,
after complaining bitterly of the sway borne by Holles and
Stapleton in the affairs of the kingdom, he added words which

[1] *C.J.* v. 275, 277–279.

[2] Declaration of the Council of the Army, Aug. 18, *L.J.* ix. 391.

[3] "The army," wrote Fairfax in Short Memorials (Somers's *Tracts*,
v. 393), "marched nearer London; and at Windsor after two days' debate in
a council of war, it was resolved to remove all of the house whom they
conceived did obstruct (as they called it) the public settlement.

"I was pressed to use all expedition in this march, but here I resolved
to use a restrictive power, when I had not a persuasive; and when the
Lieutenant-General and others did urge me to sign orders for marching, I
still delayed it, as ever dreading the consequences of breaking Parliaments,
and at a time when the kingdom was falling into a new war, which was so
near that my delaying three or four days giving out orders, diverted this
humour of the army from being statesmen to their more proper duty as
soldiers. . . . This I write to show how by providence a few days of delay
secured the Parliament above a year from the violence which soon after
was offered them."

If this took place more than a year before Pride's purge, it must have
happened before Dec. 6, 1647. If it took place at Windsor it must have
happened after Nov. 19. Between these two dates, however, no proposal to purge the House was made. Fairfax is, however, very loose
about details, and the story may safely be placed here, when a proposal to
purge was actually made.

[4] This story is told by Ludlow, who assigns it to a much earlier date;
but his regardlessness for chronology is well known, and the observation
is not only far more likely to have been made at a time when Cromwell
really advocated a purge, but the placing it at this date is strongly coun-
tenanced by a passage in Huntington's *Sundry Reasons*, p. 8, E. 548, 3.

gave bitter offence to his detractors. " I know nothing to the contrary," he said, "but that I am as well able to govern the kingdom as either of them." [1]

Cromwell's main obstacle lay with Fairfax, who refused to participate in his design of purging the House, and who post-

Fairfax resists.

poned from day to day the order for the march on which the Army Council had decided. Crom-

Cromwell prepares to act.

well determined to take the matter into his own hands. On the 20th, when the Ordinance for declaring the proceedings of Parliament in the absence of the Speakers null and void was again brought forward, he ordered a regiment of cavalry to take up a position in Hyde Park, so as to convey the impression that he intended to use it, if necessary, against the House of Commons. He then, leaving outside a party of soldiers who followed him up to the door, entered the House accompanied by those officers who were also members of Parliament,[2] and with

---

[1] *Sundry Reasons*, p. 8, E. 548, 3. This was said at Kingston; therefore between Aug. 11 and 27.

[2] " Nel medesimo tempo che stavano sopra il punto della deliberatione e per decidere il negotio, ecco che la cavalleria di Fairfax marcia verso il luogo dell' Assemblea, e che il Luogotenente Cramver [*sic*] si presenta sulla porta della Camera in compagnia di molti Colonelli e Capitani, facendo istanza a tutti insieme che tutti gl'ordini fossero annullati, e di più, che tutti quelli, i quali havevano dato il lor voto per tali ordini, fossero castigati. La più parte di quelli della camera e particolarmente li Presbiteriani che havevano travagliato intorno a tali ordini, uscirono bel bello dal Parlamento : alcuni si fuggirono dalla città ; altri hanno passato il mare, prevedendo qualche vicina tempestà, e quelli i quali continovorono nella radunanza, parte per amore, e parte per pavura votorono in favore dell' Armata, dichiarando tali ordini esser nulli." Newsletter, $\frac{\text{Aug. 27}}{\text{Sept. 6}}$, *Roman Transcripts*, *R.O.* The statement about the cavalry is confirmed by Huntington's story of a review in Hyde Park (*Sundry Reasons*, p. 8, E. 458, 3). That the retreat of the Presbyterians took place after and not before the vote is shown by the fact that the Presbyterian vote was nearly as large as it had been on the preceding day The Independent vote was higher by twenty, being no doubt increased by the presence of the military members. Holles (*Memoirs*, 172) says that there were 1,000 horse drawn up in Hyde Park, ' and guards out of the army besetting the doors and avenues.'

the aid of their votes the Ordinance was carried.[1] It did
not contain any direct provision for the punishment of those

He obtains
an Ordi-
nance an-
nulling the
votes given
under
coercion. who had taken part in coercing Parliament, but it
excepted from indemnity all who had been present when force was used, or had been cognisant
beforehand of its employment, or had afterwards
acted upon the votes obtained by force, or had
shared in the engagement to bring the King into the City.

Retreat of
Presby-
terians.

An Inde-
pendent
majority. The exceptions were somewhat sweeping, and it is,
therefore, no wonder that the passing of the Ordinance was followed by the speedy retreat of the
most prominent Presbyterians, who by their absence handed over the House to what was now an
Independent majority.

Fairfax was able to pride himself on having hindered the
purging of the House. Yet, if he had so far gained his end,
it was only because Cromwell had accomplished his design
by the display of force without actually making use of it. The
mastery of the army, thinly veiled, had made itself felt, and
one more stage had been passed on the road which was to
end in the enslavement of Parliament.

[1] The division was taken on a minor point, but the main question was
evidently settled by it. *C.J.* v. 220.

CHAPTER LIV.

CROMWELL AND THE KING.

It was possible for Cromwell to fling aside his respect for Parliamentary authority, because he still hoped to find in the
1647.
Cromwell
still builds
his hopes
on the
King. King a foundation on which to build up the civil institutions of the country in an amended form. Unfortunately it was not in Charles either to accept a compromise or to understand that Cromwell really cared for anything but his own personal advancement.

Aug. 12.
The King
merry, but
unyielding. On August 12, when he moved to Oatlands, he was observed to be 'very merry,' taking especial pleasure in the thought that, though he was himself a captive, his son was out of the rebels' reach,[1] and, therefore, it may be presumed, would refuse to be bound by any engagements which he might himself make under duress. In such thoughts there was no sign of yielding.[2] In spite of the

---

[1] Letter of Intelligence, *Clarendon MSS.* 2,573.

[2] "Let me inform you that his Majesty never trusted Cromwell, but desired that, through the differences between the Parliament and the army, and between the inferior and superior officers of the army, Cromwell should have been forced to have trusted his Majesty. It is true that Cromwell professed great matters in general, and specified those generals in the proposals beyond which he said he could not pass lest he should confirm the jealousies that had been fomented by the Presbyterians and disaffected in the army; viz. that he had deserted his party totally, and made a private agreement with the King. That these professions of his were sincere no man that I know did ever affirm; but it was most certain that if the King had consented to the proposals, he had either made an agreement with the army or discovered their villainy by their not performing what they undertook in case of his consent." Berkeley to Hyde, May 7, 1650, *Clar. St. P.* ii. 540.

A A

pleadings of his most attached servants [1] he persisted in rejecting *The Heads of the Proposals.*

On the side of the army there was still every wish to be conciliatory, and during the next week, the week in which differences between the Parliament and the soldiers were being brought to an issue, negotiations were opened in the hope that some reasonable compromise might be discovered. Charles, however, at this time stood out on two points. He asked for an amnesty for all his followers, and that there might be no diminution in the revenues of the bishops and clergy. The army, on the other hand, asked that a part of these revenues might be devoted to the payment of debts incurred in the war. Both King and army were agreed that the general toleration should include such Catholics as would take an oath of allegiance in a modified form. The scheme was approved in principle by an assembly of English Roman Catholic divines, and was then remitted to Rome for the approval of the Pope.[2]

Modifica-tions pro-posed in The Heads of the Pro-posals.

Our information on this negotiation is fragmentary, but, as a week later the discussion had passed to other points, it is to be presumed that the settlement of these questions was postponed.[3] By that time Charles was vigorously resisting the removal of the militia from under his authority, and still more the suggestion that peace and war should be subjected to the competency of Parliament. Nor was he more satisfied with a stipulation that the money to be levied for the army should be out of his own control.[4]

Aug. 20-27. Progress of the negotia-tion.

Still the army leaders did not despair. On August 24 Charles was removed to Hampton Court, and two days later head-quarters were established at Putney, half-way between Hampton Court and Westminster.

Aug. 24. Charles at Hampton Court.

---

[1] Bellièvre to Mazarin, Aug. $\frac{5}{15}$, $\frac{9}{19}$, $\frac{12}{22}$, *R.O. Transcripts.*

[2] Newsletter, Aug. $\frac{20}{30}$, *Roman Transcripts, R.O.*

[3] The army cannot have yielded, as we hear of the King's holding out on these points later on.

[4] Newsletter, $\frac{Aug. 27}{Sept. 6}$, *Roman Transcripts, R.O.*

Charles was battling as one to whom every position was of importance. With him it was no mere struggle for personal ends, as he at least believed from the bottom of his heart that the democratic innovations with which *The Heads of the Proposals* absolutely bristled would be disastrous to the well-being of the country. He knew well that those innovations had no hold on the popular mind, and he knew also that the feeling that it was impossible to make an enduring settlement from which he was himself excluded was not confined to Cromwell and the officers.

Aug. 26.
Head-
quarters at
Putney.

In this conflict of opinion the Scottish commissioners again made their voice heard with effect. They remonstrated strongly on the subject of the insult to Lauderdale, and also on the subject of the stoppage of his messenger Cheisley by the Governor of Newcastle.[1] On the 26th, to give them satisfaction, the House of Commons re-introduced the strongly Presbyterian Propositions of Newcastle,[2] which were adopted on the 27th with a few slght amendments. The rapidity with which the matter was hurried on strengthens the belief entertained by contemporaries that the Independents at least were not in earnest, their object being to convince Charles that if he persisted in refusing his consent to *The Heads of the Proposals*, a worse thing might befall him.

Intervent'on of the Scottish commissioners.

Aug. 26.
The Newcastle Propositions revived,

Aug. 27.
and
adopted.

The Independents not in earnest in supporting them.

Their motives indeed were so little of a secret, that Ireton sent Charles a message telling him not to be troubled at what was passing at Westminster, as the Independents 'intended it to no other end but to make good some promises of the Parliament which the nation of Scotland expected the performance of, and that it was not expected nor desired his Majesty should either sign or treat of them.' Parliament, said Cromwell to Charles after the vote had passed, 'intended nothing else but to satisfy the Scot.'[3]

[1] *L.J.* x. 387.
[2] Smith to Leveson, Aug. 31, *Hist. MSS. Com. Rep.* v. 172.
[3] Huntington's *Sundry Reasons*, p. 8, E. 458, 3.

If this was the truth, it may fairly be conjectured that it was not the whole truth. The Independent leaders knew that,

The Independents between King and Parliament.

unless they could win Charles over to their side, it would be impossible for them permanently to secure Parliamentary support. So strong was the universal craving for peace, that even the victorious army which was at their command could not enforce order by the sword alone. If Charles did not heartily rally to their cause, they would have to fall back on Parliament. The acceptance by the Commons of the Newcastle Propositions had indeed at first the effect of driving Charles to yield something to the importunity of the army, and though he continued to stand firm on the amnesty for his friends and the preservation of the Church lands, he gave way about the militia, and agreed that Parliament should name the great officers of State.[1] Yet the army leaders can hardly have failed to have had before their eyes the risk which they would run if Charles, having been restored to the throne after accepting their conditions, should declare that he was not bound by promises made under compulsion, and should fling them to the wild vengeance of popular indignation.[2]

[1] Newsletter, Sept. $\frac{3}{13}$, *Roman Transcripts, R.O.*

[2] The correspondent of Rome in England may not be a fair exponent of the general belief of Englishmen, but he no doubt only retailed what he heard when, in the letter just quoted, he says that the army was never nearer its ruin, ' essendo al presente un mese e più che li Capi dell' Armata con il loro consiglio di guerra non studiano altro, giorno e notte, che a ritrovare i modi per assicurare non solamente il loro stato ma ancora le loro persone, e niente di meno non lo sanno arrivare, perchè il popolo universalmente desidera, dimanda, e grida che il Rè ritorni in Londra, e nel governo dello Stato, e di fare altrimente no si può senza esporsi a una solevatione universale contro a quelli, e tale che non sarebbono capaci di resistere lungamente. Dall' altra banda, se rimettano il Rè in Londra, e nel suo Parlamento, prevegga che sarà in potere di S. M. di far concludere tutto quello che vorrà, perchè ne l'Armata, ne il Parlamento non haveranno di che resistere alla devotione del popolo che ha particolarmente apperto gl' occhi di maniera che [non] resta a gl' Independenti altra strada per assicurarli che di convenire con il Rè, e formare tutti le propositioni prima che las[ci]arlo venire a Londra ; ma questo assicuramento li sarà inutile principalmente perchè il Rè non vuol signar niente, se non è unito

On September 7, after some delay caused by the hesitation of the Scottish commissioners to accept amendments however slight without authority from their own Committee of Estates, the Parliamentary propositions were laid before the King, Lauderdale himself joining the English commissioners in presenting them. Charles was asked to give his answer within six days.[1]

For some time the Independents, having now a slight majority in the House of Commons through the absence of many of their Presbyterian opponents, had been employed in strengthening their position at Westminster. On August 13 the two Houses, finding the proceedings of the committee appointed to examine into the violence offered to the Houses[2] hampered by the action of its Presbyterian members, took the unusual course of naming by Ordinance a sub-committee to do the work of the committee itself.[3] This Independent sub-committee, if those who suffered from its proceedings are to be trusted,[4] showed itself as arbitrary as political partisans entrusted with magisterial functions usually do. On the report of this sub-committee the House of Commons expelled and imprisoned Glyn and Sir John Maynard, two of the eleven members who had remained to face the storm, and then proceeded to impeach seven peers who had continued to sit after the departure of the Speakers—Suffolk, Willoughby of Parham, Hunsdon, Maynard, Lincoln, Berkeley, and Middlesex—on the elastic charge of treason, 'for levying war against the King, Parliament, and kingdom.'[5]

Marginal notes:

Sept. 7. The Parliamentary propositions presented.

An Independent sub-committee.

Glyn and Maynard expelled and imprisoned.

Sept. 8. Impeachment of seven peers.

con li suoi membri del Parlamento : in secondo luogo quando haverebbe segnato di sua propria mano, e il Parlamento appresso havesse passato le propositioni, il Rè venendo a Londra e nel suo Parlamento potrà giustamente dichiarare, e la sua dichiaratione sarà ricevuta, che ha signato per forza, essendo nelle loro mani, e non essendo nel suo Parlamento. Di più ancora, che se il Rè per non mancar di parola non facesse una tal dichiaratione, questo sarà in potere d' un altro Parlamento, che non li sarà loro favorevole, di cassare tutti questi ordini e aggitare contro li autori di quelli como traditori e perturbatori dello Stato.'

[1] *L.J.* ix. 428. [2] See p. 345. [3] *C.J.* v. 273.
[4] Walker's *Hist. of Independency,* i. 51. [5] *C.J.* v. 295, 296.

In all this work of party vengeance Cromwell and Ireton
took no immediate part.   They were at Putney sending con-

Cromwell
gives
assurances
to the King. stant messages to Charles, urging him to refuse his
assent to the Propositions.   Charles replied by the
very pertinent question, which he conveyed to them
through Major Huntington, why, if they disliked the Propositions so much, they had not opposed them in the House of
Commons ? [1]   Their reply was that 'they only concurred with
the rest of the House that their unreasonableness might the
better appear to the kingdom.'   Cromwell next begged
Huntington to 'assure the King that, if the army remained an
army, his Majesty should trust the proposals with what was
promised [2] to be the worst of his condition which should be
made for him.' [3] Of this, added Cromwell, 'striking his hand on
his heart,' the King 'might rest confident and assured.'   Ireton

Ireton
talks of
purging
the House. went farther still.   The army, he told Huntington,
'would purge, and purge, and purge, and never leave
purging the Houses, till they had made them of such
a temper as to do his Majesty's business ; and rather than
they would fall short of what was promised, he would join with
French, Spaniard, Cavalier, or any that would join with him
to force them to it.' [4]

Neither Cromwell's nor Ireton's phrases may have been reported with complete accuracy, but in its general tenour Hun-

Object of
Cromwell
and Ireton. tington's narrative is very much what might have
been expected.   The constitutional scheme of *The
Heads of the Proposals* was Ireton's own, and Ireton
was more ready than Cromwell to use force to carry his views
into practice.   After all, could Charles have been trusted to

---

[1] There had been no vote taken, so that Cromwell's fault, if fault it
was, lay merely in not dividing the House against the Propositions.

[2] *i.e.* the suggestions for legislation appended. See *Const. Documents*,
239.

[3] Ashburnham's statement (*Narrative*, ii. 96) that Cromwell often
repeated 'that if the army continued an army, they would restore the
King,' seems to be a reminiscence of this conversation.   If so, it is a good
example of the tendency of reporters to mislead by dropping qualifi-
cations.

[4] Huntington's *Sundry Reasons*, E. 458, 3.

act in harmony with a reformed Parliament, an unconstitutional dissolution of a Parliament protected against dissolution by an unconstitutional statute might have been the best, as it certainly was the shortest, path out of the maze in which the nation had lost its way.

It is no matter of blame that Charles was as disinclined to listen to *The Heads of the Proposals* as he was to listen to the Newcastle Propositions. His fault was that he neither gave a direct negative to them nor formulated a counter-scheme of his own. He had lately received letters from Scotland which led him to believe that, by spinning out the time, he might have the support of the Scots on his own terms. Argyle's eagerness to send an army into England[1] had soon abated. On August 9 he protested in the Committee of Estates against any action which might lead to a rupture with England ; and, a few days later, he told Montreuil that Scotland would do wrong to help Charles unless he would accept Presbyterianism and the Covenant. If he could not do this let him send his eldest son to Scotland, and if the Prince, on his arrival, would give satisfaction on religion, he should at once be put at the head of an army of 16,000 men.

Charles's position.

His hopes from Scotland.

The situation in Scotland.

Argyle changes front.

As Argyle grew cool on the subject of an invasion of England, the Hamiltons began to take the King's cause up in earnest. They procured from the Committee of Estates an order for sending Lanark and Loudoun to England, and, on August 13, sent Robin Leslie in advance to prepare the way for the new commissioners.[2] By the instructions carried by Leslie it appeared that the Hamiltons wished all military movements to be postponed till the following year.[3] By that time there would be a new Parliament, and they doubtless hoped to secure the upper hand in the elections. The Hamiltons, at least, had no wish to push Charles too hard on the score of religion. Lanark wrote

The Hamiltons take up the King's cause.

---

[1] See p. 300.

[2] Montreuil to Brienne, Aug. $\frac{14}{24}$, *Carte MSS.* lxxxiii. 196 ; Montreuil to Mazarin, Aug. $\frac{21}{31}$, *Arch. des Aff. Étrangères*, lvii. fol. 201.

[3] Instructions to R. Leslie, *Burnet*, v. 113.

to him on the 23rd, excusing the delay on the ground that if help had been sent at once it could only have been given 'at the old rate of satisfaction in religion and the Covenant.'[1] Even as things were, however, the Hamiltons gained ground,

Sept. 4.
Action of the Committee of Estates.
and on September 4 the Committee of Estates ordered their commissioners in London to delay the presentation of the revised Newcastle Propositions till the arrival of Loudoun, and also to press the English Parliament to allow Charles to come to London in order that, after confirming his message of May 12—that is to say, his promise to grant Presbytery for three years—he might proceed to treat upon the remaining Propositions.[2]

These last orders arrived too late to be of service, as the Propositions were actually presented on the 7th. Lauderdale,

Batten offers the English fleet to the Scots.
however, had not been inactive on the King's behalf. Batten had made him an offer to bring the twenty-two ships under his command to declare for the Scots and the English Presbyterians, on condition that he was allowed to revictual his ships elsewhere than in England. Though Batten was aware that the Scottish authorities would object to show their hands by admitting him into one of their harbours, he fancied that, at their request, he might be allowed to seek in France the provisions of which he stood in need.[3] So conscious was Cromwell of the imminence of danger from Scotland that he assured Lauderdale of his readiness to comply with the wishes of the Scots—granting all that they could reasonably demand, if only they would abandon their intention of sending an army to the help of the King.[4]

---

[1] Lanark to the King, Aug. 23, *Burnet*, v. 114.

[2] Lanark to the King, Sept. 4, *ibid.* v. 118.

[3] Montreuil to Brienne, $\frac{\text{Aug. 28}}{\text{Sept. 7}}$, *Carte MSS.* lxxxiii. fol. 200b. Montreuil derived his information from a letter written by Lauderdale.

[4] Lauderdale, writes Montreuil in the despatch cited in the last note, had given information 'que les Independants se veulent accommoder avec les Escossais, qu'il traite avec un des plus considerables de l'armée d'Angleterre'—this can hardly be anyone but Cromwell—'pour cet effect, qui l'asseure que pourveu que l'Escosse s'accorde avec les Independants

Charles, as was too often the case, was playing a double game. On the one hand he assured Lauderdale that, if only
Charles plays a double game. the Scots would declare in his favour, they should have nothing to complain of with respect to his dealings with the Independents, though he was ominously silent as to the concessions which he was prepared
His answer to the Propositions. to make to his deliverers.[1] On the other hand, he sent to Cromwell and Ireton a draft of the answer which he proposed to send to the Houses, to the effect that he preferred *The Heads of the Proposals* to the New-castle Propositions, and that he therefore wished that Parliament would take the former into consideration and afterwards enter
He asks for a personal treaty. into a personal treaty with himself with a view to the modification of the articles to which he took objection.[2] Both Cromwell and Ireton saw in this answer far more than it really conveyed, and they engaged to support the King's demand for a personal treaty. On this the answer, which in reality bound Charles to nothing, was, on September 9, despatched by him to Westminster.[3]

It is hardly to be wondered at that the excessive eagerness of Cromwell and Ireton to accept Charles's tinsel promises as
Cromwell and Ireton suspected of too great compliance. pure gold should be received with some suspicion in the army. The soldiers, indeed, were at the time in no good humour, as their pay was considerably in arrear on account of the difficulty of levying the assessment in the city. Under such circumstances the men were ready to give ear to violent counsels which might

dans ce seul point d'abandonner leur Roy, ils demeureront aisement d'accord les uns et les autres de tout le reste.' This is vague, but I think it means what I have stated in the text.

[1] According to the same despatch, Lauderdale wrote, ' que Benfeld,' *i.e.* Bamfield, ' qui connoit M. Germain, n'avoit pu faire promettre au Roy d'Angleterre qu'il contenteroit les Escossois, mais seulement que s'ils commençoient à se declarer pour luy, il ne seroit à leur prejudice avec les Independants.'

[2] Berkeley's *Memoirs,* 43 ; The King to the Speaker of the House of Lords, Sept. 9, *L.J.* ix. 434.

[3] Huntington to Fairfax, Sept. 9, *Clarke Papers,* i. 225.

possibly lead to their entrance into the City, and to the

exaction of payment by force. Fairfax, indeed, made
an imperative demand upon the citizens for the im-

mediate payment of 50,000*l*.,[1] but the citizens had
treated many imperative demands of a similar nature
with silent contempt, and were not likely to give
way now.

If the soldiers needed a theory wherewith to justify their
actions, Lilburne was always ready to supply it. He had for

some time been teaching that Parliament had no
legal existence till it had been purged of the members who sat in the absence of the Speakers, and his
disciples repeated his arguments at head-quarters.

Sept. 9.
Major
White
expelled
from the
Army
Council.
On September 9 Major White was expelled from
the Council of the Army for maintaining that there
was 'now no visible authority in the kingdom but
the power and force of the sword;' Cromwell, as
might easily be imagined, taking a leading part in the condemnation of a doctrine so subversive of civil order.[2] On the
other hand, the principal officers did everything in their power
to obtain satisfaction for the reasonable demands of the

Sept. 14.
Words
spoken
against the
King to be
excused.
soldiers. On the 14th Fairfax forwarded to Westminster a petition in which the Agitators asked for
the release of prisoners condemned by the judges for
speaking words against the King. Amongst them was
a certain Robert White, who had said that if he met the King
at the head of his army 'he would have as soon killed him as
any other man.'[3]

It was well that at the end of a civil war rash words should
not be too readily taken into account, but it was also well
that no attempt to obtain a reasonable settlement should be

---

[1] *A Perfect Diurnal*, E. 518, 31.

[2] *The Humble Proposals*, E. 406, **21**; *The Copy of a Letter . . . by
Francis White*, E. 413, 17.

[3] *Perfect Occurrences*, E. 518, 33; *An Humble Remonstrance*, E.
407, 15. This saying has been ascribed to Cromwell on the faith of an
anonymous statement, specifying no place or date, preserved by Noble,
Mem. of the Prot. House of Cromwell, ii. 271.

neglected. Cromwell, in his efforts in this direction, was supported by a majority of the Council of the Army. On the
9th there was a long discussion at Putney on the best
way to establish a firm peace on the basis of the
King's restoration. In the course of this discussion, Cromwell reiterated his assertion that he had no wish
'to cast down the foundation of Presbytery and set up Independency.'[1] Freedom for his own party to worship in their
own way was all that he required, not its establishment in
power, or a share in the material emoluments of the Church.

Cromwell, having girt himself to the difficult task of winning Charles, had been sanguine enough to imagine that he
could also win Lilburne to his side. The fall of the
Presbyterians in Parliament had given Lilburne
fresh hopes of regaining his liberty, and it was now
expected that Marten, who was the chairman of the Committee
of the Commons in which the legality of his imprisonment had
been discussed, would be allowed to make the report, the
obstacles hitherto thrown in his way being now removed.
Lilburne had long held Cromwell to be his bitterest enemy,
but when the important day approached, he pleaded with him
for a personal interview. Cromwell was never vindictive, and
on September 6 he visited Lilburne in his cell in the Tower.
Here Lilburne discovered that Cromwell feared lest if he were
once at liberty he would spend his leisure in stirring up a
mutinous spirit in the army, and, with the generosity which
often accompanies fanaticism, he at once offered
to leave England if only a reasonable amount of
justice were done to him. That, he added, which
touched him most nearly was the interest of the public. If
only the House of Commons would deny that the Lords possessed original jurisdiction over a commoner, he would waive
all claim to compensation for his ill-treatment, at least during
the present Parliament.[2]

Cromwell spoke kindly to Lilburne, but he had to do with
a man singularly incapable of taking a broad view of political

Sept. 9.
A discussion at Putney.

Sept. 6.
Cromwell and Lilburne.

Lilburne offers to leave England.

---

[1] *Two Declarations*, E. 407, 1.
[2] *An Additional Plea*, E. 412; 11.

necessities, and when, on September 14, some days after
Marten's report had been made, Cromwell supported a motion

Sept. 14.
Cromwell
supports a
motion for a
search into
precedents.
for directing the committee from which the report
proceeded to search for precedents on the jurisdiction of the Lords, he was once more in Lilburne's
eyes the perfidious hypocrite whom no promises

Lilburne
denounces
him.
could bind. Lilburne now proposed to appeal to
the common soldiers and the labourers against the
iniquity of their superiors. He informed Marten
that he would call on ' the private soldiers of his Excellency's
army' to see what ' the hobnails and clouted shoes ' would do
for his cause.[1] A more practical reasoner might have discerned that it was undesirable in the interests of public policy
that the Commons should fulminate violent threats against
the House of Lords without, at least, making sure of the
ground on which the attack was to be conducted.

Cromwell was, no doubt, specially anxious to avert a conflict between the Houses, as the time was now approaching

Cromwell
anxious to
avoid a con-
flict between
the Houses.
when the concurrence of all men of good will would
be needed if there was to be a settlement at all.
Charles's announcement of his preference for *The
Heads of the Proposals* had stirred up the anger of
the Parliamentary Presbyterians,[2] and had left them powerless to resist the demand made by the Independents for

Delay in
considering
the King's
answer.
delay in considering the King's answer, in order to
have time to ascertain the wishes of the army as
well as to make up their own minds. For some
days negotiations were vigorously carried on between the
King's agents on the one side and the leading members of

An under-
standing
probable.
Parliament and the chiefs of the army on the other,
with the result that the explanations given on the
King's behalf were considered entirely satisfactory.[3]
Upon this the Council of the Army met at Putney on the

---

[1] *Two Letters writ by . . . John Lilburne*, E. 401, 41. *C.J.* v. 301.

[2] Newsletter, Sept. $\frac{17}{27}$, *Roman Transcripts, R.O.*

[3] "Il Rè era contento, e ciascheduno se ne stava sodisfatto della
negotiatione. Io sono stato presente a tutta istoria." Newsletter,
Sept. 24 / Oct. 4, *Roman Transcripts, R.C.*

16th, and resolved that it was expedient to proceed by steps, and that they would begin by asking Parliament to draw up

Sept. 16.
Proposals of the Council of the Army.

Bills to secure the liberties of the subject and the privileges of Parliament, as also to settle the militia, on the understanding that, as soon as these had received the royal assent, they should be followed by others securing the rights of the King.[1]

Though Cromwell was still able to carry the Army Council with him, he exposed himself to a fierce attack from

Cromwell attacked by Rainsborough.

a vigorous minority which had come to the conclusion that it was useless to negotiate further with Charles. In the course of the discussion Rainsborough, by whom this minority was led, so far lost his temper as to tell Cromwell that 'one of them must not live.' On the

A soldiers' petition on behalf of the King.

other hand the soldiers, like the officers, were divided into parties, and no less than 4,000 of them subscribed their names to a petition asking for a reconciliation with the King.[2]

It was not only at Putney that Cromwell and his supporters were attacked. In London the Royalist and Presbyterian newspapers teemed with virulent charges

Attacks of the London newspapers.

against the motives and characters of the men who were doing their best to reconcile the King and Parliament on principles of which they themselves disapproved. It is not likely that Cromwell was more ready than on other occasions to resent personal insults, but

Sept. 20.
The press to be gagged.

on the 20th Fairfax conveyed the general sense of the Council in a letter asking Parliament to put a stop to the libels.[3] Though an Ordinance intended to carry out Fairfax's wish passed through Parliament,[4] practically the press remained as free as before, and Royalist scribblers continued to call attention to Cromwell's flaming nose, or even to charge him with gross licentiousness of life.

---

[1] *The Intentions of the Army*, E. 408, 16.
[2] Ford to Hopton, Sept. 20, *Clarendon MSS.* 2,597.
[3] Fairfax to Manchester, Sept. 20, *L.J.* x. 441.
[4] *Ibid.* x. 457.

On the 21st the King's reply, expressing a preference for *The Heads of the Proposals* to the Parliamentary Propositions,

Sept. 21. The King's answer voted a denial of the Propositions.

and asking for a personal treaty, was at last formally brought before the Houses. Both Lords and Commons voted that it was a denial of the Propositions.[1] Whether this vote was to be merely a clearing of the Presbyterian scheme out of the way, or whether it was to be followed by an absolute renunciation of the King's title, depended on the course which would be taken on the following day. On the morning of the

Sept. 22. The King's imprisonment talked of.

22nd the members crowded into the House before the arrival of the Speaker, and amidst a buzz of conversation voices were heard asking that the King should be imprisoned in Warwick or Windsor Castle.[2]

After the arrival of the Speaker, a proposal was made that the House should go into Committee to consider its relations

Divisions in the Independent party.

with the King. The Independent party at once split into two fractions, the one under its old leaders still desirous of an understanding with the King; the other, which may fairly be styled Republican, aiming under the guidance of Marten and Rainsborough at

Marten proposes a vote of no addresses;

the abolition of monarchy. Marten now asked that the House instead of going into Committee should vote that no further addresses should be made to Charles, who, according to one of Marten's followers, was the Achan in Israel and the Jonah in the ship.[3]

Against this view of the case Cromwell and Ireton, followed by the old Independent leaders, Vane, St. John, and Fiennes, loudly protested, demanding that the King's request for a personal treaty should be granted.[4] In supporting his argument

[1] *L.J.* x. 440 ; *C.J.* v. 311.

[2] Newsletter, Sept. 24 / Oct. 4 , *Roman Transcripts, R.O.*

[3] W. Langley to J. Langley, Sept. 28, *Hist. MSS. Com. Rep.* v. 179.

[4] Ford to Hopton, Sept. 28, *Clarendon MSS.* 2,604. Berkeley, too, witnesses strongly as to the vigour with which Cromwell and his friends took up the King's cause. After saying that Charles's answer to the Propositions (see p. 361) had been shown to 'our friends in the army' before it was sent to Westminster, he adds that they, 'seeming infinitely

in favour of an agreement with the King, Cromwell urged that
it was worthy of consideration ' how that there was a party in
but is op
posed by
Cromwell
and the
old Inde-
pendent
leaders. the army labouring for the King, and that a great
one ; how the City was endeavouring to get another
party in the army ; and that there was a third
party . . . little dreamt of, that were endeavouring
to have no other power to rule but the sword.' [1]   The
same motive, the fear of military anarchy, which in the spring
had driven him to uphold the authority of Parliament, now
drove him in the autumn to uphold the authority of the King.

Marten's proposed vote of no addresses was rejected,
Cromwell himself acting as teller against it, by eighty-four
The vote
of no
addresses
rejected. votes to thirty-four.[2]   The majority was evidently
composed of a composite body of Presbyterians and
Independents.   Such a majority was not likely to
be coherent, and the House, as soon as it had gone into com-
Selections
to be made
from the
Parliamen-
tary Pro-
positions. mittee, decided without a division that selections
made from the last Parliamentary Propositions
should be sent to the King for his acceptance or
refusal.   The committee would not hear of Crom-
well's idea of a personal treaty.   There can be little doubt that
if a report of the proceedings of the committee were brought
to light, it would show that the combination between the
Presbyterians who wished only for a settlement on their own
terms, and the Republicans who wished to have a settlement
The
militia pro-
position
selected. without the King, was so strong that Cromwell
thought it imprudent to take a division.   Before the
end of the sitting it was agreed that the proposition
on the militia should be the first selected.

On the 23rd the discussion continued in the absence of

satisfied ' with it, ' promised to use their utmost endeavours to procure a
personal treaty, and, to my understanding, performed it ; for both Cromwell and Ireton, with Vane and all their friends, seconded with great
resolution this desire of his Majesty.'   Berkeley's *Memoirs*, 43.

[1]   Ford to Hopton, Sept. 28, *Clar. St. P.* ii. App. xxxix.   Cromwell
was afterwards accused of saying that his own opinion was the sense of the
army, which he disavowed.   See *Clarke Papers*, i. 229-232.

[2]   *C.J.* v. 312 ; Newsletter, $\frac{\text{Sept. 24}}{\text{Oct. 4}}$, *Roman Transcripts, R.O.*

Cromwell, who had duties to attend to at head-quarters.
Instead of confining its selection to merely political demands
as had been suggested by the Army Council a week before,[1]

Sept. 23.
Other
selections.

the House fixed on the propositions relating to the
abolition of episcopacy and the sale of bishops'
lands in satisfaction of the debts of the army—
everything, in short, which would be most obnoxious to

Only one
more ap-
plication
to be
made to
the King.

Charles, and then decided that application should
be 'once again made to the King,' implying that if
he refused to accept the terms thus offered, his refusal was to be final, and that no attempt to negotiate
further would be made.   Marten, who thought one application
too much, succeeded in obtaining twenty-three votes against
seventy.   It is evident that the Presbyterians voted in the
majority, who, it must be supposed, were sufficiently infatuated
to imagine that, if only they were firm enough, they would
succeed in bringing Charles on his knees.[2]

When, therefore, Cromwell returned to Westminster,[3] too
late to take part in this debate, he found that all his efforts in

Cromwell
not sup-
ported by
Charles.

the King's behalf had been thrown away.   Nor was
Charles at all ready to give him that countenance
without which all that he could do would be done in
vain.   Charles, indeed, had excellent information on all that
was passing, Lady Fairfax herself betraying to him the secrets
of the Army Council which she doubtless learnt from her com-
plaisant husband.[4]   What he learnt, however, encouraged him
to exaggerate the importance of the divisions amongst his
adversaries, and to turn a deaf ear to all offers of compromise,
in the vain hope that he would be borne back to power on the
crest of the popular wave.   Before the end of September a
Royalist who had excellent means of acquiring information
wrote that the negotiation between the King and the chiefs of

[1] See p. 365.

[2] *C.J.* v. 314.

[3] *Clarke Papers*, i. 231, 232.

[4] " La moglie di Farfax Generale appassionata per il Rè avvisa di
quanto si passa nel Consiglio secreto." Newsletter, $\frac{\text{Sept. 24}}{\text{Oct. 4}}$, *Roman Transcripts, R.O.*

the army was still kept up. " But it comes to no issue nor any likelyhood of one. The King is very resolute."[1]

Baffled by the House of Commons and unsupported by Charles, Cromwell's mediatory position was rapidly becoming *At'a ks on Ciomwell.* untenable. The split in the Independent party which wrecked his scheme in Parliament was not confined to the House of Commons. In the army itself Cromwell was denounced as a mere time-server, bent upon currying favour with Charles in the pursuit of his own private interests. Even the faithful Hugh Peters attacked him and the *Sept. 24. Cromwell on his defence.* officers who supported him as too great courtiers.[2] Cromwell could but plead his good intentions. "Though it may be for the present," he wrote, on the day after his Parliamentary defeat, "a cloud may lie over our actions to those who are not acquainted with the grounds of them, yet we doubt not but God will clear our integrity and innocence from any other ends we aim at but His glory and the public good."[3]

Cromwell, indeed, was not easily rebuffed, and the Royalist negotiators, far more eager for an arrangement than their *Cromwell and Ireton persist in treating with the King.* master, were already reporting that Ireton had given them assurances that the Parliamentary vote would not be accepted at head-quarters as decisive against the continuance of the efforts of the army to achieve a more reasonable settlement.[4] On the 24th, obviously as *Republica- tion of The Heads of the Proposals.* an appeal to popular opinion, *The Heads of the Proposals* were republished, together with certain explanations which had been made by the Council of the Army on the 16th. On the 25th the House *Sept. 25. The Lord Mayor and five aldermen impeached.* of Commons, where the majority was still Independent except when an agreement with the King was proposed, impeached the Lord Mayor, Sir John Gayer, and five aldermen as having been concerned

---

[1] Ford to Hopton, Sept. 30, *Clarendon MSS.* 2,605. Ford was Ireton's brother-in-law.

[2] Upton to Edwards, Sept. 15, *Clarendon MSS.* 2,605.

[3] Cromwell to Michael Jones, Sept. 24, *Carlyle* Letter, **xlvi.**

[4] Newsletter, $\frac{\text{Sept. 24}}{\text{Oct. 4}}$, *Roman Transcripts, R.O.*

in raising forces in the City against the army.[1] On the

Sept. 27.
Regulation
of muni-
cipalities.

27th the House ordered the preparation of an Ordinance excluding delinquents from all municipal offices, or from voting at municipal elections.[2] On

Sept. 28.
An Inde-
pendent
Lord
Mayor.

the 28th Alderman Warner, a determined Independent, was chosen Lord Mayor, the approaches to the Guildhall being guarded at the time of his elec-

Oct. 6.
Ordinance
for
municipal
elections.

tion by a strong body of soldiers.[3] The great City of London was thus cowed into submission. On October 6 the Ordinance regulating municipal elections was finally issued with the approval of both Houses.[4]

The fleet was, through jealousy of the army, almost as Presbyterian as the City, and, to secure a hold on it, the Houses

Oct. 8.
The
Commons
make
Rains-
borough
Vice-
Admiral.

voted on the 8th that Rainsborough, who had been a sailor before he was a soldier, should command it as Vice-Admiral in the place of the Presbyterian Batten.[5] Possibly those who concurred in the vote were partly actuated by a desire to separate from the army one whom they were beginning to regard as a ringleader of sedition. The party amongst the soldiers whom Cromwell had indicated as wishing ' to have no other power to rule but the sword '[6] was rapidly gaining strength, and that party regarded Rainsborough as its principal spokesman amongst the

Oct. 5.
A spirit of
parity in
the army.

officers. There was, it was said, a spirit of parity walking in the army. Many of the soldiers were asking that no Duke, Marquis, or Earl should have more than 2,000*l.* a year, and that the income of other classes should be proportionately restricted. Those in both Houses who had property began to show an unwonted desire to come to terms with the King.[7]

This feeling in favour of an accommodation could not but

---

[1] *C.J.* v. 315.

[2] *Ibid.* v. 317.

[3] Newsletter, Oct. $\frac{1}{11}$, *Roman Transcripts, R.O.*

[4] *L.J.* ix. 470.

[5] *Ibid.* ix. 476 ; *C.J.* v. 328.

[6] See p. 367.

[7] Letter of Intelligence, Oct. 5, *Clarendon MSS.* 2,611.

strengthen the hands of those members of the Army Council who had been dissatisfied with the attitude of the House of Commons. On October 6 they resolved that a fresh attempt should be made to negotiate with Charles on conditions more satisfactory to him than those which Parliament was forcing upon him.[1] In order that these conditions might be fully weighed, the Army Council was summoned to meet on the 14th, with a view to a full discussion. In the meanwhile, attempts were made to come to a preliminary understanding with Berkeley and Ashburnham, who were acting on the King's behalf. Berkeley and Ashburnham were in the highest spirits, not hesitating to express their belief that everything would be settled in a week. The army chiefs, as an evidence of their sincerity, allowed the friends from whom Charles had long been severed to gather round him at Hampton Court, and, on the 7th, the King held a council, attended by Richmond, Hertford, Ormond, Dorset, Southampton, and Seymour. No doubt the newly-suggested compromise formed the main subject of discussion.[2]

Oct. 6. The army leaders decide upon a fresh negotiation with the King.

An Army Council summoned.

Good prospect of a settlement.

Oct. 7. A Royalist council.

Charles, unfortunately, was not prepared to meet the army leaders half-way. "The secret disposition," wrote one of his partisans, "is that there is no manner of agreement between the King and the army; all this negotiation having produced no other effect but to incline some of the chief officers not to consent to his destruction, which I believe they will not, unless they be overswayed; but cannot observe that they are so truly the King's as that they will pass the Rubicon for him, which if they would do, con-

The King is not conciliatory.

---

[1] "Dopo tre giorni in quà la risolutione e stata presa per i Capi di ritornare in trattato con il Rè, e di proporgli conditioni honorabili e più adequate. A questo fine per risolvere tutte divisioni e controversie che sono fra di loro . . . hanno assegnato un luogo e determinato un giorno, che sarà li 24," *i.e.* $\frac{14}{24}$, "del corrente, per convenire tutti insieme e stabilire concordemente e di commun consenso come deono portarsi verso il Rè." Newsletter, Oct. $\frac{8}{18}$, *Roman Transcripts, R.O.*

[2] *Ibid. ; A Perfect Diurnal*, E. 518, 43.

sidering the inclination of the common soldiers, and generally
of the people, they might do what they would ; but they are
cold, and there is another faction of desperate fellows as hot
as fire." [1]

Cromwell, in short, was expected to aid in a purely
Royalist reaction.   Marten and his friends had made up their

Rumoured
offers to
Cromwell.

minds that he had already bargained for his reward.
He had, it was said, obtained from the King the
promise of the Earldom of Essex and the garter.
If this were true, said Marten, and he at least had no doubt
about its accuracy, he himself would be another Felton.[2]   So
excited were the Republicans against Cromwell, that he had
from time to time to change his quarters through fear of
assassination.[3]

The feeling amongst the soldiery that led to this exasperation against Cromwell, led also to exasperation against the

Oct. 11.
The
Royalist
council
dismissed.

King.   Cries were raised in the army for the dismissal of the Royalist noblemen who had been
admitted to Charles's presence.[4]   Charles on his
part was willing, for reasons of his own, to part with
his new counsellors.   He had come to the conclusion that the
army leaders had allowed them to come to him merely because they were frightened at the strength of popular opinion
in his favour, and that by sending the noblemen away he
would give practical evidence of his refusal to accept any terms
from Cromwell and Ireton.   On the 11th, accordingly, the
noblemen returned to London with Charles's full consent, if
not by his express orders.[5]

[1] Letter of Intelligence, Oct. 7, *Clarendon MSS.* 2,616.

[2] Wildman's *Truths Triumph*, p. 7, E. 520, 33. Marten is plainly
indicated, though his name is not given. The story may be approximately
dated by connecting it with Berkeley's statement that Cromwell believed
him to have told Lady Carlisle that Cromwell was to be Earl of Essex.
Berkeley declared, however, the supposition to have been without foundation. This was after the establishment of head-quarters at Putney. That
the earldom was offered to Cromwell is likely enough.

[3] Berkeley's *Memoirs*, 44.

[4] *A Perfect Diurnal*, E. 518, 43.

[5] "Il Rè . . . fu avvisato che il tutto non era che una apparenza per

The fact was that the approach of the two new Scottish commissioners, Loudoun and Lanark, who joined Lauderdale in London on the 11th, had inspired the King with fresh hopes, and the army leaders with fresh fears. The belief gained ground that they brought with them the menace of a Scottish invasion, and it was evident that, if the army were to march northwards to oppose that invasion, it would be in the highest degree improvident to leave Charles in his present temper in the neighbourhood of a city which was filled with his partisans. It had therefore been proposed by some of the officers, possibly by Cromwell himself, that if the army marched to the borders, the King should be compelled to accompany it. To this Charles, who was soon made aware of all that passed amongst the officers, opposed a most strenuous resistance, declaring that nothing but force would induce him to leave his present quarters.

Arrival of Scottish commissioners.

Proposal to remove Charles from Hampton Court.

Obviously the attempt of Cromwell and Ireton to come to terms with Charles had broken down ; and, as might have been expected, each party to the negotiations threw the blame on the other. Charles held that the army had only offered him terms in order to sow division between himself and his subjects. The officers held that Charles only talked of conciliating them in order to divert their attention from the general attack upon them which he was preparing.[1] When the Army Council met, as

Failure of the negotiations.

quietare il popolo, e ingannare S.M., visto che nel medesimo tempo, per ordine dell' Armata, il Parlamento faceva d' altre propositioni ripugnanti all' ottorità Regia, e medesimamente alla sua libertà ; onde doi giorni appresso, il Rè di suo moto proprio licentiò questi Signori per disingannare il popolo, e fece sapere nel medesimo tempo e al Parlamento e ai Capi dell' Armata che, se havessino intrapreso d' allontanare la sua Persona da Londra e di trasportarla altrove, come molto bene sapeva essere il loro dissegno, pensassino per questo mezzo d' allontanarlo anche dal cuore, e dall' affettione del popolo, che non lo sarebbono che con violenza e forza contra la sua persona, cosa bastante per cagionare una commutione universale per tutto il regno." Newsletter, Oct. $\frac{13}{23}$, *Roman Transcripts, R.O.*

[1] Newsletter, Oct. $\frac{13}{23}$, *Roman Transcripts, R.O.*

had been announced, on the 14th, nothing was said about any negotiation with the King. The discussion, on the other
Oct. 14.
Meeting of
the Army
Council. hand, turned on the necessity of forcing Charles to accompany the army if it was called on to resist a Scottish invasion.[1] For the present, however, no decision was arrived at, as no measures could be taken till the intentions of the Scots had been more clearly manifested.

[1] Letter of Intelligence, Oct. 14, *Clarendon MSS.* 2,624.

CHAPTER LV.

THE AGREEMENT OF THE PEOPLE.

AT the time when the last overtures of the army were rejected by Charles, there were rumours that a difference of opinion had arisen between Cromwell and Ireton, a difference which was said to be caused by Ireton's dissatisfaction with Cromwell's desertion of the King's interests.[1] Though no more than this is known, the most probable explanation is that Cromwell, though not as yet prepared for a breach with the King, perceived that it would be necessary, if he was to be brought to terms, to put stronger pressure on him than could be put by the army alone. At all events, it is at this time that Cromwell is found aiming at a compromise with the Parliamentary Presbyterians, a compromise which was embodied in a scheme accepted by the Lords on October 13, and brought on for discussion in the Commons on the same day.

1647.
Rumoured difference between Cromwell and Ireton.

Cromwell seeks a compromise with the Presbyterians.

According to this scheme, Presbyterian government was to be established in the Church for three years—the very period for which the King's assent was secured;[2] whilst, with certain exceptions, those who were desirous of worshipping in any other way were to be at liberty to do so, provided that they did nothing in disturbance of the peace of the kingdom. The exceptions were

Oct. 13.
The Lords' scheme for a settlement of religion.

---

[1] "There hath been of late some difference between Cromwell and Commissary Ireton; and I am induced to think it to be the falling off of Cromwell from the King, because that Ireton, like an honest man, stands to make good what he hath promised, and lately, in discontent, offered to quit his command in the army." Letter of Intelligence, Oct. 11, *Clarendon MSS.* 2,622. [2] See p. 252.

those who professed 'the Popish religion,' and those who departed from the Christian religion as set forth in the Apostles' Creed, or held such doctrines as would render them liable, according to the recent Ordinance, to suspension from communion. Further, no one was to be freed from the penalty attached to those who did not attend divine service on the Lord's day unless he could show either a reasonable cause of absence, 'or that he was present to hear the Word of God preached or expounded unto him elsewhere.'[1]

On the morning of the 13th, the day on which the Lords' proposal was to be discussed in the House of Commons,

A crowd in Westminster Hall. Westminster Hall was filled by a motley crowd of Roman Catholics, of seekers who professed that they were still in search of a religion, and of rationalists who declared themselves ready to conform to the

Presby-terianism to be settled till the end of the next session. dictates of reason only.[2] To these Cromwell had no help to give. Aiming at objects within the scope of practical achievement, he contented himself with supporting the scheme already adopted by the Lords. Though he acted as teller in a division in favour of the three years' limit for the Presbyterian establishment, he was beaten by 38 to 35 ; and was again beaten by 41 to 33 on an amended proposal to fix the limit to seven years. The House then adopted without a division a resolution that the Presbyterian discipline should remain in force till after the next session of Parliament, whenever that might be.[3]

The remaining clauses relating to toleration and its limits were then run through without any further division. Selden,[4]

Question of toleration for the Catholics. indeed, pleaded hard for the Catholics as believers in Jesus Christ, and was supported by Marten, who boldly asked why Presbyterians were to be tolerated if Catholics were excluded. The commonplace answers

---

[1] *The Moderate Intelligencer*, E. 410, 25 ; *L.J.* ix. 482.

[2] Newsletter, $\frac{\text{Oct. 22}}{\text{Nov. 1}}$, *Roman Transcripts, R.O.*

[3] *C.J.* v. 332.

[4] "Seldenus Independente, e tutto interamente Ecclesiastico sine ecclesiâ." Newsletter, $\frac{\text{Oct. 22}}{\text{Nov. 1}}$, *Roman Transcripts, R.O.*

were promptly forthcoming. Selden was told that the

Selden and
Marten
plead for
them. Catholics were idolaters, and Marten was answered with the argument that the Catholics unlike the Presbyterians had a foreign prince at their head.

On the following day Selden and Marten replied at length. Selden drew the well-known distinction between idolatry and

Oct. 14. prayers for the intercession of the saints ; whilst Marten, with his accustomed license of speech, carried the attack into the quarters of the Presbyterians. It was better, he said, to have one tyrant abroad than a tyrant in every parish, and even added[1] that the Protestant clergy detested the Catholic priests simply on account of their superior chastity.[2] Marten's words were not likely to carry much weight on a question of moral purity, and the House without a division persisted in refusing toleration to the

A proposed
Catholic
petition. Catholics. The victims of the Recusancy laws had indeed prepared a petition, in which they renounced the opinion that it was lawful to murder or resist excommunicated kings.[3] It was all to no purpose. Even those Independents who had hitherto supported their claims could do nothing for them, and their petition was not even presented to the House.[4] It was one thing to grant Catholics toleration in accord with a restored King. It was another thing to wring its concession from a hostile public opinion.

Even on a point on which public opinion was far less decided Cromwell was unable to reduce his new Presbyterian

Toleration
to be denied
to those who
use the
Prayer
Book. allies to reason. The House having refused to decrease the exceptions from toleration, proceeded to include amongst them all who used the Book of Common Prayer.[5] Thus amended, the Parliamentary Propositions became a direct defiance flung in Charles's face. As Cromwell did not even take a division on

---

[1] "Non e semetipso, sed a Spiritu Sancto." Newsletter, $\frac{Oct. 22}{Nov. 1}$, *Roman Transcripts, R.O.* [2] *Ibid.*

[3] Salvetti's Newsletter, $\frac{Oct. 22}{Nov. 1}$, *Add. MSS.* 27,962, L. fol. 457.

[4] Newsletter, $\frac{Oct. 22}{Nov. 1}$, *Roman Transcripts, R.O.*

[5] *C.J.* v. 333.

this proposal, it may reasonably be supposed that he saw opposition to be hopeless. On the 16th he acted with Marten

Oct. 16.
Cromwell
and Marten
urge haste.

as a teller in favour of a proposal for immediately taking into consideration 'the manner of the address to be made to the King.' [1] They were beaten by a conjunction of Independents and Presbyterians, but it is easy to understand that Cromwell desired to hasten the presentation of this impracticable scheme in order to get rid of it by the King's inevitable rejection, and thus to prepare the way for a reasonable settlement if such a settlement was to be had. Marten, on the other hand, was eager for haste because he desired no settlement in which the King should take a part.

Every day that passed in uncertainty was increasing the difficulties of Cromwell's position. In the army the anti-

Growing
divisions in
the army.

monarchical party was gathering strength. King and Parliament, it seemed, had tried their hands at bringing about a settlement, and had tried their hands in vain. Nor had Cromwell's effort to mediate failed less signally. The obvious inference was that King and Parliament were seeking nothing but their own ends, and that Cromwell was a base intriguer, as self-seeking as the rest. It was even reported that the Republicans in the army and in Parliament were preparing to impeach him. [2]

The dissatisfaction felt in the army with the policy of their

Five regi-
ments
change their
Agitators.

commanders was especially strong in five regiments. These regiments, after cashiering their Agitators, elected new ones, who set themselves, under the

Oct. 9.
The Case of
the Army,

influence of Lilburne and his disciples, to prepare a manifesto bearing the title of *The Case of the*

Oct. 18.
laid before
Fairfax.

Army truly stated. This manifesto was completed on October 9, and on the 18th was formally laid before Fairfax. [3]

---

[1] *C.J.* v. 335.

[2] Letter of Intelligence, Oct. 18, *Clarendon MSS.* 2,627.

[3] *The Case of the Army*, E. 411, 9. It was said that the new Agitators only represented a minority even in the five regiments, and one sanguine opponent reckoned the whole number of their supporters as 400. *Papers from the Army*, E. 411, 19.

In this manifesto the new Agitators, speaking in the name of the five regiments, complained that no serious step had been taken to redress those grievances of which complaint had been made in the Declarations set forth by the army in June. The remedies which they now proposed included a dissolution of Parliament in less than a year, and an immediate purging of the existing House by the exclusion of those who had continued to sit in the absence of the Speakers, the purged House being expected to give public approval to the action of the army in marching upon Westminster in August. As for the future, the views put forward had all the charm of novelty. There was to be a 'law paramount,' unalterable by future Parliaments, establishing biennial Parliaments, which were to be elected by manhood suffrage, except that delinquents were to be deprived of their electoral rights. These Parliaments were to have the supreme right of legislation and of calling public officials to account, the authority of the King and House of Lords being thus by implication abrogated. This startling innovation was justified on the ground that 'all power is originally and essentially in the whole body of the people of this nation, and' that 'their free choice or consent by their representators is the only original foundation of all just government.'

Its complaints.

Remedies proposed.

The modern reader of this document feels himself in the midst of ideas with which he is perfectly familiar. The 'paramount law' reminds him of the constitution of the United States, and the attribution of all power to 'the whole body of the people' reminds him of Rousseau's Social Contract. Yet, modern as was the character of these proposals, they had their roots in the past. Roman jurists had derived Imperial despotism from the sovereignty of the people, and this explanation had been used by Hooker to defend the control exercised by Elizabeth over the Church. Though the idea of a 'paramount law,' familiar to us from the history of our own commonwealth and of the American Republic, was indeed for the first time enunciated in set terms, yet there had been a preparation for its recep-

Modern appearance of these proposals.

tion in the notion of the existence of those fundamental and unchangeable laws to which both King and Parliament had of late been in the habit of appealing.

The immediate origin of this remarkable manifesto, however, is to be traced not to the study of the past, but to the needs of the moment. When King, Parliament, and Army Council had all failed, separately and conjointly, to give to the nation the peace and order for which it longed, it was only natural that there should be found some who imagined that their ends could be secured by sweeping away the fabric raised without design in the course of centuries, and by substituting for it a new one of their own building based on abstract principles.

To the doctrines of these men—now beginning to be known as Levellers [1]—no one could be more hostile than Cromwell. Yet it was hard to say how he could hold his ground against them. The House of Commons and the King were alike impracticable. On the 16th Charles told Bellièvre, who had come to take leave of him on his return to France, that he now counted on divisions in the army which would compel one or other party to place itself on his side. [2] Prudent Royalists might deplore the King's resolution to accept no compromise, but they were powerless to change it. There are, wrote one of them on the 18th, 'many moderate men, even amongst the Independents, who desire monarchy, and are not ill-affected to the King's person ; but do fear the King's design is, if he prevail, to root out the Puritan party, under which name both the Presbyterian and Independent are involved.' " His Majesty," wrote the same correspondent two days later, " holds firm to his first principles, not to do anything to the prejudice of his posterity, of the Church, nor of his friends ; in every one of which points, the generality of the Houses do desire to give him some satisfaction ; for I believe all men of estates do

Cromwell and the Levellers.

Oct. 16.
The King will not hear of a compromise.

Oct. 18.
Royalist forebodings.

Oct. 20.

---

[1] The name first appears in a letter of Nov. 1 (*Clarendon MSS.* 2,638), but it must obviously have been in existence before. Like most other party names, it began as a nickname.

[2] Grignon to Brienne, Oct. $\frac{18}{28}$, *R.O. Transcripts.*

fear a new war ; and no less lest the popular party in the Houses and the army should prevail." [1]

Amongst those who desired to give satisfaction to the King, Cromwell is undoubtedly to be reckoned. On the 20th he appeared in the House of Commons, and took occasion, by a motion for limiting to seven the number of Royalists excluded from pardon, to plead the cause of monarchy. For three hours he held the attention of the House, urging it to re-establish the throne with the least possible delay, giving at the same time the strongest assurances that neither himself nor Fairfax, nor any of the chief officers, had any hand in the proposals of the five regiments, and asserting positively that his aim during the whole war had been to strengthen and not to destroy monarchy.[2]

Cromwell's speech on behalf of monarchy.

If more of this remarkable speech had been preserved, it would probably be seen how far Cromwell's conception of monarchy differed from that of Charles. Little as Cromwell cared for the details of constitutional forms, he was not the man to assent to the re-establishment of the throne without some permanent constitutional checks which should render the recurrence of past abuses impossible. Yet it was precisely to this that Charles refused to agree : and when he declared that he would do nothing against his friends, his Church, and his posterity, he meant precisely what the Levellers meant by their 'paramount law,' that there was a political and ecclesiastical order which no stress of difficulty, no manifestation of the national will,

Two conceptions of monarchy.

---

[1] Letters of Intelligence, Oct. 18, 20, *Clarendon MSS.* 2,627.

[2] "Fa tre giorni, che a questo effetto Cramver . . . si usurpò una udienza di tre hore, nella quale si sforzò con tanta d' eloquenza come d' ipochrisia e di dissimulatione . . . a persuadere al resto del corpo parlamentario, che lui e il General Fairfax, e tutti li Capi dell' Armata non havevano in nessuna maniera parte nelli dissegni di quali reggimenti che si erano divisi, ma che il lor fine e la loro volontà dal principio della guerra non era stata altra che di servire al Rè, e di stabilire la monarchia nel suo potere. Parlò egli in tutto il tempo della sua arringa molto avantaggiosamente per il Rè, concludendo che bisognava restabilirlo più presto che si poteva." Newsletter, $\frac{Oct. 22}{Nov. 1}$, *Roman Transcripts, R.O.*

was of any avail to change or to overthrow. Cromwell, who knew nothing of such abstract rights, was forsooth to be counted as a self-seeking hypocrite because he lent a favourable ear to the proposals of all parties alike, whilst refusing to worship at the shrine of any one of them.

As Cromwell had stood forth as a reconciler between King and Parliament, he stood forth as a reconciler between the

Oct. 28.
An army
meeting in
Putney
Church.

parties into which the army was divided. On the 28th a meeting of the Army Council was held in Putney Church, to which Wildman and other prominent Levellers [1] were admitted, as well as the Agitators recently elected by the five regiments. At this meeting, the object of which was to find some terms of agreement between the supporters and opponents of *The Case of the Army*, Cromwell took the chair, Fairfax being absent on the

Sexby's
view of the
situation.

ground of ill-health. Sexby was the first to set forth the case of the new Agitators.[2] "We sought," he said, "to satisfy all men, and it was well; but in going to do it, we have dissatisfied all men. We have laboured to please the King; and I think, except we go about to cut all our throats we shall not please him; and we have gone to support a House which will prove rotten studs:[3] I mean the Parliament, which consists of a company of rotten members." Cromwell and Ireton, he added, had attempted to settle the kingdom on the foundations of the King and the Parliament; but he hoped that they would do no more in that direction, and that henceforth they would rely upon the army.

Sexby's last words drew forth from Cromwell and Ireton an explanation of their conduct. "I shall declare it again,"

Cromwell
and Ireton
on their
defence.

said Ireton, "that I do not seek, and would not seek the destruction either of Parliament or King; neither will I . . . concur with them who will not attempt all the ways that are possible to preserve both, and to make

---

[1] *A Perfect Diurnal*, E. 520, 1.

[2] The whole of the debate of the 28th is from the *Clarke Papers*, i. 226–279.

[3] *i.e.* rotten wooden uprights supporting a lath and plaster wall. See *Clarke Papers*, i. 228, note a.

good use, and the best use that can be of both for the kingdom."

After this personal explanation the meeting proceeded to consider *The Agreement of the People*, which had been drawn Cromwell on
The Agree-
ment of the
People. up by the new Agitators in order that the views expressed by them in *The Case of the Army* [1] might receive the definite shape of a new constitution, which would derive its authority from the direct acceptance of Many plau-
sible things
in it. the people. Cromwell at once acknowledged that it contained many things that were plausible. The question was whether it was possible to reduce them to practice. "If," he characteristically said, "we could leap out of one condition into another that had so specious things in it as this hath, I suppose there would not be much dispute; though perhaps some of these things may be very well disputed; How is it to
gain general
acceptance? and, how do we know if, whilst we are disputing these things, another company of men shall gather together, and they shall put out a paper as plausible as this? I do not know why it may not be done by that time you have agreed upon this, or got hands to it, if that be the way; and not only another and another, but many of this kind; and if so, what do you think the consequence of that It will lead
to confusion. would be? Would it not be confusion? Would it not make England like the Switzerland country, one canton against another, and one county against another? I ask you whether it be not fit for every honest man seriously to lay that upon his heart, and, if so, what would that produce but an absolute desolation to the nation; and we, in the meantime, tell the nation 'It is for your liberty! 'Tis for your privilege!' Pray God it prove so, whatever course we run.

"But, truly, I think we are not only to consider what the consequences are . . . but we are to consider the probability Difficulties
in the way. of the ways and means to accomplish [it], [2] that is to say that, according to reason and judgment, the spirits and temper of this nation are prepared to receive and go along with it, and [that] those great difficulties [which] lie

---

[1] See *Clarke Papers*, i. 237, note 1.

[2] The words in brackets are inserted to eke out the sense.

in our way [are] in a likelyhood to be either overcome or removed. Truly to anything that's good, there's no doubt on it, objections may be made and framed, but let every honest man consider whether or no there be not very real objections *Can faith re-* in point of difficulty; and I know a man may answer *move them?* all difficulties with faith, and faith will answer all difficulties really where it is, and we are very apt all of us to call that faith that perhaps may be but carnal imagination, and carnal reasoning.[1]

" Give me leave to say this :—there will be very great mountains in the way of this. . . . It is not enough to propose *It is neces-* things that are good in the end; but it is our duty *sary to cal-* as Christians and men to consider consequences. *culate con-* *sequences.* . . . But suppose this model were an excellent model and fit for England and the kingdom to receive; but really I shall speak to nothing but that that, as before the *They must* Lord, I am persuaded in my heart tends to uniting *agree among* of us in one to that that God will manifest in us to *themselves,* be the thing that he would have us prosecute; and he that meets not here with that heart, and dares not say he will stand to that, I think he is a deceiver."

Cromwell ended with a practical suggestion. Let the Council of the Army review those engagements to the neglect *and review* of which attention had been called, after which it *their engage-* would be possible to reply to the complaints of the *ments.* new Agitators. When the existing engagements of the army, entered upon at Newmarket and Triploe Heath, were fully known, it would be open to anyone who so wished ' to tender anything for the good of the public.'

This indefinite postponement of the constitutional debate was not to the taste of the Levellers. Wildman, who followed, *Wildman's* fixed on Cromwell's proposal as merely dilatory. *reply.* Abandoning the ground taken by the new Agitators, he declared that no man was bound by engagements which he himself considered unjust. As the debate threatened to take

---

[1] The usual notion that Cromwell was accustomed to make unctuous addresses to the soldiers will hardly survive this.

an angry turn, Cromwell proposed the appointment of a committee to take into consideration all questions at issue, and
more especially the binding force of the engagements
of the army. He hoped, he said, that in this way
God would unite them in one heart and mind. He
would rather resign his commission than that the kingdom
should break in pieces. Here Colonel Goffe, whose
mind was steeped in religious enthusiasm, broke in
with the suggestion of a prayer meeting, at which
God might be implored to give them the spirit of unity.
Cromwell at once assented, on condition that there should be
no delay. At his instance it was settled that the prayer meeting should be held on the following morning, and that the
committee should meet in the afternoon of the same day.[1]

Cromwell proposes a committee.

Goffe asks for a prayer meeting.

Once more Cromwell urged all present not to ' meet as two
contrary parties,' but as men desirous of giving satisfaction to
one another. " I had rather," he declared, "we
should devolve our strength to you than that the
kingdom, for our division, should suffer loss; for
that's in all our hearts to profess, above anything that's worldly,
the public good of the people; and if that be in our hearts
truly and nakedly, I am confident it is a principle that will
stand. Perhaps God may unite us and carry us both one
way."

Cromwell protests against party spirit.

Few of those to whom Cromwell now addressed himself
were in a temper to profit by his exhortation. Wildman recommended haste in coming to a decision on the
ground that Parliament might anticipate the army
by patching up some arrangement with the King to
the detriment of the natural rights of the people; whereupon
he was vehemently attacked by Ireton, whose constitutional
opinions were more definite than those of his father-in-law.
Property, said Ireton, depended on contract, not on natural
right. Wildman's assertion to the contrary contained ' venom
and poison.' Captain Audley attempted to draw aside atten-

A discussion on natural rights.

[1] "Cromwell when in difficulties," writes Mr. Firth in his preface to
vol. i. of the *Clarke Papers*, "generally moved for a committee; Goffe
invariably proposed a prayer-meeting."

tion from this unseemly charge by supporting Wildman's contention that time was precious. "If we tarry long," he said, "the King will come and say who will be hanged first." Neither Ireton nor Wildman were, however, to be recalled to such practical considerations, and a long wrangle followed between them, Cromwell occasionally intervening with a plea for a more conciliatory temper.

This painful scene had at least one satisfactory result. It taught Cromwell that it was not enough to criticise the opinions of the Levellers without the enunciation of any political faith of his own. Though the Council of the Army, he now said, was not 'wedded and glued to forms of government,' it acknowledged 'that the foundation and the supremacy is in the people—radically in them—and to be set down by them in their representations.'[1] It is probable that Cromwell failed to realise that by enunciating the doctrine of popular sovereignty he had broken with the King for ever. Cromwell would have had Charles to be king as William III. was afterwards a king. It was a condition to which Charles would never stoop. To do so would be to betray the inalienable rights of his posterity.

Cromwell declares his principles.

On the 29th,[2] when the prayer meeting had come to an end,[3] it was resolved after a long discussion to lay aside the consideration of the engagements by a committee, and to examine the *Agreement of the People.*

Oct. 29. The Agreement of the People produced.

The constitutional scheme of the Levellers was probably the shortest ever committed to paper, as it consisted of four articles only. The first required that the constituencies should be 'more indifferently proportioned according to the number of the inhahitants;' by the second, the existing Parliament was to be dissolved on September 30, 1648; by the third, future Parliaments were to be biennial, sitting every other year from the first Thursday in

Its provisions for biennial Parliaments.

---

[1] *i.e.* by means of their representatives.

[2] This day's debate is in the *Clarke Papers*, i. 280-363.

[3] There is no trace in the report in the *Clarke Papers* of Cromwell's taking any part in its prayers.

April to the last day of September, and no longer. Thus far the *Agreement of the People* was drawn on the same lines as *The Heads of the Proposals*, except so far as the demand made in the first article of the *Agreement* that representatives might be elected in proportion to the population, differed from the demand made in *The Heads of the Proposals* that they should be elected in proportion to the rates. The fourth article, widely departing from that model, was an expansion of the doctrine of a 'paramount law' set forth in *The Case of the Army*. For Authority of most purposes the biennial Parliament—consisting Parliaments to be by implication of a single elected House—was to be supreme, supreme. It might make, amend, and repeal laws; erect and abolish offices and courts; call officials to account; conduct negotiations with foreign Powers; make peace and declare war, or do anything else which was not 'expressly or implyedly reserved by the represented to themselves.'

These reservations were five in number. It was not to interfere with the most absolute religious liberty; it was not to except in press men 'to serve in the wars;' it was not to call reserved any man in question for the part taken by him in the cases. late struggle, except in carrying out sentences pronounced by the existing Parliament; it must not exempt anyone 'from the ordinary course of legal proceedings;' and finally, 'as the laws ought to be equal, so they must be good, and not evidently destructive to the safety and well-being of the people.'[1]

The *Agreement of the People* was the first example of that system which now universally prevails in the State Governments of the American Republic.[2] In both coun-The *Agree-* tries the idea of restraining the authority of the *ment of the* *People* com-legislative body by reserving certain matters to be pared with American dealt with by the people themselves, arose from the State con-stitutions. same cause—jealousy of the representative body. Yet the difference between the *Agreement of the People* and an American State constitution is enormous. In America, at the

[1] *An Agreement of the People,* E. 412, 21, is printed in the Appendix to this volume.

[2] See Bryce's *American Commonwealth,* part ii.

present day, the intervention of the people is an active, living force. The people make and unmake constitutions with decisive rapidity. The *Agreement of the People* was but the dream of a few visionaries. Its authors prescribed no way in which the people should be asked to adopt it, though they probably intended to circulate it for public subscription ; and they breathed no word of the possibility that the people, even if they once adopted it, might be inclined to change it. Their omission was by no means accidental. It arose from the stern fact, to which they wilfully closed their eyes, that the English people were irreconcilably hostile to them and to their teaching.

It was the unreality of the popular support appealed to in the *Agreement of the People* which gave strength to Cromwell
Opposition to it. and Ireton in their contention with the Levellers. As is often the case, when men are divided on questions of principle, it was on a side issue that the conflict began.
A debate on manhood suffrage. When the first article of the Agreement had been read, Ireton asked whether the declaration that the constituencies were to be 'proportioned according to the number of the inhabitants' implied that there was to be manhood suffrage, or that the old suffrage instituted 'by that constitution which was before the Conquest, that hath been beyond memory,' was still to be retained. Rainsborough at
Discussion between Rainsborough and Ireton. once declared in favour of manhood suffrage. " I think," he said, " that the poorest He that is in England hath a life to live as well as the greatest He ; and, therefore, truly, sir, I think it clear that every man that is to live under a government ought, first, by his own consent, to put himself under that government." Ireton retorted that this argument relied on 'an absolute natural right,' and denied 'all civil right.' No one, he contended, in words which came to have a familiar sound in the early part of the nineteenth century, ought to have a vote who had ' not a permanent fixed interest in the kingdom.' Those whose duty it was to choose the legislature were ' the persons who, taken together, do comprehend the local interest of this kingdom, that is, the persons in whom all land lies, and those in corporations in whom all

trading lies.' If this fundamental rule were set aside, property would be set aside as well. In reply, Rainsborough drew attention to the evil results of the existing system. "A gentleman," he urged, "lives in a country, and hath three or four lordships as some men have—God knows how they got them—and when a Parliament is called, he must be a Parliament man ; and it may be sees some poor men—they live near this man—he can crush them."

The debate grew hot, and at last Rich came to Ireton's help. Five men out of six, he said, had no permanent interest The debate in the kingdom. If votes were given to the five, grows hot. they would only sell them, as had been done at Rome, 'and thence it came that he that was the richest man, and of some considerable power among the soldiers, made himself a perpetual dictator ; and if we strain too far to avoid monarchy in kings, [let us take heed] that we do not call for emperors to deliver us from more than one tyrant.' Arguments of this kind were bandied to and fro, till agreement seemed well nigh hopeless. After a while Sexby struck in, carrying the debate outside the region of argument. There were, he said, thousands of soldiers as poor as himself, who had ventured their lives for their 'birthright and privileges as Englishmen.' Why were they to be told that unless they had a fixed estate they had no birthright ? He, for one, would surrender his birthright to no man. "Rather," replied Ireton, "than make a disturbance to a good constitution of a kingdom wherein I may live in godliness, and honesty, and peace, I will part with a great deal of my birthright."

After a while, Cromwell thought it time to intervene, expressing dissatisfaction with Sexby's language, 'because it did Cromwell savour so much of will.' Why could not the meeting intervenes. avoid abstract considerations, and content itself with discussing the question how far the existing franchise could safely be enlarged? Might not, for instance, copyholders be admitted to vote as well as freeholders ? Sir Hardress Waller was even more practical. Would the burden of the people, he asked, be lightened by papers? "If the four evangelists were here and lay free quarter on them, they will not believe you."

Doubtless Rainsborough perceived, as he glanced around, that his supporters, amongst those present, were but few, and

Rainsborough proposes a reference to the army at large.

he therefore asked that the question at issue might be referred to the whole army at a general rendezvous. The proposal found no support, and the meeting, as far as any evidence before us goes, broke up without coming to a decision.

Accordingly, on the morning of the 30th,[1] the committee proposed by Cromwell two days before met to consider the

Oct. 30. Meeting of the committee.

manifestoes put forward by the army in June, as well as the more recent *Agreement of the People*, and also 'to collect and prepare somewhat to be insisted upon and adhered unto for settling the kingdom, and to clear our proceedings hitherto.' The deliberations of the committee worked far more smoothly than those of the general meeting.

It prepares a new constitutional scheme.

Avoiding all points of controversy, it set down the heads of yet another constitutional scheme. Wisely beginning with the points least in dispute, it agreed to articles fixing the dissolution of the existing House of Commons on September 1, 1648, and establishing biennial Parliaments. It then adopted from *The Heads of the Proposals* a scheme for erecting a Council of State, taking care in so doing to introduce the King's name, which, in the *Agreement of the People*, had been passed over in silence. When the thorny question of the suffrage was at length reached, the committee contented itself with a resolution that there should be a redistribution of seats, in order to bring the representation into due proportion to the population, whilst the question of the franchise itself was left to be settled by the existing Parliament. The utmost concession which the committee made to the Levellers on this head was to couple their reference of the franchise to the Houses with the expression of a desire that the right of voting might be conferred on all who had served the Parliament during the late war, or had voluntarily assisted it with money, plate, horses, or arms; and that, on the other hand, no delinquent might be allowed to vote. Moreover, no

---

[1] *Clarke Papers,* i. 363-367.

Peer created since May 21, 1642, was to have a seat in the House of Lords without the consent of both Houses.

In the main, therefore, in spite of amendments in a popular direction, the committee, of which Sexby and Rainsborough, General character of the scheme. as well as Cromwell and Ireton, were members— upheld the general principles of *The Heads of the Proposals.* The new constitution was to be brought into existence by an understanding with the King and the House of Lords, not to be a direct emanation from the people, sweeping both King and Lords away. No better illustration of Cromwell's pertinacity in clinging to the old institutions of the realm can well be found.

APPENDIX.

——◆◆◆——

The Agreement of the People, as presented to the Council of the Army, October 28, 1647.[1]

AN Agreement of the People for a firm and present peace upon grounds of common right.

Having by our late labours and hazards made it appear to the world at how high a rate we value our just freedom, and God having so far owned our cause as to deliver the enemies thereof into our hands, we do now hold ourselves bound in mutual duty to each other to take the best care we can for the future to avoid both the danger of returning into a slavish condition and the chargeable remedy of another war; for, as it cannot be imagined that so many of our countrymen would have opposed us in this quarrel if they had understood their own good, so may we safely promise to ourselves that, when our common rights and liberties shall be cleared, their endeavours will be disappointed that seek to make themselves our masters. Since, therefore, our former oppressions and scarce-yet-ended troubles have been occasioned, either by want of frequent national meetings in Council, or by rendering those meetings ineffectual, we are fully agreed and resolved to provide that hereafter our representatives be neither left to an uncertainty for the time nor made useless to the ends for which they are intended. In order whereunto we declare :—

I.

That the people of England, being at this day very unequally distributed by Counties, Cities, and Boroughs for the election of their deputies in Parliament, ought to be more indifferently pro-

[1] *An Agreement of the People for a firm and present peace,* &c., E. 412, 21.

portioned according to the number of the Inhabitants ; the circumstances whereof for number, place, and manner are to be set down before the end of this present Parliament.

II.

That, to prevent the many inconveniences apparently arising from the long continuance of the same persons in authority, this present Parliament be dissolved upon the last day of September which shall be in the year of our Lord 1648.

III.

That the people do, of course, choose themselves a Parliament once in two years, viz. upon the first Thursday in every 2d March,[1] after the manner as shall be prescribed before the end of this Parliament, to begin to sit upon the first Thursday in April following, at Westminster or such other place as shall be appointed from time to time by the preceding Representatives, and to continue till the last day of September then next ensuing, and no longer.

IV.

That the power of this, and all future Representatives of this Nation, is inferior only to theirs who choose them, and doth extend, without the consent or concurrence of any other person or persons, to the erecting and abolishing of offices and courts, to the appointing, removing, and calling to account magistrates and officers of all degrees, to the making war and peace, to the treating with foreign States, and, generally, to whatsoever is not expressly or impliedly reserved by the represented to themselves :

Which are as followeth,

1. That matters of religion and the ways of God's worship are not at all entrusted by us to any human power, because therein we cannot remit or exceed a tittle of what our consciences dictate to be the mind of God without wilful sin : nevertheless the public way of instructing the nation (so it be not compulsive) is referred to their discretion.

2. That the matter of impresting and constraining any of us to serve in the wars is against our freedom ; and therefore we do not allow it in our Representatives ; the rather, because money (the sinews of war), being always at that disposal, they can never want numbers of men apt enough to engage in any just cause.

---

[1] *i.e.* in March in every other year.

3. That after the dissolution of this present Parliament, no person be at any time questioned for anything said or done in reference to the late public differences, otherwise than in execution of the judgments of the present Representatives or House of Commons.

4. That in all laws made or to be made every person may be bound alike, and that no tenure, estate, charter, degree, birth, or place do confer any exemption from the ordinary course of legal proceedings whereunto others are subjected.

5. That as the laws ought to be equal, so they must be good, and not evidently destructive to the safety and well-being of the people.

These things we declare to be our native rights, and therefore are agreed and resolved to maintain them with our utmost possibilities against all opposition whatsoever ; being compelled thereunto not only by the examples of our ancestors, whose blood was often spent in vain for the recovery of their freedoms, suffering themselves through fraudulent accommodations to be still deluded of the fruit of their victories, but also by our own woeful experience, who, having long expected and dearly earned the establishment of these certain rules of government, are yet made to depend for the settlement of our peace and freedom upon him that intended our bondage and brought a cruel war upon us.

END OF THE THIRD VOLUME.

**PHOENIX
PRESS**

GENERAL EDITORS:
SIMON SCHAMA AND ANTONIA FRASER

Phoenix Press publishes and re-publishes hundreds of the very best new and out of print books about the past. For a free colour catalogue listing more than 500 titles please

telephone: +44 (0) 1903 828 500
fax: +44 (0) 1903 828 802
e-mail: mailorder@lbsltd.co.uk
or visit our website at www.phoenixpress.co.uk

The following books might be of interest to you:

History of the Great Civil War
Volume I – 1642–1644
S.R. GARDINER

The first volume in S.R. Gardiner's epic four-volume history of the English Civil War traces events from the beginning of the conflict to the battle of Marston Moor which was to prove the turning point for the Parliamentarian cause.

Paperback
UK £9.99   416pp   1 84212 639 3
USA $16.95
CAN $25.95

History of the Great Civil War
Volume II – 1644–1645
S.R. GARDINER

The second volume takes the story up to 1645, a year which saw the demise of royalist hopes.

Paperback
UK £9.99   416pp   1 84212 640 7
USA $16.95
CAN $25.95

History of the Great Civil War
Volume III – 1645–1647
S.R. GARDINER

Volume three describes the victories of the New Model Army in the campaigns of 1645 and 1646 and the extraordinary political and religious upheavals of 1647.

Paperback
UK £9.99   416pp   1 84212 641 5
USA $16.95
CAN $25.95

History of the Great Civil War
Volume IV – 1647–1649
S.R. GARDINER

The fourth and final volume covers Charles' escape from his confinement at Hampton Court to the tragic climax of his execution in 1649.

Paperback
UK £9.99   416pp   1 84212 642 3
USA $16.95
CAN $25.95

Commonwealth to Protectorate
AUSTIN WOOLRYCH

The Barebones Parliament and Cromwell's response. 'It will be essential reading for all students of the period' Christopher Hill, '. . . a work to savour' T.C. Barnard, *History*

Paperback
UK £14.99   464pp   1 84212 201 0
USA $21.95
CAN $31.95

Archbishop Laud
HUGH TREVOR-ROPER

Hugh Trevor-Roper's brilliant first book about Charles I's ill-fated Archbishop of Canterbury, who became the most powerful man in

England during the Eleven Years' Tyranny from 1629–1640, only to be executed during the Civil War.

Paperback
UK £14.99   480pp + 8pp b/w   1 84212 202 9
USA $21.95
CAN $31.95

Cromwell
Our Chief of Men
ANTONIA FRASER

A magnificent recreation of the life and character of the man who has made the greatest impact on the history of England. Freed from the distortions of myth and Royalist propaganda, he is revealed warts and all. 'A great theme and a fine book' Michael Foot, *Evening Standard*

Paperback £14.99   800pp + 32pp b/w   1 84212 493 5

Battles of the English Civil War
AUSTIN WOOLRYCH

'He that draws his sword against his prince must throw away the scabbard' – so it was said in 1642, and the Civil War that ensued was an intimately bitter and bloody affair, chronicled meticulously and with style by Austin Woolrych.

Paperback
UK £12.99   208pp + 24pp b/w   1 84212 175 8
USA $19.95
CAN $29.95

The Popish Plot
JOHN KENYON

The story of how Titus Oates persuaded the British public of a Catholic conspiracy to assassinate Charles II. 'An extraordinary tale of human credulity, knavery and folly' *The Times*

Paperback
UK £12.99   368pp + 8pp b/w   1 84212 168 5
USA $19.95
CAN $29.95

Thomas Wentworth
First Earl of Strafford 1593–1641, A Revaluation
C.V. WEDGWOOD

The rise and fall of the most powerful and most hated man in the British Isles at the time of Charles I.

Paperback
UK £12.99   416pp + 8pp b/w   1 84212 081 6
USA $19.95
CAN $29.95

Memoirs of the Life of Colonel Hutchinson
Charles I's Puritan Nemesis
LUCY HUTCHINSON

The extraordinary life of one of the men who signed Charles I's death warrant, written by his wife.

Paperback
UK £9.99   422pp   1 84212 108 1
USA $16.95
CAN $24.95

Free-born John
The Biography of John Lilburne
PAULINE GREGG

The life of the leader of the Levellers, whipped, pilloried and twice put on trial for his life by Cromwell. 'Lilburne has found an admirable as well as an admiring biographer' *TLS*

Paperback
UK £12.99   432pp   1 84212 200 2
USA $19.95
CAN $29.95